A HISTORY OF
INTELLECTUAL PROPERTY
IN 50 OBJECTS

What do the Mona Lisa, the light bulb, and a Lego brick have in common? The answer—intellectual property—may be surprising, because IP laws are all about us, but go mostly unrecognized. They are complicated and arcane, and few people understand why they should care about copyright, patents, and trademarks. In this lustrous collection, Claudy Op den Kamp and Dan Hunter have brought together a group of contributors—drawn from around the globe in fields including law, history, sociology, science and technology, media, and even horticulture—to tell a history of IP in 50 objects. These objects not only demonstrate the significance of the IP system, but also show how IP has developed and how it has influenced history. Each object is at the core of a story that will be appreciated by anyone interested in how great innovations offer a unique window into our past, present, and future.

CLAUDY OP DEN KAMP is Senior Lecturer in Film and faculty member at the Centre for Intellectual Property Policy & Management (CIPPM) at Bournemouth University, UK, and Adjunct Research Fellow at Swinburne Law School, Melbourne. She has previously worked as Haghefilm Conservation's Account Manager, as a Film Restoration Project Leader at the Nederlands Filmmuseum, and as a senior research assistant in the film restoration research project DIASTOR at the Department of Film Studies at the University of Zurich. She is the author of *The Greatest Films Never Seen: The Film Archive and the Copyright Smokescreen* (2018, Amsterdam University Press).

DAN HUNTER is the founding dean of Swinburne Law School, Melbourne. He is an international expert in internet law, intellectual property, and artificial intelligence models of law. He has previously held positions at QUT Law School, New York Law School, Melbourne Law School, the Wharton School at the University of Pennsylvania, and Cambridge University. He is the author of *The Oxford Introductions to U.S. Law: Intellectual Property* (2012, Oxford University Press) and co-author of *For The Win: How Game Thinking Can Revolutionize Your Business* (2012, Wharton Digital Press).

A HISTORY OF
INTELLECTUAL PROPERTY
IN 50 OBJECTS

Edited by

CLAUDY OP DEN KAMP

Bournemouth University (UK)

DAN HUNTER

Swinburne Law School (Australia)

CAMBRIDGE
UNIVERSITY PRESS

CAMBRIDGE
UNIVERSITY PRESS

University Printing House, Cambridge CB2 8BS, United Kingdom

One Liberty Plaza, 20th Floor, New York, NY 10006, USA

477 Williamstown Road, Port Melbourne, VIC 3207, Australia

314–321, 3rd Floor, Plot 3, Splendor Forum, Jasola District Centre, New Delhi – 110025, India

79 Anson Road, #06–04/06, Singapore 079906

Cambridge University Press is part of the University of Cambridge.

It furthers the University's mission by disseminating knowledge in the pursuit of education, learning, and research at the highest international levels of excellence.

www.cambridge.org
Information on this title: www.cambridge.org/9781108420013
DOI: 10.1017/9781108325806

First published 2019

Printed and bound in Great Britain by Clays Ltd, Elcograf S.p.A.

A catalogue record for this publication is available from the British Library.

Library of Congress Cataloging-in-Publication Data
Names: Op den Kamp, Claudy, 1974– editor. | Hunter, Dan, 1966– editor.
Title: A history of intellectual property in 50 objects / edited by Claudy Op den Kamp, Bournemouth University (UK); Dan Hunter, Swinburne Law School (Australia).
Description: Cambridge, United Kingdom ; New York, NY : Cambridge University Press, 2019.
Identifiers: LCCN 2018057892 | ISBN 9781108420013
Subjects: LCSH: Intellectual property – History.
Classification: LCC K1401 .H59 2019 | DDC 346.04/8–dc23
LC record available at https://lccn.loc.gov/2018057892

ISBN 978-1-108-42001-3 Hardback

Book design, image research, and rights clearances by
Claudy Op den Kamp.

Cover images, top left to bottom right: Getty Images; Tom
Forsythe; Smithsonian Institution; The Coca-Cola Company;
Heritage Auctions; Getty Images; The Metropolitan Museum
of Art; Library of Congress NAVCC; and Getty Images.

*Aboriginal and Torres Strait Islander are advised that this book
contains names and images of people who died.*

In loving memory of Greg Lastowka (1968-2015)

Contents

Acknowledgments

As they say: it takes a village. This book could simply not have existed without Matt Gallaway, our fabulous editor at Cambridge University Press. Thank you for believing in this project from the beginning. Your communication skills and your swift, yet always thoughtful, replies to an endless stream of emails are beyond compare.

Many thanks also go to the content and production team in the United Kingdom: Catherine Smith, Jackie Grant, Ian McIver, and Janice Baiton.

This book was made possible with generous support from Swinburne University of Technology and Bournemouth University, where we would like to thank our respective executive deans Michael Gilding and Mike Wilmore (now at UNE, Australia).

This book was designed as a collaborative effort. First and foremost, we are extremely grateful to all the contributing authors. Thank you for sharing your insightful scholarship, which will surely inspire the readers of this book in myriads of ways. We also extend our gratitude to all the contributors to the several preparatory "roundtables." In Norrköping, Sweden, March 2016: Marianne Dahlén, Eva Hemmungs Wirtén, Jessica Lake, James Meese, and Amanda Scardamaglia. In Melbourne, Australia, August 2016: Mitchell Adams, David Brennan, Jake Goldenfein, Ramon Lobato, Ben Morgan, Amanda Scardamaglia, Tom Spurling, Julian Thomas, Megan Richardson, and Robin Wright. And in Rome, Italy, July 2018: Fiona McMillan, Eva Hemmungs Wirtén, Henrique Carvalho, and Giovanni Riccio; Maurizio Borghi, Melanie Brown, Elena Cooper, Marianne Dahlén, Matthew David, Peter Decherney, Stefania Fusco, Jane Ginsburg, Peter Jaszi, Mike Madison, Kathryn Raybould, Amanda Scardamaglia, Stina Teillmann-Lock, and Andrea Wallace.

During the eight months it took to put this book together, many people have played a paramount role in making sure that it could indeed visually become the crossover project between an academic publication and a coffee table book we intended it to be. Many thanks go to the following individuals, broken down by the individual object chapters: 4 • John Powell, The

Newberry Library | 6 • Margot Jones, State Library Victoria | 8 • Gregor Ruthven, Singer | 9 • Eric Colleary, Diana Leite, The Harry Ransom Center | 13 • Kelly McAnnaney, National Archives at New York City | 14 • Barry Bradford / David Hansen, Joshua Larkin Rowley, Rubenstein Library Rare Book and Manuscript Library, Duke University | 17 • Zvi Rosen / Mike Mashon, Geo Willeman, The Library of Congress NAVCC | 22 • Marc Mimler / Marcel van der Vlugt | 24 • Giuseppe Poeta, Salvatore Ferragamo SpA / Stefania Lascialfari, Alinari / John Benicewicz, Robert Dunkin, ArtResource / Caterina Belloni / Graziano Raveggi, Gallerie degli Uffizi | 25 • Courtney Matthews, Library of Congress / Piper Severance, LACMA / James McKee, Gagosian Gallery / John Benicewicz, Robert Dunkin, ArtResource | 27 • Edward Bishop, Holly Peel, Wellcome Collection / Kay Peterson, Division of Medicine and Science, National Museum of American History, Smithsonian Institution | 28 • Richard Torchia, Arcadia University Art Gallery / Sarah Oakman, National Museum of American History | 30 • Lucy Aboulian, Chanel | 32 • Ryder White, CAA / Todd Haynes / Michael Boie, Universal Music Denmark / Tom Forsythe | 33 • Marek Budzynski / Ted Ryan, Justine Fletcher, Jamie Avello, The Coca-Cola Company | 34 • Mark Davies, Sixth Floor Museum | 37 • Christopher George, Intel Museum | 40 • Karin Wholey, HBO / Anna Carboni, Wiggin LLP | 41 • Thom Rice, Hope and Glory PR / Tom Cunningham, Interpublic Group / Lucas Hilderbrand / David Hansen, Joshua Larkin Rowley, Rubenstein Library Rare Book and Manuscript Library, Duke University | 42 • Carolien Provaas, Nederlands Fotomuseum | 45 • Sara Frankel, Harvard University Collection of Historical Scientific Instruments | 47 • Annie Cavanagh | 48 • Patty Youngstein, Marc Newson Studio | 49 • Rebecca Caudell, Getty Images.

Special thanks go to Eric Bradley and Steve Lansdale at Heritage Auctions for their generous support of this publication.

For their expert advice on all matters design, thank you to Olivier van den Hoven, Andrea Wallace, and Daniëlle Dohmen. And for this book to start its own journey as "object 51," thank you for all legal advice to the inimitable Peter Jaszi. ◆

Introduction

Of People, Places, and Parlance

—Claudy Op den Kamp and Dan Hunter

INTELLECTUAL PROPERTY (OR "IP") law is the set of laws that primarily encompasses copyright, patent, and trademark law. It also includes trade secrets and publicity rights. It is one of the most important structuring systems in modern society, as it underpins vast industries such as aerospace, architecture, pharmaceutics, media, and entertainment. It is the locus of concerns about counterfeiting and piracy, it grounds arguments about trade, export, and competition, and it is at the core of discussions over knowledge-based economies, and policies relating to creativity and innovation.

IP laws are all about us, but go mostly unrecognized. They are complicated and arcane, and few people understand why they should care about, for example, copyright law, the grant of a patent, or the registration of a trademark. The IP system didn't exist in its modern form until the 18th century, and as recently as 1945, it was only important to a tiny group of people—newspaper proprietors, film studios, engineering firms, and toothpaste companies. Nowadays, the IP system profoundly affects global trade, and enables trillions of dollars of commerce.

These laws define the modern era; without them we wouldn't have famous brands like Coca-Cola or Sony, the internet would not exist, and we wouldn't have an iPhone in our pocket.

50 OBJECTS

In this book, we have brought together a group of contributors who have been drawn not only from law and history, but also from sociology, media studies, horticulture, science and technology studies, among others, while spanning a wide geographical range. In their chapters, they address the different IP regimes to tell a history of IP in 50 objects.

These objects demonstrate the importance of the IP system. They invite questions about various aspects of its multifaceted development. The objects show us how IP has developed and worked within human history, and show its influence on a range of historical events, developments, and movements. And perhaps most importantly, they are at the core of some great stories.

Some of these objects have so profoundly impacted our lives that it's hard to know what we would be without them. At the same time, their history is deeply entangled with the IP system. The Light Bulb, the Escalator, and the Wi-Fi Router are just some examples.

The objects included range from something as specific as a 16th-century Map of Rome or the Oscar Wilde Portrait No. 18 to something as ubiquitous as the Football. The objects attest to their relation with the world in which they were born as well as their enduring meaning in the world today. They have *shaped* human interactions; and they have been shaped *by* them.

But why approach the topic of intellectual property through objects at all? We could have told a history of the global IP system via a list of the laws that were enacted or the cases that were litigated. Our reasons are fourfold.

First, objects are shortcuts to the *social implications* of the laws that we're interested in addressing. An examination of the Betamax, for instance, is a story about a US Supreme Court case that rewrote copyright law, but also about the concept of "timeshifting" that was at the heart of the case, and that has come to structure modern media consumption and provide the

basis for the creation of Napster, Google, and Netflix.

Second, objects are tangible, which makes them interesting in the context of intellectual property. IP law aspires for a separation between the "thing" and the "idea of the thing." (Ideas can*not* be protected; it's their tangible expressions that can be.) But IP law also serves to remind us that it is never possible to entirely separate the "thing" from the "idea of the thing." The chapter on the Barbie Doll, for instance, shows that the doll is a tangible example not only of a toy that was originally protected by a patent, but also of a company's attempt through its litigation strategy to protect that doll's chaste image.

Third, objects are imbued with ideologies and practices of intellectual property. The contribution on the Football uses the object as a constant in the game's story of change—a story about wealth production based on intellectual property laws and the exclusivity these bring.

Fourth, we often rely on material objects to stand in for immaterial issues. The dominant metaphors for the early years of digital technology, for instance, were all material: pipes, cars, and the superhighways that would transport us to a new world. Similarly, in this volume, the entry on the Internet uses the metaphor of the hourglass to address the architecture of Internet Protocol—a different IP altogether from Intellectual Property.

"Everything is Deeply Intertwingled"

Some of the great themes of IP-history are distinctly addressed within the individual entries; it is also in their juxtaposition that they are interconnected. What follows is a random selection of examples, by no means exhaustive.

The entries on Goryeo Celadon and the Murano Glass Vase invite reflection on the process of innovation in the centuries before there even was an intellectual property system, and the chapter on the Climbing Rose highlights how the way in which the concept of "invention" was conceived within the law was altered after the patenting of the first plant, the *Rosa* "New Dawn." The latter also addresses the possibility of the absence of a human inventor, as does the contribution on the Elstar Apple,

in describing spontaneous mutations that can occur in the self-pollination of a species. The myth of the lone inventor and the flash of individual genius is a central theme in multiple entries. The chapter on the Alexander Graham Bell Telephone addresses the myth by highlighting the importance of being first in patenting, as do the entries on the Morse Telegraph and the Oral Contraceptive Pill. The piece on the Bell Transistor discusses the likelihood of success in collaborative invention. The entries on the Light Bulb and Steamboat Willie examine individuals' zeal for patenting; the former for Thomas Edison's, the latter for Walt Disney's. Inventions that are answers to other problems than originally foreseen are under scrutiny in entries as widely varied as the Post-it Note and the Viagra Pill.

We see the emergence of the right of the author, foreshadowing future narratives of copying and piracy in the pieces on the Hogarth Engraving and Tempesta's Map of Rome. The latter also queries the incentive rationale, and other philosophical pillars that underlie modern copyright. We see issues of adaptation and recognition of copyright across national borders in the

4

chapter on Uncle Tom's Cabin. Pioneering approaches to licensing are amongst the topics of the entries on the Penguin Paperback, the Lego Brick, and the Barbie Doll. Musings on the relationship between copyright, creativity, and the public domain are laid out in the chapters on the Deerstalker Hat and the Mona Lisa. How copyright effectively precluded public access to another historic document is discussed in the entry on the Zapruder Film. The chapters on the Audiotape Cassette, the 3D Printer, the CD, the Betamax, the Photocopier, and the Internet all highlight the role of and the implications for copyright in the emergence of the sharing economy and a shift toward the power of the prosumer.

The notion of what constitutes a copy is addressed in the contribution on the Photocopier, which ironically shows that a patented machine that could not be copied was "built to make copies—copies of texts, photographs, and even instructions for making or using copying machines." It is also highlighted in the entry on the Chanel 2.55, which echoes Coco Chanel's saying that "imitation is the highest form of flattery," which as a business strategy is quite the

contrary of the current House of Chanel's. The chapter on the Player Piano Roll explains that the notion of "copy" was deeply questioned in court, and that therefore the roll can be seen as the "19th century CD, DVD, and Spotify all rolled into one." The concept of the copy is also at the heart of the entry on the RAM-Chip, which fundamentally reshaped IP law and the way we regulate the entire current technical ecosystem.

We are on the verge of another fundamental shift in the way we understand IP: the contribution on the Bitcoin addresses decentralization as a promotion of individual freedom. The development of IP in response to new technologies is also discussed in the chapters on the Lithograph, the Paper Print, and the 3D Printer.

Genesis stories of products can show the importance of the political context in IP. Objects as diverse as the Ferragamo Wedge and the Aspirin Pill are described as the result of limited international trade as a consequence of war—Mussolini's war in Ethiopia and World War I, respectively. Other chapters that deal with origin stories commence with a "knock-off": the Lego Brick, the Barbie Doll, and the Coca-Cola Bottle. The doctrine of trademark genericide—a brand that morphs into its product—is discussed in the entries on the Escalator, Champagne, and the Singer Sewing Machine, the latter of which is the first subject of international branding. Multimedia approaches to merchandising are discussed in the contributions on the Lego Brick and the Action Figure.

Gendered assumptions of lawyers, judges, and the law itself are at the core of the chapters on the Corset and the Kodak Camera, two accounts that deal with the correlation of female subjects and male rightsholders. The gendered nature of pharmaceutical regulation can be seen in the chapters on the Oral Contraceptive and Viagra Pills, as they address the difference in the speed of approval of these pharmaceuticals in Japan. A different role of gender was seen in the emergence of moving images. Boxing was largely outlawed in the United States during the Kinetoscope's heyday, and where allowed, deemed improper for women and children. Yet boxing films were shown in states where live boxing was banned,

and we know that women and children frequented Kinetoscope parlors where boxing films were often on display.

Intangible design factors that add value to a product is the topic of the entry on the PH-Lamp, and how the added value also contributes to the overall success of a company is discussed in the chapter on the Qantas Skybed. More stories that find their origin Down Under, which is not surprising in light of the Australian origin of this book, are addressed in the entries on the Mike Tyson Tattoo, the Wi-Fi Router, and the Polymer Banknote.

THE COMPOSITE

There are also themes that are not specifically stated, which only emerge in seeing the collection of entries together. And these themes tell a history all of their own. A major theme is the *people* involved in the stories—Thomas Edison appears in no less than six entries. And who knew that Sherlock Holmes and Alexander Graham Bell both had a partner named Watson? It is also only in seeing this particular collection of objects together that certain *places* show their importance. Was it perhaps the long, cold winters that make Rochester the breeding ground not only of the Kodak camera but also of privacy rights *and* the Xerox photocopier? The stories also show themes in their formal similarities—in their *parlance*. Unbeknownst to the individual authors, the word "apocryphal" appears in more than a few entries, and undoubtedly hints at the many twists and turns—some cunning, some less conscious—that so often seem to underpin these histories.

HISTORY / HISTORIES

This volume is called "a" history of intellectual property and not "the" history of intellectual property, as the telling of any history is necessarily *partial*. These partial histories do meet and intersect at points, but are simultaneously also *provisional*. We're trying to tell stories and histories of an intellectual property world that was born in the Western philosophical tradition, and that is, for instance, only now beginning to come to terms with its colonial heritage—these stories and

histories are contested and shifting. Any history is also necessarily told from the *present*. As the entries on the Kinetoscope, the Paper Print, Champagne, and Steamboat Willie show us, histories are constantly being written, and being rewritten.

So why try to tell a history at all? Playwright Eugene O'Neill once said, "There is no present or future—only the past, happening over and over again, now." We have a desire to understand where intellectual property laws have come from, how they have evolved, and what they mean to our lives, now. We would like to understand how certain processes might repeat themselves. We might want to look ahead and see if we can learn anything from what has come before. We'd also like to understand our own discipline through the historic lens of another, and we'd like to understand the ramifications of the IP system on other fields of research, and vice versa.

A READER'S GUIDE

There are several ways to engage with this book. You are obviously welcome to devour its contents chronologically from cover to cover. Alternatively, you can engage with the entries within one of the discrete "ages," as indicated by the different color bars at the far outer edge of the opening page of each chapter—grey for "The Pre-Modern Period," yellow for "The Age of Invention," red for "Modern Times," green for "The Consumption Age," and blue for "The Digital Now." You can also opt for following along one regime—trademark, for instance, by following the information in the front matter at the start of the chapters.

Yet another possibility is to follow a theme. It can be a theme that has actively been planted: if you're interested in music and its relation to IP, for instance, start at the chapter on the Piano Player Roll, skip to the entry on the Audiotape Cassette, and end at the contribution on the CD. Or, if you're interested in media consumption and IP, read the chapters on the Kinetoscope, Steamboat Willie, the Zapruder Film, and the Betamax. If you'd like to follow the strand on women's history, start at the Corset and the Kodak Camera, jump to the Ferragamo Wedge, and end at the Contraceptive Pill and the Barbie Doll.

Alternatively, there is ample opportunity for you to discover your own themes.

You can also keep coming back to your favorite individual entry, and perhaps at some point let the images retell the story.

Jumping-off Points

Whether found in a gallery, an archive, a home, or a supermarket, these mundane and extraordinary objects are meant to provide astonishment about their relationship with IP. The individual objects function as jumping-off points for a larger, socially reverberating story within the chapters, and in turn, the chapters and their themes—both individually and combined—function as jumping-off points for further research beyond this volume. We rely on your own contribution and creativity here in carving your own path through these stories, whether they be familiar, of rediscovery, or entirely new.

Whichever path you choose, we hope you enjoy engaging with the stories in this book as much as we did compiling them. ◆

1100   *1200*   *1300*

--/-----/-----/-----/-----/-----/-----/-----/-----/-----/-----/-----/----

1 Goryeo Celadon

Hee-Kyoung Spiritas Cho

The line
The slender blue line
That falls gracefully
Like the shoulders of a Bodhisattva

THE KOREAN POET Park Jong Hwa rhapsodized over the beauty of Goryeo celadon like many before him over the centuries. But behind the elusive jade hue of Goryeo celadon lies a remarkable tale of a protean system of intellectual property and technology transfer practiced almost a millennium ago; a system that powered an entire industry and developed cutting-edge technology. The history of Goryeo celadon illuminates both the nature and the process of innovation long before the development of formal intellectual property rights for individuals, as well as the role of the state in the construction of these systems of innovation. It is not only a tale of intellectual property, politics, and fashion, but also an illustration of how cultural artifacts are used to enhance national prestige and to build national pride.

Although Goryeo celadon is now valued as national treasure in Korea, it had

On the left: Celadon prunus vase with plum blossom, bamboo, and crane design, Goryeo Dynasty, National Treasure 1168. (National Museum of Korea)

been forgotten for many centuries after the Kingdom of Goryeo fell in the late 14th century and celadon gave way to a new fashion for white porcelain of the Chosun dynasty. It was not until the beginning of the 20th century that Goryeo celadon was rediscovered by the Japanese colonialists who avidly collected them; even robbing graves to do so. The original celadon manufacturing know-how was long lost to history, and modern attempts to reproduce the subtle green hue never fully succeeded—spawning myths that there was some arcane trade secret in its manufacturing process and glazing technique, a technique that was supposed to have been closely guarded and passed among only a handful of masters. In this way, celadon became a source of national pride, symbolizing Korea's long history that harked back to a time when its scientific and cultural development was far superior to any of its neighbors.

The term "celadon" denotes both the jade green glaze used on ceramic ware and any porcelain made with such glaze. Celadon, like white porcelain, originated

Above: Cup and cup stand, porcelaneous stoneware with celadon glaze, inlaid glaze decoration. Goryeo Dynasty, last half 12th century. (Photo: Brooklyn Museum, Museum Collection Fund, CC BY)

in China, where the production of pottery fired at a temperature above 1,200°C necessary to achieve vitrification has been dated as far back as the Han dynasty (206 BC–220 AD). The color of celadon can vary widely from olive green, to grey green, and even brown, depending on the composition of the clay, the glaze, and the firing conditions inside the kiln. However the most desirable shade is that of a bluish green jade evoking "a clear autumnal sky after rain." The blue green celadon pottery was developed in China in imitation of jade, a stone that signifies wisdom and virtue in the Chinese culture. Despite its Chinese origin, many scholars agree that the art of celadon reached its zenith in the neighboring Korean peninsula during the Goryeo dynasty (918–1392 AD). Even the Chinese praised the Goryeo celadon as having "the most beautiful jade color under the heaven."

We now know that the jade color is the result of the presence of iron in the composition of the glaze and the clay under certain firing conditions; but even with the aid of modern science, replicating the exact hue of the Goryeo celadon has proven challenging. The difficulty of reproducing the celadon technique has led to a widely held belief that the formula behind the Goryeo celadon—like the varnish of a Stradivarius violin—was a closely guarded trade secret that died with the last Goryeo celadon master. This myth of celadon ignited popular imagination and was used as an example of the advantages and disadvantages of using trade secrets as a means to protect valuable ideas. But the real story of Goryeo celadon is far more complicated than this simple tale suggests, and it serves to show how innovations can be developed—and then lost—through complex interactions between intellectual property rights, forms of industrial organization, political interests, and war.

Archaeologists believe that Korea had already been importing celadon ware from China during the Unified Silla period (676–935 AD), mostly from the Yuezhouyao (越州窯) area near modern day Hangzhou. That porcelain manufacturing flourished around Yuezhouyao was no accident: the area was rich in kaolin, an essential

Above: Cancelled stamp from India featuring the Bodhisattva or Buddha. (Getty Images)

Below: Medical pill bowl used in the Royal Palace, Goryeo Dynasty, National Treasure 1023. The inscribed characters refer to the office in charge of preparing medication for the royal family. (National Museum of Korea)

ingredient of porcelain making that allows the raw clay to withstand the extremely high temperature required in the process of vitrification. The demand for celadon in Korea grew thanks to the rise of wealthy provincial aristocrats, many of whom had travelled to China and had acquired a taste for Chinese tea-drinking culture and the goods that went with it. The spread of Buddhism in Korea also contributed to the growing demand for celadon pieces, such as incense burners or offering plates. The supply of celadon from China, however, was not always secure nor sufficient to meet the increasing demand.

The supply problem grew worse with the demise of the Tang dynasty (618–907 AD) and the emergence of rivalrous kingdoms during a conflict-ridden period known as the "Five Dynasties and Ten Kingdoms" (907–960 AD). In the meantime, on the Korean peninsula the old and weak Shilla dynasty was replaced by the new Goryeo dynasty. The founding king of Goryeo quickly consolidated his rule, mainly by forming alliances with the powerful regional aristocratic families through marriage. The tumult in China during the "Five Dynasties" period presented an opportunity for Goryeo, which was enjoying a relatively calm and peaceful reign. By offering a safe and stable environment, with guaranteed employment and steady income, it seems that Goryeo

managed to persuade many skilled Chinese celadon makers from the Yuezhouyao area to emigrate. Excavated brick kilns and shards of pottery from archaeological sites near Songdo, the capital of Goryeo, are almost identical to those found in the Yuezhouyao area of China, and the scale and magnitude of the finds suggest that these were unlikely to have been the result of a serendipitous emigration of a few celadon makers from China. The only entity at the time with the necessary power and resources for such a large-scale construction was the state itself. Given the planning, organization and the investment required—coupled with the location of the kiln sites—it appears likely that the Goryeo government effectively facilitated the technology transfer of celadon making from China to Korea.

Initially, kiln sites in and around Songdo produced celadon for a very select market: the royal household, the aristocracy, and Buddhist ceremonies. But toward the end of the 10th and the beginning of the 11th century, the pattern of Goryeo celadon manufacture underwent a dramatic change. Starting in 992 AD, for 30 years the northern kingdom of Liao made numerous attempts to invade Goryeo. Songdo was alarmingly close to the northern border and celadon production was severely affected by a shortage of manpower and materials because of the war. The kiln sites were very close

to the capital making them vulnerable to attack. Their destruction would have resulted in a significant loss of revenue for the royal household. Thus, a decision seems to have been made around this time to move the center of celadon production to the southwestern province of Jeolla, near Gangjin and Buan, two important trading ports close to China and Japan. The new locations were chosen for a number of reasons: their proximity to the coast made it easier to transport the celadon by sea, the distance from the northern border made the production sites less vulnerable to attack, and there was the presence of the right type of clay and an abundance of fuel needed to fire the kilns. Most importantly, the southwest province was home to a powerful aristocratic clan that had helped to found the Goryeo dynasty, and who could be relied upon to protect the royal family's interests in the kiln sites.

By the time that the kilns were moved to the southwestern provinces, the production was organized in a "so" (소, 所), an administrative unit responsible for producing certain products for the royal household, such as gold, silver, bronze, iron, paper, and pottery. (Under the later Chosun dynasty, these organizations of production would become directly controlled by the state, as happened with the white porcelain production.) Many of the celadon makers belonging to a celadon *so* were Koreans who had probably been apprenticed to the original Chinese potters from Yuezhouyao. Around this time, the Korean celadon makers started to introduce a range of innovations to the production process. Unlike the original Chinese-style brick kilns, the Jeolla potters built much smaller mud kilns, which fired smaller batches, but could achieve a much higher temperature by sealing in all the heat. Inside the kiln, the potters also built an inclined plane to provide a more even, ambient heat. But perhaps the biggest innovation was to the glazing. Whereas the Chinese favored multiple coatings of thick opaque glaze and fired the pottery only once, the Koreans instead pre-fired the greenware, and then applied a thin coat of glaze for a shiny transparent finish before a second firing. The transparent

Above, from left to right: Celadon deep dish, stoneware with celadon glaze. Yuan Dynasty (1279–1368) / Ming Dynasty (1368–1644), China, ca. 1300–1499. (Rijksmuseum); Bowl, stoneware with celadon glaze. Goryeo Dynasty, 12th century. (Photo: Brooklyn Museum, The Peggy N. and Roger G. Gerry Collection, CC BY)

Above: Celadon incense burner with openwork, Goryeo Dynasty, 12th century, National Treasure 95. (National Museum of Korea)

glaze in turn allowed them to develop a further innovation, the inlaid decorations of *sanggam*. The gorgeous designs on the classic Goryeo celadon—depicting stylized flora and fauna, or sometimes even a whole landscape—are not painted on the pottery but inlaid with white and red clay. Masterful use of *sanggam* can be seen on pieces such as the Korean National Treasure No. 68, otherwise known as the "Cloud and Crane Engraved Cherry Blossom Bottle," a prosaic name for possibly the most beautiful piece of baked earth that one can imagine.

These innovations were born out of necessity rather than a purely inventive spirit. The reality was that products demanded from each *so* were a tax by the royal household, and every *so* had to provide its own resources for the production. For a celadon *so*, this meant that the residents were responsible for building their own kiln, obtaining the raw materials, and collecting the fuel necessary to produce the required quantity of celadon. Although organized by the state, the *so* residents would not have had the resources to build large brick kilns in the Chinese style, and had to make do with smaller mud kilns. They could scarcely afford the large failure rate that resulted from a single firing of greenware, and instead reduced the risk by pre-firing pottery before glazing. The only color available to decorate the pottery that could have withstood the high temperature came from cobalt, which was very rare and expensive, so they decorated by engraving rather than painting. The Korean celadon makers innovated by responding to resource constraints, cooperating with each other, sharing information and resources rather than competing with one another.

Contrary to the popular myth of a closely guarded, secret recipe of Goryeo celadon manufacture, more recent archaeological finds show a uniformity in kiln sites across the country suggesting that the celadon manufacturing technique was widely shared. It is also evident that the state encouraged as many people as they could to join celadon *so*. Among the surviving Goryeo court records from the 12th century, we find expressions of concern over

Right: Detail of bowl on page 24. Although celadon bowls seem quite plain at first glance, they often contain very delicate, hand-drawn decorations that were lightly incised into the clay before glazing. This bowl's interior has a flower floating on barely visible ripples of water; the decorators appear to have used comblike instruments to create parallel, but gestural, lines in the clay.

On the left: Detail of vase from the Chosun Dynasty, first half of the 15th century. Buncheong ware, stoneware with celadon glaze and inlaid black and white slips. (The Peggy N. and Roger G. Gerry Collection. Photo: Brooklyn Museum, in collaboration with National Research Institute of Cultural Heritage, CC BY)

the flight of celadon *so* residents and the need to recruit more people. Even though the residents of the celadon *so* were forbidden to move out without official permission, many left to escape the difficult conditions of their servitude. Those who escaped often started up their own kiln in a different part of the country thereby diffusing celadon manufacturing skill and contributing to the local economy. Scholars have likened the Goryeo celadon industry to the semiconductor industry of 20th-century Korea, in terms of its economic importance and technological advancement.

The fate of Goryeo celadon was intertwined with its eponymous dynasty. After the fall of Goryeo, celadon lay forgotten and unwanted for more than half a millennium, until its rediscovery in the early 20th century. Later, celadon became a reminder of Korea's glorious past, a tool for nation building, and source of national pride, whose myth of trade secret surrounding its manufacture added to its aura of prestige. Goryeo celadon embodies the constructed reality of intellectual property—showing us a glimpse of the hand of the state, then as now. ◆

Further Reading

Godfrey Gompertz (1963) *Korean Celadon and Other Wares of the Koryo Period*. London: Faber & Faber.

Youngsoon Pak (2002) *Earthenware and Celadon. Handbook of Korean Art*. Seoul: Yekyong.

Jeon Seungchang, Jang Sungwook, Kim Yunjeong, and Im Jin A (2013) *Goryeo Celadon*. Seoul: National Museum of Korea.

1400   *1500*   *1600*

--/-----/-----/-----/-----/-----/-----/-----/-----/-----/-----/-----/----

2 Murano Glass Vase

Stefania Fusco

On the left: Millefiori glass details. Millefiori, also known as Murrine, is one of the best-known and highly sought after techniques of Murano glassmaking. It stands for "a thousand flowers" in Italian, and the end result of this labor-intensive process are gorgeous patterns and deep intensive colors. (Getty Images)

IMPORTANT INFORMATION ABOUT a society can be learned from studying its institutions, government, industries, art, and culture. This is also true if we want to learn the way these societies lived in the past. For example, much can be learned about the Venetian society between the 13th and 18th centuries by investigating its glassmaking industry. At that time, being involved in this sector determined where you could live in Venice, your social status, whom you could marry, and whether you could travel abroad. Glassmaking was one of the two largest industries of the early modern Venetian economy—the manufacturing of silk was the other—and it employed a substantial portion of the city's corporate labor force: in the late 18th century about 30 percent of the Venetian artisans were glassmakers.

During the 12th century, the Venetian Republic became active in regulating the activity of artisans and merchants operating within its commonwealth. The making of glass, one of the Republic's most lucrative industries, was clearly a source of great interest to the Venetian government, and regulations specific to this sector were issued by the *Senato*, the *Maggior Consiglio*, and the *Consiglio dei Dieci*. The goal of this regulatory activity was, in large part, to ensure the quality of the Venetian glassware and maintain the reputation of the Republic's products in international markets. However, they were also, and perhaps more importantly, designed to keep glassmaking knowledge within Venice's borders; for example, in 1173 the Venetian Republic enacted legislation that granted to guilds the exclusive right to practice "mechanical trades." Consequently, the glassmaking industry became the domain of a system of four or five guilds that restricted their art to Venetian, male glassmakers. Foreigners and women were generally excluded from membership.

Although it was strongly protectionist, the 13th-century Venetian Republic also energetically promoted innovation, and specifically sought to attract inventors from abroad. The Senate began issuing licenses to practice skills and technologies unknown in Venice, in fields that were

18

Above: A 17th century map of the island of Murano. (Photo by Bojan Brecelj / CORBIS / Corbis via Getty Images)

normally reserved to the guilds. Venice is universally recognized as being responsible for the origin of patent protection, but the strength and flexibility of the patent system came about in significant part as a result of the foreign inventors Venice was attracting. The foreign licensees were not allowed to become members of the related guild, and although Venice used patents of importation to induce them to bring their inventions to the lagoon, these forms of protection did not prevent Venetian guild-members from copying them. The foreign inventors must have complained to the Senate and requested the more valuable *exclusive right to practice* their knowledge in Venice. The first patent that we know about—one that incorporated the all-important "right to exclude"—was issued in 1416 with a term of 50 years. It was granted to Ser Franciscus Petri, a foreigner, for a device to transform wool into felt. Later, in 1474 the Venetian Senate passed the first patent statute in history, with a vote of 116 in favor, ten against, and three abstaining. Venice continued to issue ad hoc patents to inventors until the end of the Republic in 1796.

While patent protection did not play a significant role in the *development* of the Venetian glassmaking technology, it proved fundamental to revealing this art to other countries in Europe, as Venetian glassmaking masters began escaping the strict control of the Republic, selling their knowledge and skills to other cities. As Venice began to decline in the 16th century, other European markets became coveted destinations for the Venetian glassmakers and the grant of patents facilitated the transfer of the glassmaking knowledge to these new locations. The history of Venetian glassmaking, and its patent protection,

is therefore a perfect illustration of the interplay between patents, trade secret and global trade. Murano glassware is central to the development of intellectual property throughout Europe, and ultimately the United States.

The technology of glassmaking is considered to have existed since about 3500 BC. Various types of glassware have been found in Egypt, Mesopotamia, Greece, and later throughout the Roman Empire. Staples of the later Venetian glass industry—objects such as *rosette*, *margherite*, and *millefiori*, often made of glassy earthenware, but, sometimes, also of pure glass—were known to ancient populations. The main difference that distinguishes those earlier objects from the ones created much later by the Venetian artisans is the refinement of the manufacturing, new methods of production, and the high quality of the ingredients used. Earlier glassmakers very rarely blew glass, instead relying on stamps and lathes to produce their glass objects. Venetian glassmakers instead mastered the art of glassblowing, using scissors and other small tools to create ethereal forms, and found new recipes and techniques to improve the transparency and colors of the glass.

In the mid-13th century, the Venice glassmaking industry began flourishing, and it consequently began to be strictly regulated through guild-specific statutes, called *mariegole*. By 1291 the Republic had issued a law prescribing that all the furnaces employed in glassmaking activities had to be moved out of the city and relocated to Murano, a small island in the Venetian lagoon about one mile north of the city. The official reason for this decision was to protect Venice from the significant risk of fire, due to the presence of the furnaces in the city. At the same time, though, this law served the very important purpose of ensuring that the Republic had full control of the glassmaking technology now concentrated in a single, confined location. Thus, the art of glassmaking gradually became the subject of highly guarded secrets developed through the fierce competition that characterized the activity of the guild members working in Murano. But while secrecy was strictly enforced outside the various glassmaking guilds both by their members and the Republic, the situation was very different when it came to keeping secrets *within* these organizations. The furnaces used to make glass were all located on one street on the island, and the most creative masters found it difficult to prevent other members of the same guild from copying their techniques and using them as a basis for experimentation. The result was the emergence of remarkable innovation in this field, driven by geographic proximity and commercial need.

Being a glassmaker in Venice conferred significant benefits, including a higher social status and greater economic well-being. Skilled glassmakers were in high demand and very well compensated for their services, and their daughters were allowed to marry into the wealthiest and noblest Venetian families. However, in 1295 the price of these privileges became much steeper as the Venetian Republic—seeking to intensify its control over the glassmaking secrets and consolidate its supremacy in this sector—decided to prohibit the glassmakers from leaving the Republic. The penalties for those who violated this rule included banishment, prohibitions on working in Venice, and in, some cases, even death.

During the 14th century, high-quality transparent colored glasses, enamels, beads, lenses, and eyeglasses were introduced into international markets by Venetian glassmakers, causing Venice to become the leading glass manufacturing center in Europe. In the 15th century, the process of making crystal glass was discovered, and Venetian glassmakers began using it to manufacture mirrors. By the 17th century, large, flat mirrors of superior quality could be bought in Venice. As a result, other European countries engaged in significant espionage in an effort to copy the Venetian methods of production. Famously, in 1665–1666 Jean-Baptist Colbert, the French Minister of Finance, managed to attract a group of Venetian glassmakers to Paris to create the *Manufacture Royale des Glaces de Miroirs* for the large-scale production of mirrors—much of this operation was conducted behind the Venetian Senate's back. There are substantial narrative reports indicating that this situation lasted more than hundred years, and that during that period numerous Venetian glassmakers who sold their secrets were poisoned abroad by order

of the Senate. Meanwhile, other important glassmaking techniques were introduced in Venice, such as *enameling, gilding glass*, and the making of the *filigrana glass*.

Innovation occurred both as a consequence of the patent system and also as a trade secret. The guild members in Murano hired outside laborers to lower the costs of production and to manage the economic fluctuations of the market. Two notable groups were the women living in the city, and immigrants from Friuli—a region in the northeast of Italy—who were employed at very low salaries to refine final products, such as small mirrors and beads. The new techniques that these laborers and guild members developed were often documented in the recipe books of the masters supervising the various activities, but not disclosed in the petitions to the *Doge*, the Prince, to grant a patent. As a result, the Venetian glassmaking patents of the period still in existence focus almost exclusively on the tools of glass production, rather than its methods.

The decline of the Venetian glassmaking industry occurred concurrently with the decline of the Venetian Republic itself. The 17th century saw the emergence of important competitors in Bohemia, England, and France. Some innovation occurred during the 18th century, but it was not very significant. Ultimately, the Venetian glassmaking industry reached its darkest moment after Napoleon invaded Venice in 1797 and decided to abolish the guilds.

However, the decline of Venetian glassmaking created the conditions for the dispersal of the patent system from its Venetian home. During the 16th century, as glassmakers began leaving Venice—relocating to more promising European markets, and revealing the secrets of their art—they took with them their understanding of the benefits of an exclusive right to practice their inventions. Because they had come from Venice, where the system of patent protection was well established, they often agreed to reveal their glassmaking knowledge to other countries only in exchange for the grant of a monopoly. These patents were issued either directly to the Venetian glassmakers, or to other individuals who were nationals of the

Above, left: Transparent violet glass wares with enamel painted and gilt. Venice, ca. 1500–1525. The State Hermitage Museum, Saint Petersburg. (Photo by PHAS / UIG via Getty Images)

Above, right: Glassblower of Murano glass, illustration from the Illustrated book of Venetian Costumes, by Jan Grevenbroeck (1731–1807). (Photo by DeAgostini / Getty Images)

Above: A pair of Murano glass penguin lamps. (Courtesy of Heritage Auctions, HA.com)

Thus, through the mediating vector of the glassblowing art, and the widespread desire for high-quality glassware of all sorts, the Venetian patent system spread throughout Europe and eventually reached England. Then, from England, it was transported to the United States and then the rest of the world. The history of glassmaking is, then, a history of the development of the patent system; and it highlights the fundamental role patent protection plays in both divulging knowledge *and* shaping societies, by allowing the custodians of knowledge the freedom to travel abroad, find new homes, and practice their art and commerce. ◆

Further Reading

Bartolomeo Cecchetti, *et al.* (1874) *Monografia della Vetraria Veneziana e Muranese*. Venice: Tipografia Antonelli.

Maximilian Frumkin (1945) "The Origin of Patents," *Journal of the Patent Office Society*, 27(3), pp. 143–149.

Maximilian Frumkin (1947) "The Early History of Patents and Innovation," *Transactions of the Newcomen Society*, 26, pp. 47–55.

Ted Sichelman and Sean O'Connor (2012) "Patents as Promoters of Competition: The Guild Origins of Patent Law in the Venetian Republic," *San Diego Law Review*, 49, pp. 1267–1282.

Francesca Trivellato (2008) "Guilds, Technology, and Economic Change in Early Modern Venice," in Stephan R. Epstein and Maarten Prak (eds.) *Guilds, Innovation, and the European Economy, 1400–1800*. Cambridge: Cambridge University Press.

granting country, sometimes associated with the Venetians, sometimes operating independently. In some cases, these initial patents issued by various European countries did not refer to the making of glass, but rather to other manufacturing trades. But there was always some connection with Italy, and in particular with Venice, and the emergence of glassmaking industries in various European countries was closely followed by the emergence of a patent system modeled on the one in Venice. This can be clearly seen in Belgium, England, and France—examples of European patents for glass include a patent issued in Belgium in 1541 to a patentee called Cornachini, a patent issued in France in 1551 to an Italian named Mutio, and a patent issued in England in 1552 to one Smyth.

1400   *1500*   *1600*

--/-----/-----/-----/-----/-/----/-----/-----/-----/-----/-----/-----/----

3 Mona Lisa
Andrea Wallace

On the left: Salvador Dali in the studio beside his gallery of mustached personalities, including his own "Self Portrait Mona Lisa" (1973). (Getty Images)

For centuries, business models have been based on reproducing copyright-free works using the available technologies, often claiming new rights and commercializing the results. In part this is why the public domain exists: to copy or make new works that attract new copyrights, so long as they are sufficiently original. In the past two decades, however, new technologies have made this practice exponentially easier and its products much more available. Meanwhile, the role of copyright during the digitization of public domain works has become the focus of significant legal and social controversy.

There is no better artwork to illustrate how these phenomena have played out than Leonardo da Vinci's *Mona Lisa*, a painting recently valued at nearly one billion dollars, and said to be the most reproduced, written about, referenced, and parodied artwork in the world—a work that in its five centuries of existence has never once been protected by copyright.

When Leonardo set out to capture Lisa del Giocondo's likeness in 1503, copyright did not exist. Privileges, the precursor to modern copyright, were granted as a means to protect investment in the technologies necessary for reproduction in the book trade and printing industry. When modern copyright debuted in England with the 1710 Statute of Anne, it inherited its rationale for protecting reproducible subject matter from the privileges system. Yet, paintings lacked protection for centuries—not until the end of the 18th century in France, the 19th century in Italy, and in some countries like the Netherlands not until the 20th century. Similarly, no legal protection would have been awarded to Leonardo's sketches of Lisa del Giocondo, had any been made. The irony is, therefore, that printed reproductions generally received some form of copyright protection centuries before the masterpieces they reproduced.

For a work as captivating as *La Joconde*, as she is called in France, or *La Gioconda* in Italy, this meant anyone with access to da Vinci's painting could attempt its reproduction—attempt, of course, being the operative word. Leonardo's masterpiece possessed a *je ne sais quoi* which artists

found difficult to capture due to his *sfumato* (smoke-like) technique of rendering light and darkness in her flesh and fabric. This did not stop court artists and others from trying. The production of high-quality surrogates was a respected and lucrative industry, one through which aspiring artists could become well known via their copies. With each copy's completion, a new source entered the world that could be used to make subsequent *Mona Lisa* reproductions. And though many of the artists' names have long been lost to history, at the time their painted reproductions similarly received no legal protection.

Unlike painted copies, print-based images could be reproduced in multiples and sold to many, fetching a greater profit than a single painting. As technologies developed and reproduction became cheaper and easier, new print houses emerged, dedicated to slavishly copying the engravings realized through the labor of others. By the 18th century, legislative measures sought to protect this effort—the 1735 Engravers' Act in Britain, for example, awarded a 14-year copyright on the basis of the work's design to the designer who also engraved it.

Technology has come a long way since Leonardo's time, reducing the cost and creative input required to make an accurate reproduction; but so has copyright. Today, an original work receives protection for 70 years from the author's death.

And legal determinations of originality can hinge on a number of factors, including the geographical jurisdiction and the technology used—depending on where the reproduction is made, different treatment may exist for versions made with a copy machine, a scanner, or a camera.

But it was the *absence* of copyright—coupled with technology—that created the cultural artifact that we know as the *Mona Lisa*. Leonardo kept the painting with him at the Castle of Clos Lucé until his death in 1519, after which King François I purchased it from his heir. It moved from room to room at Versailles until the monarchy was abolished in 1792, and it was subsequently selected for inclusion in a new public museum at the Louvre. There, the painting caught the eye of Napoleon, who reportedly removed it to his bedroom and enjoyed its company until 1804, before permanently reinstalling it on the Louvre's walls.

By the end of the 19th century, Lisa Gherardini had returned the gaze of royalty, emperors, politicians, artists, authors, musicians, and many, many others. Her image had been reproduced and referenced in culture countless times by those enjoying her company personally or publicly. Yet, the image was not thus far the icon of public consumption it is today. It was *fin-de-siècle* technological advancements that were responsible for making this possible; but it

Above, left: A woman examines "Thirty Are Better Than One" (1963) by Andy Warhol. (Alberto Pizzoli / AFP / Getty Images)

Above, right: A woman examines "Double Mona Lisa, After Warhol (Peanut Butter and Jelly)" (1999) by Vik Muniz. (Gerard Julien / AFP / Getty Images)

was the remarkable theft of the painting in 1911 that has been credited for catapulting the *Mona Lisa* to international recognition. At 7:30 am on Monday, 21 August 1911, Vincenzo Peruggia walked through the Louvre's back door wearing a white smock, entered the gallery exhibiting the *Mona Lisa*, and unhooked it from the wall. He then slipped into a stairwell, removed the frame, and tucked the painting under his smock. Peruggia attempted to exit through the service door at the foot of the stairs, but it was locked. Along came a workman who, rather than catch the thief red-handed and become a hero, helped open the door.

It took two days for the Louvre to notice. Newspapers reported her disappearance, speculating on the motive. It must have been a blue-eyed visitor, who had been seen gazing at the painting, enamored. No, it was a wealthy American who took it to make a copy but would later return it. Suddenly everyone was an expert on the painting, spinning tales of the dancing jesters that the strikingly-handsome Leonardo had employed in his studio to keep Lisa's face in a perpetual smile. On the front pages of newspapers worldwide that smile could be admired; but on her wall at the Louvre *La Joconde*'s place remained empty. A larger number of visitors than ever came to witness her absence, including Franz Kafka. Postcards and reproductions exploded through Parisian streets. Musicians wrote songs of her theft. A reward was offered, arrests were made—even Pablo Picasso was a suspect.

The mystery continued for two years, until Florence antique dealer Alfredo Geri received a letter signed by "Leonardo." The sender claimed to have the painting and wanted to discuss a price. Inviting Leonardo to Florence, Geri and Uffizi Gallery curator Giovanni Poggi met with Peruggia and verified the painting's authenticity using photographic reproductions. Peruggia was arrested.

Once again, front pages around the world reported *Mona Lisa*'s recovery, the trial, and the painting's Italian tour, until she was restored to her wall in the Louvre. Another vandalism attempt in 1956 and subsequent world tours provided more reportable content in the following years. In 1963, the Kennedys paid homage to Lisa at the National Gallery of Art during her first trip outside Europe; afterward she traveled to the Metropolitan Museum of Art to greet more than one million visitors in less than a month. Ten years later, she visited Japan and Russia, accompanied this time by a massive merchandizing campaign, before returning to France to retire behind the bulletproof glass where she remains today.

Like the artists Marcel Duchamp, Salvador Dali, and Andy Warhol, we may all use the *Mona Lisa* without paying a copyright fee, just as we may use the majority of the historical reproductions of the painting fee-free. However—public domain or not—one cannot simply walk into the Louvre and remove the *Mona Lisa* from the wall to make a reproduction, and it remains no small feat to make one within the gallery. Those who travel to Paris and pay the admission fee will find difficulty getting close enough to capture her with any fidelity. Regardless, under the Louvre's visitor photography policy, any photograph is restricted to *private* use only.

Without the ability to make our own reproduction, we must rely on stewards of public domain works to make and release surrogates for others to use. This endeavor is easier than ever to accomplish, due to advancements in digital technologies and industry guidelines that have not only simplified the process but also eliminated many of the creative choices once

On the following pages: "Mona Lisa Mural, Columbus Ohio" (2009) by Carol M. Highsmith. (Carol M. Highsmith's America, Library of Congress, Prints and Photographs Division)

recognized as bestowing originality on the surrogate. Despite this, a new copyright is usually claimed during the transition from analog to digital, potentially restricting use of the surrogate unless permission is granted by the alleged rightsholder.

The internet provides few reliable alternatives. An extensive online search for copyright-free surrogates of the *Mona Lisa* and her reproductions made available by legitimate sources reveal that the majority come with copyright-strings attached, sometimes hidden among the many reproduction layers that a single image can hold. Even the image in Wikipedia's *Mona Lisa* entry is taken from a surrogate that is subject to a copyright claim, a detail that potentially exposes users to secondary infringement. Few institutions openly license the digital surrogates in their collection—an image that, in some cases, might be a surrogate of a surrogate of a surrogate. A visualization of this relationship and the difficulty in finding copyright-free surrogates online is illustrated across pages 44–51. In truth, the reproduction timeline should follow not a linear path, but that of

a family tree with each off-shoot spawning its own lineage of surrogates. Considering the lack of information about many reproductions—early and contemporary—such a reconstruction is likely impossible.

Despite this difficulty and uncertainty, it is impossible to escape the image of the *Mona Lisa* in modern culture. Over the years, reproductions have appeared on playing cards, cigarettes, coffee mugs, postcards, t-shirts, in advertising, and in various corners of pop culture. She provoked Théophile Gautier's cult of the femme fatale, and surfaced among the writings of authors like Oscar Wilde, Marcel Proust, Henry James, D.H. Lawrence, Jean-Paul Sartre, and Mary McCarthy. Sigmund Freud theorized Lisa's smile was Leonardo's attempt to reproduce his mother's. The film THE THEFT OF THE MONA LISA (1931) follows Vincenzo Peruggia's saga, and a fictional theft occurs in GOOD MORNING BOYS (1937). She makes a cameo in THE PRIME OF MISS JEAN BRODIE (1969) during an art history lesson with Maggie Smith. Both Lucile Ball in the *I Love Lucy Show* ("Lucy Goes to Art Class," 1963)

Above: "Mona Lisa Barn Art, Wisconsin" (1990) by Carol M. Highsmith. (Carol M. Highsmith Archive, Library of Congress, Prints and Photographs Division)

Further Reading

Taylor Bayouth (2016) *How to Steal the Mona Lisa: And Six Other World-Famous Treasures*. New York: Perigee.

Susan M. Bielstein (2006) *Permissions, A Survival Guide: Blunt Talk about Art as Intellectual Property*. Chicago: University of Chicago Press.

Michael Burrell (2006) "Reynolds's Mona Lisa," *Apollo*, Vol. CLXIV, No. 535.

Martin Kemp and Giuseppe Pallanti (2017) *Mona Lisa: The People and the Painting*. Oxford: Oxford University Press.

Darian Leader (2002) *Stealing the Mona Lisa: What Art Stops Us From Seeing*. London: Faber & Faber.

Donald Sassoon (2006) *Leonardo and the Mona Lisa Story: The History of a Painting Told in Pictures*. London: Duckworth.

Andrea Wallace and Ronan Deazley (2016) *Display at Your Own Risk: An Experimental Exhibition of Digital Cultural Heritage*. Available at: displayatyourownrisk.org

Above, left: The "Mona Lisa" handbag from Jeff Koons' collection entitled "Masters" (2017) made in collaboration with Louis Vuitton. (Alamy)

Above, right: Marlon Brando sitting before Mona Lisa portrait in a scene from ONE-EYED JACKS (US 1961, Dir. Marlon Brando). (Getty Images)

On the following pages: "Mona Lisa: A Reproduction Timeline, ca. 1503–2017," by Andrea Wallace.

and Elizabeth Montgomery in *Bewitched* ("Mona Sammy," 1970) transform into Lisa del Giocondo before audiences. She has been serenaded by Nat King Cole, Bob Dylan, The Fugees, and will.i.am; her face has been plastered across surfaces from barns to luxury handbags.

Regardless of how far technology has come, the *Mona Lisa* cannot yet be cloned to satisfy public consumption—nor can we accurately predict how such a thing might be treated by copyright law. Still, imagine what we might learn by analyzing the historical, technological, and geographical path taken by Leonardo's image, a task potentially achieved via meaningful online access to her surrogates (and their surrogates). A champion in the pursuit of knowledge, Leonardo gave us the ideal opportunity to study not only the generation of knowledge over five centuries from a single painting, but also an ideal example of the public domain's potential once truly freed from copyright claims. ◆

Musée du Louvre, Paris

Leonardo da Vinci (1452–1519)

Mona Lisa

€11

1503–1516

Icon made by Freepik from www.flaticon.com

Mona Lisa:
A Reproduction Timeline
ca. 1503–2017

1500

---

jpg
date unknown,
© RMN-Grand Palais (musée du Louvre) / Michel Urtado | RMN Photo, €75.90

jpg
date unknown,
© RMN-Grand Palais / Art Resource, NY / Lewandowski / Le Mage / Gattelet | Art Resource, $150

jpg
date unknown,
© RMN-Grand Palais / Art Resource, NY, René-Gabriel Ojéda | Art Resource, $150

jpg
date unknown,
© Scala / Art Resource, NY | Art Resource, $150

jpg
2007, © Eric Vandeville / Gamma-Rapho via Getty Images | Getty Images, £485

---

jpg
date unknown,
© Erich Lessing / ART RESOURCE, NY | Artstor Digital Library

jpg
date unknown,
Art History Survey Collection, Art Images for College Teaching, copyright unclear | Artstor Digital Library

slide
date unknown,
Unknown, copyright unclear | ARTstor Slide Gallery

jpg
date unknown,
copyright unclear, University of California San Diego | Artstor Digital Library

slide
date unknown,
Unknown, copyright unclear | ARTstor Slide Gallery

jpg
date unknown,
University of California San Diego, copyright unclear | Artstor Digital Library

jpg
date unknown,
The Archive for Research on Archetypal Symbolism, copyright unclear | Artstor Digital Library

---

jpg
date unknown,
The Archive for Research on Archetypal Symbolism, copyright unclear | Artstor Digital Library

jpg
date unknown,
Harvard University Library, copyright unclear | HOLLIS

jpg
date unknown,
Harvard University Library, copyright unclear | HOLLIS

jpg
date unknown,
Harvard University Library, copyright unclear | HOLLIS

jpg
date unknown,
Harvard University Library, copyright unclear | HOLLIS

jpg
date unknown,
Harvard University Library, copyright unclear | HOLLIS

jpg
date unknown,
Harvard University Library, copyright unclear | HOLLIS

---

jpg
date unknown,
Harvard University Library, copyright unclear | HOLLIS

jpg
2011, © RMN-Grand Palais / Art Resource, NY / Michel Urtado | Art Resource, $150

jpg
1999, © Musée du Louvre, © Direction des Musées de France, © Réunion des musées nationaux - utilisation soumise à autorisation, © Hervé Lewandowski, © Thierry Le Mage | Europeana

jpg
1999, © Musée du Louvre, © Direction des Musées de France, © Réunion des musées nationaux - utilisation soumise à autorisation, © Hervé Lewandowski, © Thierry Le Mage | Joconde

unclear
date unknown,
Musée du Louvre, copyright unclear | focus.louvre.fr

jpg
2017, Elsbeere, copyright unclear | Wikimedia Commons

---

unclear
date unknown,
Musée du Louvre, copyright unclear | focus.louvre.fr

jpg
2010, Amandajm, copyright unclear | Wikimedia Commons

jpg
2014, ANGELUS, copyright unclear | Wikimedia Commons

jpg
2011, Cybershot800i, copyright unclear, | Wikimedia Commons

painting
date unknown,
Unknown / Fracnesco Melzi, public domain | Museo Nacional del Prado

unclear
2012, © AFP PHOTO / JAVIER SORIANO | location unclear

jpg
2012, © Antonforever CC BY-SA 3.0 | Wikimedia Commons

---

unclear
2013, © 2013 C2RMF | C2RMF

jpg
2011, Amandajm, copyright unclear | Wikimedia Commons

unclear
2013, © 2013 C2RMF | C2RMF

jpg
2011, Cybershot800i, copyright unclear | Wikimedia Commons

jpg
2012, Jeff G., copyright unclear | Wikimedia Commons

unclear
2013, © 2013 C2RMF | C2RMF

jpg
2011, Dcoetzee, copyright unclear | Wikimedia Commons

jpg
2013, © Cicada 021 CC BY-SA 3.0 | Wikimedia Commons

unclear
date unknown,
© RMN-Grand Palais (musée du Louvre) / Michel Urtado | cartelen.louvre.fr

jpg
2010, Amandajm, copyright unclear | Wikimedia Commons

---

unclear
2013, © 2013 C2RMF | C2RMF

jpg
2011, Dcoetzee, copyright unclear | Wikimedia Commons

unclear
date unknown,
© RMN-Grand Palais (musée du Louvre) / Michel Urtado | cartelen.louvre.fr

jpg
2013, Slick-o-bot, copyright unclear | Wikimedia Commons

unclear
1754, Unknown, public domain | Hulton Fine Art Collection

jpg
date unknown,
© Hulton Archive / Getty Images | Getty Images, £485

unclear
1934, copyright unclear, *The World's Greatest Paintings,* Odhams Press, London

jpg
2013, © Universal History Archive | Getty Images, £485

---

unclear
1924, *The Outline of Art,* Sir William Orpen (ed.), George Newnes Limited, London, copyright unclear

jpg
date unknown,
© Hulton Fine Art Collection / Print Collector | Getty Images, £485

slide
date unknown,
Unknown, copyright unclear | ARTstor Slide Gallery

jpg
date unknown,
University of California San Diego, copyright unclear | Artstor Digital Library

slide
date unknown,
Unknown, copyright unclear | ARTstor Slide Gallery

jpg
date unknown,
University of California San Diego, copyright unclear | Artstor Digital Library

Based on extensive web research, this timeline depicts the online availability of digital surrogates of the Mona Lisa and her reproductions.

The timeline divides the source Mona Lisa from her surrogates: above the timeline is a representation of the painting, which cannot be accessed without visiting the Louvre in Paris and paying an €11 admissions fee. Below the timeline are her surrogates, starting with the earliest known copy, believed to have been painted alongside da Vinci by an unknown artist in his workshop.

Notably, each host institution or licensing organization maintains different information about each material surrogate and most claim copyright in the digital surrogate they make available online.

1

Museo Nacional del Prado

Workshop of da Vinci, after Leonardo da Vinci, *Earliest known copy*
1503–1519

oil on walnut
1503–1519, Anonymous, public domain

jpg
date unknown, © Museo Nacional del Prado | Museo Nacional del Prado, €169 + VAT

unclear
date unknown, Leonardo da Vinci, Copia, public domain

fotografía
date unknown, J. Laurent, public domain | Instituto del Patrimonio Cultural de España

jpg
2017, © Ministerio de Educación, Cultura y Deporte; © Instituto del Patrimonio Cultural de España; Fotografía: © Instituto del Patrimonio Cultural de España, CC BY-NC-ND | Europeana

painting
15th century, Leonardo da Vinci, public domain

unclear
date unknown, Unknown, copyright unclear | Universal History Archive

jpg
date unknown, © Universal History Archive/ IUG via Getty Images | Getty Images, £485

unclear
date unknown, Leonardo da Vinci, Copia, public domain

fotografía
1860–1886, J. Laurent, public domain | Instituto del Patrimonio Cultural de España

jpg
2017, © Ministerio de Educación, Cultura y Deporte; © Instituto del Patrimonio Cultural de España; Fotografía: © Instituto del Patrimonio Cultural de España, CC BY-NC-ND | Europeana

painting
1503–1516, Apprentice of Leonardo da Vinci, public domain

unclear
2012, Alberto Otero, copyright unclear

jpg
2012, Outisnn, copyright unclear | Wikimedia Commons

jpg
2012, Escarlati, copyright unclear | Wikimedia Commons

unclear
date unknown, Leonardo da Vinci, Copia, public domain

negativo fotográfico
date unknown, Unknown, copyright unclear | Instituto del Patrimonio Cultural de España

jpg
2017, © Ministerio de Educación, Cultura y Deporte; © Instituto del Patrimonio Cultural de España; Fotografía: © Instituto del Patrimonio Cultural de España, CC BY-NC-ND | Europeana

huile sur bois
1503–1516, Vinci Léonard, atelier de, public domain

jpg
date unknown, © Museo Nacional del Prado, Dist. RMN-GP / image du Prado | RMN Photo

unclear
date unknown, Leonardo da Vinci, Copia, public domain

vidrio a la gelatina
date unknown, Unknown, copyright unclear | Instituto del Patrimonio Cultural de España

jpg
2017, © Ministerio de Educación, Cultura y Deporte; © Instituto del Patrimonio Cultural de España; Fotografía: © Instituto del Patrimonio Cultural de España, CC BY-NC-ND | Europeana

oil on walnut
1503–1516, Leonardo da Vinci (workshop), public domain

jpg
date unknown, © Museo Nacional del Prado / Art Resource, NY | Art Resource, $150

unclear
date unknown, Leonardo da Vinci, Copia, public domain

vidrio a la gelatina
date unknown, Unknown, copyright unclear | Instituto del Patrimonio Cultural de España

jpg
2017, © Ministerio de Educación, Cultura y Deporte; © Instituto del Patrimonio Cultural de España; Fotografía: © Instituto del Patrimonio Cultural de España, CC BY-NC-ND | Europeana

unclear
date unknown, Leonardo da Vinci, Copia, public domain

vidrio a la gelatina
date unknown, Unknown, copyright unclear | Instituto del Patrimonio Cultural de España

jpg
2017, © Ministerio de Educación, Cultura y Deporte; © Instituto del Patrimonio Cultural de España; Fotografía: © Instituto del Patrimonio Cultural de España, CC BY-NC-ND | Europeana

unclear
date unknown, Leonardo da Vinci, Copia, public domain

vidrio a la gelatina
date unknown, Unknown, copyright unclear | Instituto del Patrimonio Cultural de España

jpg
2017, © Ministerio de Educación, Cultura y Deporte; © Instituto del Patrimonio Cultural de España; Fotografía: © Instituto del Patrimonio Cultural de España, CC BY-NC-ND | Europeana

1600

2

Private collection

Unknown, after Leonardo da Vinci, *Isleworth Mona Lisa*

16th century

oil on canvas
unknown date, before WWI, Unknown, public domain

jpg
date unknown, Unknown, copyright unclear | monalisa.org

jpg
2012, Shakko, copyright unclear | Wikimedia Commons

3

Private collection

Unknown, after Leonardo da Vinci, *Flemish School Mona Lisa*

16th century

unclear
16th century, Flemish School, public domain

jpg
date unknown, © Bonhams, London, UK / Bridgeman Images | Bridgeman Art Library, £150

4

The State Hermitage Museum

Unknown, after Leonardo da Vinci, *State Hermitage Mona Lisa*

16th century

oil on canvas
16th century, Anonymous Artist, public domain

jpg
date unknown, © The State Hermitage Museum | State Hermitage Museum, €0–70

5

Château du Clos Lucé

Ambroise Dubois, after Leonardo da Vinci

16th century

oil paint and canvas
XVIth century–2009, Ambroise Dubois, public domain

jpg
date unknown, Unknown, copyright unclear | Google Arts & Culture

6

The Walters Art Museum

Unknown, after Leonardo da Vinci, *Walters Mona Lisa*

ca. 1635–1660

oil on canvas
ca. 1635–1660, Copy after Leonardo da Vinci, public domain

jpg
date unknown, Unknown, copyright unclear | Artstor Digital Library

unclear
sec. XVI, Anonimo, public domain

gelatina ai sali d'argento
ca. 1946–1976, Shirley Hobbs, copyright unclear | Fondazione Frederico Zeri, Università di Bologna

jpg
date unknown, © Federico Zeri Foundation, CC BY-NC-ND | Fondazione Frederico Zeri Online Photo Archive

oil on canvas
ca. 1635–1660, Copy after Leonardo da Vinci, public domain | The Walters Art Museum

jpg
date unknown, CC0 | The Walters Art Museum Website

7

Location Unclear

Charles Errard (1606–1689), after Leonardo da Vinci

1651

unclear
date unknown, Unknown, public domain | location unclear

jpg
2007, © Eric Vandeville / Gamma-Rapho via Getty Images | Getty Images, £485

8

Private Collection

Unknown, after Leonardo da Vinci, *Reynolds Mona Lisa*

17th century

unclear
probably early 17th century, French School, public domain

jpg
2006, Unknown, copyright unclear | Saatchi Gallery Website / Courtauld Photographic Survey

9

Walker Art Gallery

Unknown, after Leonardo da Vinci

17th century

oil on poplar
date unknown, Leonardo da Vinci (after), public domain

jpg
date unknown, © All Rights Reserved | ArtUK.org

10

Location Unclear

Unknown, after Leonardo da Vinci, *Vernon Mona Lisa*

16th–17th century

olio su tela
1503–1599, Anonimo, public domain

foto
1950–1979, Unknown, copyright unclear | Fondazione Frederico Zeri, Università di Bologna

jpg
date unknown, International Foundation for Art Research, Inc. (IFAR), © Alma Mater Studiorum Università di Bologna | Artstor Digital Library

unclear
16th to 17th century, Unknown, public domain | Louvre Museum

unclear
1966, *The World of Leonardo*, Robert Wallace, Time-life Books, copyright unclear

jpg
2010, Shakko, copyright unclear | Wikimedia Commons

unclear
sec. XVI, 1503–1599, Anonimo, public domain

gelatina ai sali d'argento
1950–1979, International Foundation for Art Research, Inc. (IFAR), copyright unclear | Fondazione Frederico Zeri, Università di Bologna

jpg
date unknown, © Federico Zeri Foundation, CC BY-NC-ND | Fondazione Frederico Zeri Online Photo Archive

unclear
sec. XVI, 1503–1599, Anonimo, public domain

gelatina ai sali d'argento
1970–1989, Anonimo, copyright unclear | Fondazione Frederico Zeri, Università di Bologna

jpg
date unknown, © Federico Zeri Foundation, CC BY-NC-ND | Fondazione Frederico Zeri Online Photo Archive

unclear
sec. XVI, 1503–1599, Anonimo, public domain

gelatina ai sali d'argento
1930–1950, Soichi Sunami, copyright unclear | Fondazione Frederico Zeri, Università di Bologna

jpg
date unknown, © Federico Zeri Foundation, CC BY-NC-ND | Fondazione Frederico Zeri Online Photo Archive

11

Portland Art Museum

Unknown, after Leonardo da Vinci, *Portland Mona Lisa*

16th–18th century

oil on canvas on panel
16th to 18th century, After Leonardo da Vinci, public domain

jpg
2015, © Portland Museum of Art | Portland Museum of Art Website

12

Alte Pinakothek

Unknown, after Leonardo da Vinci

17th–18th century

leinwand
17th to 18th century, Leonardo da Vinci (Kopie nach), public domain

jpg
date unknown, © Bayerische Staatsgemälde-sammlungen, CC BY-SA 4.0 | Sammlung, Alte Pinakothek

Often, an image may sustain multiple format transfers before access to the digital version is extended online. These layers of surrogacy and the corresponding copyright considerations have been captured and communicated according to each surrogate.

Although a material surrogate may exist as a single copy, multiple digital surrogates of the work may be found online, as with The Walters Mona Lisa (no. 6). The research revealed three organizations that make digital surrogates of the Walters painting available online, with two claiming copyright in their version.

Other institutions may permit reuse of a digital surrogate through the website terms and conditions or via an open license, yet continue to claim copyright in the digital versions (no. 4 & no. 12).

1800

13

Multiple
J.B. Rapael Urbain Massard (1775–1843), after Leonardo da Vinci

ca. 1803–1809

engraving
date unknown, Massard, public domain | Harvard University Library

jpg
date unknown, © President and Fellows of Harvard College | HOLLIS

engraving
ca. 1803–1809, Massard, public domain | The British Museum

jpg
date unknown, © Trustees of the British Museum, CC BY-NC-SA 4.0 | The British Museum, £63 + VAT

engraving
late 18th to early 19th century, Massard, public domain | Victoria and Albert Museum

jpg
date unknown, © Victoria and Albert Museum, London | Victoria and Albert Search the Collections

14

Multiple
Constant Louis Antoine Lorichon (1800–1855), after Leonardo da Vinci

ca. 1804–1816

etching and engraving
ca. 1804–1815, Constant Louis Antoine Lorichon, public domain | The British Museum

jpg
date unknown, © Trustees of the British Museum, CC BY-NC-SA 4.0 | The British Museum Collection Online, £63 + VAT

etching and engraving
ca. 1816, Constant Louis Antoine Lorichon, public domain | Philadelphia Museum of Art

jpg
date unknown, © Philadelphia Museum of Art | Philadelphia Museum of Art Website

15

The British Museum
Zéphirin Belliard (1798–1861), after Leonardo da Vinci

ca. 1815–1861

lithograph
ca. 1815–1861, Zéphirin Belliard, public domain

jpg
date unknown, © Trustees of the British Museum, CC BY-NC-SA 4.0 | The British Museum, £63 + VAT

16

The British Museum
Louis Victor Jean Baptiste Aubry-Lecomte (1787–1858), after Leonardo da Vinci

1824

lithograph
1824, Louis Victor Jean Baptiste Aubry-Lecomte, public domain

jpg
date unknown, © Trustees of the British Museum, CC BY-NC-SA 4.0 | The British Museum, £63 + VAT

17

Multiple
Gustave Le Gray (1820–1884), after Aimé Millet (1819–1891), *Millet's Drawing of the Mona Lisa*

1849–1850

unclear
1848, Aimé Millet, public domain | location unclear

photographie
1855, Gustave Le Gray, public domain | Bibliothèque nationale de France

jpg
date unknown, Unknown, copyright unclear | BnF Gallica, €25

unclear
date unknown, Unknown, public domain | location unclear

photographie
19e siècle, Gustave Le Gray, public domain | Musée Gustave Moreau

jpg
1999, © Musée Gustave Moreau, © Direction des Musées de France, © René-Gabriel Ojeda | Joconde

drawing
date unknown, Aimé Millet, public domain | location unclear

albumen silver print
1854–1855, Gustave Le Gray, public domain | The J. Paul Getty Museum

jpg
2016, public domain | The J. Paul Getty Museum Website

18

Multiple
Luigi Calamatta (1801–1869), 1857 engraving of 1825–1826 drawing, after Leonardo da Vinci

1857

unclear
date unknown, Unknown, public domain | location unclear

engraving
1857, Luigi Calamatta, public domain | Philadelphia Museum of Art

jpg
2010, © Philadelphia Museum of Art | Philadelphia Museum of Art Website

unclear
date unknown, Unknown, public domain | location unclear

grafiek
1821–1869, Luigi Calamatta, public domain | Teylers Museum

jpg
date unknown, © Teylers Museum, CC BY-NC | Europeana

unclear
date unknown, Unknown, public domain | location unclear

etching and engraving
1857, Luigi Calamatta, public domain | Philadelphia Museum of Art

jpg
2010, © Philadelphia Museum of Art | Philadelphia Museum of Art Website

19	20	21	22	23		24

19

The British Museum

Hermann Eichens (1813–1886), after Leonardo da Vinci

ca. 1865–1871

lithograph
ca. 1865–1871, Hermann Eichens, after Leonardo da Vinci, public domain

jpg
date unknown, © Trustees of the British Museum, CC BY-NC-SA 4.0 | The British Museum Collection Online, £63 + VAT

lithograph
ca. 1865–1871, Hermann Eichens, after Leonardo da Vinci, public domain

jpg
date unknown, © Trustees of the British Museum, CC BY-NC-SA 4.0 | The British Museum Collection Online, £63 + VAT

20

Multiple

Laurent Hotelin, after Claude Ferdinand Galliard (1834–1887), *Galliard's Drawing of the Mona Lisa*

1867

drawing
date unknown, Gaillard, public domain | location unclear

engraving
1867, Hotelin, public domain | Paris-Guide, Volume 1, Science-Art-Biblioteca Ambrosiana

jpg
2016, © DeAgostini / Getty Images | Getty Images, £485

drawing
date unknown, C.F. Gaillard, public domain | location unclear

drzeworyt
1867, Laurent Hotelin, public domain | Biblioteki Uniwersytetu Wrocławskiego

djvu
date unknown, Unknown, copyright unclear | Digital Library of University of Wroclaw

21

The J. Paul Getty Museum

Goupil & Cie (1839–1860s), Leonardo da Vinci's *Mona Lisa*

ca. 1870

albumen silver print
about 1870, Goupil & Cie (French, active 1839–1860s), public domain

tif
2016, public domain | The J. Paul Getty Museum Website

22

Rijksmuseum, Amsterdam

Pompeo Pozzi (1817–1888), after Leonardo da Vinci

ca. 1850–1880

drawing, sketch
date unknown, unknown, public domain | location unclear

photograph
ca. 1850–1880, Pompeo Pozzi, public domain

tif
2011, Staeske Rebers, public domain / © Rijksmuseum, Amsterdam | Rijksmuseum, Rijksstudio

23

Multiple

Claude Ferdinand Galliard (1834–1887), after Leonardo da Vinci

1886–1887

etching
1886–1887, Claude-Ferdinand Galliard, public domain | Louvre, (Museum), Paris, France

jpg
date unknown, Thierry le Mage, © RMN-Grand Palais / Art Resource, NY | Art Resource, $150

etching
1886–1887, Claude Ferdinand Galliard, public domain | Musée du Louvre

jpg
date unknown, Réunion des Musées Nationaux / Art Resource, NY, copyright unclear | Artstor Digital Library

eau-forte
1886–1887, Claude-Ferdinand Galliard, after Léonard de Vinci, public domain | Saint-Denis, ateliers d'art des musées nationaux

jpg
date unknown, © RMN-Grand Palais / Thierry Le Mage | RMN Photo

engraving
1886, Ferdinand Galliard, public domain | The British Museum

jpg
date unknown, © Trustees of the British Museum, CC BY-NC-SA 4.0 | The British Museum Collection Online, £63 + VAT

24

Multiple

Carlo Brogi, (1850–1925), Unknown (ca. 1503–1599), after Leonardo da Vinci's *Mona Lisa*

ca. 1881–1900

dipinto
sec. XVI, Anonimo, public domain | Roma - Galleria Corsinio

gelatina ai sali d'argento
1912, Brogi, public domain | Fondazione Frederico Zeri, Università di Bologna

jpg
date unknown, © Federico Zeri Foundation, CC BY-NC-ND | Fondazione Frederico Zeri Online Photo Archive

malerei
date unknown, Unknown, public domain | Roma, Galleria Corsini

fotografie
ca. 1881–1900, Carlo Brogi, public domain | MK&G Hamburg

jpg
date unknown, public domain | MK&G Hamburg Collection Online

dipinto
sec. XVI, Anonimo, public domain | location unclear

gelatina ai sali d'argento
ca. 1920, Brogi, public domain | Fondazione Frederico Zeri, Università di Bologna

jpg
date unknown, © Federico Zeri Foundation, CC BY-NC-ND | Fondazione Frederico Zeri Online Photo Archive

1900

25

Harvard Art Museums
Augustin Fauchery, (1800–1843), after Leonardo da Vinci
19th century

engraving
19th century, Augustin Fauchery, public domain

jpg
date unknown, © President and Fellows of Harvard College | Harvard Art Museums Website

26

Harvard University
Albert Teichel (1822–1873), after Leonardo da Vinci
19th century

engraving
date unknown, Albert Teichel, public domain

jpg
date unknown, © President and Fellows of Harvard College | HOLLIS

27

The British Museum
Léon Boisson (1854–1941), after Leonardo da Vinci
19th century

engraving
1891, Léon Boisson, public domain

jpg
date unknown, © Trustees of the British Museum, CC BY-NC-SA 4.0 | The British Museum Collection Online, £63 + VAT

28

Saint-Denis
Augustin Bridoux (1813–1892), after Leonardo da Vinci
19th century

burin, eau-forte
19e siècle, Augustin Bridoux, d'aprés Léonard de Vinci, public domain | Saint-Denis, ateliers d'art des musées nationaux

jpg
date unknown, © RMN-Grand Palais / image RMN-GP | RMN Photo

29

Multiple
Antoine-François Dezarrois (1864–1949), after Leonardo da Vinci
19th century

engraving
19th century, Antoine-François Dezarrois, public domain | Musée du Louvre, Paris, France

jpg
date unknown, ©Thierry Le Mage, RMN-Grand Palais / Art Resource, NY | Art Resource, $150

burin, eau-forte
19e siècle, Derrarois, public domain | Saint-Denis, ateliers d'art des musées nationaux

jpg
date unknown, © RMN-Grand Palais (musée du Louvre) / Michel Urtado | RMN Photo

30

Multiple
Unknown, after Leonardo da Vinci
19th century

print reproduction
19th century, Unknown, public domain | Hulton Archive

jpg
date unknown, © Hulton Archive | Getty Images, £485

unclear
1900, Unknown, public domain | Bettmann

jpg
date unknown, © Bettmann | Getty Images, £485

31

Trinity College Watkinson Library
Unknown, Leonardo da Vinci's *Mona Lisa*
ca. 1907–1914

picture postcard
ca. 1907–1914, Neurdein et Cie (publisher, French, act. 1860s–1919), public domain | Trinity College Watkinson Library

jpg
date unknown, © Trinity College Watkinson Library | Artstor Digital Library

picture postcard
ca. 1907–1914, Braun, Clement and Comany (publisher, French, act. 1907–1914), public domain | Trinity College Watkinson Library

jpg
date unknown, © Trinity College Watkinson Library | Artstor Digital Library

32

National Archives, The Hague
Unknown, Leonardo da Vinci's *Mona Lisa*
ca. 1911

photograph
1911, Spaarnestad Photo collection illustrated magazine Het Leven (1906–1941), copyright unclear

png
date unknown, copyright unclear | Memory of the Netherlands Website

33

Library of Congress

Detroit Publishing Company, Leonardo da Vinci's *Mona Lisa*

ca. 1900–1915

glass negative between 1900–1912, Detroit Publishing Co., copyright claimant and publisher, no known restrictions on publication

tif date *unknown*, public domain | Library of Congress Website

glass negative between 1900–1915, Detroit Publishing Co., copyright claimant and publisher, no known restrictions on publication

tif date *unknown*, public domain | Library of Congress Website

34

Multiple

Timothy Cole (1852–1931), after Leonardo da Vinci

1914

jpg date *unknown*, © Art Institute of Chicago | Art Institute of Chicago Website

wood engraving on Japanese paper 1892, Timothy Cole, Leonardo da Vinci (after), del Sarto, public domain | Smith College Museum of Art

jpg date *unknown*, © Smith College Museum of Art | Artstor Digital Library

wood engraving date *unknown*, Timothy Cole, public domain | Harvard Art Museums

jpg date *unknown*, © President and Fellows of Harvard College | HOLLIS

wood engraving 1914, Timothy Cole, after Leonardo da Vinci, public domain | Art Institute of Chicago

wood engraving 1914, Timothy Cole, no known copyright restrictions | Brooklyn Museum

jpg date *unknown*, public domain | Brooklyn Museum Online Collection

35

Biblioteca Berenson

Unknown, Bernard Berenson's photos, of various Mona Lisas

ca. 1920–1958

painting 1st quarter of 16th century, Unknown, copy after Leonardo da Vinci, public domain | location unclear

photograph ca. 1920–1959, Unknown photographer unknown, copyright unclear | Biblioteca Berenson, Fototeca, Villa I Tatti

jpg date *unknown*, copyright unclear | HOLLIS

painting 1st quarter of 16th century, Unknown, copy after Leonardo da Vinci, public domain | location unclear

photograph ca. 1920–1959, Unknown photographer unknown, copyright unclear | Biblioteca Berenson, Fototeca, Villa I Tatti

jpg date *unknown*, copyright unclear | HOLLIS

painting date *unknown*, Unknown, copy after Leonardo da Vinci, public domain | location unclear

photograph ca. 1920–1957, Unknown photographer unknown, copyright unclear | Biblioteca Berenson, Fototeca, Villa I Tatti

jpg date *unknown*, copyright unclear | HOLLIS

36

Library of Congress

Unknown, Leonardo da Vinci's *Mona Lisa*

1936 or 1937

glass negative 1936 or 1937, Unknown, no known restrictions on publication

tif date *unknown*, public domain | Library of Congress Website

It is worth noting that surrogates made available via Wikimedia Commons are often alleged to be public domain material, but without conclusive provenance as to their origin, their copyright-free status cannot be confirmed. Moreover, in many instances, the source cited as the surrogate's origin revealed the user had uploaded an image subject to a clear copyright claim.

In total, 113 digital surrogates of the Mona Lisa and 36 of her reproductions were archived from a number of host institutions and licensing organizations. Only nine were made available copyright-free for any type of reuse. Six of those were reproductions of the Mona Lisa by subsequent artists. Only three were attributed to Leonardo da Vinci (no. 33 & no. 36).

1400   1500   1600

--/-----/-----/-----/-----/-----/-----/-----/----/-/-----/-----/-----/----

4 Tempesta Map of Rome

Jane C. Ginsburg

IN THE LATE 1580s, Florentine painter and printmaker Antonio Tempesta (1555–1630), having thrived under the earlier Pope Gregory XIII, found himself on the ebbing end of the next Pope, Sixtus V's patronage. Tempesta's commissions to fresco churches or residences had fallen off, but the burgeoning print market offered new opportunities. Printed images of Rome proved increasingly popular with pilgrims, particularly in anticipation of the Jubilee of 1600. Moreover, Rome's urban transformation under Sixtus V refocused attention from the ruined glories of the imperial past to the grandiose design of new thoroughfares, piazzas, fountains, and edifices. The newly mastered engineering feat of transporting obelisks symbolized the passage of grandeur from Roman emperors to Popes—obelisks displaced from their pagan settings now rose throughout the city, facing churches and ecclesiastical palaces. An immense bird's-eye view depiction of the city, greater in size and detail than any predecessor, would celebrate the new Rome, and would advertise Tempesta's representational accomplishments

On the left: Detail of Tempesta's Map of Rome, Recens provt hodie iacet almae vrbis Romae, 1593. (Novacco 4F 256, The Newberry Library)

to prospective papal patrons and other benefactors. It would also enhance his reputation as a printmaker.

Tempesta may have perceived even greater need for alternative sources of income as the early demise of Sixtus V, and the fleeting reigns of his immediate successors—three popes in two of the years during which Tempesta would have been developing his map—rendered the prospect of papal patronage ever more precarious. When Tempesta completed his map, Clement VIII, a fellow-Florentine, was in the second year of an eventual 13-year papacy. By this point, however, if Tempesta was still hoping for lucrative work as a painter of large-scale frescos, he was also extensively exploiting the print market. Wary, it seems, of papal inconstancy in largess or longevity, Tempesta dedicated his map not to Clement VIII, but to Jacobo Bosio, the representative of the Knights of Malta to the Holy See. The map was monumental in every sense—it measured 103.5 × 244 cm, and gave a comprehensive coverage of imposing new buildings as well as ordinary dwellings—and it set

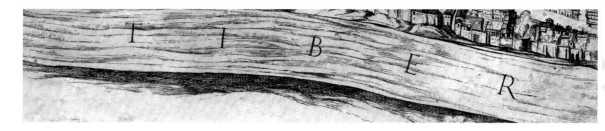

a new standard for visual representations of contemporary Rome. Thenceforth, throughout the 17th century, maps of Rome would literally as well as figuratively derive from Tempesta's template, as subsequent publishers following Tempesta's death reworked the plates that he had etched. (The art historian Eckhard Leuschner notes that publisher Giovanni Battista de Rossi reworked Tempesta's plates for his 1665 edition of the map, and suggests that, although during his life Tempesta sold the plates for many of his prints to various publishers, he appears to have kept the plates for the map, which were probably not dispersed until after his death.)

Tempesta anticipated great success for his map, and accordingly sought to ensure that he would retain the profits. He not only drew the underlying images and etched them himself, but also kept the plates rather than selling them to one of the established Italian or Flemish print publishers in Rome. In a step unusual for artists and print designers, he thus became his own publisher. Most importantly from an intellectual property perspective, he obtained privileges granting him a ten-year monopoly on printing or selling his map. Tempesta was by no means the first mapmaker or printmaker of Roman images to seek exclusive rights from the Pope and other sovereigns. For example, as early as the 1550s, Leonardo Bufalini received papal and French, Spanish and Venetian privileges for his 1551 map of Rome. In 1587 Venetian publisher Girolamo Francino obtained a papal privilege for *Le cose maravigliose dell'alma città di Roma*, with text and engravings celebrating the great public works of Sixtus V, and Flemish publisher Nicolaus van Aelst (who would publish

other prints by Tempesta) received a papal privilege in 1588 for engravings of Roman obelisks. But Tempesta's papal privilege stands out for the arguments he made to support his application for the grant. Tempesta wrote:

Antonio Tempesta, Florentine painter, having in this city [Rome] printed a work of a new Rome, of which he is not only the creator, but also has drawn and engraved it with his own hand, with much personal expense, effort, and care for many years, and fearing that others may usurp this work from him by copying it, and consequently gather the fruits of his efforts, therefore approaches Your Holiness and humbly requests him to deign to grant him a special privilege as is usually granted to every creator of new works, so that no one in the Papal States may for ten years print, have printed, or have others make the said work, and [further requests] that all other works that the Petitioner shall in the future create or publish with permission of the superiors [papal censorship authorities] may enjoy the same Privilege as well so that he may with so much greater eagerness attend to and labor every day [to create] new things for the utility of all, and for his own honor, which he will receive by the singular grace from Your Holiness. (Archivio segreto vaticano, Sec. Brev. Reg. 208 F. 74, at F. 76r (13 October 1593). *Author's translation.*)

The petition evokes justifications spanning the full range of modern intellectual property rhetoric, from fear of unscrupulous competitors, to author-centric rationales. Invocations of labor and investment ("with much personal expense, effort, and care for many years") and unfair competition-based justifications ("fearing that others may usurp this work from him

Above: Detail of Tempesta's Map of Rome, 1593. (The Newberry Library)

Above: Detail of Tempesta's Map of Rome, 1593. (The Newberry Library)

by copying it, and consequently gather the fruits of his efforts") were familiar, indeed ubiquitous, in Tempesta's time; and they still echo today. From the earliest Roman printing privileges in the late 15th century, these rationales figured prominently in petitions by and privileges granted both to authors and to publishers. Petitions and privileges would frequently emphasize the public benefit that publishing the work would confer, while stressing that the author or publisher hesitates to bring the work forth lest others unfairly reap the fruits of their labors, to the great detriment of the author or publisher. Other petitions made explicit the incentive rationale that underlies investment-protection arguments. They urged, as did Tempesta, that the grant of a privilege would encourage not only immediate publication of the identified work, but also future productivity, to even greater public benefit ("so that he may with so much greater eagerness attend to and labor every day [to create] new things for the utility of all"). We can see that long before the 1710 Statute of Anne—the first Act vesting exclusive rights in authors, and the event which is commonly accepted as the birth of the modern era of intellectual property—the precursor regime of printing privileges understood

monopolies as incentives to intellectual and financial investment. The pre-copyright system had thus already firmly established one of the philosophical pillars of modern copyright law.

Tempesta's petition, however, went further than its antecedents with respect to the second pillar of modern copyright law, that is, the justification based on the natural rights of the author, a rationale that roots exclusive authorial rights in personal creativity. Tempesta's contention that new works routinely receive privileges was not novel, but he focused on the rights of the creator ("as is usually granted to every creator of new works") and equated creativity with his personal honor. This argument foreshadowed the modern moral rights conception of copyright. It would be anachronistic to argue that Tempesta claimed that exclusive rights inherently arise out of the creation of a work of authorship, rather than solely by sovereign grant—on the contrary, Tempesta carefully acknowledged both that privileges are a "singular grace" from the Pope, and that all works must receive a license from the papal censors. Nonetheless, in advancing the then-unusual request that the privilege cover "all other works that the Petitioner shall in the future create or publish," Tempesta

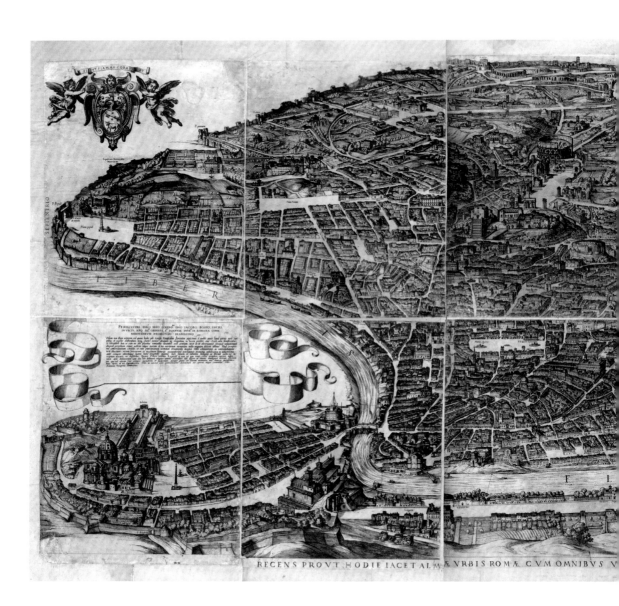

RECENS PROVT HODIE IACET ALMÆ VRBIS ROMÆ CVM OMNIBVS V

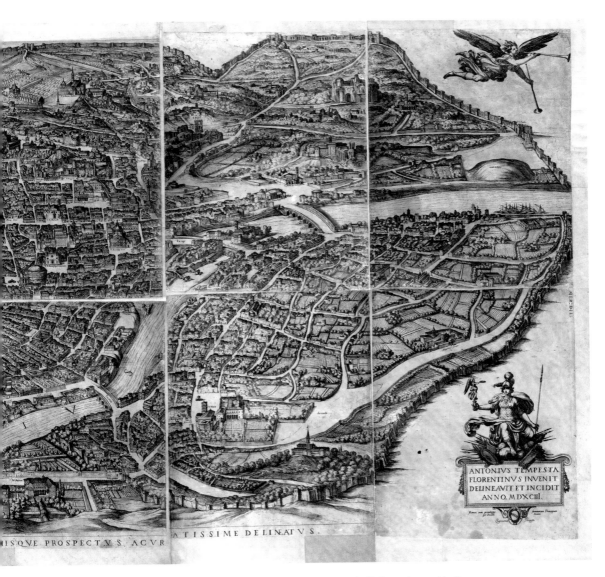

Above: Antonio Tempesta's Map of Rome, Recens provt hodie iacet almae vrbis Romae,
1593. (Novacco 4F 256, The Newberry Library), 103.5 × 244 cm

was urging that his entire future production should automatically enjoy a ten-year monopoly on reproduction and distribution in the Papal States (a claim that was subject, of course, to the censors' approval of each work Tempesta would bring forth). In more modern terms, Tempesta was seeking a result equivalent to "I created it, it's mine." Tempesta also tied his request to incentive rationales—a broad grant of rights would spur him ever more eagerly to greater creativity—and this conflation of creativity-based and labor-incentive conceptions anticipates the frequent oscillation and overlap in modern copyright between natural rights and social contract theories of copyright.

The privilege that Clement VIII eventually granted to Tempesta, while broad, fell short of the full range of Tempesta's aspiration. The Pope did not cover all of Tempesta's future print production, but he did grant exclusive rights not only in the map of Rome, but "also in maps of whatever other places and cities that he will invent and will have engraved onto copper plates." Moreover, the scope of the monopoly in the map of Rome (and, potentially, of other locations) extended to what copyright lawyers today call "derivative works," that is, works based on the initially protected source, such as adaptations and new editions. The privilege thus included "whatsoever form, whether larger or smaller, or in any form different from the version initially printed." Coverage of different size versions of the map would ensure Tempesta's control over smaller, less expensive, editions, whether to exploit that market, or as appears to be the case, to decline to exploit that market in order to preserve the monumental cachet of the immense original. It seems no smaller size editions of the map were published during Tempesta's lifetime.

Yet, the large-scale version may not have sold widely, either. Scholars of Roman printmaking have nonetheless speculated that the number of copies sold does not indicate the measure of the map's success. Jessica Maier and Francesca Consagra suggest that wealthy landowners of the time

Above: Details of Tempesta's Map of Rome, 1593. (The Newberry Library)

liked to decorate their houses with maps and city views; they reference 17th-century architect and author Joseph Furttenbach who advised the affluent to adorn their residences with maps of Rome, mentioning the Tempesta Map as one particularly well suited for a well-appointed study. In other words, Tempesta's map may have attracted an elite clientele prepared both to pay prices three to twenty times higher than smaller prints commanded and, Tempesta may have hoped, to commission even more expensive painted decorations for their villas.

Tempesta's privilege thus served multiple purposes. It allowed him to control the market for his work, matching the public for his map to his self-conception as an innovative painter-printmaker, a polyvalent artist who not only invented the image, but also with his own hand prepared it for the print medium and executed the transfer of the drawing to the copper plate. The exclusive rights the privilege conveyed thus provided legal certainty sufficient to warrant the undertaking of creating and disseminating the map and, Tempesta asserted, stimulating further creative endeavors. And it enhanced the author's honor by conferring the prestige of the approval of the Pope and other sovereigns, a prestige that carried market value. This latter value is clear from the persistent appearance of the original notice of "privileges of the highest princes" through the 1645 reprinting of the map, long after the original privileges would have expired.

The Tempesta Map is an important waypoint in the development of copyright and intellectual property. Over 400 years later, many of the financial and artistic concerns that motivated Tempesta's claim for exclusive rights in his creative output continue to underlie authors' aspirations for the copyright system today. ◆

Further Reading

Giovanni Baglione (1642) *Le vite de' pittori, scultori, architetti, ed intagliatori, dal pontificato di Gregorio XIII. del 1572. fino a' tempi di papa Urbano Ottavo. nel 1642.* Rome.

Stefano Borsi (1986) *Roma di Sisto V: La pianta di Antonio Tempesta, 1593.* Rome: Officina.

Eckhard Leuschner (2012) "Prolegomena to a Study of Antonio Tempesta's 'Map of Rome,'" in Mario Bevilacqua and Marcello Fagiolo (eds.) *Piante di Roma dal Rinascimento ai catasti.* Rome: Artemide.

Eckhard Leuschner (2005) "Note on Antonio Tempesta," p. 4, entry 3501 in *Antonio Tempesta: Commentary, Part 1 (Illustrated Bartsch),* 35. New York: Abaris.

Eckhard Leuschner (2003) "Censorship and the Market: Antonio Tempesta's 'New' Subjects in the Context of Roman Printmaking, ca. 1600," in Marcello Fantoni, Louisa C. Matthew, and Sara F. Matthews-Grieco (eds.) *The Art Market in Italy 15th–17th Centuries.* Modena: F.C. Panini.

Eckhard Leuschner (1998) "The Papal Printing Privilege," *Print Quarterly,* XV, p. 359.

Jessica Maier (2015) *Rome Measured and Imagined: Early Modern Maps of the Eternal City.* Chicago: University of Chicago Press.

Christopher Witcombe (2004) *Copyright in the Renaissance: Prints and the Privilegio in Sixteenth-Century Venice and Rome.* Leiden: Brill.

ΑΠΟΛΛΩΝΙΟ
ΝΕΣΤΟΡΟΣ
ΕΠΟΙΕΙ

1500   *1600*   *1700*

--/-----/-----/-----/-----/-----/-----/-----/-----/-----/-----/-/----/----

5 Hogarth Engraving
Michael Punt

On the left: Detail of "The Analysis of Beauty, Plate I: A Statuary's Yard," William Hogarth, 1753. (Yale Center for British Art)

WILLIAM HOGARTH (1697–1764) was, like Jonathan Swift (1667–1745) before him, an artist whose work represents a set of ideas that are both indicative of his period and transferable to the present. Their significance is such that we describe things as "Hogarthian" or "Swiftian," and the periods in which they lived saw dramatic social, economic, and political change, in which the power of art to express and marshal political criticism has rarely been matched. The biting satires of Swift and Hogarth were advance warning of the political turmoil of the period, a tumult that would boil over across Europe and spill into the United States of America.

Before 1735, artists and engravers such as Hogarth did not enjoy legal protection for their works and were, thus, open to exploitation by print sellers who simply copied popular images if the original engravers held out for too high a price. Hogarth and his fellow artists lobbied parliament to revise copyright laws to protect their images, and this can be seen as merely an act of financial necessity. But the effect of these changes were more important politically than this reading would indicate: extending copyright protections to satirists like Hogarth meant that he could use them to develop vivid visual political analogies, whose potency become stronger through wide publication and even wider reuse.

Hogarth initially had ambitions to be taken seriously as a history painter, but found that the market for such works was led by an aristocracy whose taste was informed by a style from an earlier age. For him this was not just a rejection of his style and oeuvre, but also a social and political iniquity. It meant that those with the means to propagate an English national style were besotted to the aesthetics and values of the Italian Renaissance. To challenge this, Hogarth devoted his painting and image-making to important moral statements. He made images that were powerful interventions in the disputes between artists and their critics about taste; debates that had been conducted to this point only by prominent and wealthy individuals, in a closed discourse. He opened out the debate by a familiar artistic tactic. He used the precise and particular observation of the

everyday to speak of a general condition. His style was to construct analogies in a visual language of caricature and lampoon, and he was able to summon the aesthetic of the everyday to connect with the experience of the viewer in ways that inspired moral reflection, as well as political action. His paintings, and the subsequent engravings that he made of them, aspire neither to the nostalgic depiction of a lost civilization, nor to a frisson of the sensual license of the arts of the French Court. Instead, Hogarth presented arguments in vernacular images.

The directness of his language, the clarity of his intention, and the relevance of his work to the daily experience of his clientele made Hogarth a valuable target for exploitative print-sellers. At the beginning of Hogarth's working life, engravers' work had no protections. Thus, print-sellers of the day were able to operate an abusive publishing business model, commissioning copyists to make cheap copies of his work

in ways that undercut Hogarth's credibility as an artist, diminished his aesthetic project and, of course, diluted his share of the market. This was not personal, it was a widespread practice that yielded profits to the print-sellers, at the expense of the originating engravers and poorly paid copyists alike.

Hogarth was understandably aggrieved by this state of affairs, and his injury was made more acute by the fact that the status of artists and engravers was very different from novelists and authors, who had enjoyed copyright protection for more than two decades. Not only was this unjust in principle, it was financially crippling, and inconsistent with Hogarth's desire to create a new, English style of art. He threw his weight behind the cause of law reform to give artists similar parliamentary protection to that enjoyed by authors. In the end he was successful, and the Engravers' Copyright Act of 1734 extended to engravers of original work a number of

Above: "The Analysis of Beauty, Plate I: A Statuary's Yard," William Hogarth, 1753. (Yale Center for British Art)

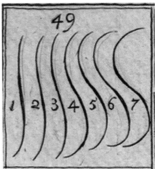

Above, left: "The Painter and his Pug", William Hogarth, 1745, self-portrait of the artist and his dog, Trump. (Photo by Hulton Archive / Getty Images)

Above, right: Detail from "The Analysis of Beauty," Plate I: A Statuary's Yard, William Hogarth, 1753. (Yale Center for British Art)

the protections that had applied to novels for years.

To coincide with the beginning of the Act's operation, on 25 June 1735 Hogarth released a series of engravings of his cycle of paintings called *The Rake's Progress*. The new laws meant that he was able, for the first time, to bypass (what he regarded as) the extortion of the print-sellers. The response of the sellers was immediate, forceful, and devious: they published crude copies of the engravings in order to undermine the novelty of his work. But the copies lacked Hogarth's crisp observation of the particular, from which general moral messages could be understood. The counterfeit works were unsuccessful, and the engravings of *The Rake's Progress* returned a handsome profit to Hogarth, allowing him to operate with both political vigor and some financial security.

In this way, the Engravers' Copyright Act 1734 was a necessary precursor to the development of English art. The successes that followed *The Rake's Progress*—and the confidence engendered by his new legal rights—allowed Hogarth to produce a treatise that challenged the regressive orthodoxies of taste of his time. This treatise, entitled *The Analysis of Beauty*, was published in 1753. In six important principles it set out where beauty was to be found and how it was organized. It was widely read, and sparked considerable controversy, even animosity. Its key assertion was that the most elegant and beautiful is in the world and, in that world, there is the recurrent motif of the serpentine line. Wherever one troubled to look, the line was there. To confirm this, he presented two large engravings along with a frontispiece that included a serpentine line: Plate I, depicting a dance, and Plate II, a sculptor's yard. Both plates follow the same arrangement of a centerpiece surrounded by small numbered illustrations in boxes. The serpentine line is instrumental in the central composition of the two plates, and it flows through both scenes, as well as appearing in several of the numbered boxes. Details in the images and boxes are referred to by Hogarth in the text as though they are diagrams; but, independently, the plates also articulate the philosophical and political argument of

the text using specific social and historical references. The densely coded iconography of these engravings has been the subject of much scholarship and interpretation, and Ronald Paulson's authoritative reading of the engravings gives some indication of the complexity of the philosophical commentary and critique within and between the images. The capacity of these engravings to carry such an argument is a measure both of the intellectual importance of the image in the 18th century and of Hogarth's command of its visual rhetoric.

The Analysis of Beauty is a complex set of ideas that occupied Hogarth for many years. Its most potent and recurring motif, the serpentine line, appears nearly a decade earlier in the 1745 self-portrait, *The Painter and His Pug*. This image, as the underpainting reveals, was begun in the middle of the 1730s as a relatively formal self-portrait of Hogarth as a well-dressed 18th-century gentleman. But progressively, it seems, a more artisanal depiction developed, that of the artist as a person of sensitivity and candor. The formal clothing gives way to a cap, and the intangible aspects of the character are offered not by fashion but by a witty commentary offered through the pose of his favorite dog, called Trump. In 1749 Hogarth made a print after the painting in which the artist's appearance is captured in an oval painting behind his dog, who takes the foreground to both contemplate and guard the line of beauty resting lightly on the artist's palette. The image, entitled *Gulielmus Hogarth*, represents the work of an artist at the top of his game, and it's little surprise that he later used the engraving as the

On the left: "Gulielmus Hogarth," William Hogarth, 1749, Engraving. (Yale Center for British Art)

frontispiece to a published album of his collected works. In the four years between the painting and the engraving, the artist seems to have become more relaxed (and younger), in direct proportion to the dog's more troubled demeanor, as he appears to bear the burden of his master's inner world. The engraving marks, as many have noticed, bespeak a growing self-confidence in the artist who had successfully fashioned a career that was independent of the established routes of patronage. This independence—made possible by the new copyright laws—allowed him to articulate views contrary to the orthodoxies of the aristocracy. Hogarth's mature work was a call to the people to seek beauty in the everyday and not be led by the whims and fashions of connoisseurs.

Hogarth's self-reflection and pugnacious political style did not temper with age, nor did his tactic of using the image in the cause of political confrontation. In 1763, he reworked *Gulielmus Hogarth* and called it *The Bruiser*. In this version, the artist was replaced by a drunken bear in ragged clerical dress, intended to represent Charles Churchill. This act of self-erasure was a bitter volley in the political battles that Hogarth waged against John Wilkes who had, among other things, critiqued the populist emphasis of *The Analysis of Beauty*. Hogarth had earlier depicted Wilkes as an unprincipled criminal, and Churchill had defended him, with a personal attack on the artist citing his vanity and flawed character. In *The Bruiser* the line of beauty has been burnished and replaced by a crude vignette, in which Hogarth, reduced to a comic miniature, whips the bear. There

THE BRUISER, C. CHURCHILL (once the Rev.ᵈ) in the Character of a Russian Hercules, Regaling
himself after having Kill'd the Monster Caricatura that so Sorely Gall'd his Virtuous friend, the Heaven born WILKES.

—— But he had a Club this Dragon to Drub,   Or he had ne'er don't I warrant ye.—— Dragon of Wantley

Design'd and Engraved by W.ᵐ Hogarth Price 1. 6.°   Publish'd according to Act of Parliament August 1. 1763.

is much discussion about the significance of Hogarth using this old plate—whether for example it amplifies the insult because it suggests Churchill does not warrant a new one, or whether it is symptomatic of the aging artist losing his confidence and his rhetorical skills to sheer temper. Whatever the reason, the most striking figure in this engraving is Trump, the beloved pug who, now apparently more distracted by his own thoughts, urinates on Churchill's manuscript. Trump, the established avatar of the artist, manages to both insult and ignore his enemy's epistle at the same time.

Whatever the state of mind Hogarth was in when he modified his triumphal self-portrait and turned it into *The Bruiser*, the complete appropriation of the artist by his analogy in the form of Trump reveals a belief in the endurance of an image as the property of its creator. Art may, or may not, be subject to the patronage of a foppish elite or the whims and fancies of a fickle market; but, as Hogarth argues in *The Analysis of Beauty*, when beauty is drawn from the world of the everyday it becomes invested with a quality that, if protected, will always belong to its author. In the case of Hogarth the pursuit of intellectual property rights was not solely an issue of reward and ownership. With the new rights of the Engraving Copyright Act of 1734 he was able to own an image sufficiently to develop vivid visual analogies whose potency could be leveraged through reuse. And, as we see with the case of *Gulielmus Hogarth* and *The Bruiser*, through copyright

On the left: "The Bruiser," William Hogarth, 1763, Line engraving on medium, slightly textured, cream laid paper. (Gift of Thomas S. Holman, New York, NY, Yale Center for British Art)

he was able completely to own his image, vision, and sensibility.

It is not too much to say then that the new copyright laws of the 18th century are responsible for a range of Hogarth's remarkable innovations. They were responsible for the creation of *The Analysis of Beauty*, and they gave Hogarth the financial security to use art and aesthetics as instrument of political resistance. In this way copyright did give us the term "Hogarthian." The word has become synonymous with the corrupt politics and exploitative society of Britain in the last half of the 18th century, and its use as an adjective to describe unacceptable social inequality everywhere, in part because of the changes that occurred to copyright in the mid-18th century. ◆

Further Reading

Lionel Bently and Martin Kretschmer (eds.) *Primary Sources on Copyright (1450–1900).* Available at: www.copyrighthistory.org

Mark Hallett (1999) *The Spectacle of Difference: Graphic Satire in the Age of Hogarth.* New Haven: Yale University Press.

Ronald Paulson (1971) *Hogarth: His Life, Art, and Times.* New Haven: Yale University Press.

Joachim Möller (ed.) (1996) *Hogarth in Context: Ten Essays and a Bibliography.* Marburg: Jonas Verlag.

1600   1700   1800

--/-----/-----/-----/-----/-----/-----/-----/----/-/-----/-----/-----/----

6 Lithograph
Amanda Scardamaglia

On the left: Advertising for Lewis & Whitty's Diamond Starch, ca. 1881–1890, Troedel & Co. Lithographers. (State Library Victoria)

THE LEGACY OF the lithograph is understated, crowded out by our perception of the importance of the printing press. Although there were clear parallels between both processes, in terms of technical achievement and social consequence, the lithograph was responsible for changing print advertising practices around the world.

Lithography, a method of chemical printing based on the incompatibility of oil and water, was invented by Alois Senefelder sometime around 1796 in Bavaria as a cheap and efficient alternative to the existing processes for print reproduction using metal and wood engraving. Its invention had a profound impact on the categories of intellectual property, and transformed the production of print advertising in the same way the printing press transformed the production of literary works. It paved the way for the registration of commercial artifacts as trademarks for the first time. And it casts an illuminating shadow on the glow in which the printing press has basked, and especially on the prevailing accounts of how intellectual property law has developed in response to new technologies.

It is a popular myth that Senefelder invented lithography by chance: the story goes that he penned a list for his mother on a flat stone with a grease pencil and, on a hunch, covered the surface with acid, only to discover the greasy pencil protected the stone and revealed the list. In reality, Senefelder was an accomplished playwright who struggled to pay the printing fees, and was motivated to develop an affordable way to print his theatrical works.

Senefelder was conferred exclusive printing rights for 15 years from the Prince of Bavaria on 3 September 1799 for "Chemical Printing for Bavaria and the Electorate." Soon after, he set up a number of presses in Offenbach in Germany and London, later securing patent rights across Europe, including in England, where he obtained a patent in 1801 for "A New Method and Process of Performing the Various Branches of the Art of Printing on Paper, Linen, Cotton, Woollen and other Articles." To produce a lithograph using Senefelder's method, the artist draws on the

surface of a limestone or other plate with greasy crayons or a grease-like ink. When the drawing is complete, a solution of gum arabic and nitric acid is washed across the stone to prevent the grease from bleeding. The entire surface of the limestone is then washed with water, and the stone is rolled with printing ink. Since grease and water repel each other, the ink adheres only to the greasy drawing. Thereafter, paper is laid across the stone and together they are pulled through a press. This transfers the image from the stone to the paper, producing a mirror image of the original image, to complete the printing process.

The invention of the lithograph could not be more significant to the media age in which we now live. To some, the printing press is the most significant development leading to the advent of advertising. The printing press facilitated the first forms of print advertising. These were featured in the newly established newspapers and magazines and were a marked departure from the earlier methods of word of mouth advertising and town-criers. The printing press also allowed for mass advertising, including the mass publication of posters, handbills, flyers, pamphlets, and other promotional material.

But from a design perspective, these ads lacked visual appeal. Early print advertising was dominated by black and white textual matter and only began to incorporate trademarks and graphics in the 1850s,

although this was dictated by the limits of the mechanical printing processes available at the time. Enter the lithograph, dramatically changing the face of advertising, most notably from the 1870s, thanks to developments such as chromolithography which facilitated the layering of color.

During the latter part of the 19th century, advertising evolved from the simple text and devices used in early classified advertising, to artistic masterpieces. Lithography allowed for the production of low-cost, high-quality illustrations on labels and other ephemera. Lithography also enabled the reproduction of original paintings, delicate oil-and-water drawings and other sketches, which were used as full-page advertisements and more frequently, for advertising posters.

The advertising poster really owes its existence to lithography. Early advertising posters were produced using wood or metal engravings with little color or design, but the production quality did not compare to the possibility offered by lithography and color lithography. Jules Chéret, who became a master of The Belle Époque and the French poster art movement, showcased this possibility in a way that promoted lithography as a legitimate art form. Chéret's work inspired a troupe of other designers, with the growing popularity of poster art culminating in a major exhibition in Paris in 1884. The public bought into this hype and started to demand these

Above: Advertisements for Red Cross Raspberries and Red Currants, ca. 1880, and Comet Pears, date unknown, Troedel & Co. Lithographers. (State Library Victoria)

Above: Advertisement for Australian Trent Brewery's Pure Malt & Hop Ales, ca. 1881–1900, Troedel & Co. Lithographers. (State Library Victoria)

advertising posters for their own personal collections, with the aesthetic appeal soon surpassing their advertising function.

There is no doubt that this palpable shift in style would have been impossible without lithography, and its ability to produce inexpensive, first-class illustrations in a way that traditional printing methods could not. It is no wonder that lithography quickly became the printing medium of choice in the late 19th to early 20th centuries. Lithography was warmly embraced by artists, particularly in Europe with notable names including Pablo Picasso, Edgar Degas, and Édouard Manet all working with lithographs at various times during their careers.

Obviously, the transition from textual to graphical advertising was not due to the lithograph alone, in the same way that one cannot claim the printing press was singularly responsible for revolutionizing the production of the written word. The shift in advertising aesthetic was assisted by other innovations in production techniques, notably the development of new fonts. Changes in advertising practices were also influenced by new practices in product packaging. Advances in paperboard packaging and the invention of the metal can and methods in canned food preservation were particularly important, providing a packaging canvas upon which producers could affix their labels, bringing advertising into people's homes.

Many of these product labels and advertising posters were registered for copyright protection, with international copyright registers littered with lithographs. This appears strange, for copyright is supposed to protect authorial works, not commercial descriptors, and many of these works, particularly product labels, were largely descriptive, and not at all similar to the kinds

Above: Advertisement for Fragrant Capstan Health Soap, ca. 1921–1930, Troedel & Cooper. (State Library Victoria)

of creative works normally associated with copyright protection and artistic works. The labels were merely instructional, conveying information about the product and the proprietor, having no meaning beyond the associations to the products to which they were affixed.

Controversy quickly ensued. In the 1840s, the American courts limited the scope of protection for the owners of these commercial artifacts. The high point was a case involving the reproduction of a medicine label for "Doctor Rodgers' Compound Syrup of Liverwort and Tar," which had been registered for copyright protection. The court rejected the plaintiff's claim, holding the labels served a purely commercial purpose of identifying goods for sale and therefore could not be protected as copyright works. Notwithstanding this decision, the distinction between the various categories of lithographs was not always applied in practice, with thousands of labels registered as copyright works across the continents.

In response, the US State Department distributed a circular to the district courts not to register these types of labels because it was contrary to the purpose of copyright, which was designed to promote the acquisition and diffusion of knowledge, and to encourage the production and publication of works of art. But again, the practice continued until 1903 when the US Supreme Court confirmed the legality of these registrations, deciding that a picture is a picture and nonetheless a subject of copyright, even if used for an advertisement.

While copyright was never intended to protect trade labels or advertising posters for that matter, this practice was allowed for some years because there was at the time no proper legislative machinery for the registration of trademarks. And were it not for the habit of registering these commercial works as copyright, the necessity of legislation permitting trademark registration would have likely arisen sooner.

Copyright was never intended to protect commercial interests and brand identity. This is clear from the limits to the protection afforded to trade material by the copyright system. While copyright

Above: Advertisement for Robert Harper & Co. New Seasons Teas, ca. 1891–1892, Troedel & Co. Lithographers. (State Library Victoria)

registration did serve as notice to other traders that a claim had been made over a work, in the case of infringement, the owner was only entitled to an award of damages for copying. Moreover, a copyright owner was not eligible for damages for trade diversion or lost sales caused by consumer confusion. Copyright registration therefore only gave rise to the right against copying; it did not give authors the exclusive right to use those works in the course of trade.

Trademark registration overcame these limitations and provided the kind of protection for brands and commercial reputation that copyright did not. There were a number of factors leading to the introduction of trademark registers in the common law world. Lithography was part of this complex matrix. Stone press printing made the reproduction of trademarks and advertising materials easier than ever before and so facilitated the production of counterfeits and imitations. Lithography also made it possible to produce content that was commercially valuable and worth protecting.

Firms realized this, and took advantage of the registered trademark system. Many of these early registered trademarks were advertising posters. Many more were labels. These labels, which became increasingly ornate and featured bright and often gaudy colors, were primitive in their attempt to distinguish the products on which they were affixed. Early labels were mostly descriptive of the product and lacked features that would serve to differentiate a brand or trader. Some labels were little more than a long descriptive text, without any distinctive elements at all; other than, perhaps, the border of the label. Nevertheless, the practice continued largely unabated, thanks to the broad definition of a trademark.

The production of lithographs posed a legal problem. These objects did not fit the traditional copyright mold, but they also did not sit squarely within the definition of a trademark. Today, we understand copyright and trademarks to be conceptually different, albeit with some overlap. Lawmakers, the courts, and the bureaucrats responsible for administering these registration systems recognized a conceptual difference between the registered copyright and trademark systems in the 19th century too, as these regimes were still in their infancy, but it took some time for these legal differences to fully develop.

Over time, the definition of a trademark was interpreted more strictly to relate to distinctive and not descriptive signs, to the exclusion of labels lacking any distinctive indicia. But this was only following a decades-long process which eventually carved out a more distinct delineation between copyright and trademarks—a delineation that was only brought to bear by the invention of lithography and the lithograph. In this way, the lithograph was to trademark law what the printing press was to copyright, transforming the production of print advertising in the same way that the printing press transformed the production of literary works. ◆

Further Reading

Pat Gilmour (ed.) (1988) *Lasting Impressions: Lithographs as Art*. Philadelphia: University of Pennsylvania Press.

Amanda Scardamaglia (2019) *Charles Troedel: From Stone to Print*. Melbourne: Melbourne Books.

Alois Senefelder (1819) *A Complete Course on Lithography*. London: Ackermann.

1600   1700   1800

--/-----/-----/-----/-----/-----/-----/-----/-----/-----/----/-/-----/----

7 Morse Telegraph

Adam Mossoff

O N 24 MAY 1844, Samuel Finley Breese Morse tapped out the first message on the first fully operational electro-magnetic telegraph line: "What hath God wrought!" Reflecting his deeply held religious convictions, Morse chose a line from the Bible, which he sent in the now-famous dot-and-dash transmission code he also invented, the eponymous "Morse Code." One might accuse Morse of hyperbole in this transmission, but his invention of the electro-magnetic telegraph was a radical innovation that fundamentally transformed human communication. It was part of a wide-ranging upheaval in early 19th-century American society, in a country that was transforming itself from a primarily agrarian economy based on the Eastern seaboard to one that stretched across the continent with a fast-growing industrial and commercial economy, driven by technological innovation that dazzled world representatives when displayed in 1851 at the Crystal Palace Exhibition in London.

At the Crystal Palace, Morse's telegraph was included along with other American innovations, such as Eli Whitney's cotton gin, Samuel Colt's repeating firearm, Charles Goodyear's vulcanized rubber, and Cyrus McCormick's mechanized reaper. Together these inventions caused a radical technological, social, and economic transformation of American life in the 19th century. Yet, the telegraph was unique if only because it was the product of cutting-edge discoveries in both mechanics and science (called "natural philosophy" at the time) that created an immediately practical benefit unknown before in human history—fast and efficient communication over vast distances.

Americans were enthralled with what they called the "Lightning Line" and with the man who invented it, whom they called the "Lightning Man." One newspaper proclaimed that the telegraph's instantaneous communication "annihilated space and time." The *New York Sun* waxed poetic that Morse's telegraph was "the greatest revolution of modern times and indeed of all time, for the amelioration of Society." Another newspaper embraced Morse's own nationalist chauvinism in

On the left: Telegraph key on an antique map. (Getty Images)

calling the telegraph "the most wonderful climax of American inventive genius."

It may be hard for the modern reader to appreciate such praise for the telegraph, but in its historical context, the telegraph portended a communications revolution, the likes of which society had never seen. Until the invention of the telegraph in the 1830s, the speed of communication had been inextricably linked with the speed of human transportation, whether by foot, sailing ship, or horseback. Systems of long-distance communication had been devised—such as smoke signals and later the French semaphore system, which used flags—but these were labor intensive, crude, and highly limited in the information that they could send. The unfortunate results of these natural limits on human communication over vast distances were well known. One of the more famous examples in the early 19th century was the Battle of New Orleans, the only battle in the War of 1812 won by the Americans, which occurred three weeks *after* the Treaty of Ghent officially ended hostilities between the United States and Great Britain. But

for the lack of a telegraph in 1815, General Andrew Jackson, the commander of the US forces in New Orleans, may not have garnered some of his early fame that eventually helped propel him to the presidency in 1832.

The lightning simile for the telegraph was apt, given its use of electricity, a subject little understood but of increasing scientific and technological interest at the time. Morse was not the only early American who found inspiration in electricity: Benjamin Franklin famously experimented with it in the 18th century, as did others. Joseph Henry, a nationally renowned physicist at Princeton University and the first Secretary of the Smithsonian Institution, experimented with it, using a battery and wires to ring a bell in another building on the Princeton campus in an experiment in the late 1820s. Morse used the fascination with electricity at the time to help promote his telegraph: in the 1830s, he teamed up with Samuel Colt, the inventor of the famous revolver, to give a public demonstration before 40,000 people in New York City of how he could send electrical signals

Above: American painter-turned-inventor Samuel Morse sends the first public telegram from the Supreme Court chamber in the Capitol, Washington, DC, to Baltimore, 24 May 1844. Morse sent the message "What hath God Wrought?" (Photo by Authenticated News / Getty Images)

Above: Concept of Manifest Destiny: Allegorical female figure carrying electric telegraph wire, leads American pioneers and railroads westwards, Native American Indians and buffalo and bear retreating before them. Chromolithograph, ca. 1873. (Photo by Universal History Archive / Getty Images)

through underwater wires by remotely detonating a ship in the Hudson River.

Lightning is also an excellent simile for the telegraph because Morse conceived of the electro-magnetic telegraph in 1832 in a classic "flash of genius." During an ocean voyage back to the United States after a long sojourn in Paris, Morse's dinner conversations focused on recent advances in electricity and mechanics, as well as the defects of the French semaphore system as a communication system. At one dinner, he excitedly proclaimed, "If the presence of electricity can be made visible in any part of the circuit, I see no reason why intelligence may not be transmitted instantaneously by electricity." (Many people consider these claims to a "flash of genius" to be apocryphal, but Morse's story is corroborated by substantial letters, notes, and sketches, all of which were preserved for posterity in legal records in his patent infringement lawsuits in the 1840s and 1850s, known at the time as the "Telegraphic War in the West.")

Although Morse conceived of his telegraph in 1832, it still took six years of experimentation and development before he perfected the technical details and submitted his first patent application in 1838. Like many American innovators at this time, he was not trained in science or mechanics. He was a well-known artist and he was working as a professor of art at New York University in the 1830s while experimenting to perfect his electro-magnetic telegraph. Morse was the 19th-century version of the modern "garage inventor."

His six years of research and development was also due to the fact that he needed assistance. This was provided by another NYU colleague, Leonard Gale, a chemistry professor, and a former student, Alfred Vail, who provided mechanical assistance and, even more importantly, funds to support their inventive labors. Morse also corresponded with Dr. Henry, who was impressed with Morse's invention, stating in one letter that although many people had been pursuing the "idea of

transmitting intelligence to a distance by means of electrical action ... all attempts to reduce it to practice were necessarily unsuccessful." But with Morse's telegraph, he wrote, "science is now fully ripe for this application, and I have not the least doubt, if proper means be afforded, of the perfect success of [your] invention."

Morse's first patent on his invention was issued on 20 June 1840, titled "American Electro-Magnetic Telegraph." It showed an electrical circuit powered by a battery to activate an electro-magnet. In using a switch to toggle the flow of electricity on and off, the electro-magnet alternately moved a magnetized lever back and forth, causing it to make tic marks on a strip of paper. These marks represented the transmission code also invented by Morse—the famous dots and dashes that we now call "Morse Code" and which long outlived his telegraph. The telegraph was made obsolete long ago by the telephone, fax, and the internet, but Morse Code was only officially phased out of service by maritime and military communications systems at the end of the 20th century.

As Dr. Henry's letter to Morse made clear, other innovators were working on telegraphs at the same time as Morse, including the British inventor Charles Wheatstone, but Morse beat them to the punch. He did so in large part because his invention was the epitome of the engineer's "elegant solution." The simplicity of a binary code with an equally straightforward battery-powered circuit cum electro-magnet was innovation par excellence. Morse's binary code and the electro-magnetic telegraph went hand in hand, just like the modern union of software and hardware in computers and smartphones.

Morse was not just first in inventing a working electro-magnetic telegraph; his telegraph was technically superior to the complicated circuitry and error-prone machinery that others independently invented shortly after him in the late 1830s and early 1840s. This explains why the Lightning Man's electro-magnetic telegraph became *the* telegraph, the technology that ushered in the communications revolution. Morse saw the potential value in his invention, and patented all of the inventive elements comprising his technological innovation— his transmission code, the circuit, and the machinery itself.

The excitement about the Lightning Line was very real, as everyone recognized the commercial, industrial, and political implications of long-distance communication at the speed of light. But Morse faced a problem familiar to modern entrepreneurs: how could he commercialize the invention? Morse's telegraph was the exemplar of out-of-the-box innovation by a nonspecialist, and this was a problem: he was an artist,

Above, from left to right: Aerial Telegraph: Ancient Greek soldiers tending a signal fire, ca. 1900. It is claimed that news could be transmitted 525km in a night; Maritime Telegraph, ca. 1900. Sailors hoisting flags which have been assembled to convey a message to a nearby vessel. For centuries signals were sent from vessel to vessel using flags, each of which represented a phrase or word. Trade cards for Liebig Meat Extract. (Photo by Ann Ronan Pictures / Print Collector / Getty Images)

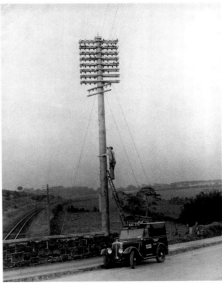

not a businessperson. Morse realized that he could extract the value in the property rights in his patents by selling and licensing his ownership interests to others with the business acumen to convert the invention he created in his New York City apartment into real-world technology used across the United States. He transferred control of his patent in the American Magnetic Telegraph to Amos Kendall, who then created the Magnetic Telegraph Company, which used patent licensing in an innovative commercial organization that we now call the franchise business model. As a result, numerous people and companies began building and operating telegraph lines across the country.

The ability to communicate instantaneously across vast distances was an essential building block to increasing the speed of all human activity, especially in industry and commerce. The railroads used the telegraph to expand their railway lines and operations; in fact, railroad and telegraph companies were largely born together through a marriage of commercial convenience. Kendall and his franchise operators needed access rights to land to lay telegraph wires and the railroad companies needed faster and more efficient communication about their long-distance operations. Thus, the railroads allowed the telegraph lines to be constructed along the easements they already acquired for laying their tracks and telegraph lines sprung up as fast as railway tracks were laid.

As with all innovation, the telegraph led to follow-on improvements that produced unintended and sometimes surprising consequences. For example, Morse and his associates originally planned to install telegraph wires underground, but this idea proved a failure given the lack of proper materials and know-how in the early 1840s in insulating electrical wires to protect them from water in the soil. The solution was provided by Ezra Cornell, who first conceived of stringing transmission wires from the tops of wooden poles. Telegraph

A	·—		N	—·
B	—···		O	———
C	—·—·		P	·——·
D	—··		Q	——·—
E	·		R	·—·
F	··—·		S	···
G	——·		T	—
H	····		U	··—
I	··		V	···—
J	·———		W	·——
K	—·—		X	—··—
L	·—··		Y	—·——
M	——		Z	——··

Above: The signboard of the Telegraph Café in Vienna. (Photo by Claudy Op den Kamp)

On the left: The table of the encoded alphabet deposited by Samuel Morse on 3 October 1837. (Photo by Fototeca Gilardi / Getty Images)

poles installed alongside railroad tracks were used in the first telegraph line on which Morse sent his famous message in 1844. Cornell made a fortune on his idea, founding the famous telegraph company, Western Union—which is still in business today—and later using his wealth to found Cornell University. It is perhaps fitting that an institution of higher learning—the enlightenment ideal—was brought into existence by harnessing the power of lightning to communicate.

The telegraph didn't just revolutionize the United States. Replacing sailing ships that took weeks or months to convey letters across oceans, the first transatlantic telegraph line between North America and England was laid in the late 1850s and was fully operational by the 1860s—a mere 20 years after Morse's first patent was issued on the technology. The telegraph thus played a key role in making the world a smaller place. Many of today's undersea cables that form the backbone of the internet's communication system follow the same paths of these first undersea telegraph lines laid in the mid-19th century.

One modern historian has referred to the telegraph as the "Victorian internet,"

which is not far off in terms of the technological advances it represented, the legal and political issues raised by the large corporations that came to own and control it, and even the disruption of social norms. The rise of acronyms and shortened slang, for instance, far predates today's emails and text messages: in the 19th century, grammarians bemoaned the impact that the telegraph was having on the English language given its incentive to create acronyms and slang to save on both time and cost in sending messages—users were charged per letter in telegraph messages. Somewhere in America in the late 19th century a recipient of a telegraph message might have had difficulties deciphering its mangled English, paving the way for today's parents reading one of their children's text messages exclaiming "What has God wrought!" ◆

Further Reading

David Hochfelder (2012) *The Telegraph in America, 1832–1920*. Baltimore: Johns Hopkins University Press.

Daniel Walker Howe (2007) *What Hath God Wrought: The Transformation of America, 1815–1848*. Oxford: Oxford University Press.

David McCullough (2011) *The Greater Journey: Americans in Paris*. New York: Simon & Shuster.

Adam Mossoff, *O'Reilly v. Morse*. Available at: https://ssrn.com/abstract=2448363

Kenneth Silverman (2003) *Lightning Man: The Accursed Life of Samuel F.B. Morse*. Cambridge: Da Capo Press.

Tom Standage (1998) *The Victorian Internet: The Remarkable Story of the Telegraph and the Nineteenth Century's On-line Pioneers*. London: Bloomsbury.

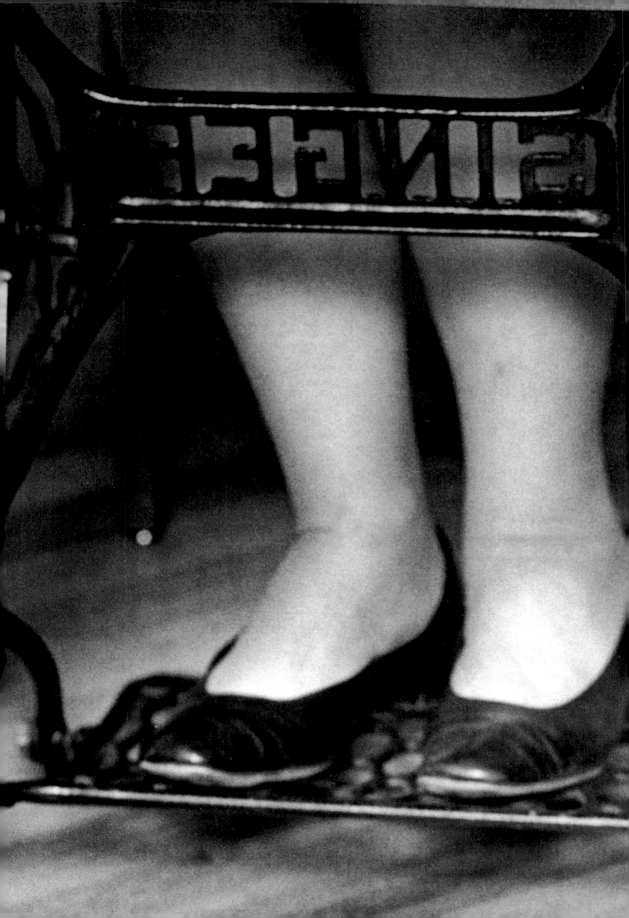

8 Singer Sewing Machine

Lionel Bently

On the left: Many hours of treadling on a vintage Singer sewing machine helped Mrs. Mario Iona win a new Touch and Sew Zig-Zag machine and a host of prizes in National Grange sewing contest in 1973. (Denver Post via Getty Images)

THE SEWING MACHINE was one of the most important innovations of the 19th century. Arising out of a series of individual breakthroughs, workable sewing machines emerged on the market in the United States, Britain, and Europe in the mid-1850s. The innovation was described by contemporaries as one of the "wonders of the age," transforming the labor of all those who worked in the garment industry—seamstresses, tailors, shirt- and collar-makers, cap-makers, glove-makers, hosiers, and more. But the sewing machine also generated disquiet, leading to strikes and protests from tailors and bootmakers, paving the way for the emergence of the ready-made clothing industry, and eventually the sweatshop. In this way, the sewing machine was little different from many 19th century innovations; but the real watershed was how the machine entered the home, as, perhaps, the first domestic appliance. Indeed, one commentator, Andrew Gordon, suggests that the marketing of the sewing machine not only created modern selling practices, but also created the concept of the modern consumer, someone who was

engaged in the world of branded products and also dependent on credit for access to these products.

Intellectual property was central to the development of the sewing machine. In 1864, the *Sydney Morning Herald* reported that the "history of the sewing machine is simply a record of legal proceedings in every possible shape"—by which the paper mostly meant patent litigation, in particular questions of novelty and proper disclosure. In the following decades, the litigation would take a different shape, as sewing machine manufacturers fought each other over the use of trade names and trademarks. In doing so, they would unknowingly lay the foundations for much of modern day trademark law.

Most commentators agree that a workable sewing machine depended on eight or nine inter-related breakthroughs. Perhaps not surprisingly, patent rights were obtained by different persons over each of these elements. The most important was Elias Howe's "lockstitch" invention, in which a needle would carry a thread through a piece of cloth so as to create a

Above, from left to right: Elias Howe's patent model, using an eye-pointed needle and a shuttle to form a lock-stitch (Getty Images); Early model of Singer sewing machine (Harris & Ewing Collection, Library of Congress, Prints and Photographs Division); A woman sewing on a Singer sewing machine, ca. 1900. (Photo by Zander & Labisch / ullstein bild via Getty Images)

On the left: "Singer sewing machines lead all others." (Library of Congress, Prints and Photographs Division)

loop, through which a second thread was laced, before the first needle was withdrawn carrying the thread back to the other side of the cloth. Other inventions, including ways to hold the cloth steady and move it on, were soon developed by others.

In the United States, intense litigation emerged from this—nicknamed the "patent wars"—where Howe fought a range of manufacturers—Singer & Co., Wheeler & Wilson, and Grover & Baker—over a range of alleged patent infringements. The chief protagonists of the wars eventually formed a "patent pool," or cartel, where each was licensed to use the pooled patents to make its own style of sewing machine, paying Howe $5 per machine produced. If the market was not fully satisfied by the pool members, nonpool members could be licensed at $15 a time, and those outside the pool who did not negotiate licenses would be subject to infringement proceedings. Through these means, Elias Howe became a millionaire, and the members of the cartel thrived. Today's scholars debate the merits of this pooling arrangement on innovation of the time; but whether

good or bad for innovation, it was certainly lucrative for those within the pool.

In the UK, many of the sewing machine patent rights were in different hands, and these patentees did not cartelize in the same way as in the United States. The right to patent the lockstitch invention was assigned by Elias Howe to the corset-maker, William Thomas, who allowed his son to attempt to exploit the invention. However, he did so without the benefit of the rights to use the other inventions necessary for a commercially useful machine, and so, while he was able to use his exclusivity to control the market, his commercial success was limited. Rather, much of his energy seems to have been spent litigating the patent to keep others, such as Grover & Baker, out of the market; a strategy that led to the repeated amendment of the patent and, at the end of 1860, its expiry.

It is instructive to compare the effects of the two arrangements in the different jurisdictions: the one in the United States involving co-operation, the one in the United Kingdom applying individual exclusivity. According to *Mechanics*

Magazine, as of 1860, the number of machines per capita in the United Kingdom was about one-tenth of the penetration that had occurred in the United States. Not surprisingly, with the lapse of the Thomas lockstitch patent, the British market was immediately invaded by American manufacturers, and in particular the patent pool operators, Wheeler & Wilson, Grover & Baker, and the Singer Manufacturing Co. With the benefit of their experience in refining their products, as well as advertising and selling—for example, through another innovation, the hire-purchase scheme—they quickly established reputations for high-quality products and became the dominant players in this fast-growing market. The sewing machine thus became the first subject of international branding, that is, the centrally controlled use of trademarks as a means to project particular product values, attributes, and meanings.

Even with the lapse of the Thomas patent, the patent wars were not over in the United Kingdom. Instead, other patentees sought to enforce related sewing machine patents—most remarkably, in a case from 1864 when Daniel Foxwell issued separate proceedings against some 134 manufacturers, importers, sellers, and users of sewing machines. The Lord Chancellor sought to manage the litigation by trying only a few chosen representative cases, but the matter highlighted in many ways both ongoing problems with the patent system and with the system of litigation in England at the time. The patent ended up being invalidated, confirming that the market was now free for the sale of working machines. A by-product of this litigation was the creation of the Makers, Dealers, and Users of Sewing Machines' Central Association, a group formed to defend businesses from the impact of the sewing machine patents. This group worked together, seeking to defeat intellectual property rights, rather than to enforce them, as was the case in the United States. This idea seems to have mutated into the British Sewing Machine Trade Association in the 1870s; a group with the stated desire to defeat the "American monopoly."

After the expiry of the Thomas patent, and especially from 1864 onward, British makers imitated the American market leaders in the construction of the machines, and in their advertising and sale. The British firm Newton, Wilson & Co., for example, established a huge shop at 144 High Holborn, that was strikingly similar to I.M. Singer & Co.'s shop on Broadway in New York, a store that opened a decade earlier. These emporiums were akin, in their day, to the Apple stores of the present. Newton, Wilson & Co. also exhibited their machines at international exhibitions and

Above, left: the Newton, Wilson & Co. High Holborn shop in London. (Gale Cengage's 19th century UK periodicals)

Above, right: the I.M. Singer & Co.'s shop on Broadway in New York. (Library of Congress)

advertised in newspapers and journals and on billboards, typically depicting a woman sitting at the machine. Sewing machines were described as the perfect Christmas present or wedding gift.

American manufacturers, like Singer & Co. and Wheeler & Wilson, began using the trademark system to push back on the attempts by British and German manufacturers and retailers to make inroads on their market share. Early targets were former British selling-agents of the American companies who had set themselves up in competition with their former licensors. Tom Shakspear, who had previously sold Wheeler & Wilson machines, was eventually enjoined from describing his business as if he were still an agent for the American company. Another former licensee, Alonzo Kimball, and his partner, John Morton, were sued by Singer & Co., for using the name "Singer" to describe aspects of their "Lion" sewing machine that they produced and sold in Scotland. Lord President Inglis in the Scottish Court of Session interdicted the firm from using the word "Singer" in relation to their sewing machines. He said that the name "Singer" was "a great favourite with the public," the use of which created "a certain guarantee of excellence in the machine sold," and which "carries off machines, and produces a greater sale than any other name going."

Lord Inglis' language seems to anticipate by half a century Frank Schechter's idea that courts should protect the "selling power" of a mark—a theory that was only implemented decades later in the development of trademark dilution laws. But whatever the underlying theory, the American companies were clear about the practical value of their marks in monopolizing the trade: if British manufacturers could not refer to their machines using the terms with which the public had become familiar—"Wheeler & Wilson," "Singer," or "Grover & Baker"—then they simply would not make machines in those configurations. Writing in June 1872, just after securing the interdict against Kimball & Morton, one of Singer & Co.'s British managers stated that maintaining the trademarks was far better than having any patent.

Having prevailed in Scotland, Singer & Co. turned its attention south. In 1875 it commenced proceedings against Newton, Wilson & Co., on the basis that the British firm had advertised its models using the term "Singer." Seeking to stop British manufacturers from what we would nowadays call "passing off," Singer & Co. was infuriated when Sir Georg Jessel ruled—even without hearing the evidence for the defence—that there could be no infringement, because there was no possibility of purchasers being deceived. The judge indicated that the use of the word as a sign on the goods would be illegal, but that its use in advertising was permissible unless the plaintiff could demonstrate fraud. On appeal to the House of Lords, Lord Cairns, the Lord Chancellor ruled that there was no principled distinction between the use of a mark as a sign on goods and its use in advertising, finding that some purchasers might have been deceived by the English firm's advertising. The case was remitted back to the trial

court, but Newton, Wilson and Co. could not afford to defend further proceedings, and went out of business.

Even before the House of Lords had allowed the appeal in the case against Newton, Wilson & Co., Singer & Co. had started proceedings against another seller, Hermann Loog. Loog was selling machines made by the leading German firm, Frister & Rossmann, and his advertising materials referred to the models being sold by reference to the "Wheeler & Wilson" and "Singer" names. Singer & Co. won at trial, but on the eventual appeal to the House of Lords, the new Lord Chancellor gave the leading speech in a decision that ruled for Loog. Without determining that the word "Singer" was generic in describing sewing machines, Lord Selborne observed that:

[i]f the defendant has … a right to make and sell, in competition with the plaintiffs, articles similar in form and construction to those made and sold by the plaintiffs, he must also have a right to say that he does so, and to employ for that purpose terminology common in his trade, provided that he does this in a fair, distinct and unequivocal way.

This was an important step toward the principle that these days we know as "genericide," the limiting doctrine that recognizes that words that were once trademarks—such as cellophane, escalator, or bandaid—may over time come to describe the class of products themselves and lose trademark protection.

Although England was first to begin to limit the control that incumbents like Singer & Co. could exert via trademark, once the patent pool lapsed in the United States similar battles ensued. After a series of state decisions, the issue of whether traders were free to use the term "Singer" descriptively came before the Supreme Court. In *Singer Manuf'g Co.* v. *June Manuf'g Co.* the Court reviewed American, English and French case law and concluded:

[t]hat where, during the life of a monopoly created by a patent, a name … has become, by his consent … the identifying and generic name of the thing patented, this name passes to the public with the cessation of the monopoly which the patent created. Where another avails himself of this public dedication to make the machine and use the generic designation, he can do so in all forms, with the fullest liberty, by affixing such name to the machines, by referring to it in advertisements, and by other means, subject, however, to the condition that the name must be so used as not to deprive others of their rights, or to deceive the public; and, therefore, that the name must be accompanied with such indications that the thing manufactured is the work of the one making it, as will unmistakably inform the public of that fact.

This case is widely considered to be the genesis of the concept of the public domain, an idea that was fundamental to intellectual property reform movements more than a century later. And this case—along with *Loog* in the United Kingdom—is an

Above: Singer sewing machine advertisement cards, distributed at World Columbian Exposition, Chicago, 1893, showing six people from Zululand, and two people from Ceylon, with Singer sewing machines. (Singer Manufacturing Co. / J. Ottmann Lith. Co., NY, Library of Congress, Prints and Photographs Division)

Singer Viking Pfaff (SVP) Worldwide was not able to confirm whether they owned the copyright to these two images. They stated that they would not do anything legally to stop us, but that they also weren't giving their approval to move forward. Instead, they suggested to list the company. So, if any of the readers of this book are interested to learn more about SINGER®, or buy one of their machines, please visit www.singer.com.

Above, left: Two men looking in a window display of Singer sewing machines, Iran, ca. 1935.

Above, right: The Singer Sewing Machine Company in Irkutsk, Siberia, ca. 1910–1920. (Library of Congress, Prints and Photographs Division)

early signal of the later tensions that would emerge between the laws that regulate consumer protection, commercial fraud, and trademarks. Taken together with its significance to the creation of the doctrine of genericide and to our understanding of patent pools, it is probably fair to say that no one object has been as central to the evolution of our modern intellectual property system as the sewing machine. ◆

Further Reading

Grace R. Cooper (1976) *The Sewing Machine: Its Invention and Development* (2nd edn). Washington, DC: Smithsonian Institution Press.

Robert B. Davies, "'Peacefully Working to Conquer the World': The Singer Manufacturing Company in Foreign Markets, 1854–1889," *The Business History Review*, 43(3), pp. 299–325.

Andrew Gordon (2011) *Fabricating Consumers: The Sewing Machine in Modern Japan*. Berkeley: University of California Press.

Ryan Lampe and Petra Moser (2010) "Do Patent Pools Encourage Innovation? Evidence from the Nineteenth-Century Sewing Machine Industry," 70(4), *The Journal of Economic History*, pp. 898–920.

Adam Mossoff (2011) "The Rise and Fall of the First American Patent Thicket: The Sewing Machine War of the 1850s," 53, *Arizona Law Review*, pp. 165–211.

Tim Putnam (1999) "The Sewing Machine Comes Home," in Barbara Burman (ed.) *The Culture of Sewing: Gender, Consumption and Home Dressmaking*. Oxford: Berg, pp. 269–270.

Foxwell v. *Webster and Seventy-Six Other Suits* (1863) 4 De Gex J & S 77, 46 ER 844 (Lord Chancellor)

Singer Manufacturing Co v. *Wilson* (1877) 3 App. Cas. 376 (House of Lords)

Singer Manufacturing Co v. *Loog* (1882) LR 8 HL 15 (House of Lords)

Singer Manuf'g Co v. *June Manuf'g Co* (1896) 163 US 169

135,000 SETS, 270,000 VOLUMES SOLD.

UNCLE TOM'S CABIN

FOR SALE HERE.

AN EDITION FOR THE MILLION, COMPLETE IN 1 Vol., PRICE 37 1-2 CENTS.

"   "   IN GERMAN, IN 1 Vol., PRICE 50 CENTS.

"   "   IN 2 Vols,. CLOTH, 6 PLATES, PRICE $1.50.

SUPERB ILLUSTRATED EDITION, IN 1 Vol., WITH 153 ENGRAVINGS,

PRICES FROM $2.50 TO $5.00.

The Greatest Book of the Age.

1600   1700   1800

--/-----/-----/-----/-----/-----/-----/-----/-----/-----/-----/-----/----

9 Uncle Tom's Cabin

Peter Jaszi

Notwithstanding the apocryphal story, it seems that Abraham Lincoln never actually characterized Harriet Beecher Stowe as "the little woman who made this big war;" and it's equally doubtful that her 1852 novel, *Uncle Tom's Cabin: or Life Among the Lowly*, had a similar effect. But that is not to cast doubt on the book's importance. It was the first entirely successful American blockbuster-by-design, and it changed the nature of the book world forever. Unbeknownst to Stowe—or to John Jewett, the small-time Boston publisher who engineered its remarkable commercial and cultural coup—the book helped light a slow fuse that, in time, detonated an explosion that lit the way for the modern copyright system.

We know copyright today as an intrusive and ubiquitous regulatory scheme, global in both the literal and the physical senses, spanning both time and space. The qualified monopoly it confers on a wide range of more or less imaginative creations generally lasts longer than the value of those objects. Copyright embraces a wider variety of works than could ever have been imagined at its birth, and it extends to the most geographically remote corners of the world. Its ubiquity gives rise both to triumphalist celebrations of copyright's contributions to global trade in cultural commodities, and to anguished and anxious expressions of its chilling effects.

When *Uncle Tom's Cabin* first appeared, however, copyright was still struggling to establish its contemporary form. A few years before the book's publication, the English historian and politician, T.B. Macaulay, would warn against the dangers of copyright's monopoly. He wrote in support of remunerating authors, but warned of the evil of monopolistic control: "For the sake of the good we must submit to the evil; but the evil ought not to last a day longer than is necessary for the purpose of securing the good." The history of *Uncle Tom's Cabin* shows the winding path that copyright trod in the 19th and the 20th centuries, as legislators sought to meet these conflicting demands.

Stowe hadn't expected much from the book publication of her serialized magazine story. Calvin, her hapless, washed-up,

On the left: An 1859 poster for Uncle Tom's Cabin by Harriet Beecher Stowe. (Getty Images)

Above: Portrait of Harriet Beecher Stowe, photographed in 1876 by Napoleon Sarony. (Alamy)

academic husband, served as her de facto literary agent, and struck a bargain that he hoped would pay for a good new silk dress. They did rather better than this, as it turned out, thanks to the publisher's unexpected marketing genius. Sales in the first year or so of publication exceeded 300,000 copies, and the Stowes seem to have pocketed $30,000—roughly $2 million in 2018 dollars—despite Calvin's deficient negotiating skills.

The book's success was, in retrospect, implausible. *Uncle Tom's Cabin* was launched into a book market where mid-century innovations in printing technology and the rise of a literate middle class had led to the rise of cheap reprint publishing, so that "book piracy" was rife. The Stowe–Jewett team seems to have done a reasonable job, at least initially, of using the legal system to keep direct competitors at bay. Secondary markets were another matter, however, and in short order the book had generated 27 copycat novels—many taking a pro-slavery perspective—along with numerous stage shows, plays, songs, candies, statuettes, tableware, board games, and so forth. Under copyright laws of the time, none of these were subject to any licensing restrictions, nor did they require the payment of royalties to Stowe and Jewett.

This aside, there was the nontrivial question of translation rights. This issue soon came to the head in a lawsuit, *Stowe* v. *Thomas*, brought against a cheap,

unauthorized German version of the novel that—at least among German-Americans in Philadelphia—was undercutting demand for the authorized translation. The case was heard by Robert Grier, a faithful Democrat who presided part time in the Pennsylvania Federal Circuit Court by virtue of his elevation to the US Supreme Court by President James K. Polk.

In 1857, Grier would earn undying opprobrium by joining the majority in the *Dred Scott case*. But all that lay ahead. In 1853, Judge Grier opined that Mrs. Stowe's actual words were entitled to protection, but *only* the actual words. Everything else was up for grabs. "All her conceptions and inventions may be used and abused by imitators, playwrights and poetasters." And since a translation might be characterized as a "copy of her thoughts or conceptions" it was not a copy of the book. As a result, an unauthorized translation was not a copyright infringement.

Stowe and Jewett also faced the fact that mid-19th-century copyright was

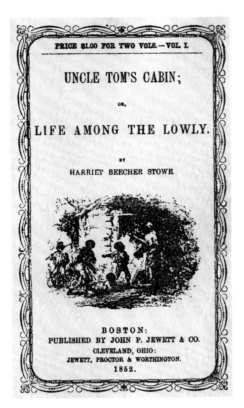

PRICE $1.00 FOR TWO VOLS.—VOL. I.

UNCLE TOM'S CABIN;

OR,

LIFE AMONG THE LOWLY.

BY

HARRIET BEECHER STOWE.

BOSTON:
PUBLISHED BY JOHN P. JEWETT & CO.
CLEVELAND, OHIO:
JEWETT, PROCTOR & WORTHINGTON.
1852.

Above: Title page of Harriet Beecher Stowe's Uncle Tom's Cabin; or, Life Among the Lowly *(Vol. 1) Boston, 1852, printed for John P. Jewett & Co., first edition. (Getty Images)*

would suggest. But the benefit flowed mostly in one direction. The few American writers whose reputations made the crossing to the United Kingdom had a harder time of it, since the pirates who seized most enthusiastically on their works were outsiders to the respectable publishing world and did not recognize trade courtesy at all. From the 1870s, Mark Twain inveighed in colorful terms—although without immediate noticeable effect—against the sins of literary freebooter and sometime-pornographer John Camden Hotten:

My books are bad enough just as they are written; then what must they be after Mr. John Camden Hotten has composed half-a-dozen chapters and added the same to them? ... If a friend of yours, or if even you yourself, were to write a book and set it adrift among the people, with the gravest apprehensions that it was not up to what it ought to be intellectually, how would you like to have John Camden Hotten sit down and stimulate his powers, and drool two or three original chapters on to the end of that book? Would not the world seem cold and hollow to you? Would you not feel that you wanted to die and be at rest?

In 1881, Twain attempted to secure Imperial copyright for *The Prince and the Pauper* by publishing it first in Canada—a copyright granted there was good throughout the rest of the Empire, including Britain. It's not clear, though, that the gambit had much effect on pirates of Hotten's ilk.

Stowe (who happened to be Twain's next-door-neighbor) had better luck in the

territorially circumscribed, such that the two great markets for English-language books existed in legal isolation. US-based publishers could, and did, legally reprint British bestsellers and classics, much to the chagrin of writers like Charles Dickens who wore out his fabulous transatlantic welcome in 1842 by persistently campaigning for transatlantic copyright protection. Although, he said, he would "rather have the affectionate regard of my fellowmen as I would have heaps and mines of gold," he saw no reason why he should not have both. Except, of course, the US law of the time did not recognize UK copyright.

Thanks to the institutional custom known as "trade courtesy," some popular British authors did derive more benefit from the US market than Dickens' complaints

British market. She received voluntary compensation for at least three mainstream reprints of *Uncle Tom's Cabin*, and while visiting England in 1853 she was ceremonially presented with the $20,000 proceeds of a public "Penny Offering," intended to compensate her for royalties that had gone unpaid. Nevertheless, when the US campaign for international copyright began in earnest, Stowe's experience with *Uncle Tom's Cabin* was singled out to illustrate how the lack of legislation harmed American authors.

That campaign led to the Chace International Copyright Act of 1891, authorizing the United States to establish reciprocal copyright relations with Great Britain, among other nations. This new bilateral arrangement contributed as much or more to the larger cause of international copyright as did the original 1886 iteration of the Berne Convention, a treaty to which the United States remained an outsider for more than a century. Ultimately, both of these late 19th-century laws foreshadowed the move in the 20th century for the general recognition of copyrights across national borders. The vexed and variable protection of *Uncle Tom's Cabin* reminds us of where copyright was in the 1850s, and the new course that was charted for it in the final decades of the 19th century.

A subsequent episode reveals another sense in which *Uncle Tom's Cabin* offers a double perspective on change in copyright culture. Today, we are accustomed to copyright terms that endure for the life of the author and (typically) 70 years after their death. But it was not always so, either in the United States or elsewhere. In 1894, the maximum US term copyright on *Uncle Tom's Cabin* was 28 years, plus a 14-year renewal. When this term expired, the book enjoyed a dramatic revival in its country of origin; it became widely and legally available to US reprint publishers, who operated at various price points and served an ever-expanding universe of readers. Stowe's death in 1896 triggered a series of elaborate "memorial" and (eventually) a number of scholarly editions. All in all, the book's altered copyright status helped to secure both its continued popularity and its lasting literary reputation, ultimately enabling a 1932 edition introduced by

the poet Langston Hughes ("a moral battle cry"), and a 1944 Classics Illustrated comic book—No. 15 in the long-running series, following *Westward Ho!* and preceding *Gulliver's Travels*.

But, by the time *Uncle Tom's Cabin* was published, the days of meaningfully limited copyright protection were numbered. Shortly after the 19th century rolled around, England had unexpectedly imitated the French mode by adopting a term based on the life of the author. In 1814, the English term of protection was extended to the life of the author or 28 years, whichever was longer. In 1842, the alternatives became the author's life plus seven years, or a fixed term of 42 years. During the 19th century, many European countries moved to a "life plus" formula for copyright duration.

The United States was a holdout, refusing to embrace a life-based term until 1978. Nevertheless, the grant of a 14-year extension in the Copyright Act of 1909

Uncle Tom's Cabin

by

Mrs. H. B. Stowe

with
George Cruikshank's
Original
Illustrations

was the first step of many toward what we have today, a copyright term that is nearly perpetual. This legislation eventually came about thanks in part to some late career lobbying by Mark Twain. Decades before its introduction, he had sought to provide for his own old age—unnecessarily as it turns out—and to assure the wellbeing of his immediate offspring. It took nearly 70 years after Twain's death for the United States to embrace his proposal; but such was his cultural significance that his endorsement of the idea was pressed into service as Congress was considering the question in the 1970s.

The changes to copyright since the publication of *Uncle Tom's Cabin* are quite remarkable. The difficulties Stowe and Jewett faced in protecting against various types of copying—in translations, overseas editions, various unlicensed rip-offs, and so on—were fundamental in the development of the US law. These days, almost every form and kind of sequel, adaptation, and spinoff has been brought within the reach of copyright regulation, and copyright's term of protection has extended beyond the wildest imaginations of Stowe and her contemporaries. The popularity of *Uncle Tom's Cabin*, and the effect of its publication on the development of an indigenous American publishing industry, played a guiding role in the seemingly limitless expansion of copyright's empire.

On the left: The cover of Cassell's 1852 pirated British edition of Uncle Tom's Cabin. (Alamy)

There is both piquancy and irony, then, in the fact that the plaintiff who mounted the unsuccessful 2003 constitutional challenge to US copyright term extensions in *Eldred* v. *Ashcroft* was a principal of Dover Books—a reprint publisher that helped to assure that the works of Twain, Stowe, and other 19th-century American authors remain available to this day in cheap, uncopyrighted paperback editions. ◆

Further Reading

Scott E. Casper, Jeffrey D. Groves, Stephen W. Nissenbaum, and Michael Winship (eds.) (2007) *A History of the Book in America (Vol. 3): The Industrial Book, 1840–1880*. Chapel Hill: University of North Carolina Press.

Thomas F. Gossett (1985) *Uncle Tom's Cabin and American Culture*. Dallas: Southern Methodist University Press.

Joan D. Hedrick (1994) *Harriet Beecher Stowe: A Life*. New York: Oxford University Press.

Claire Parfitt (2007) *The Publishing History of Uncle Tom's Cabin, 1852–2002*. Abingdon: Ashgate.

Robert Spoo (2013) *Without Copyrights: Piracy, Publishing, and the Public Domain*. Oxford: Oxford University Press.

1600   *1700*   *1800*

==/-----/-----/-----/-----/-----/-----/-----/-----/-----/-----/---/--/----

10 Corset

Kara W. Swanson

On the left: "Studio di donna col busto," (Study of Woman with the Bust), by Giuseppe de Nittis (1846–1884), undated. (Photo by Mondadori Portfolio via Getty Images)

Two centuries ago, women and girls throughout the United States reached for one piece of technology first thing in the morning, and kept it with them all day long—the corset. Although men had worn corsets in earlier periods, the corset's purpose by the mid-19th century was to create the public shape of the female body. It emphasized (or depending on the whims of fashion, deemphasized), bust, waist, and hips in ways intended to accentuate differences between male and female. Today, the corset still fascinates, an emblem of femininity that appears on fashion runways, the concert stage (famously worn by pop star Madonna), and in blockbuster movies (The Rocky Horror Picture Show, Gone with the Wind). Less visible are the ways the corset as an object of intellectual property has exposed the masculine assumptions in our understanding of technology, patents, and law.

When we think of technology, we think of machines, not underwear. This understanding of technology is the product of the Industrial Revolution. The development of factories separated mass-produced technologies from home-made technologies. As women's work remained home-based, "technology" became something made, and better understood, by men. The results of that gendering have been profound, reflected in the gender gap in Science, Technology, Engineering and Mathematics (STEM) participation, and the wage gap between men and women in industrialized nations, as women's work outside the home was less valued.

Patent laws drafted and interpreted in the 19th century helped reinforce the masculinity of technology, invention, and inventors by the legal definition of "invention." To this day, an innovative, collapsible playpen made by a carpenter or in a factory can be patent-protected; a baby quilt made in a novel design, stitched lovingly at home, cannot. In the golden age of invention, the famous inventors were men, like Samuel Morse, Thomas Edison, and Alexander Graham Bell, all patent-holders. By one count, women obtained fewer than 100 patents in the United States before 1860, and while the number of female patentees increased significantly

after the Civil War (1861–1865), less than one percent of late 19th-century patents were granted to women.

The corset, as an oh-so-feminine technology, challenged the association of technology, patents, and invention with masculinity.

During the late 19th century, the corset became a mass-produced, factory-made consumer good, like plows, sewing machines, and horseless carriages. But the purpose of this technology was to make its user feminine. Middle and upper class women wore corsets as part of their assigned social role of ornament, adorning the home by their well-dressed presence. The corset not only created a pleasing body shape, but also produced specific behavior. The corset influenced how its wearers walked, sat, danced, and even breathed. Tight lacing could induce pallor, breathlessness, and a tendency to faint. The corset thus promoted a performance of delicate femininity that reinforced a common belief that females were the weaker sex. Corsets were also required wear for female prisoners and worn by servants and factory girls. Social pressures that kept women of all classes corseted were intended to police female behavior in another way—to control female sexuality. The corset "is an ever-present monitor indirectly bidding its wearer to exercise self-restraint; it is evidence of a well-disciplined mind and well-regulated feelings." A corseted woman was unavailable, and thus, chaste.

Attaining the perfect silhouette was neither comfortable nor simple. Corsets were marvels of engineering. Containing as many as 50 separate pieces of cloth, reinforced by stiffening stays, busks, and steels, and fastened with laces, eyelets, and clasps, they could be made at home only by the most ambitious amateur, and more often were made in small workshops. As industrial techniques came to the textile industry, the goal of weaving corsets on power looms became a sought-after commercial prize. As in other business sectors, corset makers turned to intellectual property law, with patents protecting innovations and heavily advertised trademarks used to market these consumer goods.

Above, left: Madonna during her 1990 "Blond Ambition" tour, in a design by Jean Paul Gaultier. (Getty Images)

Above, right: Tim Curry in THE ROCKY HORROR PICTURE SHOW (US 1975, Dir. Jim Sharman). (Alamy)

A corset inventor was literally patenting an ideal female form—not in metal, like seamstress dummies, or in plastic, as in the later Barbie doll—but in a tool to mold living flesh into a shape admired by men. During the corset's heyday, inventors obtained hundreds of patents annually. Their inventions claimed to make corsets stronger, less cumbersome, easier to wash, or quicker to manufacture. Like other innovators, corset inventors licensed their patents for royalty payments, and sued competitors for infringement. As a patented technology, corsets were merely one type of the inventions pouring into the US patent office in the 19th century. But the corset stood out in two ways. First, as a technology well known to women, the corset proved accessible to women as inventors and entrepreneurs. Second, in the language of patent law, the corset's utility (usefulness) was inextricably linked to its production of femininity and control of female sexuality. In these differences, the corset as an object of intellectual property challenged and exposed the gendered assumptions of lawyers, judges, and the law itself.

Though women faced daunting barriers, they earned almost one-quarter of corset patents. Women lacked access to education, capital, business networks, and, as married women, even the legal capacity to own inventions and enter contracts to commercialize them. But they had first-hand experience wearing and washing corsets. Most learned sewing skills at home. Dressmaking was already a women's trade. As corsets became a booming business, these experiences helped some women enter the market as inventors and entrepreneurs.

Sarah Dake, in rural Eureka, Wisconsin, used the patent system to turn her knowledge of corsets into dollars, obtaining a patent and then finding 38 different licensees to commercialize her invention. In New York City, Mina Sebille, owner of a corset workshop, obtained a patent, and then used the same patent lawyer later employed by Thomas Edison to represent her interests. Several Massachusetts women licensed their patents to a Boston corset firm, while another, Lavinia Foy, turned her corset innovation into a long-lasting business. Based in New Haven, Connecticut, Foy's company employed over two hundred workers, and reportedly brought her an annual income of $25,000 in the 1870s, when most workers earned less than $500 a year. Although she was in business with her husband and later her son, Foy was the inventor, obtaining at least 13 patents.

Each of these women used their expertise in corsetry for economic gain. At the same time, the corsets these businesswomen wore marked them as feminine, serving as a constant reminder of the limitations imposed by Victorian gender roles.

Those gender roles ultimately cost another female corset entrepreneur her patent. Frances Egbert earned royalties from her deceased husband's patent for 15 years, suing numerous competitors for infringement. One competitor fought back, claiming that the patent was invalid. Frances pursued her case all the way to the US Supreme Court in 1881. There, the femininity of the corset changed patent law. Despite the common assumption that technology—and thus law interpreting technology—is rational, value-free,

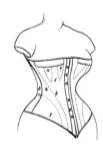

Above: Corset patent drawing, US Patent No. 202,038 (1878).

On the following pages: The 'corset scene' from GONE WITH THE WIND (US 1938, Dir. Victor Fleming), illustrating the corset as a technology of race as well as of gender. (Getty Images)

and gender-neutral, patent law proved no different than any other area of law in reflecting society and culture.

Frances' troubles stemmed from her dual role. She was the patent owner and a businesswoman, but she was also a key witness, testifying as the "intimate friend" (and future wife) of Samuel Barnes at the time of his invention. In 1855, neither Samuel nor Frances were in the corset business. Frances wore corsets, and she complained to Samuel about her steels breaking. These vertical pieces of metal were worn in pairs to keep the front of a corset rigid, and also served as anchors for fasteners that closed the corset. The strain of lacing the corset in back, however, could cause steels to give way. Samuel crafted a set of reinforced steels and gave his prototype to Frances, who wore the pair, sewn into her corset, for 11 years before Samuel filed his patent application. Patent law, then and now, provides that if an invention was in public use before its inventor seeks a patent, a patent cannot be granted. Frances argued that her use was very private. The Supreme Court decided otherwise, ruling her use a public use of the invention.

To 21st-century sensibilities, this ruling seems odd. If steels sewn into one woman's undergarments are in public use, it is hard to imagine what use is private. The justices, however, considered the transfer of the steels as if Frances and Samuel were two businessmen, contemplating a partnership. They declared that since Samuel had failed to extract any promise of confidentiality from Frances, she was free to show others the steels or develop the invention commercially, making her a public user. Of course, it probably never occurred to Samuel to ask Frances, his "intimate friend" and later his wife, to sign a confidentiality agreement. He would assume that Frances would not be showing her corset, or its steels, to anyone but him.

Samuel, Frances, and the justices knew, as Victorians, the power of the corset to contain female sexuality and signal respectable femininity. In both law and

Above: Model wearing a back-lacing corset by Detolle for Mainbocher, 1939. (Photo by Horst P. Horst / Condé Nast via Getty Images)

society, removing a corset in the presence of a man, or even discussing it, as Frances had with Samuel, was evidence of a sexual relationship. In a divorce case in that era, evidence that a woman had been in the same room as a man, fully clothed except for a corset, was evidence of adultery. A man who was found to have talked about buying a corset for a woman was ruled the father of her child. Frances' testimony about her corset indicated that she was sexually available to Samuel, an intimacy that eventually led to marriage, and underlay their mutual understanding that her corset steels remained secret.

The justices chose to ignore the implications of Frances' actions regarding her corset, actions suggesting female sexuality insufficiently restrained. Instead, they interpreted her actions as if she were the businessperson she later became, to whom corsets were manufactured goods bought and sold in bulk, rather than a personal technology of self-presentation. In that choice, they not only avoided acknowledging a nonmarital sexual relationship, but also refused to reward the female partner in that relationship with an enforceable patent. The gendered meanings of Frances' corset had long-term consequences for all inventors, as the Court broadened the legal meaning of public use.

Frances was only one of many women who challenged socially imposed limitations on their behavior. Eventually, the restrictive corset itself faded from popularity, defeated by the bicycle craze, flapper fashions, and new elastics that allowed more comfortable girdles and garters. Women still innovated, however, in what became known as "intimates," echoing Frances' term. Seeking an undergarment that wouldn't show under her dress, New York City debutante Caresse Crosby invented an early version of the modern bra out of two handkerchiefs in 1910. As both inventor and wearer, Crosby patented her invention

and sold the patent rights to male-founded Warner Brothers Corset Company for the "munificent" sum of $1,500, allowing Warner Brothers to commercialize the latest in feminine technologies. ◆

Further Reading

C. Willet Cunnington and Phillis Cunnington (1992) *The History of Underclothes.* Mineola: Dover. (quoted above from p. 180)

Wendy Gamber (1995) "'Reduced to Science': Gender, Technology, and Power in the American Dressmaking Trade, 1860–1910," *Technology and Culture*, 36(3), pp. 455–482.

B. Zorina Kahn (2000) "'Not for Ornament': Patenting Activity by Nineteenth-Century Women Inventors," *Journal of Interdisciplinary History*, 31, pp. 159–195.

Clarence D. Long (1960) *Wages and Earnings in the United States, 1860–1890.* Princeton: Princeton University Press.

Anne L. MacDonald (1992) *Feminine Ingenuity: Women and Invention in America.* New York: Ballantine Books.

Deborah J. Merritt (1991) "Hypatia in the Patent Office: Women Inventors and the Law, 1865–1900," *American Journal of Legal History*, 35, pp. 235–306.

Denise E. Pilato (2000) *Retrieval of a Legacy: Nineteenth-Century American Women Inventors.* Santa Barbara: Praeger.

Valerie Steele (2001) *The Corset: A Cultural History.* New Haven: Yale University Press.

Kara W. Swanson (2011) "Getting a Grip on the Corset: Gender, Sexuality and Patent Law," *Yale Journal of Law & Feminism*, 23, pp. 57–115.

1700   *1800*   *1900*

--/-----/-----/-----/-----/-----/-----/-----/-----/-----/-----/-----/----

11 A.G. Bell Telephone

Christopher Beauchamp

WHO INVENTED THE telephone? It is a famous question in the history of invention, partly because the standard answer—Alexander Graham Bell—is so widely known, and partly because Bell's claim to be the first inventor was shadowed from the start by a host of rival candidates. Versions of Bell's story appear in innumerable biographies and textbooks, scholarly works and movies. But for all the ink that has been spilled on the invention of the telephone, an under-appreciated fact remains: the very question "who invented the telephone?" is above all a *legal* artifact. What does it mean to invent a new technology? Who should receive credit, and with what result? Why do we care so much about identifying a first inventor? In the United States, these are questions that have persistently been asked and answered by the legal process, and nowhere more dramatically than in the case of Bell's telephone patent.

Alexander Graham Bell began experimenting with electrical sound transmission in Boston in the early 1870s. He did not initially aim to transmit speech. Instead, he joined a race to develop the "acoustic telegraph," a type of high-capacity telegraph system that would carry multiple signals simultaneously on a single wire using sounds of different pitch. Many well-known inventors of the day were chasing the same objective, including Thomas Edison and the electrical engineer Elisha Gray. But it was Bell—a teacher of the deaf who came to electrical invention from the study of sound, rather than the other way around—who had the crucial insight. Bell recognized that complex sounds could be transmitted using a continuous and fluctuating ("undulatory") current, rather than the intermittent make-and-break current of the telegraph. By 1875, Bell's experiments with his assistant Thomas Watson were reproducing sounds with ever greater sensitivity: first the sound of a plucked reed, then inarticulate vocal noises.

With the help of his business partners and the elite patent lawyers they hired, Bell filed a patent application on 14 February 1876. The patent described a system of acoustic telegraphy based on Bell's undulatory current. It contained only two

On the left: Alexander Graham Bell at the New York end of the first long-distance telephone call to Chicago in 1892. (Getty Images)

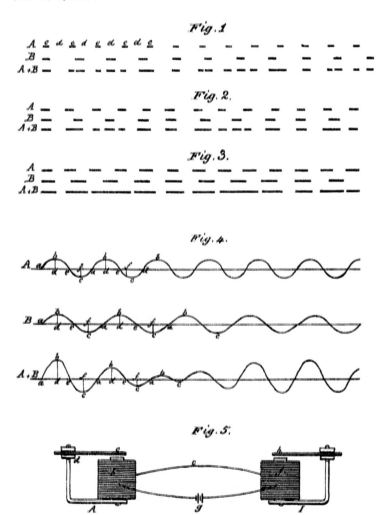

A. G. BELL.

TELEGRAPHY.

No. 174,465. Patented March 7, 1876.

Fig. 1

Fig. 2.

Fig. 3.

Fig. 4.

Fig. 5.

Witnesses

Ewell A. Dick

H. J. Hutchinson

Inventor:

A. Graham Bell

by atty Pollok & Bailey

glancing references to the human voice, and no mention of speech communication as such, although the patent did include one claim for the transmission of "vocal or other sounds." The Patent Office granted US Patent No. 174,465, for "Improvements in Telegraphy," a mere three weeks later. Three days after that, and using a device somewhat different from the one described in the patent, Bell and Watson managed to transmit their first intelligible words: "Mr. Watson—come here—I want to see you."

Obtaining a patent was just a first step, but it was the seed from which the telephone business grew. Bell and his partners organized the new technology around their patent rights, licensing local operating companies that leased rather than sold telephones. (This would remain the basic model of the telephone industry for a century.) The telegraph giant Western Union notoriously declined an offer to buy Bell's patent for $100,000, but soon afterward decided to enter the market and quickly outpaced Bell operations in several major cities. The litigation that followed provided the first real test of Bell's patent rights. What, after all, had he truly invented? And more importantly, what did his patent cover?

At this point, Bell's lawyers made a consequential decision—and did so against the inventor's wishes. The eve of argument found Bell's attorneys "dissecting" the language of his patent in order to decide on the most promising interpretation of the text. Their client wailed that "[t]hey have plucked out the *heart* of the invention and have thrown it away." The lawyers chose instead to focus solely on Bell's practical claim to transmitting "vocal or other sounds ... by causing electrical undulations," disregarding much of the patent's technical content—or as Bell put it, "all that I thought most valuable." Their aim was to paint Bell as a pioneer inventor,

deserving broad rights over the undulatory current idea and thus over telephone technology in general. To Bell's surprise and delight, the strategy was a smashing success. The judge ruled that Bell had "discovered a new art—that of transmitting speech by electricity." *Scientific American* observed, correctly, that the decision handed the Bell Company "the exclusive right of talking over a wire by electricity." This judicial view of the scope of Bell's rights had a profound effect. The actual device invented by Bell hardly mattered. It was obsolete anyway by 1880; even the earliest commercial telephones depended upon transmitters and switchboards invented by others. Yet as a legal matter Bell's patent controlled every form of telephone, regardless of how it worked.

What followed was a decade-long legal war over Bell's patent monopoly. With no way around Bell's rights, challengers tried to invalidate the patent by putting forward earlier inventors. Some of these were credible figures, such as the German scientist Philipp Reis and Bell's rival Elisha Gray, who had filed a preliminary description of his own telephone device with the Patent Office on 14 February 1876, mere hours after Bell's patent application. Other contenders were more obscure. The Italian-American Antonio Meucci claimed to have invented a telephone in Havana in 1849, but lamented that he had been unable to pursue a patent after being injured in an explosion on the Staten Island ferry. Dr. Sylvanus Cushman located his breakthrough in Racine, Wisconsin in 1851, after experiments with a lightning rod enabled him to hear the piping of frogs from a nearby swamp. Daniel Drawbaugh, self-described as "one of the greatest inventive geniuses of this age," declared that he had invented several forms of telephone in Pennsylvania in the 1860s and 1870s. All of these claims were taken up by the promoters of new telephone companies (many

As far as I can r...

...ts of my Telephone

... transmission of vocal...

...these are the ...
... or instrument for ...
... by telegraph ...
A. Gra...

of them largely speculative enterprises), which sprang up to defy Bell.

Even the unlikely pretenders had support, and some hope of success, because of the political climate surrounding Bell's patent. By the mid-1880s, "who invented the telephone?" was no mere question of scientific curiosity: it had become a raging public battle, closely covered in the newspapers. The tightening monopoly and high prices of the Bell companies generated fierce resistance: state rate regulation laws in Indiana and the Midwest; a mass subscriber strike in Rochester, New York. Bell's own lawyer would later confide that "The Bell Company has had a monopoly more profitable and more controlling—and more generally hated—than any ever given by any patent." Not for nothing did the anti-Bell telephone companies bear populist names like "the People's Telephone Company."

At the same time, the telephone question was engulfed in scandal. Bell's opponents began asserting that Bell had obtained his patent by fraud, pointing to the timing of Bell's application right before Elisha Gray's submission and to some suspicious procedural moves within the Patent Office. The patent examiner who had handled Bell's application swore to a number of misdeeds, including an allegation that Bell had copied portions of his patent from Gray. Compounding the chaos, the US government filed suit against Bell to cancel his patent for fraud—only for that case to collapse in scandal when it emerged that the US Attorney General was a major shareholder in the anti-Bell company behind the suit. Finally, New York newspapers revealed that two federal judges who had earlier ruled for Bell had family members with large stakes in the Bell company. One of them, Supreme Court Justice Horace Gray, was forced to recuse himself from the Court's upcoming consideration of Bell's case.

The Bell patent swept into the Supreme Court in 1887 undefeated, but trailing a poisonous cloud of corruption and controversy. Arguments before the justices took two full weeks, after which the court deliberated for more than a year. The decision, when it came, was four-to-three for Bell over Daniel Drawbaugh. The bare majority of the justices accepted both Bell's priority and the pioneering nature of his invention. The three dissenters purported to find Drawbaugh's evidence "overwhelming, with regard both to the number and character of the witnesses," but were probably motivated more by hostility to the monopoly than by the quality of the testimony.

The Bell interests' control of the telephone lasted until the foundational patent rights expired in 1893. Subsequent events confirmed how far-reaching the effects of Bell's patent had been. Bell Company leaders had always regarded the telephone as a high-cost, high-quality service for urban businessmen and the well-off. And so it was, with approximately one telephone for every 250 Americans in 1895. Once the patent expired and competition began to

Above: Alexander Graham Bell, Scottish-born inventor, who patented the telephone in 1876, as a young man. (Getty Images)

I BELL'S NEW TELEPONE.

Above, left: Illustration of exterior view and cross-section of mouthpiece apparatus of Alexander Graham Bell's first telephone. (Getty Images)

Above, right: Early Bell telephone and terminal panel, 1877. (Getty Images)

enter the market, the telephone service was transformed: suddenly even small towns had telephone companies or farmers' lines; in the cities, apartment buildings gained party-line service and cheap nickel-in-the-slot telephones. By 1907, there was one telephone for every 14 people in the United States.

The legacy of the patent was far from extinguished, though. The erstwhile monopolist, now under the name American Telephone and Telegraph (AT&T), gradually brought competition to heel. American communications in the 20th century were dominated by AT&T's so-called Bell System of companies, which kept the reputation of the eponymous inventor at the forefront of American technology. It made sense for Alexander Graham Bell to be a household name when the Bell System, based on his original patent-holding company, was the largest business organization in the world.

More subtly, the saga of Bell's patent framed the way that the origins of the telephone have been understood ever since. We now take for granted that the telephone was a single invention, arrived at by a single person in a decisive break from the prior art. These are all contestable propositions as a factual matter, and were once hotly contested. But as arguments advanced by Bell's lawyers more than 130 years ago, they first triumphed in court and then went on to conquer popular culture and posterity.

Bell is not the only American inventor whose reputation was made by the patent system. In fact, generating tales of individual genius is one of the things that the patent law does best. The history of the telephone suggests that we might think differently about our stories of heroic invention, just maybe by giving more credit to their lawyerly authors. After all, the single most important object in the invention of the telephone was not the fragile machine of Bell's first telephone call; it was his patent. ◆

Further Reading

Christopher Beauchamp (2015) *Invented by Law: Alexander Graham Bell and the Patent that Changed America.* Cambridge: Harvard University Press.

Richard R. John (2010) *Network Nation. Inventing American Telecommunications.* Cambridge, MA: Harvard University Press.

Robert MacDougall (2013) *The People's Network. The Political Economy of the Telephone in the Gilded Age.* Philadelphia: University of Pennsylvania Press.

US Supreme Court, *The Telephone Cases,* 126 US 1, 1888.

1700 *1800* *1900*

==/=====/=====/=====/=====/=====/=====/=====/=/====/=====/=====/=====/====

12 Light Bulb

Stef van Gompel

ANKIND HAS BEEN using artificial light for millennia. Starting with camp-fires and torches in ancient times, lighting improved slowly but incrementally with the introduction of candles, oil lamps, kerosene lamps, and gas lighting.

Artificial lighting was lifted to another dimension by the invention of the electric light bulb, which effectively extended day into night at the switch of a button. However, electric light not merely prolonged the usable hours in a day: by illuminating homes, schools, factories, offices, shop windows, theaters, street corners and parks, it also improved conditions for learning and reading, furthered economic and commercial progress, created opportunities for leisure and night life, and brought about a sense of safety. It transformed the world.

Of course, electric light required a network of wires and power generators to bring electricity to the people, and this spurred the development of the electric power industry. As Thomas Edison explained in the *New York Sun* of 16 September 1878: "The same wire that brings the light will also bring power and heat." The widespread use of electric light facilitated the invention of various electric home appliances and industrial equipment. Without electric lighting, everyday life would look completely different and contemporary concepts like the "24-hour economy," or even the "city that never sleeps," could not exist. And the story of the electric light bulb is one that relies on patent law, (outrageous) exercise of monopoly control, and a hefty serving of marketing brilliance.

Like many other famous inventions, the light bulb was not the result of a spark of genius of a sole inventor. While Thomas Edison or Joseph Swan are often credited as "the" inventors of the light bulb, the truth is that the concept of incandescent light existed long before they entered the scene. In 1802, Humphry Davy and Vasily Petrov simultaneously invented the arc lamp, by lighting an electric arc between carbon electrodes. Because arc lamps were too bright for indoor use and suitable only for large spaces, other 19th-century scientists experimented with a range of electrically heated wires or rods inside semi-vacuum glass tubes, trying out various combinations

On the left: American inventor Thomas Alva Edison holding a light bulb in his laboratory in Menlo Park, NJ. (Getty Images)

of iridium, platinum, carbon, and other materials. However, none of these early experimental bulbs were commercially attractive—they were too costly to produce, or they burnt out too quickly. This was where Edison, Swan, and their teams of inventors stepped in.

In 1878, Swan was the first to create a light bulb consisting of an enclosed vacuum glass tube, platinum wiring, and a filament of carbonized cotton. It gave off light but was short-lived. Having a low-resistance filament, it moreover required larger conductors to supply the necessary electric current, making it ill-suited for commercial application. Meanwhile, in the United States, Edison had developed an incandescent lamp based on similar principles to Swan's, but which used a high-resistance carbon filament. This increased the durability of the lamp, as it required a lower current for the filament to glow. On 22 October 1879, Edison successfully demonstrated a lamp that burned 13.5 hours at his home laboratory in Menlo Park, NJ, and, in 1880, he created a light bulb with an improved filament of carbonized bamboo that lasted over 1,200 hours.

Swan did not seek patent protection for the light bulb he created, as he assumed that its technical details were public knowledge and lacked patentable innovations. However, Edison sought and eventually obtained patents in the United States, Britain, and elsewhere on his invention of the 1879 carbon-filament lamp and its subsequent improvements. In his zeal for patenting, he was not alone: already by 1878, Sawyer and Man had obtained patents on a filament improvement process

called "flashing," and in the 1880s Swan obtained a series of patents for a method to avoid bulb-blackening, a process to produce "parchmentized" cotton filaments, and a process to create high-resistance cellulose filaments. Not only were many inventors working on incandescent lighting at the same time, but they also all realized the significance of the patent system to secure and maintain their position in the newly emerging lamp market.

Patent holders enjoy strong commercial advantages, of course, since their patents can be used to prevent competitors from entering new markets. Unsurprisingly, the early days of the incandescent lamp industry witnessed fierce patent wars. The most contested patent was undoubtedly Edison's basic patent on the 1879 light bulb: it was central because of its broad scope, and so its validity was widely questioned by competitors who maintained that Edison's invention was not genuinely new, and was, instead, based on existing knowledge and prior art.

The battles over this and other patents played out differently in different territories.

Above: Edison's filament lamp, 1879. Edison's lamp had a single loop of carbon which glowed when a current flowed through it. The glass bulb contained a partial vacuum; there was so little oxygen in the bulb that the filament could get very hot without catching fire. (Photo by SSPL / Getty Images)

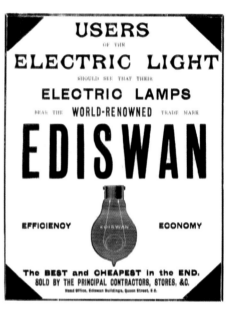

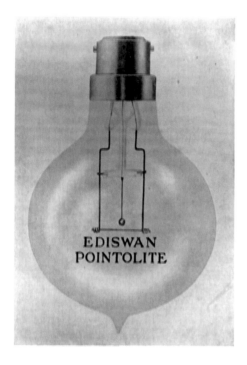

Above, left: The Ediswan Pointolite, ca. 1916. From "All About Inventions and Discoveries," printed by Cassell and Company Ltd., 1918. (Photo by The Print Collector / Print Collector / Getty Images)

Above, right: Advertisement for Ediswan incandescent light bulbs, 1898. (Photo by Oxford Science Archive / Print Collector / Getty Images)

In Britain, for example, a near-monopoly on electric lamps was established after Edison and Swan joined forces in the Ediswan Company in 1883. This merger was mutually beneficial, as Edison's broadly formulated patent on the 1879 light bulb made Swan's business vulnerable, while Edison was uncertain about his patent being upheld in court if Swan could establish priority of invention. Ediswan's rich patent portfolio—which also included Sawyer and Man's flashing patent and lamp patents purchased from others—formed the basis for systematic litigation against competitors. After winning a series of patent infringement cases against rival manufacturers in the mid-1880s, Ediswan's near-monopoly in the British incandescent lamp industry was firmly secured. Oddly, Swan was asked to testify as an expert witness in those cases as to the validity of Edison's basic patent. His business interests forced him to agree that Edison was the rightful owner of the patent, and so Swan downplayed his own contribution to the invention of the light bulb. This act of willful self-erasure doubtlessly contributed to the myth that Edison was the sole inventor of the light bulb.

Outside Britain, the lamp industries in other territories were more competitive. This was particularly so in continental Europe, where unfettered competition reigned, especially from foreign lamp producers whose economic sustainability greatly depended on export markets. Despite the existence of patents—including Edison's basic patent held by local subsidiaries such as AEG in Germany and the Compagnie Générale des Lampes Incandescentes in France—competition in Europe could roam freely, as French and German courts rendered the validity of some key lamp patents uncertain, while light bulbs could be manufactured without restrictions in the Netherlands and Switzerland, which had no patent protection at the

time. This also explains the establishment in the Netherlands of the Philips company in 1891, which later grew out to be one of the largest lamp producers in Europe, next to AEG and Siemens-Halske.

Likewise, while the early US lamp industry faced little foreign competition due to high import taxes, domestic competition was intense. In the United States in the 1880s numerous lamp manufacturers existed, and despite litigation over various lamp patents, few of them took out licenses: they either ignored the patents, or designed around them. Ultimately, in the early 1890s US courts upheld the validity of Edison's basic patent; but by then it was too late to confer monopoly powers on the Edison General Electric Company. Still, General Electric led the US lamp industry with a 50 percent market share throughout the 1890s—partly caused by the success of Edison's bamboo filament lamp, but also because fierce competition had, by then, driven many competing lamp manufacturers out of business.

Consistent with the economic literature on monopolies, the dominant market position of a few large companies caused drawbacks for consumers. During the period of Ediswan's near-monopoly in Britain, innovations in filament development halted, and lamps cost almost three times the price charged in Europe. Only after Edison's basic patent expired in 1893 was the British market flooded with foreign lamps, often of a better quality and costing less than Ediswan's lamps. But the monopoly was not all bad: the public benefited from the monopoly rents extracted from the sale of lamps, as part of these profits were reinvested in the development of the electricity network. This brought advantages to all, rich and poor. Edison's famous quote in the *New York Herald* of 4 January 1880 captures some of this: "After the electric light goes into general use, none but the extravagant will burn tallow candles."

However, monopoly powers derived from lamp patents impeded the public interest more seriously in the first half of the 20th century, when carbon-filament lamps were replaced by metal-filament lamps which significantly improved the lifetime and intensity of light bulbs. The basic patents on these new lamps were owned by a few large companies, which repeatedly strengthened their patent portfolios by amassing improvement patents through corporate invention, mergers and takeovers, and the purchase of patent portfolios. The incumbents controlled domestic competition, and had the power to speed up or delay introduction of new innovations, depending on their commercial interests.

In the United States, the market was controlled largely by General Electric, which owned most metal-filament patents. General Electric was able to fix prices and set strict production quotas for licensees. Although in 1911 a federal antitrust case was successfully brought against General Electric, it did not seriously affect the company's patent domination and its market-restricting licensing practices in the US market.

In other territories, lamp producers established market control through collaboration, by establishing national cartels—such as the British Carbon Lamp Association—or by using patent pools to jointly regulate competition, quality, and prices in the metal-filament lamp industry. Examples of these pools include the UK Tungsten Lamp Association founded in 1912; and the German *Patentgemeinschaft* established in 1911 by AEG, Siemens-Halske and the Deutsche Gasglühlicht AG, which sought to control competition on the European mainland. After World War I, as the balance of power in the European lamp industry changed, the three German firms merged into the Osram company to secure their position.

Around this time, the world's leading lamp producers also began to organize themselves internationally. While in continental Europe, regional markets were allocated and prices and production quotas were fixed through international lamp cartels such as the Internationale Glühlampen Preisvereinigung, transatlantic trade was controlled by cross-licensing contracts between General Electric and leading European lamp producers, which agreed to exchange technological advances but not to invade each other's markets. In 1924, lamp producers in continental Europe, the United Kingdom, and Japan set up the Phoebus cartel, which regulated prices, quality, and sales quotas; facilitated the exchange of patents and knowhow; and introduced technological standardization in the lamp industry. Meanwhile, General Electric continued its patent licensing and exclusive sales territory agreements with lamp producers around the world, while securing its interests in the Phoebus cartel through foreign subsidiaries.

The outbreak of World War II rendered the cartel ineffective. Moreover, postwar antitrust actions filed against lamp producers, mostly in the United States, soon banned the industry practices of international cartelization, exclusive patent licensing, price fixing, and market division. Cooperation and knowledge exchange between lamp producers continued, but this was now based on the principle of

*Above: Thomas Edison
Patent Infringement
Case Court Exhibits.
(Courtesy of Heritage
Auctions, HA.com)*

formal nonexclusivity. However, while competition increased, large pre-war companies like Osram, Philips, and General Electric continued to dominate the postwar global lighting market.

Today, in many countries worldwide, incandescent light bulbs are gradually being phased-out in favor of more energy-efficient lighting like halogen, CFL, and LED lamps. Yet, the history of the light bulb remains and holds important lessons for current and future generations. From questions of inventorship and patent grants for incremental innovations built on existing ideas, to patent wars that established early market positions, collaborative strategies of pooling patents to eliminate competition, and exclusive sales territory and cartel agreements to divide markets, the chain of events in the history of the light bulb is characteristic of how industries emerging around new paradigm technologies behave. Utilizing the commercial power of intellectual property was central to the history of the light bulb, and studying this history helps us to better understand how these cycles might repeat themselves in the future. ◆

Further Reading

Stathis Arapostathis and Graeme Gooday (2013) *Patently Contestable: Electrical Technologies and Inventor Identities on Trial in Britain.* Cambridge, MA: MIT Press.

Arthur A. Bright, Jr. (1949) *The Electric-Lamp Industry: Technological Change and Economic Development from 1800 to 1947.* New York: Macmillan Co.

A. Heerding (1986–1988) *The History of N.V. Philips' Gloeilampenfabrieken, Volume I: The Origins of the Dutch Incandescent Lamp Industry; Volume 2: A Company of Many Parts.* Cambridge: Cambridge University Press.

1700   *1800*   *1900*

--/-----/-----/-----/-----/-----/-----/-----/-/----/-----/-----/-----/----

13 Oscar Wilde Portrait

Megan Richardson

On the left: Oscar Wilde Portrait No. 18. (National Archives and Records Administration)

IT IS SAID that celebrity is a combination of the celebrity producer, the celebrity figure and the public. And all three are evident in Napoleon Sarony's iconic portrait of Oscar Wilde—No. 18 of a set of 27—taken in Sarony's studio in New York at the beginning of Wilde's American tour in January 1882. Sarony created the portrait, posing Wilde, arranging his contours and approving his expression (intelligent and thoughtful), selecting the props (Wilde's dandified clothes and the book in his hand signifying the idea of the intellectual aesthete), and ordering the background (the rich Persian carpet on the floor adding to the impression of cultivated aestheticism, drawing here on the Orientalism that Wilde and other British aesthetes favored). Sarony's recognizable customized signature at the bottom of each image completes the suggestion that America's leading celebrity photographer was responsible for the remarkable image. But without Wilde's distinctive figure, face, and personal renown as a literary celebrity even at this relatively early stage of his literary life, the photograph would mean

nothing to the audience. And without an audience to be impressed, amused, scandalized, and mesmerized, in turn, there would be no point in the photographic author or his (in)famous subject taking part in the project.

The project was initiated by the entertainment entrepreneur Richard D'Oyly Carte, 'Oily' Carte as he was sometimes known, for the Gilbert and Sullivan comic opera *Patience* that Carte was producing, which was now commencing its American tour after a successful season in London. The show featured J.H. Ryley in the role of the poet-dandy Reginald Bunthorne and, concerned that the American public might not appreciate that such British dandies actually existed, Wilde was approached with the proposition that he tour alongside the musical to provide the necessary evidence, including sitting in the audience when the opera was performed, appropriately dressed and coiffured to reflect the character on stage—a clever play on things that worked to foster confusion as to just who was the copy and who was the original here. Wilde readily assented to the congenial plan. No doubt he was influenced in part by the money he was offered (his expenses covered and a share of the profits from his appearances) at a time when he was enjoying an extravagant existence beyond his income as the 27-year-old author of a beautifully produced book of *Poems*—possibly the book that featured in his hands in photograph No. 18. His financial success as the author of *The Importance of Being Earnest* and other major theatrical productions was still to come in later years, being plays that to an extent emulated the comic parodying of contemporary life of Gilbert and Sullivan's *Patience*. But the project also offered an irresistible opportunity for ready fame to this ambitious talented rising star.

As it turned out, the project designed to publicize *Patience* soon became Wilde's personal project as his press interviews and lectures throughout America and Canada drew their own audiences and income, with his year-long sojourn long outlasting the three-month *Patience* tour. Sarony's promotional portraits were also probably Wilde's initiation, aware of the tremendous success of his friend Sarah Bernhardt's portraits taken by Sarony the year before for her American tour. So keen, some have said, were Wilde and Carte's agent W.F. Morse to have the photographs that they waived the customary fee paid to celebrities in their contractual arrangements with Sarony, which specified that Sarony would enjoy "the sole and exclusive right to make, publish, sell, and dispose of portraits of him, said Wilde, in the United States" (as spelt out in Sarony's claim in his later case against the lithographer Burrow-Giles). But

I have found no evidence to support any notion that less than "good and valuable consideration" was paid for the entitlement that Sarony was granted (as also specified in the claim). In any event, there was a *quid pro quo* for the contractual arrangement even apart from the money. For on Wilde's and Carte's side the photographs provided a way to introduce Wilde to a vast new audience as he toured American and Canadian cities in a period before film, television, and the reproduction of photographs in newspapers (with the technology of photogravure mainstream in the 1890s) provided for easy circulation of accurate visual images. Wilde himself actively participated in the idea that the images should be widely distributed in advance of his physical arrival, for instance writing to Carte in March 1882 that "I think if some large lithographs of me were got up it would help business in these small cities, where the local men spend so little on advertising" (presumably to be done on agreed terms with Sarony pursuant to their contract). Interestingly, the image he preferred for the task was not Oscar Wilde No. 18 but rather "the photograph of me with my head looking over my shoulder," just showing "the head and fur collar"—probably referring here to photograph No. 23 in the session with Sarony.

Perhaps the choice of No. 23 over No. 18 was due to the widespread pirating of Oscar Wilde No. 18 that was already occurring by March 1882. In general, an enormous number and variety of unauthorized trade cards featuring Wilde in Saronian-style poses circulated during his

On the right: Oscar Wilde Portrait No. 23. (Alamy)

OSCAR WILDE.

Copyright 1882, by N. Sarony

NEW YORK.

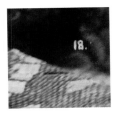

tour. But a particularly extreme source of the pirated images was the Burrow-Giles Lithographic Company. Eighty-five thousand copies of photograph No. 18 were exposed for sale in the city and southern district of New York and throughout the United States, including the ones featuring in advertisements for Erich Bros. in New York and Mandel Bros. in Chicago. By April 1882 proceedings were initiated in the southern district of New York for damages. Sarony claimed that Burrow-Giles' unlawful acts undercut his efforts to "receive the profits to be derived from the exclusive and sole liberties so to him secured" and which, prior to Burrow-Giles' acts, had been a source of "great gains and profits by his [Sarony's] said copyright and the publication and vending of the said copyrighted photograph." To avoid any argument that his actions in producing the photograph were merely mechanical, Sarony claimed specifically that the photograph was

the original invention and design of this plaintiff, for the reason that it was made by this plaintiff entirely from his own original mental conception, to which he gave visible form by posing the said Oscar Wilde in front of the camera, selecting and arranging the costume, draperies and other various accessories in said photograph, arranging the subject so as to present graceful outlines, arranging and disposing the light and shade, suggesting and

evoking the desired expression, and from such disposition, arrangement, or representation, made entirely by this plaintiff, producing the picture which is the subject of this suit.

Further details of the case can be found in the case file held at the National Archives and Records Administration in Washington, DC. They can also be found on the Gale online archive of primary sources. Suffice for present purposes to note that Sarony's account of the way that the photograph had come into being was not essentially questioned (although commentators since have said that he did not actually push the button which activated the mechanism of photography, leaving that to his assistant Benjamin Richardson). Burrow-Giles limited its defence to the questions of the constitutionality of granting copyright in photographs and the proper registration of any copyright in the Library of Congress, disputing that the signature "N Sarony" was sufficient for the purpose. The circuit judge, Alfred Coxe, held for Sarony in a judgment issued on 11 June 1883. Burrow-Giles appealed, and in the end the legal dispute over Sarony's copyright was only finally resolved in Sarony's favor in the US Supreme Court in March 1884. As Mark Rose puts it in his excellent chapter on the case in *Authors in Court*, "[t]he court's decision thus ratified Sarony's status as an artist not a mechanic." But the

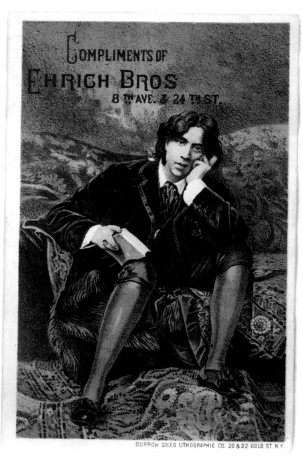

Supreme Court's decision gives a sense that the deeper question of mechanical reproduction and its effect on the traditional idea of creative authorial production was still not finally resolved. The unanswered question continues to resonate even now when there remains continuing debate about the level of creativity and human involvement that an author must be able to demonstrate in order to claim copyright.

Nevertheless, to focus only on copyright gives a rather limited account of the multiple interests at stake in the case. Some distinguished commentators, including Rose, Jane Gaines in a classic essay, and Peter Decherney in Chapter 15 of this book on the "The Kinetoscope," have observed that the Supreme Court's decision seemed to pay little heed to Wilde's interests in his portrait. What were those interests?

Michael North writing in the *Publications of the Modern Language Association of America* (PMLA) refers interestingly to privacy, as discussed by Samuel Warren and Louis Brandeis in the 1890 *Harvard Law Review*. But I have found nothing to indicate that Wilde was concerned about the effect of the advertising ventures involving his portraits on his right to be "let alone," as Warren and Brandeis termed the right to privacy. This is not to say that he was unaware of the value of maintaining a private sphere. But he may have felt that he gave this up—at least temporarily—in his quest for celebrity on his American tour. When interviewers in Washington and St. Louis raised the issue of his "private life," he responded mildly that "I wished I had one." Indeed, his most significant concerns about privacy seem to have developed later in the wake of the virulent publicity he received following publication

Above, from left to right: USCC SDNY Law Case A-802, Exhibit B. (National Archives and Records Administration); Compliments of Ehrich Bros. 8th Ave. & 24th St. (Library of Congress)

of his novel *The Picture of Dorian Gray* in Lippincott's *Monthly Magazine* in 1890. So we see some bitter comments about the press and public's treatment of private life in *The Soul of Man Under Socialism* published shortly after Warren and Brandeis' article. As to these authors, in their discussions of privacy they seemed more concerned about George Eastman's recently invented "instantaneous" photography (the subject of the next chapter), "newspaper enterprise" and the public's propensity for gossip than commercial advertising practices, notwithstanding passing references to the problem of unauthorized circulation of portraits. In the 20th century we see arguments about privacy extending to unwanted publicity involving the use of a person's name or likeness in advertising, as reflected, for instance, in the enactment of "the right of privacy" in §§ 50 and 51 of the New York Civil Rights Law in 1903. Even then, the interests of many celebrities, including Wilde, in the circulation and use of their name or likeness in advertising may have less to do with privacy than with something else entirely.

Returning to the multifaceted idea of celebrity put forward at the beginning of this piece, Wilde's interests in *Burrow-Giles v. Sarony* may be most closely aligned to the "right of publicity" recognized in another case decided in a New York court some 50 years later. That is the case of *Haelan Laboratories, Inc. v. Topps Chewing Gum, Inc.*, where Frank, Circuit Judge, for the Court of Appeals, second circuit, in 1953 observed that, despite the rhetoric of privacy, "many prominent persons (especially actors and ball-players), far from having their feelings bruised through public exposure of their likenesses, would feel sorely deprived if they no longer received money for authorizing advertisements, popularizing their countenances," and accepted that such rights may be assigned by contract (as in that case for use of ball-players' images on chewing-gum cards). Had Frank acknowledged that celebrities and their publics may be more interested in celebrity than anything much else, the parallel would have been even clearer with Wilde who in his contract with Sarony seemed to be pursuing something that was more ephemeral but ultimately more significant than the ability to receive money for commercial advertising. It was fame. ◆

Further Reading

Jane Gaines (1991) *Contested Culture: The Image, the Voice, and the Law.* Chapel Hill: University of North Carolina Press. (Chapter 2, Photography "Surprises" the Law: The Portrait of Oscar Wilde)

Matthew Hofer and Gary Scharnhorst (eds.) (2010) *Oscar Wilde in America: The Interviews.* Champaign: University of Illinois Press.

Merlin Holland and Rupert Hart-Davis (eds.) (2000) *Complete Letters of Oscar Wilde.* London: 4th Estate.

Michael North (2010) "The Picture of Oscar Wilde," *PMLA*, 125(1), pp. 185–191.

Mark Rose (2016) *Authors in Court: Scenes from the Theatre of Copyright.* Cambridge, MA: Harvard University Press. (Chapter 4, Creating Oscar Wilde: *Burrow-Giles* v. *Sarony* (1884))

1700   1800   1900

--/-----/-----/-----/-----/-----/-----/-----/---/--/-----/-----/-----/----

14 Kodak Camera

Jessica Lake

On the left: Kodak advertisement from 1904, originally published in the Saturday Evening Post. (Ellis Collection of Kodakiana, Rubenstein Library Rare Book and Manuscript Library, Duke University)

"IT MUST BE confessed that the etiquette of the 'kodaker' has not kept pace with the development of the 'kodak.' It is difficult for some people to understand that there are those who have a strong prejudice against being promiscuously 'snapped at' through a camera," opined an article from the *Ladies Home Journal* in 1900. The invention and release of the Kodak camera by New York entrepreneur George Eastman in 1888 heralded a new generation of photographic cameras, intensified debates about the unauthorized capture and circulation of people's (particularly women's) images at a time of shifting and unstable gender roles, and contributed to the recognition of a right to privacy in the United States, the first in the common law world.

When Eastman first introduced the trademarked and patented Kodak camera to the world at the Convention of the Photographic Association of America in Minneapolis, he cemented his role as the father of modern photography. In previous decades, photography had been an expensive and time-consuming pursuit requiring expert knowledge, complicated bulky equipment and the ambient conditions of light and stillness only generally achievable indoors within a studio setting. Individuals who desired likenesses of themselves or their family members sat for professionals in their studios or shops. This was a popular pastime, sought after by a growing new middle class (of shopkeepers, managers, clerks, and small traders) as well as budding "celebrities" (such as Oscar Wilde, as discussed in the previous chapter). By 1850, Americans were spending between eight and 12 million dollars a year on photographic portraits, and portraits constituted an astonishing 95 percent of all photographic production.

Photography, from its beginnings in the 1830s as Louis Daguerre's "daguerreotype" and William Henry Fox Talbot's "calotype," had radically altered the nature of portraiture, creating images that were simultaneously more authentic and more autonomous than their drawn or painted equivalents. As a form of writing with light (with all the attendant theological and philosophical associations), photography occupied a unique relationship to

truth. Via this new medium, the uncanny likeness of an individual could be lifted with mechanical ease from its possessor and cast upon paper, to be reproduced, handled, disseminated, and published on an unprecedented scale. This ability to uniquely capture human subjects was, from its beginnings, problematic. On the one hand, a photograph of a loved one brought that person closer to those who loved them. On the other hand, photography detached a subject from him or herself. Photographic portraits could be snapped, developed, and presented to loved ones for them to cherish or honor, just as they could be stolen, lost, and trafficked. In 1888, one of New York's most renowned photographers, 30-year-old Le Grange Brown, was accused of exhibiting and offering for sale (in local saloons) photographs of "undraped women." Apparently Brown had taken the photographic portraits of hundreds of young high society ladies during various social events and then pasted their heads on to indecent images of naked women.

Photographic portraits (particularly those of women) clearly held more than sentimental value—and were soon being used voyeuristically as advertisements, greeting cards, and sexual commodities. This practice was so widespread that in 1888 Republican Congressman John Robert Thomas, particularly incensed by the use of the First Lady Frances Cleveland's image on advertisements for tobacco and pharmaceuticals, introduced a bill to the House of Representatives proposing "to prohibit the use of likenesses, portraits or representations of females for advertising purposes, without consent in writing." As newspapers began discussing the "Bill to Protect Ladies" in terms of women's rights to "privacy," professional photographers rallied against it to defend their recently secured intellectual property rights as authors (i.e., their copyright) and they won—the bill was never passed.

The same year that the Bill to Protect Ladies was introduced to Congress, George Eastman released his Kodak camera, which heralded the transformation of photography into a "delightful pastime" for ordinary people and intensified debate

Above, left: The Kodak, 1888, invented by George Eastman, is perhaps the most significant commercial camera ever produced. The important feature of the Kodak was not the camera itself but the new photographic system marketed to support it. It was sold pre-loaded with enough film to take 100 photographs. (Getty Images)

Above, right: An 1888 ad for the Kodak camera, originally published in Outing Magazine. (Ellis Collection of Kodakiana, Rubenstein Library Rare Book and Manuscript Library, Duke University)

about the image rights of photographed subjects. Though there were many photographic companies at the time, Eastman and the Kodak trademark quickly became synonymous with the new "amateur photography" craze. Since the early 1870s, when Eastman had worked by day at the Rochester Savings Bank to support his widowed mother, he displayed a fascination for photography and a mission to simplify the process. In the 1870s and early 1880s he invented a number of innovative photographic products—dry plates, machine-coated paper, a roll holder, stripping film coated with gelatin and then his first so-called "detective" camera in 1886. However, this model was soon abandoned by Eastman as he set to work on the lightweight and affordable "Kodak" camera. The Kodak proved immensely popular. By 1896, the Eastman Kodak Company had sold more than a hundred thousand of them.

In September 1888, an advertisement for the new Kodak camera appeared in the *Scientific American*: "100 instantaneous pictures! Anybody can use it. No knowledge of photography is necessary. The latest and best outfit for amateurs." Kodaks were sold as "easy" portable devices to accompany an active outdoors American life, to document local landscapes, sporting hobbies and the exotic curiosities of foreign lands as well as the warm hearth of domesticity.

While there were of course some women who identified as photographers and some men whose images were used without their permission, advertising and commentary encouraged a general delineation between men as active photographers and women as passive photographic subjects. Marketing commonly employed hunting and shooting metaphors and framed it as a masculine hobby. "There are no game laws for those who hunt with a Kodak," declared one early advertisement.

The Kodak camera also contributed to a boom in surreptitious and uninvited photography during the late 19th century. It was categorized as a "detective camera," as its small size and ease of use allowed it to be more readily hidden from view. On 6 December 1889, an article titled "The Kodak Camera" in *The Detective* newspaper (published in Cedar Rapids, Iowa) declared: "This device enables us to obtain (instantaneously) perfect pictures of faces, objects, or scenes which may be secured without the knowledge or exciting the suspicion of the person or persons whose picture is being taken … As a detective camera, the Kodak is unequalled." Now, anyone with a portable $25 Kodak camera could snap and circulate someone's likeness and more often than not, it was men capturing the images of unwilling or unsuspecting women. A 1889 *New York Times* article described amateur photographers as

Above: Ironstone Sparks' kidney tonic advertising tray with a portrait of the First Lady as the central theme. From the U.I. "Chick" and Cecilia Harris Collection. (Courtesy of Heritage Auctions, HA.com)

On the left: Frances Folsom Cleveland, First Lady of the United States and wife of President Grover Cleveland. (Photo by Library of Congress / Corbis / VCG via Getty Images)

"young knights of the camera" and "pretty girls" as their "natural prey" and discussed the issue in terms of conflicting "rights": "It is a question of debate what rights the amateur has in securing pictures, and of course there are some who consider a party of young women as free subjects of photography as a waterfall or clump of trees."

The battle over image rights that arose in the late 19th century represented a collision of new technology (photography) and rapidly changing social, cultural, and political circumstances. In the growing ocular-centric culture of this period, photographic images became a new and valuable dimension of individual personality. Photography offered a radical new way of representing and addressing people. No longer were individuals simply framed by the stories told or opinions held about them by others; by their social status or the conditions or circumstances of their labor; or with the manners or display they affected in public space. Now, visual images could define and determine a person. Women experienced the personal consequences of photography's growing ubiquity most acutely as cultural and social forces combined to emphasize their place in front of the lens and their images became imbued with special significance. As the turn of the 20th century approached, American women were in a state of heady transition—they were entering the paid workforce and higher education in ever growing numbers, calling for rights of citizenship and choosing to lead lives others than as wives and mothers. As Elizabeth Otto and Vanessa Rocco argue in their book, *New Woman International*, it was primarily through images that the New Woman—a figure of liberation and agency and a threat to traditional values of womanhood—was contested and identified at the turn of the last century, the camera functioning as an "instrument of self-determination."

At the end of the 19th century, the Kodak camera accelerated the image rights debate and posed the question as to whether photographic subjects should have legal rights to control their images? Two cases involving surreptitious photography worked to answer this question and ultimately spurred the establishment of a legal "right to privacy" in the United States—the first such right or cause of action in the common law world.

Kodak knows no dark days

With its allies, the Kodak flash sheets and a Kodak flash sheet holder, your Kodak camera is ready for every Christmas opportunity.

The guests at the house-party, the Christmas tree itself, a chronicle of all the good times are all easily within its scope. Snap-shots out-of-doors, time exposures in-doors and flashlights at night are all the same to the Kodak.

And such pictures are easy to take by the simple Kodak method.

Ask your dealer or write us for a Kodak catalogue and a copy of our little booklet "By Flashlight." There's no charge.

EASTMAN KODAK COMPANY, ROCHESTER, N. Y., *The Kodak City.*

In the 1890 case of *Manola* v. *Stevens*, comic opera star Marion Manola had her photograph surreptitiously snapped by a theater manager and a professional photographer while she was on a Broadway stage playing the role of Bul-Bul in the comic opera *Castle in the Sky* by the DeWolf Hopper Opera Company. She wore a (at the time revealing) costume of tights. The image was intended to be used as publicity for the theater but Manola took the photographer and manager to court. She protested that she did not want to become an object of the voyeuristic male gaze, for her picture to become, in her own words, "common property, circulated from hand to hand, and treasured by every fellow who can raise the price demanded." Manola won her case but only because the defendants failed to appear in court. In 1890, she had no cause of action upon which to rest her claim.

Boston jurists Samuel Warren and Louis Brandeis cited Manola's case when they advocated for the recognition of a new common law right to privacy in their seminal article, "A Right to Privacy," published by the *Harvard Law Review* in 1890. They argued that recent inventions and business methods meant the law must move to protect an individual's right "to be let alone." Lamenting the incursion of "instantaneous photographs" such as those produced by the Kodak camera, Warren and Brandeis noted that "for years there has been a feeling that the law must afford some remedy for the unauthorized circulation of portraits of private persons" and referred to Manola's recent predicament. Warren and Brandeis' logical and eloquent plea for a new form of legal redress to combat the hazards posed by modern industry and innovation, particularly the snapshot camera, has been labelled by some commentators in the United States as the most influential law review article ever published.

Some years later, another young woman from New York, Abigail Roberson, had her image captured without her knowledge and plastered on packets of flour and other advertising material, in the United States and around the world,

Above: An ad for Kodak photography, 1917, originally published in Ladies' Home Journal. (Ellis Collection of Kodakiana, Rubenstein Library Rare Book and Manuscript Library, Duke University)

Above: Kodak advertisements to encourage readers to have a picture taken of their family, originally published in the Saturday Evening Post. (Ellis Collection of Kodakiana, Rubenstein Library Rare Book and Manuscript Library, Duke University)

for Franklin Mills Flour. Under a photograph of her profile was the witty caption: "The Flour of the Family." Distressed and outraged, 17-year-old Roberson took Franklin Mills Flour and the advertiser, Rochester Folding Box, to court. Her suffragist championing attorney, Milton E. Gibbs, argued that they had violated her right to privacy and her property right in her own beauty. He formulated his arguments upon the article penned by Warren and Brandeis ten years earlier. Unlike Manola, Roberson lost her case. But such was the outrage by the community about the decision—lawyers and lay people alike—across the United States, that the New York legislature responded by enacting a statutory case of action for "a right to privacy." This law, which prohibited the use of an individual's name or likeness for trade or advertising purposes without their consent, was the first privacy right in the common law world and the first time photographed subjects gained specific legal protection.

It is fitting that a girl from the town of Rochester, New York, forged the first rights for photographed subjects when a young man from the very same town invented the Kodak and ignited the passions of photographers 12 years earlier. Eastman, entrepreneur and inventor, was the amateur photographer's hero and, on the other side of the lens, Roberson became, in legal scholarship of the time and subsequently, the "pinup" girl for privacy rights. ◆

Further Reading

Douglas Collins (1990) *The Story of Kodak.* New York: H.N. Abrams.

Jessica Lake (2016) *The Face that Launched a Thousand Lawsuits: The American Women Who Forged a Right to Privacy.* New Haven: Yale University Press.

Samuel D. Warren and Louis D. Brandeis (1890) "The Right to Privacy," *Harvard Law Review*, 4, pp. 193–220.

1700   1800   1900

--/-----/-----/-----/-----/-----/-----/-----/---/--/-----/-----/-----/----

15 Kinetoscope
Peter Decherney

THE HISTORY OF film and media technology often seems to move backwards as well as forwards. Synchronized sound and color films, for example, appeared and disappeared for decades before they became industry standards. And 3D movies continue to come and go in waves. The stops and starts of media history can have many causes: technologies are insufficiently developed, businesses fail to promote them effectively, or the social integration of new media technology takes a wrong turn. Media revolutions may begin in the laboratory, but they don't take hold unless all of the pieces are aligned. And it is not uncommon for technological advances to lay dormant for centuries until they can be successfully employed and enjoyed.

When motion pictures emerged simultaneously in Europe and the United States in the last decade of the 19th century, they existed in a heterogeneous environment filled with possibilities, ultimately ending with a mix of success stories and failures. Some investors incorporated movies into amusement parks and world's fairs, creating early film rides. Others projected

film in vaudeville and music hall theaters, extending the traditions of popular theater. And Thomas Edison's short-lived Kinetoscope created a personalized viewing experience that disrupted social norms and legal regulation before it submerged again, only to be reborn, we might argue, more than a century later.

Edison first set a team in his lab working on motion picture technology in 1888 after he witnessed photographer Eadweard Muybridge's studies of animal locomotion. Over the next few years, the team experimented with many different methods of reproducing moving images, and they incorporated ideas from collaborators and competitors. After trying a number of unsuccessful formats, Edison's lab settled on George Eastman's flexible celluloid film, which proved to be both pliable and tough enough to wind through the gears of a film camera. Edison soon added sprocket holes to move the celluloid even more effectively, as French scientist Etienne-Jules Marey and others had done. Sometime between the summer of 1889 and fall of 1890, Edison's lead assistant on the project,

W.K.L. Dickson, successfully recorded a short movie, Monkey Shines No. 1, and in 1891 Edison filed three patents describing the Kinetograph camera and Kinetoscope viewer. Eventually, all three patents were overturned, because they were overly broad and insufficiently novel. Edison claimed to be the sole inventor of film, when he clearly stood on the shoulders of many predecessors and contemporaries.

The judge who wrote the decision may have gone a little too far when he claimed, "It is obvious that Mr. Edison was not a pioneer, in the large sense of the term, or in the more limited sense in which he would have been if he had also invented the film." Although Edison claimed credit for the entirety of the film medium, his vision for technology differed significantly from his competitors. When the Edison laboratory developed the Kinetoscope, they were most specifically trying to expand Edison's already successful phonograph business. As Edison explained in his 1888 caveat (a precursor to a patent), he wanted to "do for the Eye what the phonograph does for the Ear."

Edison had struck gold with the arcade-like phonograph parlors where patrons listened to recordings of popular songs or famous speeches on coin-operated machines. Edison initially envisioned building on this business by adding peep show devices for spectators to peer into while listening to phonographs through primitive headphones. This multimedia device, also known as the Kinetophonograph, never made it past an experimental stage, but Edison and Dickson produced films for it and promoted it to the public. Clearly a vision of the future, one promotional photograph of a man using a Kinetophonograph with prominently displayed white headphones resembles nothing so much as an early iPod advertisement.

From the beginning, Edison imagined a wide range of media devices, even beyond the personal sound and image viewer. His initial caveat described a spectator experiencing an opera as if he or she was there, as we tend to fantasize about virtual reality today. Edison's subsequent patent application made reference to the possibility of showing stereoscopic (i.e., 3D) images,

although he never realized that dream either. And at one point, Edison marketed (and sold a few) devices for watching movies at home.

Surprisingly, one form of movie consumption Edison did not envision at first was projection. The always commercially minded inventor calculated that selling single-viewer devices was a better business than selling projectors. Kinetoscope viewers consumed one film at a time, while images projected on a screen entertained hundreds.

Edison may have bet on the wrong technology, or he may have been a 100 or so years ahead of his time. The Kinetoscope, optimized for personal viewing of short movies, anticipated 21st-century phones and YouTube videos. Indeed, many Kinetoscope movies resemble the astonishing and voyeuristic content available on internet video sites. In fact, Edison's 1894 cute cat video, Boxing Cats, hasn't lost its appeal and has attracted over three-quarters of a million views on YouTube to date.

Whether the Kinetoscope represents a road not taken or a route technology companies eventually circled back to, it occupied a formative moment in which the movies had the potential to develop in multiple directions. And the Kinetoscope forced audiences, filmmakers, and regulators to confront the many disruptions introduced by the new technology and artform. In addition to cat videos, popular subjects for Kinetoscope films included episodic narratives, like passion plays, which unfolded in scenes, or boxing matches with multiple rounds. The suspense built by the episodic form would inevitably compel patrons to move from one Kinetoscope scene to the next, binge watching early films while depositing plenty of coins along the

way. Other films played with the peephole design of the Kinetoscope and showed private scenes as though seen through a keyhole. And star power was a draw from the very beginning. Many of Edison's films showed vaudeville celebrities who traveled from New York City to his New Jersey studio to be recorded. Audiences clamored for the virtual, close-up experience of famous performers and politicians like Annie Oakley and President William McKinley.

These new Kinetoscope experiences of faux proximity to important people and events and of private experience acquired in a public led to new business practices, new forms of regulation, and new social norms. How, for example, did Edison pay the dancers, strongmen, and comic actors who performed before his camera? They were paid a flat fee for their one-time performance, for their labor. Some even did it for free. But performers were never

Above: Sharpshooter Annie Oakley shooting over her shoulder using a hand mirror. (Getty Images)

given residual payments for subsequent showings, as TV actors have been paid since the 1940s. If a film was a hit, it boosted a vaudevillian's reputation, but it did not increase his or her pocketbook. Performers did not retain any rights to the films they appeared in either, and since the 1880s Supreme Court case involving Napoleon Sarony's picture of Oscar Wilde, discussed as object 13 of this collection, American copyright law has not recognized the subjects of photographs or movies as a co-authors. It is a question, however, that has continued to arise, igniting intense controversy again in the 2010s when an actress asked YouTube to remove an inflammatory anti-Islamic short video claiming to be the trailer for a film called THE INNOCENCE OF MUSLIMS. Protests over the video in Egypt and other countries resulted in more than 50 deaths. At first the Ninth Circuit Court of Appeals decided that, as a performer, the actress was in fact a co-author who shared the film's copyright, giving her the right to request that the video be removed from YouTube. But the court later reversed its decision, returning to the norm set by the Oscar Wilde case.

In addition to opening new territory in the regulation of authorship and representation, the Kinetoscope upset laws and norms that governed public space. Just how close was seeing a film to seeing the real thing? And what were the implications for viewers? Boxing, for example, was largely outlawed in the United States during the Kinetoscope's heyday. And even where boxing was allowed it was deemed improper for women and children to witness the bloodsport of half naked brawling

men. Yet boxing films were shown in states where live boxing was banned, and we know that women and children frequented Kinetoscope parlors and later nickelodeons where boxing films were frequently on display. Movies offered virtual experiences that we tend to regulate differently than their live counterparts.

Kinetoscope parlors also reconfigured the social composition of public space, bringing together women and men, children and adults, and middle- and working-class patrons. Regulators cautiously adjusted to these new diverse spaces. A 1908 New York ordinance, for example, insisted that lights remain on in movie venues to deter crime. Edison responded to panic over movie content and exhibition spaces by partnering with a private censoring board, self-editing before the city or state could do it. Later, in 1915 the Supreme Court deemed filmmaking to be "a business pure and simple." Films, the Court determined, could be regulated like food to ensure public safety, and movies were routinely sanitized or banned entirely by state censor boards until the Supreme Court finally granted filmmakers first amendment protection in the 1950s.

Despite his early patent setbacks, Edison never gave up his ambition to control the entire film industry. Edison may have obstinately pursued the personal media technology of the Kinetoscope when audiences prefered the theatrical experience of projection, but that did not stop him. He eventually adapted to the market and shifted his focus away from the Kinetoscope. Instead of developing a new projector in his laboratory, Edison licensed a

EDISON'S GREATEST MARVEL

THE VITASCOPE

"Wonderful is The Vitascope. Pictures life size and full of color. Makes a thrilling show."
NEW YORK HERALD, April 24, '96.

projector invented by two young engineers and rebranded it "Edison's Vitascope." Undeterred by his crushing patent defeat, Edison reapplied for several narrower patents on small changes that his team had made to film technology, including his particular arrangement of sprocket holes. With his weakened legal position, Edison pooled his patents with those of the other major film companies, and in 1909 he started the Motion Picture Patents Company, informally known as the Edison Trust. The Trust vertically and horizontally integrated the industry, making it almost impossible for non-Trust members to make or show films in the United States.

Edison's Trust quickly grew to be large and powerful, and it dominated American movies for several years. But its tight control also discouraged innovation, an especially dangerous situation in the rapidly developing early film business. By the mid-1910s, the independent companies that banded together to oppose the Trust began to win over audiences with better films and bigger stars. And Edison's movie business declined in the mid-1910s as quickly as it had risen. The final nail

in the coffin for the business that Edison started with the Kinetoscope came in 1915 when a federal court found the Trust to be in violation of the Sherman Antitrust Act. Edison's movie business was soon shuttered entirely.

Edison's second act in the film industry failed as the Kinetoscope had, but all of Edison's early visions for the industry from synchronized sound to 3D images to home viewing came to pass. And the personal experience of the Kinetoscope proved prescient as well. Late 19th- and early 20th-century audiences were much more comfortable watching projected images, because they closely resembled the familiar experience of enjoying a vaudeville show or play in a theater. The act of privately watching a movie in public took some adjustment, and the descendants of the Kinetoscope continued to encounter social resistance. When the first Sony Walkman was introduced in the 1970s, almost a century after the phonograph and Kinetoscope, it contained two headphone jacks, because the company was reluctant to introduce a completely solitary media technology. Years later, Apple CEO

Above: The earliest showings of movies were done on competing projectors; the Thomas Edison version was known as the Vitascope. (Getty Images)

Above, left: Portrait of Thomas Edison, ca. 1878. (Getty Images)

Above, right: Portrait of Steve Jobs at the first West Coast Computer Faire, where the Apple II computer was debuted, San Francisco 1977. (Photo by Tom Munnecke / Getty Images)

Steve Jobs expressed great reluctance to introducing an iPod that played video. In 2003, just two years before changing course and releasing the fifth generation iPod with video, Jobs told reporter Walt Mossberg, "I'm not convinced people want to watch movies on a tiny little screen." In retrospect, it can be difficult to imagine a world in which thoroughly domesticated technologies like personal media players seemed impractical, immoral, or illegal. But new technologies routinely require multiple attempts before they become staples of our existence, and we continually return to nodal points in technological history, like the early days of the film industry, to pick up lost threads and move in new directions. ◆

Further Reading

Brian X. Chen (2010) "Steve Jobs Sneakiest Statements," *Wired*, 16 February.

Peter Decherney (2012) *Hollywood's Copyright Wars: From Edison to the Internet*. New York: Columbia University Press.

W.K.L. Dickson and Antonia Dickson (1895) *History of the Kinetograph, Kinetoscope, and Kineto-Phonograph*. New York: Albert Dunn.

Charles Musser (1991) *Before the Nickelodeon: Edwin S. Porter and the Edison Manufacturing Company*. Berkeley: University of California Press.

Edison v. *American Mutoscope Co*, 114 F. 926 [2d Cir. 1902]

Mutual Film Corporation v. *Industrial Commission of Ohio*, 236 US 230 (1915)

Thomas A. Edison, caveat 110, 8 (Filed Oct. 17, 1888).

Further Viewing

"Inventing Entertainment: The Early Motion Pictures and Sound Recordings of the Edison Companies" (Library of Congress), *web exhibit*. 341 motion pictures available at: www.loc.gov/collections/edison-company-motion-pictures-and-sound-recordings/

1700   *1800*   *1900*

--/----/----/----/----/----/----/----/---/--/----/----/----/----

16 Deerstalker Hat

Ronan Deazley

On the left: Basil Rathbone as Sherlock Holmes and Ida Lupino as Ann Brandon in THE ADVENTURES OF SHERLOCK HOLMES *(US 1939, Dir. Alfred Werker). (Photo by Silver Screen Collection / Getty Images)*

IN MILLER'S CROSSING, the prohibition era gangster movie by the Coen brothers, Gabriel Byrne plays Tom Reagan, a rumpled, whiskey-soaked, antihero—the brooding right-hand man to Irish kingpin, Leo O'Bannon. Reagan's hat—a simple fedora—is more than costume or prop: it is central to his character and the narrative. In the film's title sequence, the hat blows along a forest path, caught in the breeze, dancing between the trees in what might be a fairy tale scene. Later, Tom recounts a dream to his lover Verna about walking in the woods when the wind blows his hat off; she preempts the ending: "And you chased it right? You ran and ran, and finally caught up to it … picked it up. But it wasn't a hat anymore, it had changed into something else, something wonderful." "Nah," he responds, "it stayed a hat and no, I didn't chase it. Nothing more foolish than a man chasing his hat." Tom's curt, irritable dismissal is playful and sly. The Coen brothers have remained famously gnomic about the hat's significance, but its place on screen is deliberate, purposeful and integral. It is one of the most iconic

hats in cinematic history. With its roots in mid-19th-century Scotland, the humble deerstalker *has* been transformed into "something else, something wonderful." It has become a metonym. Show someone a picture of a fedora and they are unlikely to think: Tom Reagan. But, show someone a deerstalker?

In many respects, the deerstalker's place within this history of intellectual property is ambiguous and improbable. But that also imbues it with relevance and resonance. It shimmers, speaking not to one story but many. The story of the deerstalker is the story of Sherlock Holmes, and the story of Holmes is Scheherazadian, offering up an abundance of tales: about the contingent nature of intellectual property rights, their territoriality, and longevity; about authorship, co-creation, and the collective construction of cultural value; about copyright's public domain, and the afterlife of characters beyond the stories that define them; about intertextuality, making meaning, and making money; and, about the mysteriousness of copyright, its unknowability, and ubiquity. In *The Blue*

Carbuncle, an "ordinary black hat" offers Holmes insights into the owner's circumstances and demeanor: he is an intellectual man who leads a sedentary life, he has fallen on difficult times, has likely taken to drink, and his wife has ceased to love him. The deerstalker offers more.

Most of these stories must wait to be told another time, like the unchronicled cases crammed into John Watson's battered old dispatch box. Here, we consider only a few.

Sherlock has a long-established iconography that includes hat, cape, pipe, and magnifying glass, but the deerstalker remains most iconic. It personifies—perhaps reifies—the myth that is Holmes. And yet, this was not prescribed by Doyle. Unlike the Coen Brothers, Doyle did not cultivate meaning in this particular hat. He describes Holmes wearing a "close-fitting cloth cap," and an "ear-flapped travelling cap," but never actually refers to him wearing a deerstalker. Moreover, throughout the canon of 60 stories published between 1887 and 1927 you are more likely to encounter Holmes in a silk top hat, a bowler, a boater and—yes—a fedora. Clearly, something else is afoot.

It was the illustrator Sidney Paget who first gave the detective a deerstalker in *The Boscombe Valley Mystery*, establishing an association that soon became set in aspic. Basil Rathbone is best known for sporting the deerstalker on screen, but he was preceded by many others: James Braginton, John Barrymore, Clive Brook, and more. In turn, each helped to concretize the indelible relationship between Holmes and the hat.

And Doyle acknowledged how instrumental others were in shaping and molding Holmes. He authorized Stoll Pictures to produce 47 films in the early 1920s starring Eille Norwood. At a dinner organized by Stoll in 1921, Doyle proposed the toast: if Sherlock had survived longer than he deserved, "it is very largely due to those gentlemen, who have, apart from myself, associated themselves with him." He named Paget and Norwood, as well as Harry Arthur Saintsbury, who played Holmes over 1000 times on stage, and William Gillette. Gillette was the American playwright and actor whose play, *Sherlock Holmes*, eclipsed Doyle's own success in adapting Sherlock for the theater. Notionally co-authored with Doyle, Gillette's play also formed the basis for an influential silent film adaptation in 1916. Like so many others, Gillette sported the deerstalker on stage and screen.

Paget, Norwood, Saintsbury, and Gillette all contributed to the public persona of Sherlock Holmes with Doyle's approval.

Above: Holmes with different hats. From left to right: A top hat, drawing by Sidney Paget of Sherlock Holmes visiting friend Dr. John Watson, from "The Adventure of the Stockbroker's Clerk" (Photo by Time Life Pictures / Mansell / The LIFE Picture Collection / Getty Images);
A bowler, "You are the very man," from "The Blue Carbuncle." Image by Sidney Paget (Photo by The Print Collector / Getty Images);
And a fedora, drawing by Sidney Paget of Sherlock Holmes removing bath sponge from his Gladstone bag, from "The Man with the Twisted Lip." (Photo by Time Life Pictures / Mansell / The LIFE Picture Collection / Getty Images)

Above: Daffy Duck as Sherlock Holmes parody Dorlock Homes and Porky Pig as Watkins as they try to capture the "Shropshire Slasher" in the Warner Bros. cartoon DEDUCE, YOU SAY! (US 1956, Dir. Chuck Jones).

But there were many others who did so without endorsement or permission. Holmes has remained at the forefront of popular consciousness since the late 19th century through a multiplicity of authorized and unauthorized editions, adaptations and imitations in a manner unrivalled by any other literary character. Parody and pastiche have played a key role in this process.

Within a year of Doyle's stories appearing in *The Strand*, parodies began to mushroom, ludicrous tales of erroneous detection featuring the exploits of Sherlaw Kombs, Thinlock Bones, Sherlock Shamrock, and Sheerluck Gnomes. Later parodies would tackle the theft of the Mona Lisa, Doyle's interest in Spiritualism, and civil unrest in Ireland. A.A. Milne, P.G. Wodehouse, and Dashiell Hammett each tried their hand. In 1956, Daffy Duck starred as Dorlock Homes in DEDUCE, YOU SAY! (Dorlock's favorite pastime is "deducting.") Over 20 years later, Mickey Mouse first played sidekick to Sureluck Sleuth, an inept but well-intentioned canine detective.

As for pastiche, the spotlight must fall on the detective Solar Pons, created by writer and publisher August Derleth. Pons operated in Holmes' London, albeit Georgian London. In lieu of Watson, Mrs. Hudson and Mycroft, Pons has Parker, Mrs. Johnson and Bancroft. Between 1929 and 1971, they featured in a corpus of stories that outstripped Doyle's own canon, in quantity at least. And after his death, this body of Pontine tales continued to grow, with the approval of Derleth's estate, under the direction of Basil Copper.

No other Holmsian pasticheur can match the remarkable Derleth, although many others—like Stephen King and Ellery Queen—have contributed to the genre. And these manifold works have allowed the real and the imaginary their place in the Baker Street tableau, whether it's Harry Houdini or Karl Marx, Dracula or the Ripper. Indeed, Robert B. DeWaal's 1994 bibliography, *The Universal Sherlock Holmes*, offers over 25,000 listings of licensed and unlicensed, faithful and irreverent, serious-minded and more ephemeral manifestations of Holmes. And to these, we must add the online world of fan fiction. FanFiction.net, founded in 1998, currently hosts over 45,000 stories tagged "Sherlock Holmes." Archive of Our Own—a not-for-profit open source repository established in 2008—lists over 100,000. I am Sherlock. You are Sherlock. He is ubiquitous … and we are all complicit in the plot.

Above: From 9 December 1910 until February 1913, illustrator Gus Mager drew Sherlocko the Monk for the Hearst newspaper syndication group. He would draw over 270 strips under this title, featuring the characters of Sherlocko and Watso. Journal Gazette (Mattoon, Illinois), 17 April 1912.

On the left: Poster for Gillette's adaptation of Sherlock Holmes at The Lyceum Theatre, London, notionally co-authored with Conan Doyle, ca. 1905. (Photo by Buyenlarge / Getty Images)

Sherlock's ubiquity is matched—has been fueled—by his longevity. It is more than 130 years since Holmes appeared in print. When *A Study in Scarlet* was first published in the United Kingdom, literary copyright lasted for the life of the author plus seven years, or 42 years following publication, whichever was longer. By the time Doyle published his last story in April 1927, copyright duration had been extended by the 1911 Copyright Act to the life of the author plus 50 years. Doyle died just over three years later, in July 1930, and his work entered the public domain on 1 January 1981. However, following the harmonisation of the standard copyright term in Europe to life plus 70 years, Doyle's canon came back into copyright on 1 January 1996, only to expire once again on 31 December 2000.

To reflect on the duration of copyright in Doyle's canon—and its variability over time—prompts questions about more fundamental aspects of the copyright regime: its purpose, scope and logic. Famously, Holmes inhabits a world bounded by observation and deduction. "I never guess," he declares in *The Sign of Four*, "It is a shocking habit—destructive to the logical faculty." But, he overstates his case. Many writers have pointed out that Holmes rarely engages in deduction, classically defined. With deduction, conclusions drawn from the available data must inevitably be true. Holmes, however, more often engages in abductive reasoning: he offers the best

available account of events that may or may not be true. In other words, there is considerable guesswork in his method, albeit with a veneer of seemingly inexorable logic. The same might be said for much copyright policy and law-making.

To reflect on duration is also to consider the public domain. Today, in the United Kingdom, all Doyle's published works are out of copyright. But copyright is territorial, and so too is the public domain. In the United States, for example, Holmes is currently only *mostly* in the public domain. The first 50 stories in Doyle's canon were published before 1923 and as such, under US copyright law, are no longer in copyright. However, copyright in the remaining ten stories—published between 1923 and 1927—will only expire in the United States between 2018 and 2022. Moreover, the Conan Doyle estate has attempted to rely on the copyright status of these later stories to leverage an overreaching protection in the character of Holmes himself. In 2013, the Doyle estate argued before the US Seventh Circuit Court of Appeals that Holmes, as a character, was not fully realised until the entire canon had been published (e.g., in *The Lion's Mane* we learn that Holmes has retired to Sussex); as such, the estate continued, Holmes remains in copyright so long as any part of that canon remains in copyright. They were unsuccessful. Judge Richard Posner rejected their argument unequivocally: "We cannot

find any basis in statute or case law for extending copyright beyond its expiration." In his words, their claim bordered on the "quixotic." (And yet, as we have already seen, this is precisely what happened to Holmes in the United Kingdom.)

Judge Posner also spoke to the relationship between copyright and the public domain. Extending copyright protection, he commented, is a double-edged sword from the standpoint of encouraging creativity. To increase copyright protection is to shrink the public domain, and a smaller public domain might impact negatively on authors and creators interested in creating new and original—albeit derivative—works, such as pastiches involving characters like Holmes and Watson. And great authors have always demonstrated an appetite for revisiting the work of those who have gone before. Think of *Foe* by J.M. Coetzee, retelling *Robinson Crusoe* from the perspective of a female character that is absent from Daniel Defoe's original novel. Or *Jack Maggs* by Peter Carey, a reworking of *Great Expectations*, in which Carey borrows from the story while also taking inspiration from Charles Dickens himself in creating the character of Tobias Oates, an ambitious, often disagreeable, novelist.

Both Coetzee and Carey were, of course, drawing on material already in the public domain, but copyright also allows space for reimagining the work of contemporary authors. In *The Wind Done Gone*, Alice Randall retells Margaret Mitchell's *Gone With the Wind* from the perspective of Cynara, one of Scarlett O'Hara's slaves. The Mitchell estate sued for copyright infringement in the United States, but Randall's work

was deemed to be fair use and so lawful. Fredrik Colting had more trouble with *60 Years Later: Coming Through the Rye*, his 2009 novel featuring a 76-year-old Holden Caulfield, the teenage protagonist of J.D. Salinger's *Catcher in the Rye*. At a hearing for a preliminary injunction, Colting's fair use defense was considered unlikely to succeed at full trial; an injunction was granted. On appeal, the injunction was lifted, although the appellate court expressed similar concerns about the weak nature of the fair use claim. In 2011, Colting settled with Salinger's estate, agreeing not to publish his book in the United States or Canada until *The Catcher in the Rye* is in the public domain. Salinger, of course, was always extraordinarily litigious regarding both his work and his privacy. His estate has continued in that vein: Holden remains firmly under their control. So too does a third iconic hat: Holden's red hunting hat—not a hat for hunting deer apparently, but a hat for hunting humans.

Above: BIFF! POW! BANG! CRUNCH! The poster for the film A Study in Terror *(UK 1965, Dir. James Hill) featuring the famous detective played by John Neville— obviously influenced by the Batman comic book. The poster also preempts the Batman TV series that would launch the next year (1966) with its long list of infamous on-screen Bat-Fight words: POWIE! KLONK! ZLOPP! and BAM! (Photo by Fototeca Gilardi / Getty Images)*

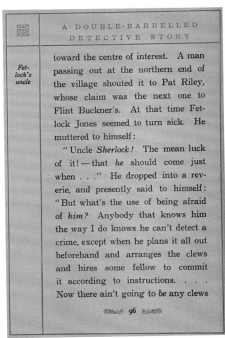

Above, left: Batman— The World's Greatest Detective—crosses paths with Sherlock Holmes in the double-sized 50th Anniversary edition of Detective Comics (Detective Comics, Vol. 1, #572). The cover art includes a framed copy of Detective Comics #27, in which Batman made his first appearance in 1939. (ComiXology)

Above, right: A page from Mark Twain's parody "A Double-Barrelled Detective Story" (New York: Harper & Bros., 1902): Fetlock Jones, Sherlock's nephew, provides the reader with an alternative take on Sherlock's renowned powers of deduction. (Roy J. Friedman Mark Twain Collection / Library of Congress)

Were the outcomes for *The Wind Done Gone* and *60 Years Later* appropriate or correct? In a way, it doesn't matter, at least not in this context. Suffice it to say, it is notoriously difficult to gauge or predict when lawful appropriation might spill over into infringing activity, both for copyright owner as well as creative re-user. Each situation is fact specific, depends on flexible legal concepts, and—if it ever makes it to court—will turn on questions of judgment exercised by different judges with different worldviews. In this respect, copyright and the public domain have always been prickly and unpredictable bedfellows. The boundary between them is a fog, and there be dragons, and hounds, and the devil himself. Above all else, perhaps, the deerstalker reminds us that copyright has a history which is still being written—a history, and a future, that is shifting and elusive, complex and contested. ◆

Further Reading

Keith Akoi, James Boyle, and Jennifer Jenkins (2006) *Tales from the Public Domain: Bound by Law?* Durham: Duke University Press.

Marcus Boon (2010) *In Praise of Copying.* Cambridge, MA: Harvard University Press.

Sabine Vanacker and Catherine Wynne (eds.) (2013) *Sherlock Holmes and Conan Doyle: Multi-Media Afterlives.* Basingstoke: Palgrave Macmillan.

Peter Ridgway Watt and Joseph Green (2003) *The Alternative Sherlock Holmes: Pastiches, Parodies and Copies.* Farnham: Ashgate.

Further Viewing

DEDUCE, YOU SAY (US 1956, Dir. Chuck Jones)

THE GAME IS ON! (UK 2015–18, Dir. Ronan Deazley and Bartolomeo Meletti). Available at: www.copyrightuser.org/educate/the-game-is-on/

1700   *1800*   *1900*

--/-----/-----/-----/-----/-----/-----/-----/----/-/-----/-----/-----/----

17 Paper Print

Claudy Op den Kamp

DEAR AINSWORTH,
   You don't know me. I am writing to you from 125 years in the future and I would like to thank you. I have long felt the need to thank someone. You might not even realize what you've done, and you certainly might not understand the magnitude of the consequences of what might have been a fleeting decision.

   It's strange. Often you don't register the important moments in your life as they happen. Only when you look back do you see that they were important. How certain moments were clearly an ending, and how others were the beginning of something. The *shadow line*, Joseph Conrad called it, that line you know you've crossed only after you've crossed it and can look back over it. Like the invisible line between adolescence and adulthood. Like the equator. And in your case, like the invention of cinema. It's hard for us to imagine now, but it took a while to figure out what cinema was. Was the new invention an extension of an existing medium or was it something different? The 20-year period between 1893 and 1912 now marks that *shadow line*.

In 1864, you were 49 years old when Abraham Lincoln appointed you the 6th Librarian of Congress. You also acted as the Register of Copyrights—not by title but in practice, as that job had not yet been made a formal position.

   By advocating for the passage of the Copyright Law of 1870, you made it your quest to move all US copyright activities that were once dispersed among the Smithsonian Institution and the Patent Office to the Library of Congress. The new law required all copyright applicants to send the Library two copies of their work. You argued that if both copies were mailed directly to Washington fresh off the press, instead of having to go through their authors' District Courts, the labor involved would be cut by half. You also argued that having copyright records readily available where their related publications are stored would simplify and facilitate reference to the utmost degree. The number, too, of copyright publications issued in the United States would now be known, and such a precise accounting would prevent copyrights from being invalidated.

On the left: Ainsworth Rand Spofford (1825–1908). Sixth Librarian of Congress, 1864–1897, ca. 1900. (Photo by Library of Congress / Corbis / VCG via Getty Images)

During 1871, the first full year of the law's operation, some 20,000 books, periodicals, musical and dramatic compositions, photographs, prints, and maps were acquired exclusively through the new copyright requirements. A photograph of your charge desk shows stacks of books and newspapers that are piled on the floor and around the upper-level railings due to overcrowded storage conditions. You understood very early on that this situation couldn't last. Seeking to grow a repository of American culture, you persuaded Congress to complement the existing library with a new building—now known as the Thomas Jefferson Building.

You saw no conflict between the functions of a legal and a national library. You wrote that "public intelligence and welfare are promoted by every extension of the means of acquiring knowledge." You were occupied above all with making the library a national institution, not just a congressional resource.

This was before anyone could even fathom the idea of being the spider in a web on which all other libraries could depend for inspiration, guidance, and practical help.

Centralized cataloging and interlibrary loans would become indispensable tools of that web. My 19-year-old students can hardly wrap their heads around a world that is not online. You have never heard of the interconnected space we call online. (It would blow your mind.)

In an 1896 transcript of congressional hearings about the library's workings, you state that each work that came in for copyright registration, though perhaps pre-checked by one of your team's 24 clerks, received your personal sign-off. Precisely because of that interconnected space I just mentioned, I was able to lay eyes on your signature of January 1894 at the bottom of the registration of "Edison Kinetoscopic Record of a Sneeze," a film now colloquially known as FRED OTT'S SNEEZE. In the film we see funny Fred, one of Edison's engineers, as he pinches some snuff up

Above, left: The crowded interior view of the old Congressional Library in the US Capitol building. In the middle background is Spofford's charge desk, ca. 1897. (Library of Congress Prints and Photographs Division Washington, DC)

Above, right: Ainsworth Rand Spofford standing amid stacks of books and library shelves. (Library of Congress Prints and Photographs Division Washington, DC)

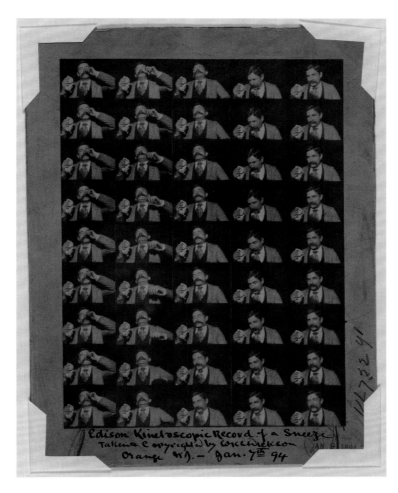

Edison Kinetoscopic Record of a Sneeze,
Taken & Copyright by W.K.L.Dickson
Orange N.J. — Jan. 7th 94

his nose, then sneezes—a story told in a mere five seconds—the very first paper print that survives.

You have never seen this sneeze as a film. This work was registered not as a film but as a *photograph*. You don't even know motion pictures to be a subject category. That emerged in 1912 with the Townsend Amendment—four years after you died.

Looking at a copy of that photograph leaves an extraordinary impression. Not only did you accept a *moving* image as a *still* image; you accepted a *multitude* of still images as *one* image. W.K.L. Dickson, Thomas Edison's assistant, registered this "paper print" for copyright after the Edison company had produced it as an advertisement to show off its latest invention for *Harper's Weekly*.

FRED OTT'S SNEEZE, it seems, was registered rather "fully formed." There is, however, an earlier registration, in 1893, also signed by you, where it seems you were trying to work things out. It reads "Edison Kinetoscopic Records." The actual titles of that registration seem lost to history. Or, in fact, it's likely that the title page for that entry currently sits in a Maryland storage facility somewhere. Digitizing that backlog will likely take decades. (Digitization, trust me, would also blow your mind.)

The 1893 registration prompts some confusion. Where it asks to identify the type of work, it says "Book or Form." Form could have meant several things. And we know that *book* wouldn't have meant a print, or a photograph, because you probably would have used one of those terms. It

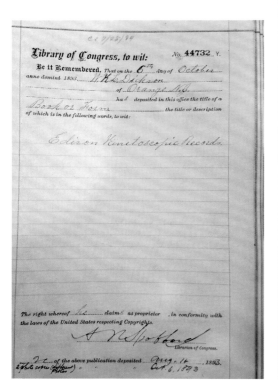

could have meant a pamphlet, a one-sheet, or anything else with minimal graphic content. Possibly a description of the film? With a little stub? Or a frame? The several dates on the form tell us that it took less than two months to reach some sort of decision, and three months after that, FRED OTT'S SNEEZE was registered as a photograph.

What you don't know is that allowing this method of compliance with a technicality in the copyright law inadvertently led to the preservation of the earliest chapter in US motion picture history, which might otherwise have been lost. Nearly 4,000 such titles were registered, sometimes in the form of photographs, sometimes as rolls of film printed on paper—now known as the Paper Print Collection.

One of the consequences of your decision was that the films themselves weren't kept at the library. This makes sense to me. Until the early 1950s films were shot on inflammable nitrate stock, and the library lacked the proper storage to safely house them. So when, more than 30 years after you died, the paper prints were "re-discovered" in the basement of that same Jefferson Building (curious that we call it "re-discovered," they'd been stored there all along), they were often all that remained of the work. The original films had perished, or were recycled for their silver content, or were lost due to some other reason.

The paper rolls couldn't be projected, so thus began a painstaking process of printing them back to film. Not until the 1950s did some of these titles flicker again. And can you believe that the restoration of the collection is still happening? Insights into film restoration keep changing and

Above, from left to right: The 1893 title registration for "Edison Kinetoscopic Records" as a Book or Form; The 1894 title registration for "Edison Kinetoscopic Record of a Sneeze" as a Photograph. (Photos by Zvi Rosen)

Above, left: A paper print of The Great Train Robbery *(US 1903, Dir. Edwin S. Porter). (Courtesy of Library of Congress NAVCC)*

Above, right: A little boy in the back of a horse-drawn buggy in A Trip Down Market Street *(US 1906, Dir. Miles Brothers). (Available on www. archive.org)*

technological developments keep being made, so we return to the source material again and again.

But I'd like to talk to you a little about what's *in* the collection, do you even know? The Great Train Robbery! Edwin S. Porter's milestone in filmmaking. Some of the earliest examples of advertisements. A Trip Down Market Street! Have you ever been to San Francisco? If so, you probably saw the city before the devastating earthquake of 1906. A Trip is the only moving-image record we have of the city from before the quake. The film is astonishing. For 13 minutes we follow the view of a camera mounted on the front of a cablecar—a phantom ride. There's this cute little boy who plays hide-and-seek with the cameraman while sitting in the back of a horse-drawn buggy that's driving in front of the cablecar. You can't take your eyes off him (you also can't take your eyes off Rita Hayworth when many years later

she sang that Mame should be blamed for the Frisco quake, but that's another story).

You pursued your vision of a national library with an intensity that far outweighed your commitment to any other idea. So, I realize you might not even have *liked* film. I do know you loved *books*. In 1900, you published *A Book for All Readers*, on the collection and preservation of books and the founding of libraries. You speak about the spacing of a font across a page. You speak about the way a well-bound book should always open out flat, and stay open. And that it should also shut up completely, and when closed stay shut. The level of detail here is incredible.

The way you feel about books, that's how I feel about film. As one of my favorite screenwriters once said, "I can't get enough flicks to quiet my addiction." You didn't really like it that the duties of recording copyrights occupied the larger proportion of your time as Librarian. You certainly thought that copyright deposits should be used to enrich libraries, but you kept recommending a separate copyright department and a full-time register of copyright. But I was elated at the sight of your signature. As I said, I have long felt the need to thank *some*one, because I just can't accept that the past houses all these anonymous decision-makers, often masked as historical accidents.

When you voiced your ideas about public intelligence and welfare, you might not have realized that these can be threatened in ways beyond anything you can even start to imagine. But your dream of a "truly great and comprehensive library," which would be "universal in both its range and its usefulness," has until further notice come true. When you joined the Library of Congress, it had a staff of seven. Currently it employs some 5,000 people and houses documents in more than 470 languages. It is also still the home of the Copyright Office. And you might like to hear that the jobs of Librarian of Congress and Register of Copyrights are now formally two separate jobs. (You might also like to know that we no longer register copyright in the way you understand it. But, I digress.)

As a historian, I try to reconstruct a past from the fragments that are left. So when the original film is lost, the paper prints become sort of stand-in objects, the fragments. And there is so much left to figure out. As C.S. Lewis (an author you don't know, but I think you'd like him) has said: "What you see and what you hear depends a great deal on where you are standing."

So you can perhaps see that from where I am standing the story of the paper print collection looks a peculiar way. It's a story that has always been told, replete with the names of other men. Thomas Edison. As if having invented the light bulb and the

phonograph wouldn't provide an impressive enough epitaph, he also helped invent motion pictures. His name is all over this story. And you knew him, right? Didn't your son Charles work with him? W.K.L. Dickson, Edison's assistant, whose name is on the copyright registrations. Most of your business was done via mail, but I wonder if there was any informal interaction. Did he come by with a few examples, and did you discuss them at length? And then there are a few men you certainly never did meet: Kemp Niver and Howard Walls, both involved in the first restoration attempts. But what about *your* contribution to this story? Why hasn't your name come up?

I grew up believing in the magic of a DeLorean time machine (this requires a separate letter). I wish I had one, so that I could visit you and pick your brain. I'd ask you what happened. What about that 1893 registration? Why do we know so little about those early years of film copyright?

Above: Rita Hayworth singing "Put the Blame on Mame" in GILDA *(US 1946, Dir Charles Vidor). (Photo by George Rinhart / Corbis via Getty Images)*

Above: A DeLorean time machine, as first seen in BACK TO THE FUTURE *(US 1985, Dir. Robert Zemeckis). (Photo by Noel Vasquez / Getty Images)*

Why were motion pictures not made a subject matter category in 1909 with the omnibus revision of the Copyright Act? Why did we have to wait instead until 1912? That was after you passed away, so you might not know either.

The most optimistic current estimates say that only 20 percent of all the silent films ever produced survives in archives worldwide. And the paper print collection is a significant part of that. The collection represents the survivors. It is not a novel idea to think that history is written by the survivors. But what might be novel to you is the thought that what has survived is colored by the people who were wary of their competitors, and good at registering their films!

This letter is probably a bit startling to you, I get that. But do you know what truly blows *my* mind? It's not only that the collection forms the basis for nearly our entire understanding of the earliest period in US cinema. It's also that our understanding of film's earliest chapter starts with an understanding of the intellectual property system.

Perhaps you were just doing your job. Just working your way along, anonymously, doing your best to make everything hold together till morning. But it makes me happy, very happy, to think that you and I are tiny spots in each other's histories.

With gratitude,
—Claudy. ◆

Further Reading

John Cole (ed.) (1975) *Ainsworth Rand Spofford. Bookman and Librarian*. Littleton: Libraries Unlimited, Inc.

"Mostly IP History." Available at: www.zvirosen.com

Gabriel Paletz (2001) "Archives and Archivists Remade: The Paper Print Collection and THE FILM OF HER," *The Moving Image*, 1(1), pp. 68–79.

Dan Streible (2017) "THE FILM OF HER: The Cine-Poet Laureate of Orphan Films," in Bernd Herzogenrath (ed.) *The Films of Bill Morrison. Aesthetics of the Archive*. Amsterdam: Amsterdam University Press.

Further Viewing

Mike Mashon (2013) "Early Motion Pictures," *American Artifacts*, 27 March. Available at: www.c-span.org/video/?313371-1/early-motion-pictures.

18 Player Piano Roll

Maurizio Borghi

On the left: A snapshot photograph of a young woman seated at a player-piano, taken by an unknown photographer, ca. 1910. This type of piano has a player mechanism inside the case that "reads" the rolls of music fed through it and plays them automatically. (Photo by SSPL / Getty Images)

T HE PLAYER PIANO—ALSO known as the "Pianola" or the "Aeolian Pianola," from the brand of the leading manufacturer in the early 1900s—is a mechanical instrument capable of automatically playing music scores converted into perforated paper rolls. It was the first technology for mechanical reproduction of music that was mass-produced and had widespread application and success. It fundamentally changed the way that we experience music; and the copyright battle that the technology generated was the beginning of a war over the control of music and content that is being fought to this day.

In the course of the 19th century, music performance increasingly became an activity played not only in theaters, concert halls, and other public places, but also in the intimacy of private homes. Parlor music—music written to be performed in the parlors of bourgeois homes by amateur singers and pianists—gained immense popularity among a rapidly expanding middle-class in industrialized countries. The sale of arrangements for piano became the core of the business of musical publishers such as Casa Ricordi, Boosey & Sons, Chappell & Co., and Novello.

On the back of a flourishing industry of mass-produced pianos, manufacturers started developing systems to automate the playing of music scores. Early prototypes were a feature of the Universal Exposition of 1876 in Philadelphia. An example of the innovations of the era can be found in the patent applications of Edwin Scott Votey, who invented a semi-automatic player piano mechanism, powered by air suction generated by foot treadles. The keyboard was activated by an ingenious system of valves that opened corresponding to the holes punched in a paper roll which moved over a pickup bar with 88 openings, one for each key of the piano. The sequence of unevenly spaced holes in the roll "translated" a musical score into instructions for the mechanically assisted piano. This invention meant that virtually every piece for piano could be made automatically playable, with just a little human intervention. The Aeolian Corporation acquired the rights from Votey, and launched their player piano in 1897

with a massive advertisement campaign. They called it the Pianola™ and its success was immense. Soon piano manufacturers all over the world started developing and marketing their own models. Not only did they rapidly become a must-have equipment for home entertainment, but also the name "pianola" quickly came to denote all player pianos—an early example of trademark genericide. By 1908 the market was sufficiently well established that standards became necessary. So, in that year, US piano producers signed the Buffalo Convention, establishing a standard format for piano rolls. Any instrument that conformed to the standard could now play rolls from any producer. The production expanded and reached its peak in the mid-1920s, when it started declining due to the competition of a new, disruptive, and cheaper technology of music reproduction, the gramophone.

Throughout its golden age, the pianola continued to improve technically and evolved into an autonomous self-playing instrument, fully independent from human intervention. This unprecedented feature not only changed the habits of music consumption, but also opened up the possibility of a new language in musical composition. This attracted the imagination of composers, such as Igor Stravinsky, Paul Hindemith, and Ferruccio Busoni. Busoni was a renowned virtuoso, and the new technology allowed him to record his unparalleled piano executions. The music historian Thomas Patteson notes the enthusiasm for this new style of composition, translating an article from a German newspaper of 1926, reporting on a concerto for player piano only:

The piano began to play: music like an étude, toccatas with otherwise unplayable harmonic progressions, with a speed that could never be approached even by the most virtuosic of players, with an exactitude of which a human could never be capable, with a superhuman sonic force, with a geometrical clarity of rhythm, tempo, dynamics, and phrasing, which only a machine can produce.

One of the contributing factors to the success of the pianola was the lack of enforceable intellectual property rights in the music. Copyright in musical compositions

Above: A pianist at London's Perforated Music Company recording music onto punched paper roll to use on a player piano. (Photo by Hulton-Deutsch Collection / CORBIS / Corbis via Getty Images)

Above, left: A group of player piano rolls. (Courtesy of Heritage Auctions, HA.com)

Above, right: Maggie Hunt of Hunt Estate Sales displays a player piano roll at the former home of the M. Steinert & Sons store on Boylston Street in Boston, 2017. The company put over a century's worth of items up for sale to the public as the 120-year-old building began extensive renovation work. (Photo by Craig F. Walker / The Boston Globe via Getty Images)

had been recognized in most jurisdictions at least since the late 18th century, and it was clearly reaffirmed by the Berne Convention, the central international treaty on copyright, in 1886. But while the *existence* of the right was undisputed, its *scope* was still unsettled. Although mechanical reproduction of music was not completely unknown at the end of the 19th century, copyright statutes were mostly silent on the subject. Until the arrival of the pianola the main technologies for music reproduction were music boxes and carillons, and owners of musical copyrights did not consider these toys to be a threat worthy of their attention. To be on the safe side, Switzerland, the main producer of music boxes at the time, had included an express provision exempting "mechanical instruments" from copyright infringement in its bilateral copyright agreement with France in 1864. The issue was tabled at the Diplomatic Conferences in preparation of the Berne Convention, and a provision mirroring the "music box immunity" of the Swiss-French treaty eventually made its way into the closing protocol, exempting the manufacture and sale of instruments for the mechanical reproduction of musical airs from copyright infringement.

The provision—which commentators suggested was "a slight act of courtesy" to the hosting country of the Conferences—became one of the most hotly disputed issues in the subsequent revisions of the Berne Convention. Especially contentious was a subtle ambiguity in the treaty language: did the immunity apply only to the manufacture and sale of the pianola, or did it extend to the perforated rolls as well? The rolls were the major source of concern for copyright holders, because they were easy to create and reproduce, and they were sold by the thousands on the shelves of music stores, often appearing alongside the copyrighted sheet music.

Aside from the dispute about the extent of the immunity, there was a more mystifying metaphysical question: were the piano player rolls "copies" of music scores at all? The question was at the core of a number of lawsuits brought by music publishers all over the world at the turn of the 20th century. Perhaps at no other point in copyright history has the notion of "copy" been so deeply questioned in court. In the 1899 landmark English case of *Boosey* v. *Whight*, the members of the court gave a range of reasons why there could be no copyright infringement by

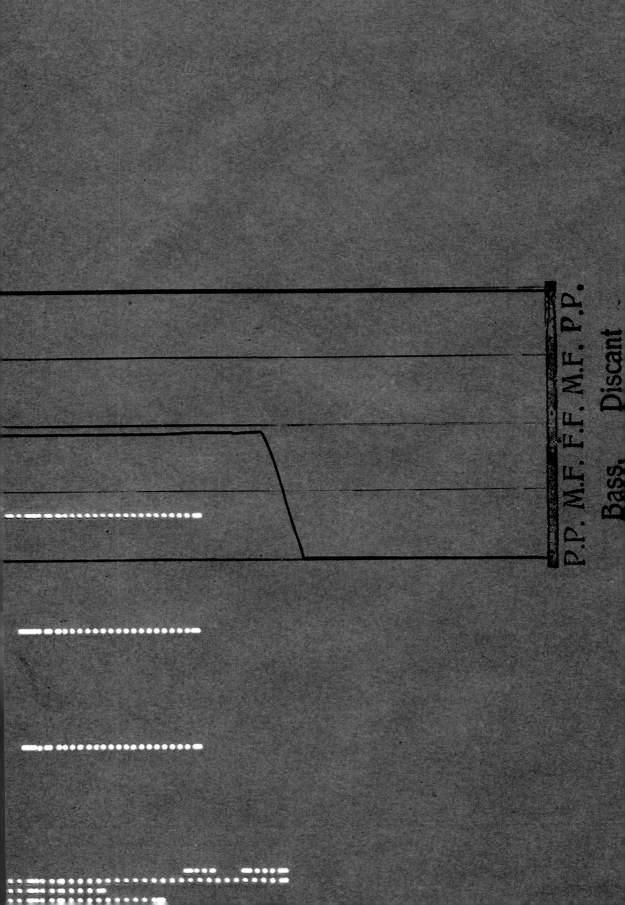

P.P. M.F. F.F. M.F. P.P.

Bass.   Discant

Above, from left to right: Advertisement for the Pianola piano by The Aeolian Company, New York, 1901; Advertisement for the Simplex piano player by Theodore P. Brown, Worcester, Massachusetts, 1902. (Photos by Jay Paull / Getty Images)

On the left: Welte-Mignon piano roll with lines for manual expression if played on not-reproducing pianos, ca. 1919. (Photo by Gerhard51, CC BY-SA 3.0)

player piano rolls. Most interesting was the conclusion that piano rolls are not actually copies of sheet music, as they are not meant to *indicate* music, but rather to *cause* music to be played by a mechanical instrument. Accordingly, they were strictly part of a mechanical contrivance and are not covered by copyright law—although they might be appropriate subject matter for patent. The court also concluded that pianola music is played in private homes, and the plaintiff had no rights over the performance in private of the copyrighted sheet music.

The position expressed by the English court, as is often the case, was not widely shared in the rest of Europe. In Germany, for instance, where the publisher Waldmann brought a number of lawsuits against player piano manufacturers, the prevailing view was that the closing protocol of the Berne Convention did not apply to mechanical instruments with interchangeable parts—hence, player pianos were not immune from infringement. The exclusion of player pianos from immunity was

reinforced by an Act of 1901, in which reproduction by mechanical instruments was declared to be permitted, except when the instrument was one "by which the work can, as regards strength and duration of tone and tempo, be rendered in a manner resembling a personal performance." By that time, pianola performances were already "resembling" many German virtuosi, including the much-acclaimed Carl Reinecke, author of some of the oldest piano rolls recordings still audible today.

The English approach to the pianola infringement problem had greater influence on the other side of the Atlantic. When the US Supreme Court decided *White-Smith Music Publishing* v. *Apollo* in 1909, it refused to find infringement in the making of objects that were not "made to be addressed to the eye as sheet music," but formed part of a machine. However, the judges did wrestle with the troubling question of what do we mean by "copy?" Justice Oliver Wendell Holmes, renowned as one of the most brilliant judges in US legal history, supported a nuanced and expansive

interpretation of "copying," holding in his dissenting opinion that a musical composition was a "rational collocation of sounds," and that this collocation could be reproduced "either with or without continuous human intervention."

The conflict between music publishers and the pianola industry changed the face of music copyright law. William Briggs, the author of the influential early 20th-century treatise *The Law of International Copyright*, argued for the complete assimilation of mechanical reproduction to other, traditional forms of music reproduction. The time was ripe for a change, and so the Berne Convention was amended in 1908 to incorporate a right for authors of musical works to authorize the adaptation of their works to "instruments which can reproduce them mechanically." Reproduction for mechanical instruments was progressively included in national laws, either as an exclusive right of the composer or as an entitlement to equitable remuneration under a compulsory license scheme. The UK Copyright Act 1911 vested authors of literary, dramatic, and musical works with the right "to make any record, perforated rolls ... or other contrivance by means of which the work may be mechanically performed." Other countries chose instead to introduce a compulsory license system. The US Copyright Act 1909 made the use of musical works for "mechanical reproduction" free to anyone upon payment of a royalty, after the first authorization by the

Above: "Pianola Helps Dad Relax." Vintage photograph of a man sitting at pianola in his living room in the 1970s. (Photo by Found Image Holdings / Corbis via Getty Images)

Above, right: A dog portraying a player piano for a Halloween costume contest, New York. (Photo Keith Getter / Getty Images)

copyright owner, and a similar provision was adopted in Germany with the Law of 22 May 1910.

This was the dawn of what nowadays represents the core economic interest of music composers, the right to reproduce and distribute copyrighted musical compositions in various forms, like sound recordings as CDs, ringtones, or internet streams. Even though the player piano is long dead, we still today call these "mechanical rights," or just "mechanicals."

The history of the pianola tells the emergence of modern musical copyright, with its tangle of overlapping rights of different scope, duration, and conditions of exercise. The pianola created the conditions for the debut of some the most litigious issues of recent copyright history: the status of intermediate "technical" copying, the scope of private use, and the limits of liability for the makers of reproduction devices. These are issues that have resurfaced upon every

new technological shift in the way we experience, perform, and generally appreciate music. In this way, the player piano and its rolls were the 19th-century CD, DVD, and Spotify, all rolled into one. ◆

Further Reading

Walter Benjamin (2008 [1936]) *The Work of Art in the Age of Mechanical Reproduction*, trans. J.A. Underwood. New York: Penguin Books.

Maurizio Borghi and Stavroula Karapapa (2013) *Copyright and Mass Digitization*. Oxford: Oxford University Press.

Ronan Deazley (2006) *Rethinking Copyright: History, Theory, Language*. Cheltenham: Edward Elgar.

Thomas Patteson (2016) *Instruments for New Music. Sound, Technology and Modernism*. Oakland: University of California Press.

1800   *1900*   *2000*

--/-----/-----/-----/-----/----/-/-----/-----/-----/-----/-----/-----/----

19 Champagne
Dev S. Gangjee

Pleasure without Champagne is purely artificial.
—Oscar Wilde

OF ALL THE products that qualify as protected geographical indications, Champagne's prominence is undeniable; it veritably sparkles. Within its enticingly translucent green-glass walls of reinforced thickness, the bottle successfully contains the burgeoning effervescence arising from successive fermentations. All is seemingly calm until the celebratory uncorking. Champagne is therefore the perfect metaphor for understanding geographical indication protection systems, and wine appellation regimes in particular.

Beneath the surface of the "naturalized" claim—that the geographical features of a region influence product quality—lies considerable agitation and volatility. Indeed, the very question of whether we call the wine "champagne" or "Champagne" is still argued over, much like the disputes that arose over which locations could produce Champagne. The intertwined socio-economic and legal histories of Champagne show these fault lines,

and help to explain how a distinct or *sui generis* legal regime came to protect regional brands.

Modern intellectual property law has grappled with the question of how to protect such potentially valuable regional brands since at least the 19th century. Trademark law seems to be the obvious choice. However, signs such as Champagne are inexorably considered descriptive—they describe the geographical region of origin, such as Parma for ham or Colombia for coffee—and cannot distinctively identify a specific commercial undertaking, like Coke®.

These designations can also be used collectively by all legitimate producers within the region, whereas trademark law presumes that an individual commercial entity is claiming exclusive use over a sign. To some extent, these hurdles have been overcome within trademark regimes, in the form of certification marks or collective marks. However, these (initially significant) obstacles led to the adoption of a distinct, registration-based system of protection for such regional brands and Champagne was deeply implicated in its emergence.

On the left: A bottle of Moët & Chandon champagne popping. (Getty Images)

Over the past half-millennium, the wine's journey to iconic status has been neither smooth nor inevitable. Originating as a mediocre, nonsparkling red wine it was, in the word of Joonas Rokka, "transformed from a practically insignificant no-brand wine label in the 15th century to a holy elixir served and elaborated by Benedictine monks; to an ostentatious and seductive fashion item in the court of the Sun King Louis XIV; to a crucial symbol of the French national soul and values; and, toward the late nineteenth century, Champagne established itself as an expression of modernity and icon for the global leisure class and celebration." In common with other regional specialities, its appeal was bolstered by the claim that certain products owe their distinctive or typical qualities to the particular features of physical geography, including soil and climate, which exist within defined regions. French wine appellations in general and Champagne in particular helped to articulate and give legal substance to this claim, via the concept of *terroir*, over the course of the late 19th and early 20th centuries. Put differently, French legislation embraced, reinforced and rearticulated this notion of a causal link between place and product.

Historically *terroir* referred to an area whose soil and micro-climate imparted distinctive qualities to agricultural products, including products of the vine. Over the years the concept has gained legal traction, appearing in judicial pronouncements in courts as far afield as England and New Zealand. In determining whether those from outside the region can use the term "champagne"—the lower case indicates generic usage for a type of product—to describe their sparkling wine, judges have acknowledged that the chalky, flinty soil of the French region and its wide variations of temperature are said to influence the quality of the grapes and consequently the wine produced there. Today *terroir* encompasses human factors alongside natural ones: not just the soil and climate, but also the social and cultural dimensions of food production, and the regionally specific experimentation directed at sustaining and improving product quality. Although this concept predates the 19th century, its legal significance can be traced to the epistemological quest by French regulators to discover a means of measuring authenticity,

Above: Workers in Champagne install frosting supports to protect young grape vines from freezing temperatures. (Photo by Sasha / Getty Images)

Above: Thousands of bottles of champagne maturing in one of the Roman cellars at Reims, France, where they are left to acquire their famed "bubbly" qualities, ca. 1910. (Photo by Sasha / Getty Images)

Above: Map of Champagne-Ardenne, France. (Planet Observer / UIG / Getty Images)

a method for distinguishing the genuine from the fake.

The French appellation regime, as well as much of contemporary geographical indications law that is influenced by it, results from a crisis—*la crise du vin*—in the latter half of the 19th century. During this period, French grape production was significantly impeded by a range of fungal diseases and blights, but above all by *phylloxera*, the tiny sap-sucking, aphid-like root-louse that feeds on the roots of grape-vines. Vineyards were decimated in the aftermath of this infestation, just as the demand for quality wines increased. Fraud-ulently labeled inferior wines began to fill this gap, putting long-established regional reputations at risk. While there was a con-sensus that falsehoods should be stamped out, identifying the baseline—the genuine article—proved far more divisive.

There was intense debate across France as to what should count as authentic or be condemned as counterfeit. Differences of opinion arose between *négociants* (merchant manufacturers) and *vignerons* (wine growers) as to the definition of genuine Champagne. Could merchants based in the *département* of Marne source their grapes from outside

the region and still label the end-product as Champagne? What about Champagne houses based within the traditional re-gion of production, which exported grapes to Germany for crushing and bottling? Would leading producers rely on their individual brands at the cost of the collec-tive appellation? As the historian Kolleen Guy asks: "What *was* Champagne? Was it a blend of certain types of grapes? Was it a blend of grapes from an exclusive region? What were the boundaries of that region? [And] what was the basis for these limits and boundaries?" To take one specific ex-ample, the vine shortages had forced mer-chants to search for new sources of supply, sometimes from other countries, or through the production of artificial wines. If the genuine article could only be produced by grapes from within the designated region, then this degree of greater flexibility would not be surrendered without protest by those reliant on external sources.

Besides the sourcing of grapes another controversial issue related to the method for delimiting the region of origin. Since boundaries affected prices and determined livelihoods, this was not some abstract dis-cussion. The scourge of *phylloxera* combined

with crop losses over successive years, resulting in reduced yields within the traditional Champagne regions. Vine growers became suspicious that the large chateaus were sourcing their grapes from without. They were outraged, since the resulting wines could not claim to represent the *terroir* of the region. Grape prices were being driven down and desperation set in. Finally in 1908 the French government proposed an official delimitation that excluded the Aube region, which contained Troyes, the historic capital of the Champagne region. The controversy boiled over in 1910 and 1911, unleashing riots in Damery, Hautvilliers, and the village of Aÿ, where the warehouses, stocks, and even the homes of those suspected of "fraudulent practices" were destroyed. To quell this the army had to be deployed, and the regional boundaries were eventually renegotiated following the conclusion of World War I. Place proved difficult to find—it had to be actively constructed.

The late 19th and early 20th century was therefore a period of great regulatory experimentation in France. In terms of guaranteeing authenticity, the consensus shifted, from merely guaranteeing geographical origin under the *Appellation d'Origine* legislation to guaranteeing both origin as well as quality. Wine was required to be produced in accordance with "loyal, local and constant" production methods—historically stabilized and consensually adopted methods, which sought to preserve quality. The recognition of this human experimentation would deemphasize the significance of purely natural "authorship" for such products. It led

Above: Cary Grant pouring a glass of champagne for Ingrid Bergman in INDISCREET *(US 1958, Dir. Stanley Donen). (Alamy)*

Above: Every film archivist's nightmare. French singer Patachou uses a bottle of Moët & Chandon in the Epernay cellars in France to baptize a film can containing Maurice Chevalier's film MA POMME (JUST ME; F 1950, Dir. Marc-Gilbert Sauvajon). (Photo by Keystone-France / Gamma-Rapho via Getty Images)

to the adoption of the *Appellation d'Origine Contrôlée* regime, which in turn has greatly influenced contemporary geographical indications legislation in the European Union. Although *where* a product originated continued to be important, *how* it was made also began to matter. As for geographical boundary setting, various approaches were tried. These included the establishment of local commissions, which had local expertise but were vulnerable to co-option by local interests; judicially determined boundaries, where objectivity and neutrality might be achieved but at the cost of technical expertise and local knowledge; and eventually the emergence of a dedicated public sector agency—the *Institut National des Appellations d'Origine*—which worked collaboratively with producer collectives to establish regions on a scientific and historically inclusive basis.

While the experiences with Champagne proved influential in the design

of legislative and institutional machinery for defining wine appellations in general, this valuable regional brand has also been at the forefront of campaigns to expand the scope of geographical indications protection. Today in *sui generis* geographical indications regimes, such designations are protected not only against misleading or deceptive uses but also those that take unfair advantage of the reputation of a protected term or mentally evoke it. The *Comité Interprofessionnel du Vin de Champagne* has proactively, and sometimes perplexingly, litigated to prevent the so-called free-riding uses of Champagne on a range of unrelated products, including perfume, mineral water, biscuits, bread, bubble bath, and computers. Notwithstanding the CIVC's vigilant and aggressive enforcement practices, Champagne also showcases the process of genericide, which remains a major obstacle to international geographical indication protection efforts. Where a term is treated

of winemaking regions in Europe may become completely inhospitable to grape production by 2050. By contrast, the climate of southern England is increasingly coming to resemble that of the Champagne region, and its sparkling wine production is gathering pace. Truth may indeed be stranger than fiction! The story of Champagne is still being written and its symbolism will continue to exert a powerful influence on all geographical indications, for better or worse. ◆

Further Reading

Dev S. Gangjee (2012) *Relocating the Law of Geographical Indications.* Cambridge: Cambridge University Press.

Kolleen M. Guy (2003) *When Champagne Became French: Wine and the Making of a National Identity.* Baltimore: Johns Hopkins University Press.

Michelle R. Mozelle and Liz Thach (2014) "The Impact of Climate Change on the Global Wine Industry: Challenges and Solutions," *Wine Economics and Policy*, 3(2), pp. 81–89.

Joonas Rokka (2017) "Champagne: Marketplace Icon," *Consumption Markets & Culture*, 20(3), pp. 275–283.

Charles K. Warner (1960) *The Winegrowers of France and the Government since 1875.* New York: Columbia University Press.

Above: Champagne Joseph Perrier Poster by Colette Stall. (Corbis via Getty Images)

On the left: 1940s French poster makes champagne irresistably attractive. (Alamy)

as the reference for a class or category or products regardless of their origin—think cheddar cheese or dijon mustard—it remains available to all to use, and cannot be controled by one person or group. Over the years, major sparkling wine producing countries, including Germany and Spain within the EU, as well as the United Status, Australia, South Africa, and Switzerland have contested the status of Champagne/ champagne on this basis.

Finally, Champagne gives us a flavor of the tensions between innovation and tradition, which beset all such regional products. At this moment, minds are turning toward the impact of climate change on all geographical indications. Research suggests that over the coming decades, vast tracts

1800   *1900*   *2000*

--/-----/-----/-----/-----/-----/-/----/-----/-----/-----/-----/-----/----

20 Steamboat Willie

Peter Decherney

WHEN YOU WALK down Disney World's Main Street, the seven-minute long 1928 Mickey Mouse film STEAMBOAT WILLIE is likely to be playing. STEAMBOAT WILLIE was not the first animated sound film, as is often claimed. It was not even the first Mickey Mouse film. But STEAMBOAT WILLIE was the first widely released film featuring the iconic mouse, and it immediately captured audiences' imaginations when it premiered before the now-forgotten feature film GANG WAR. The rest, as they say, is history. Mickey Mouse became the foundation on which the Disney Company was built, and today, the movie plays on a perpetual loop in Disney theme parks, cruise ships, and hotels as a reminder of the company's humble beginnings and as a link to its creator and namesake, Walt Disney.

Like most myths, there is some truth to this story of a founding genius whose quaint movie grew into a global media empire. Indeed, it would be hard to think of a company more connected with its founder. Millions of people around the world, for example, recognize Walt Disney's signature as the Disney Company's trademarked

On the left: Mickey Mouse in STEAMBOAT WILLIE (US 1928, Dir. Walt Disney). (Courtesy of Heritage Auctions, HA.com)

logo, and the opening of every Disney film gives the impression of being signed personally by Walt.

But the myth of the lone inventor masks the legal, cultural, and industrial context that led to Disney's success, and that familiar signature also belies the layers of infrastructure beneath Disney's authorship. That signature was the brainchild of a graphic designer, not Walt Disney's personal signature, and it always perturbed Disney that he could not convincingly recreate it. To avoid embarrassment, Disney often resorted to carrying presigned cards to give out when fans asked for autographs.

Shortly before the birth of Mickey Mouse, in the spring of 1928, Walt Disney found himself in a tough spot. He had a falling out with his producer at Universal, the studio that distributed his popular animated series featuring the character Oswald the Lucky Rabbit. And, as a result of their licensing agreement, Universal and not Disney ended up with the rights to Oswald. Disney found himself desperately in need of a new character, and he vowed to own his intellectual property in the future. As he had in the past, Disney found inspiration from existing stories and characters, and he worked with his team to craft a new series. There were already many animated cats in circulation (most popularly Felix and Krazy Kat), and Disney seemed to have an affinity for mice—at least that is how he remembered it years later. There were also fables about mice to serve as source material, and, perhaps most importantly, a mouse with a circular head and two circular ears would be easy to draw. In his earliest incarnation, Mickey Mouse also looks strikingly like Oswald the Lucky Rabbit, who Disney's animators were already adept at drawing.

Animators Hugh Harman, Rudolf Ising, and Ub Iwerks had all worked with Disney since his early days in Kansas City, and they were the the primary architects of both Oswald and Mickey Mouse's appearance. According to one story, the initial idea for Mickey Mouse came from mice that Harman had sketched around a photograph of Disney. When Disney and Universal parted ways, Harman and Ising stayed on with the studio to continue to animate Oswald; later they founded Warner Bros.' successful animation division. Iwerks sided with Disney and the two worked together to craft the Mickey Mouse character and make the early Disney cartoons.

Walt Disney owned the newly reconfigured company with his brother Roy, and Iwerks worked as their salaried employee. Iwerks did all of the drawings while Walt and Roy took care of the business. Walt, it seems clear, also guided the overarching vision of the company, and he provided the voices for the early films, to the extent that they spoke.

Above: Portrait of Walt Disney, 1945. (Alamy)

Iwerks is generously credited on STEAM-BOAT WILLIE. The title card announces the movie as as "A Walt Disney Comic" on one line with the tag "by Ub Iwerks" immediately below. Iwerks' name appears on the other early Mickey Mouse shorts and on Disney's "Silly Symphony" series as well. But Iwerks was never satisfied with his credit line, his compensation, or his contract. Under copyright law's work-for-hire doctrine, Iwerks' creations belonged to the company, no matter how much of the genius was his, and in 1930, Iwerks struck out on his own. After a decade of ups and downs, however, Iwerks returned to the Disney family, where not only Ub but also his son Don and granddaughter Leslie have enjoyed stellar careers.

The break with Iwerks foreshadowed the tension that continued to exist between

Walt Disney and his animators, who collectively went on strike in 1941 after years of disputes. Disney never really recovered from the pain he felt over the strike, and it pushed him politically to the right, culminating in his anti-Communist testimony before the House of Representatives' Committee on Un-American Activities (known as HUAC). Disney used his time to recount the story of the strike, blaming one "commie" union organizer for stirring up his otherwise contented animators.

The Disney Company was not only built on fraught work-for-hire labor relations, but it has also depended heavily on stories adapted from freely available public domain fables (*The Tortoise and the Hare, The Little Tailor, Mulan*) and exclusive licenses to characters from classic works of literature (Mary Poppins, Winnie the Pooh, Mowgli). Walt Disney learned early to reduce the risk of technical and creative innovation by erecting his experiments on top of time-tested stories and characters. When the company moved from making short films to making its first feature film, for example, it adapted the Grimm's fairy tale *Snow White and the Seven Dwarfs* (1937). In return, the Academy of Motion Picture Arts and Sciences awarded Walt Disney one large and seven miniature Oscar statuettes. When the Disney Company made its first fully live-action feature film in 1950, it adapted Robert Louis Stevenson's 1883

novel *Treasure Island*. Both works were in the public domain, free of all copyright restrictions.

The first Mickey Mouse cartoons were no exception: Disney and Iwerks drew on established stories, characters, and public domain material to make their new character appear familiar. The first Mickey Mouse cartoons, for example, all relied on the fair use exception to US copyright law in order to parody public figures, actors, and movies. The first Mickey Mouse cartoon that Iwerks animated, PLANE CRAZY (1928), had Mickey Mouse imitate Charles Lindberg's hair style, airplane design, and general attitude just one year after Lindbergh's famous transatlantic flight. The second Mickey Mouse film, THE GALLOPIN' GAUCHO (1928), parodied Douglas Fairbanks' movie THE GAUCHO (1927). And the third film, STEAMBOAT WILLIE, parodied Buster Keaton's blockbuster film STEAMBOAT BILL JR. (1928). In addition to riffing on Keaton's title and plot, Mickey displays Keaton's brand of slapstick comedy, especially Keaton's Rube Goldberg-like facility with technology.

STEAMBOAT WILLIE was the first Mickey Mouse cartoon to be released with synchronized sound (sound was added later to both PLANE CRAZY and THE GALLOPIN' GAUCHO). And for the first Disney soundtrack, arrangers Wilfred Jackson and Bert Lewis used popular songs that Disney

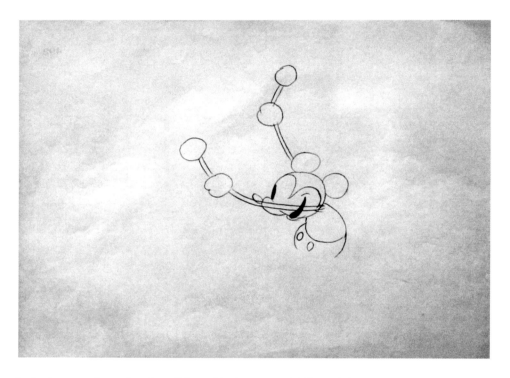

and Iwerks had woven into the plot. Of course the song "Steamboat Bill" had to be included; it served as the inspiration for Keaton's title and had remained popular since ragtime singer Billy Collins' 1911 recording. Jackson and Lewis also used the American folk classic "Turkey in the Straw," which is an integral part of STEAM-BOAT WILLIE's plot. In the film, after a goat eats the sheet music for the song, Mickey and Minnie turn him into a street organ by winding his tail while music wafts out of his mouth. At the time, "Turkey in the Straw" was a widely recognized public domain standard that had been made popular with the addition of offensive racist lyrics used in 19th-century minstrel shows. (As many

critics have noted, Mickey Mouse owes a lot to blackface minstrelsy, especially his later white-gloved incarnations.) All of these elements of Disney's overall style—parody, public domain source material, and reliance on popular music and theatrical forms—allowed him to create something novel buttressed by familiar culture.

Adding sound to Disney cartoons required technological as well as aesthetic decisions, and Walt had to choose a synchronized sound system for STEAM-BOAT WILLIE. Only a year after THE JAZZ SINGER's 1927 premiere, there were competing sound formats available in Hollywood. Disney's largest competitors, the animation team of Max and Dave Fleischer,

Above: A sketch by Ub Iwerks of Mickey Mouse, which was used for STEAMBOAT WILLIE. (Photo: Jim Watson / AFP / Getty Images)

Above: Mickey Mouse and the cow in STEAMBOAT WILLIE. *(Alamy)*

were some of the first filmmakers to embrace synchronized sound film. As early as 1924 (three years before THE JAZZ SINGER), they produced animated sound films using inventor Lee DeForest's Phonofilm system. (The Fleischers also produced a feature-length animated version of SNOW WHITE in 1933, four years before Disney.)

Disney investigated the options. Warner Bros. Studio was promoting its Vitaphone system, and 20th Century Fox championed its Movietone system. In the end, Disney chose the cheapest available technology for his fledgling company: a system called Powers Cinephone being sold by the crafty businessman Pat Powers. Cinephone was cheap, because it was built on patent infringement. Aside from the Fleischer brothers, DeForest did not have much luck licensing his film sound system, and Phonofilm declared bankruptcy in 1926. After an unsuccessful takeover bid, Pat Powers hired away DeForest's lead technician to create a

Phonofilm clone, which he rebranded with his own name. Powers correctly calculated that DeForest's financial situation was too desperate for him to sue. It's unclear if Disney knew that he was using a pirated sound technology, but he soon learned to distrust Powers for other reasons. First, Powers' financial terms became untenable, and then Powers turned Ub Iwerks against Disney. Powers was the scoundrel who lured Iwerks away in 1930 and set him up with his own company.

Since STEAMBOAT WILLIE, Mickey Mouse has starred in hundreds of movies, television shows, comic books, and video games. His short film, LEND A PAW, won an Academy Award in 1941, and Mickey was the first animated character to receive a star on the Hollywood Walk of Fame. In 1998, STEAMBOAT WILLIE was named to the Library of Congress' National Film Registry with the promise of perpetual preservation. The Disney Company eventually

trademarked Mickey Mouse in addition to holding the copyright to STEAMBOAT WILLIE, because the mouse's image had become synonymous with the company.

Although Mickey Mouse and STEAMBOAT WILLIE benefited greatly from fair use and the public domain, the company has fought many legal battles to thwart parodies of Mickey Mouse and to keep him from entering the public domain. In the 1970s, for example, the Disney Company successfully sued a group of artists who were producing a parodic comic called AIR PIRATES FUNNIES, a countercultural statement that depicted Mickey Mouse and Minnie having sex and doing drugs. Disney also aggressively polices the use of the trademarked Mickey Mouse image, once going so far as to send cease-and-desist letters to daycare centers in Florida that had Disney characters on their walls.

In Washington, the Disney Company has regularly lobbied to prolong the length of copyright protection, keeping STEAMBOAT WILLIE and millions of other works from entering the public domain. Partly as a result of Disney's efforts, US Congress has extended the length of copyright protection every time STEAMBOAT WILLIE's copyright term nears its end. Most recently, Disney's influence on the passage of the 1998 Copyright Term Extension Act, which extended the length of copyright to 70 years after an author's death, caused many people to nickname the law the Mickey Mouse Protection Act. Even more dramatically, the company threatened to sue when a law student's research pointed out that STEAMBOAT WILLIE's copyright notice may have failed to follow the proper format, invalidating the film's copyright altogether. We might conclude that the Disney Company is preventing a new generation of Walt Disneys from benefiting from the intellectual

property system that launched Mickey Mouse, or we might see the company as successfully taking advantage of copyright law and policy.

Bringing the story of Mickey Mouse full circle, Disney CEO Bob Iger reversed the deal that initially led to the birth of Mickey Mouse and the Disney Company. In a 2006 exchange with NBCUniversal, Disney traded sportscaster Al Michaels and other properties for Oswald the Lucky Rabbit, who finally took his place among the pantheon of Disney characters. The story continues, however, and we will have to wait and see what Disney will do in 2023 and 2024, when first Oswald and then STEAMBOAT WILLIE are expected— if nothing changes—to enter the public domain. ◆

Further Reading

Neal Gabler (2007) *Walt Disney: The Triumph of the American Imagination.* New York: Vintage.

Douglas A. Hedenkamp (2003) "Free Mickey Mouse: Copyright Notice, Derivative Works, and the Copyright Act of 1909," *Virginia Sports & Entertainment Law Journal,* 2, pp. 254–278.

Lawrence Lessig (2004) *Free Culture: The Nature and Future of Creativity.* New York: Penguin.

Further Viewing

MICKEY MOUSE IN BLACK AND WHITE (2 volume DVD collection)

PLANE CRAZY (US 1928, Dir. Walt Disney)

SHERLOCK JR (US 1924, Dir. Buster Keaton)

On the left: Colorful paper Mickeys in the sky. (Eli Hayasaka / Getty Images)

1800   *1900*   *2000*

--/-----/-----/-----/-----/-----/-/----/-----/-----/-----/-----/-----/----

21 PH-Lamp
Stina Teilmann-Lock

THE "PH-LAMP" IS a Danish design classic. It comes in different variants—pendant lamps, table lamps, and floor lamps, in different sizes and colors—but all are characterized by a three-shade design that enables glare-free lighting. Since the 1920s, when the manufacturer Louis Poulsen Lighting Aps first marketed the lamp, it has been popular in Denmark and beyond among cultural elites and design connoisseurs alike. It has been awarded design prizes, displayed in museums, used in art projects and—importantly for us—it has been copied endlessly by rivals in the market for designer goods.

The lamp was created by the Danish designer Poul Henningsen (1894–1967) in accordance with Louis H. Sullivan's famous aphorism, "form ever follows function." In modern Danish design this dictum was turned into a strategy that promoted the ideal of a perfect unity between the aesthetic and the useful. The Danish Modern movement was personified by Henningsen, along with Arne Jacobsen, Finn Juhl, Hans Wegner, Børge Mogensen, Mogens Lassen, Grethe Jalk, and others.

Their chairs, tables, sofas, cutlery, lamps, door handles, and more have been widely celebrated for the aesthetic stripped of ornament, allowing, it is said, the sheer beauty of functionality to shine through. The PH-lamp captures in some measure how the concept of "Danish Modern" emerged—a concept created by a savvy mixture of intellectual property law reform, national interest, and marketing.

Since the beginning of the 20th century the indivisibility of form and function has been celebrated as a defining value of Danish design. Yet, in the context of intellectual property law the marriage between the aesthetic and the functional turned out to be complicated. Intellectual property law categorically allocates the aesthetic and the functional to different branches of law: aesthetic considerations are generally covered by design laws or copyright; while the functional has always been the province of patent. As a result, in the first half of the twentieth century, intellectual property protection of design was erratic. A Danish *sui generis* law of 1905 protecting registered designs did little to

On the left: A 1970s-style style living room with two PH5 Lamps. (Lena Koller / Getty Images)

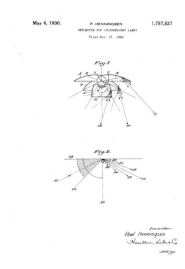

change this state of affairs—in effect, it came to protect ornamental designs only. It is, thus, an historical irony of design law that it remained inconsequential for Danish Modern designers, whose designs were ostentatiously nonornamental and not covered by the designs protection system. Further, in the first half of the 20th century modernist designers could not rely on copyright protection, as Danish courts consistently ruled it inapplicable to designed objects.

The PH-lamp fell squarely within this gap, and despite its significance it was initially denied intellectual property protection. However, by continuous lobbying Poul Henningsen and his generation of designers shaped a new legal paradigm for design. Thus, by the 1960s copyright protection of design in Denmark was among the most comprehensive in the world.

Today, the PH-lamp—along with many other pieces of "designer furniture" of the Danish Modern era—has become a status symbol for the middle classes. The lamp also remains a symbol of particular social and cultural developments in 20th-century Scandinavia. The emergence of modern Scandinavian design was closely tied to the evolution of the welfare state and to a new role that designers played in it as self-pronounced facilitators of the good life. Functionalist design ideology was motivated by notions of increased well-being. Designers considered themselves shapers of norms, with a moral obligation to promote public good through design. Linked to these developments was reform of the intellectual property system, in particular of copyright law.

Henningsen's lamp bears the mark of these movements and reforms. It was one among an abundance of items designed to furnish the homes of the citizens of the evolving Scandinavian welfare state. "Reflector for incandescent lamps" was the title of a series of patents issued first in Denmark and then in the United States on 6 May 1930 to Henningsen, as the inventor, and Louis Poulsen, the manufacturer and assignee of the invention. The patented invention was a system of lampshades that completely surrounded the source of light such that no radiating rays could meet the eye directly. The patent claimed:

A reflector for diffusing the light of incandescent lamps comprising a plurality of concentric

Above, left: US Patent No. 1,757,527A, "Reflector for Incandescent Lamps."

Above, right: PH desklamp, 1941. (Photo by Sandstein, CC BY 3.0)

Above, from left to right:
PH5 Lamp, designed in
1958. (Photo by Holger
Ellgaard, CC BY-SA
3.0);
PH Artichoke lamp,
1958. (Photo by Kri,
CC BY-SA 3.0)

downwardly concave shades disposed above and below the plane of the source of light, the inner surfaces of said shades being directed toward the source of light, the surfaces of said shades making at all points angles of less than 45° with a line to the source of light, the inner surfaces of the shades being dulled.

However, patenting the lamp in Denmark and abroad was a business strategy that turned out to have serious limitations. The patent was of little use in the fight against counterfeiters; competitors and consumers alike cared little for the underlying invention; they simply liked the lamp's shape.

To stop the copying of the lamp, Henningsen and Poulsen sought refuge in copyright law, which, under Danish law, had covered the applied arts since 1908. Thus in 1929, Henningsen sued the lighting manufacturer Lyfa for copyright infringement, based on a series of lamp designs from the competitor. The Lyfa lamps were

based on its own patent, but their appearance were very similar to the PH-lamp. In 1930 the Eastern High Court of Denmark heard the case.

A string of expert statements were presented in court, each of which in their own way demonstrate the difficulty of channeling protection of modernist design into the categories that intellectual property had developed by the early part of the 20th century. One expert, an art historian, said the PH-lamp possessed all the qualities of a distinguished work of art that, replete with the curves and contours of the shades, displayed an artistic intent and unity of execution. An engineer presented the view that if the two lamps looked the same it was most likely a sign that the technical development had reached an "optimum," and that the similarity occurred because of the technical need from the two companies to solve the same problem. A court-appointed expert proposed that, insofar as the designs of the PH and the

On the left: A pair of The Chairs. The Chair best represents Hans Wegner's design philosophy of cutting down to the simplest possible elements of four legs, a seat, and a combined top rail and armrest. The Chair was a collaboration of Wegner and furniture maker Johannes Hansen, and was offered with a solid upholstered seat, or a seat of airy woven caning. It rose to prominence in the 1960 televised debate between Richard Nixon and John F. Kennedy. Both presidential candidates sat in The Chair during the debate. (Courtesy of Heritage Auctions, HA.com)

On the right: St. Catherine's College, Oxford University. Architects: Arne Jacobsen, original design, Hodder Associates, refurbishement and additions. (Photo by Arcaid / UIG via Getty Images)

Lyfa lamps were technically determined, the latter could not be a copy. A different, court-appointed expert argued that design had moved on from the earlier, artisanal period, into a new technological age that focused on the function of the object. The designs of both lamps were, therefore, determined more by technique, design, and material science, than by the styles of the past where ornamentation was the major design consideration.

Faced with this wealth of opinion it is, perhaps, not surprising that the court took the middle course. It ruled that the PH-lamp as a whole was an artistic work protected by copyright, and that a number of Lyfa's lamp designs had indeed infringed the copyright in the PH's design. But it also concluded that there was no patent infringement.

But how could this be so? The court ruled that one of Lyfa's lamps infringed Henningsen's copyright because the feet of both lamps were very similar. However, the three-shade design—which was the subject matter of the patent and the truly revolutionary aspect of the Henningsen

lamp—was determined by technical considerations, and therefore irrelevant to the determination of copyright infringement. Copyright, after all, only applied to the artistic elements of the lamp. Thus, any outer similarity in shape between the lamp-shades should be considered inevitable and legitimate, since the similarity was a question of "technical effect" rather than an artistry. The forgettable foot of the lamp therefore was protected, but the iconic and radical shade was not. The irony must have been hard for Henningsen to accept: his functionalistic design ideology had worked to his own disadvantage.

Since this case, copyright has become even more central to the protection of the Danish Modern movement. In 1961, the Danish Copyright Act specifically mentioned design—that is "applied art"—as an object of protection; and around that time the most iconic of Danish designs, Hans Wegner's "The Chair," was held by a Danish court to be protected by copyright as an artistic work—even though its key function is to support someone merely to sit down.

Henningsen and his Scandinavian colleagues designed for a vision of society with citizens freed from the constraints of heavily ornamented Victorian culture. The PH-lamp sought to express this vision, and other iconic designs shared this aim: Børge Mogensen's "Viking Chair," Arne Jacobsen's interior for St. Catherine's College, Hans Wegner's "Wishbone Chair," and Piet Hein's "Ellipse Table," all played a part in imagining a better future. The rejection by designers of ornament had implications of social reform. As the Austrian architect Adolf Loos phrased it in his 1908 manifest *Ornament and Crime*, ornament should be banned because it belonged to an earlier stage in human evolution. Modern design viewed itself as a remedy for the depraved industrial culture advanced during the 19th century,

where the quality of consumer goods spiraled downwards, leading to a diminution of people's capacity to lead good lives. Functionalism in Scandinavia, William Morris and the Arts & Crafts Movement in Britain, the *Deutsche Werkbund* in Germany, and the *Wiener Werkstätte* in Austria were all responses to this decline in the quality of everyday goods and lives—a decline which was linked to an alleged failure to live authentically in modernity.

Today, the PH-lamp reflects the ideology of these movements—even if the lamp has, somewhat paradoxically, been embraced by the leisure class in its desire for high-end, luxury designer goods. But Henningsen would probably be comfortable with this tension. Notwithstanding their grand claims for design as serving a higher social purpose, the

In 2002 SUPERFLEX modified an original PH5 lamp into a biogas lamp. The Biogas PH5 Lamp is a rethinking of the original concept; to industrially produce lamps to make them accessible for the general population—adapted for a globalized world. When SUPERFLEX created the Biogas PH5 Lamp it was met with a series of lawsuits and demands of destruction of the lamps. As a reference to the cease-and-desist action by lawyers representing

Danish Modernists were careful capitalists and significant promoters of the protection of their designs by the intellectual property system. In their capacities as court-appointed experts, opinion makers, and lobbyists, Danish Modern designers were actively involved in the shaping of design-related intellectual property laws in Denmark. It's no accident that the Danish intellectual property system in time came to grant broad protection to their beloved functional aesthetic. Today, unlike the approach in countries like the United States or Australia, copyright law has become a major regulator of the market for industrial designs in Denmark; and because it is generally seen as weaker, the registered design right now plays a marginal role.

In recent decades the PH-lamp has been acclaimed as a design icon, a political-cultural statement, a collector's item, a status symbol, and more. It is no longer spoken of in terms of its technical specifications—as an invention for living, as Henningsen and his colleagues of the time might have put it. Crucially, today, it is the aesthetic qualities and the cultural implications of the lamp that account for its importance.

In 2002, the Copenhagen-based artist group Superflex created the artwork titled "Biogas PH5 Lamp." The group modified a pendant variant of the PH-lamp—the 1958 PH5 lamp—to allow it to use biogas, thereby rethinking Danish Design for a globalized world and seeking to make it accessible to people living in areas with no access to electricity. When "Biogas PH5 Lamp" was first displayed, the exhibition was quickly closed, after Louis Poulsen Lighting made threats of legal action for copyright infringement of its design. In an out-of-court settlement, the parties agreed that to avoid a lawsuit over copyright infringement "Biogas PH5 Lamp" was to be exhibited only in its transportation box.

This was, we might say, yet another layer in the aesthetic, social, and cultural significance of the PH-lamp—and its intellectual property record. ◆

Further Reading

Kjetil Fallan (ed.) (2012) *Scandinavian Design: Alternative Histories*. Oxford: Berg Publishers.

Jens Hemmingsen Schovsbo and Stina Teilmann-Lock (2016) "We Wanted More Arne Jacobsen Chairs But All We Got Was Boxes – Experiences from the Protection of Designs in Scandinavia from 1970 Till the Directive," *International Review of Intellectual Property and Competition Law*, 47(4), pp. 418–437.

Annette Kur, Marianne Levin, and Jens Schovsbo (eds.) (2018) *The EU Design Approach: A Global Appraisal*. Cheltenham: Edward Elgar.

US Patent No. 1,757,527A (issued May 6, 1930), "Reflector for Incandescent Lamps."

the copyright holder concerning the work Supercopy / Biogas PH5 Lamp, SUPERFLEX and Rirkrit Tiravanija made a new blackout version. Making the lamp black is SUPERFLEX' comment on the censorship in question—and underlining the irony in painting a light source black to prevent someone from seeing it. (Courtesy of SUPERFLEX)

22 Climbing Rose

Brad Sherman

On the left: The Rosa "New Dawn," advertised as the first patented plant in Peter Henderson & Co.'s Catalogue, 1931. (Author's own)

IN THE MID-1920s, Henry F. Bosenberg, a landscape gardener from New Brunswick, NJ, purchased a number of roses for use in his landscape business. These included several "Dr. Van Fleet" roses, the climbing rose which had been bred by Dr. Walter Van Fleet at the US Department of Agriculture Plant Introduction Station, and introduced in 1926. The Dr. Van Fleet rose, which had been developed by crossing a tea rose with *Rosa wichuraiana,* was one of Van Fleet's "backyard roses" that were marketed as roses with beautiful flowers, luxuriant foliage, colorful hips, and that were resistant to disease and able to thrive in America's harsh climates. While Dr. Van Fleet roses typically only bloomed once a year for around two weeks, Bosenberg noticed that one of the Dr. Van Fleet roses that he had bought continued to bloom after the other Dr. Van Fleets had finished flowering. After watching the aberrant plant for two seasons, Bosenberg used the ever-blooming rose to propagate a number of new plants. Bosenberg noted that because the propagated plants bloomed the very first year and continued to bloom, and because plants

that were budded from those young plants also continued to bloom, there would be little danger of it reverting to the original Dr. Van Fleet. As a result, a new variety of rose—the *Rosa* "New Dawn"—was born.

Unlike the ordinary Dr. Van Fleet rose, which—in New Jersey, at least—usually bloomed for around two weeks in early June, with the occasional rare flower in mid-summer or fall, the New Dawn rose flowered continuously from early June until growth was stopped by frost, usually in late October. Recognizing the potential value of this repeat-flowering rose, Bosenberg filed for plant patent protection on 6 August 1930 from the US Patent and Trademark Office under the 1930 Plant Patent Act. After some initial problems—primarily caused by the US Department of Agriculture's demand for proof of the New Dawn's "everblooming characteristics"—*Plant Patent Number 1* was granted for the New Dawn rose on 18 August 1931. The Plant Patent Act, which had been signed by President Hoover on 23 May 1930, had emerged in response to complaints from the nursery industry that the future of the plant breeding industry

was being jeopardized by the "pirating" of new plant varieties. After early attempts to amend trademark law to provide a remedy against the misuse of plant names failed, the nursery industry successfully lobbied to have the patent legislation amended to allow for plant patents to be granted to breeders, in return for the public disclosure of a new plant.

The New Dawn rose was a plant pioneer. As well as being the first plant to be patented, it was also the first repeat-flowering climbing rose to be commercialized. This history-making rose—still commercially available today—has become the benchmark against which repeat-flowering climbing roses are judged. The New Dawn also spawned a host of successful climbing roses, including the Aloha, Blossomtime, Cadenza, Penny Lane, Don Juan, Pearl Drift, Parade, and Pink Perpétue. The success of the New Dawn was formally recognized in 1997, when it was voted the most popular rose in the world at the 11th World Convention of Rose Societies, and inducted into the Rose Hall of Fame by the World Federation of Rose Societies.

The New Dawn rose was also a legal pioneer. As the first plant to be patented, it paved the way for the patenting of thousands of plants, many of which are roses. The first plant patent also outlined an approach to plant patenting that continues today. Of particular importance was the way the invention was claimed. The plant patent scheme was based upon the system of design patents, and applicants for a plant patent were limited to a single claim, which was meant to set out the distinguishing characteristics of the plant. While the details of the claim varied, they tended to follow a similar pattern, in which, after linking the claim to "the plant as

described," applicants would highlight the distinctive features of the invention. This pattern was established in *Plant Patent 1*, which claimed: "A climbing rose as herein shown and described, characterized by its everblooming habit."

Another notable feature of *Plant Patent Number 1* was the way it described the New Dawn rose. What was particularly interesting was the way the legal description of the new rose built upon and linked to the taxonomic and botanical practices that were used to describe and demarcate plants. Here, the scientific name of the plant—*Rosa* "New Dawn," or more accurately the *Rosa* "Dr. Van Fleet" on which the New Dawn was based—played a key role in determining its legal status. The scientific name of the rose, combined with the myriad of rules, practices, and conventions used for naming, describing, and identifying roses, linked roses in nurseries to the object protected by *Plant Patent Number 1*.

While a rose by any other name may smell as sweet, for the purposes of plant patent law and the emerging field of horticulture, "any other name" would not do. Instead what was needed was a name that was stable and fixed, one that could be relied upon to demarcate and identify a specific plant. While it may have taken some time for naming practices to be standardized in other areas of botany, this was not the case with roses. This was largely a result of the American Rose Society, which had helped to standardize names and develop a common language to describe and identify roses. The standardization of plant names was an essential precursor to the grant of intellectual property rights in botanical innovations. When combined with type specimens, which emerged officially in

the 1940s, and a detailed official description of novel plants—roles performed by the American Rose Society—the name acted as a mechanism that enabled the patented plant to be identified and the boundaries of the intangible property to be set. Over time, the role and place of the scientific name in demarcating and defining botanical innovations has become even more pronounced. One issue that took some time to clarify was whether trademarked names, which have been very important in the sale of roses and other nursery plants, could be included in the scientific name. After some uncertainty, it became clear that this was not permissible, primarily to ensure that the trademark owner could not restrict the use of the scientific name. As the American Rose Society's guidelines for the naming of roses states: "Trademarks, claimed or registered, cannot be accepted epithets." Thus, while some of New Dawn's offspring have been sold under trademarked names, trademarked names have never been able to form part of either the official name registered at the American Rose Society, or the name used in plant patents.

One of the most important consequences of patents such as the one granted for the New Dawn rose was that it helped to change the way the "invention" was conceived within the law. At the time there was little scientific breeding in the nursery industries: new roses, like most nursery plants, were developed using one of two traditional breeding techniques. In some cases, breeders produced a large number of artificial hybrids, from which they selected a few desirable plants for further propagation and study. Often this was a large scale and arduous process that required great skill. For example, over 65,000 hybrid bushes had been grown and eliminated in the development of the white blackberry, while Luther Burbank selected his famous seedless plum from 300,000 artificially produced variations. This was also the case with the Dr. Van Fleet rose, which had been selected from thousands of crosses.

While many plants were the product of systematic breeding and selection, in the majority of cases the industry relied on nature's own "breeding experiments" to provide new plants. As with the New Dawn, the industry relied on seedlings, bud mutations, and sports that were discovered in orchards, greenhouses, gardens, and fields. A sport or bud variation occurs where a plant or a portion of a plant spontaneously assumes an appearance or character distinct from that which normally characterizes the variety or species; whereas, a mutant is a new and distinct variety that results from seedling variations from the self-pollination of a species.

While it was accepted that the efforts of breeders such as Dr. Van Fleet were worthy of protection, this was not the case with plants such as the New Dawn that were the result of chance finds. Giving protection to someone for merely finding a sport, bud, or mutation seemed like the Patent Office was granting a monopoly to someone who had not invented anything, but was lucky enough merely to find a naturally occurring variation. While the origin of inventions such as the Singer Sewing machine can be traced to efforts of a human inventor—who conceived, planned, and brought the tangible object into existence—this was not the case with the New Dawn rose. It seemed that, in light of these concerns, the law would have to exclude chance finds such as the New Dawn from plant patent protection. However, this did not eventuate,

On the left:
Marcel van der Vlugt.
Rose 131, 2001, from
the series BUDS.
Dye diffusion transfer
print / Polaroid.
(Courtesy of Marcel
van der Vlugt)

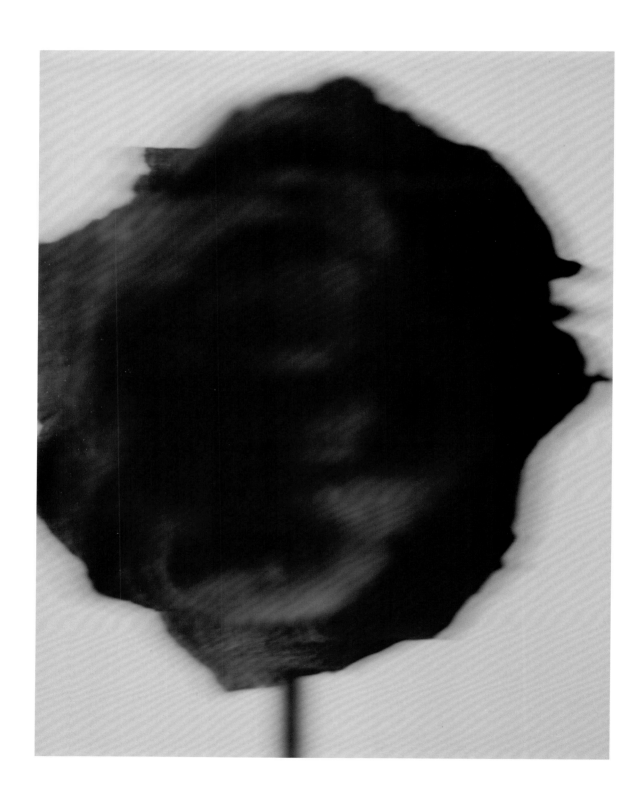

and instead the role of the inventor—and with it the invention—was reconfigured to accommodate chance finds. While breeders sometimes played an important role in stimulating genetic changes, for the most part the role of the "innovator" in the plant patent systems was limited to recognizing the genetic aberration that had been created by nature—the sport or mutant—and preserving it for future generations. Importantly, this was the case irrespective of whether the plant was the result of sophisticated selection process, as with the Dr. Van Fleet, or the result of a chance discovery, as with the New Dawn. In both cases, the role of the breeder was not that of an inventor in the usual sense of the word; rather, the role of the breeder was to identify and then preserve, capture, and retain what nature had spontaneously created but was unable to repeat unaided. Once a novel bud, sport, or mutation had been discovered, the task of the breeder was to asexually reproduce (or clone) the genetic aberration. In this sense, the role of the breeder, and the law, was to normalize the abnormal, to stabilize and standardize nature's deviants, mutations, and aberrations, to "save this freak or abnormality in plant life to make it useful to mankind." In a sense, plant patent law saw the breeder and nature as something akin to joint inventors of a new variety. It was only when the skill and effort of the two were combined that a plant invention was ever able to come into existence—in this particular association of humans and nonhumans, neither nature nor breeders could operate independently of each other to develop a novel plant invention.

In finding a feasible solution to the question highlighted by the New Dawn patent—namely, "what does it mean to invent a plant?"—a key problem in relation to the operation of the plant patent law was resolved. In so doing, it not only laid the foundation for the ongoing application of plant patents in the nursery industry, but it also marked the beginning of a widespread interest in intellectual property more generally. The modern nursery industry now relies widely on plant patent protection—since 1930, nearly 30,000 plant patents have been granted in the United States, of which approximately 40 percent have been for roses—and many industry participants have used trademark law to differentiate their branded plants from those of their competitors. As advances in biotechnology start to play a more important role in the nursery sector, there has also been an increase in the number of utility patents, for things such as technologies that extend the shelf life of cut roses, and the use of molecular markers to speed up the breeding process. The significance of intellectual property in all parts of the plant breeding industry seems likely to increase in the future—a significance that stems from the early efforts to protect the first repeat-flowering climbing rose. ◆

Further Reading

Robert Starr Allyn, John G. Townsend, and Fred S. Purnell (eds.) (1934) *The First Plant Patent: A Discussion on the New Law and Patent Office Practice.* Brooklyn: Educational Foundations.

Robert C. Cook (1931) "The First Plant Patent," *Journal of Heredity*, 22(10), pp. 313–319.

Alain Pottage and Brad Sherman (2007) "Organisms and Manufactures: On the History of Plant Inventions," *Melbourne University Law Review*, 31(2), pp. 539–568.

On the left:
Marcel van der Vlugt.
Rose 43, 1996, from
the series BUDS.
Dye diffusion transfer
print / Polaroid.
(Courtesy of Marcel
van der Vlugt)

1800   *1900*   *2000*

--/-----/-----/-----/-----/-----/--/---/-----/-----/-----/-----/-----/----

23 Penguin Paperback
Stuart Kells

THE PENGUIN PAPERBACK is an icon of publishing and design. The first covers were attractively simple. A rectangular shape, 181 × 112 mm, adhering to the golden ratio of 1.61 and based on work by Leonardo da Vinci on the ideal page size. Friendly bands of orange, white, and orange—like the map of an imaginary European country, tilted on its side. The words "Penguin Books" in a stylish escutcheon. And most recognizable of all, the cheerful, irreverent Penguin logo.

How recognizable? In 1987 militants kidnapped Terry Waite in Beirut. Years of solitary confinement followed. When Waite asked his captors for a book, he decided the best way to transcend language barriers, and the best way to ensure he received something decent to read, was to draw the Penguin logo.

Now part of the global Penguin Random group, and with thriving subsidiaries in Europe, China, India, the Americas, and Australia, Penguin Books is the world's best-known publishing imprint. Its rise to prominence and profitability was anything but inevitable; but in attaining both ends, it transformed the way that the public read, and the way that publishers use the intellectual property system.

Like many famous brands, Penguin sprang from humble and precarious circumstances. In the early 1930s, three brothers—Allen, Richard, and John Lane—were working at their family firm, The Bodley Head. At the end of the 19th century, that firm had published groundbreaking and somewhat-scandalous books in London and New York. By the time of the Great Depression, however, the imprint was somewhat crusty—and on the way to bankruptcy.

The Lane brothers needed a lifeline. In the 1930s, a typical, new hardcover volume cost seven shillings and sixpence, a price that made them an unaffordable luxury for many readers. The brothers decided to launch a new venture from within The Bodley Head: a series of paperbacks that would sell at the remarkably low price of sixpence.

The brothers launched the series with an initial tranche of ten titles. The sourcing of the ten texts was a key part of what

On the left: A general view of a collection of Penguin books on display in Foyles bookshop in London, 2015. (Photo by Ben Pruchnie / Getty Images)

made the new venture innovative. The Lanes negotiated with rival publishers to sub-lease the paperback rights for titles that had previously appeared in hardcover. Of the first ten titles, six came from Jonathan Cape, one from Chatto & Windus, one from Benn, and the remaining two from The Bodley Head. Though privately Cape wished the new venture well, his public line was that the Lanes would certainly fail and, he said, "I thought I'd take four-hundred quid off you before you did."

The brothers' effort to convince hardback publishers to agree to a paperback appearance under someone else's imprint foreshadowed the kind of copyright licensing that is now a mainstay of media and consumer industries, such as film-making and toy manufacturing. And—similar to Lego's debt to Kiddicraft and Barbie's to the Bild Lilli Doll—the new imprint copied a foreign predecessor.

Founded in 1932, Albatross Verlag was owned by a South African and managed through an Italian chairman and a British holding company. From Germany, Kurt Enoch controlled marketing and

distribution; in Paris, Max Wegner handled editorial and production; and the firm's German designer, Hans Mardersteig, was based in Italy. For tourists and continental readers alike, Albatross published the best of modern literature as well as popular fiction—but in English, and in paper covers.

Each genre in Albatross's Modern Continental Library had its own cover color, so customers knew straightaway what they were getting. The Lanes saw the value in the way that Albatross issued its books, and soon appropriated multiple aspects of the German company's design: the format, the paper covers, the color coding, the simple sans-serif titling. They even copied the ornithological branding.

To settle on the precise brand for their new series, the brothers convened a conference meeting and invited members of The Bodley Head's editorial and sales staff to participate. The attendees assembled a long list of potential names, then subjected them to a grueling selection process to arrive at a winning name and logo. Albatross was naturally the starting point for the long list. But what comparable real or imaginary

Above: The Lane brothers outside the company's office and warehouse in London, 1940. From left to right: Richard Lane, finance and production manager; Allen Lane, managing director; and John Lane, export manager. (Photo by © Hulton-Deutsch Collection / CORBIS / Corbis via Getty Images)

Above, from left to right: Child film actress Binkie Stuart hand in hand with a penguin pal during a visit to London Zoo, 1937. (Photo by Fox Photos / Getty Images); The Penguin logo in 1937. (Alamy)

creature might best capture what the Lanes were trying to do, and serve as title, logo, and emblem for the new venture? Among the names considered were "phoenix," "kiwi," and "woodpecker."

For many reasons, penguins were in several minds at the meeting. The London Zoo's ultra-modern penguin enclosure had just opened, its well-dressed inhabitants featuring prolifically in the press. In 1925, The Bodley Head had issued Anatole France's *Penguin Island*. Tudor had published Stuart Palmer's *The Penguin Pool Murder* with a striking penguin blocked on the cover. There were penguin-branded chocolate bars and sports teams, and "Squeak the Penguin" was one third of a much loved comic strip. In other forms, too, penguins had colonized the popular imagination. Around the conference table, the name "penguin" was ready to leap from the tips of several tongues.

The brothers sent Edward Young to the Zoo to sketch penguins. It was a hot day and he complained that the birds stank. Back in the office, he presented the Lanes with his (odor-free) drawings. Only then was the name for the series settled upon.

The Penguin brand, and indeed the whole Penguin package, was immediately successful. People vacuumed up Penguins as quickly as new titles could be issued. Within four months of the imprint's launch, sales reached one million copies. Within a year, they surpassed three million. In the firm's first decade, the Lane brothers would sell a hundred million paperbacks.

There is a huge significance to intellectual property for this enormous success, one that sounds in trademark law and branding, not in the usual copyright law that we expect with books. Purchasers of Penguins were immediately doing something new: they were "buying on imprint,"

on their acceptance of the brand, as much as on author, subject, or genre. University lecturers might have routinely bought the latest Oxford University Press titles, and romance readers might have flocked to the latest Mills and Boon; but, in general, it was rare for customers to buy consciously on the strength of the publisher's brand.

Penguin embraced this new practice of imprint buying. The firm pioneered the use of "shops within shops": large and stylish displays of exclusively Penguin books, to be set up inside bookshops. In its marketing, the firm playfully showcased the Penguin brand, seeking to make it a signal of accessibility and also excellence. According to the firm's corporate marketing, the "bird in the oval represents an assurance of integrity and quality to readers around the world."

Just as the Lanes had copied Albatross, so the success of the new imprint attracted a flock of imitators. Knock-offs sprang up all over the world, even in Britain. Hutchinson's Pocket Library, for example, copied Penguin's stripes, binding, dust jackets, typefaces, and price.

The Penguin brand had become a valuable piece of intellectual property, separate from the books. And yet the Lanes' attitude to the brand was remarkably cavalier. For the firm's first company outing to Paris, a printer equipped the traveling party with posters and cardboard medallions featuring the logo. During the evening, one of the staff went to a brothel where "the girls were lined up for his inspection, one girl's clothes consisted of a pair of high-heeled shoes and, around her neck, a Penguin medallion."

The same relaxed attitude saw different penguins appear on different books. Some of the penguins looked sinister and potato-like, while others looked oddly unfinished and overweight. In the firm's first decades, Penguin books carried advertising for a carelessly diverse range of products and institutions. Nora Waln's *Reaching for the Stars*, for example, featured a jaunty advertisement for Communist Radio. Gradually the Lanes became aware of the value of their brand, and grew more protective of it. One of their fears was that the imitators might eat into Penguin's market. The name "pelican" was a particular vulnerability: people were misaddressing letters to "Pelican," and asking for "Pelicans" in shops when they meant Penguins. As soon as the brothers had the opportunity, they grabbed the Pelican brand, repurposing it for a nonfiction series.

After World War II—in which John Lane was tragically killed—Allen and Richard Lane employed the greatest European typographer to improve Penguin's logo and layout. Wooed by a salary that exceeded the owners' combined remuneration, Jan Tschichold spent two and a half

years at Penguin, paying close attention to every book, and establishing exacting quality control systems that spread from the office to Penguin's printers. He conferred typographical beauty on the standard Penguin and Pelican covers, and, after dozens of attempts to improve the logo that he labeled "deformed" and "corrupted," he eventually hit upon the sharp and elegant bird that became the design icon that we recognize today.

At the same time that Tschichold was working his magic, Allen and Richard came into conflict with the leaders of their American subsidiary. Fraught negotiations followed. The Lanes' main anxiety was that they might lose control of the Penguin brand in America, and so, to prevent that eventuality, they were willing to sacrifice all their American operations. Penguin's former American executives took control of the subsidiary and operated it under a new name, Signet. The Lanes had to start from scratch in America; but the Penguin brand was saved.

Despite this new awareness of the centrality of trademark and branding, the firm still made missteps. By mid-century, the Australian subsidiary had prospered to such an extent that it was preparing to move to larger premises. In 1953, plans for the new building were finished, and the construction was about to start. Penguin's Australian manager, Bob Maynard, came up with a clever tease to display on the hoarding: "A Sanctuary for Penguins and Pelicans is being erected on this site." The sign caused no end of trouble. Bob recalled later that one firm wanted to tender for tiling the pools, and a bus company wanted to arrange tours. Old ladies wrote to the press complaining of cruelty to birds.

The Penguin brand family grew to include Porpoise, Peacock, Peregrine, Ptarmigan and the children's imprint, Puffin. But there were limits to the P-fun. A London schoolboy submitted a new Puffin slogan: "It's a P'Super—It's a Psychedelic." Puffin's editor Kaye Webb embraced the suggestion—until she was informed that "psychedelic" came from the "hipster world of drugs." The *Daily Mail* ran the story, "Censored: Sir Allen orders the Puffin Club to drop psychedelic."

Above, from left to right:
Legend has it that Lane conceived the idea of producing good-quality, affordable paperbacks after a visit to Agatha Christie in 1934, when he found himself stranded on the platform at Exeter St. Davids train station with nothing to read. (Photo by Elizabeth Chat / Picture Post / Getty Images);
Poster produced by Cancol Ltd. for British Rail to advertise Intercity services, featuring the Penguin Books symbol resting. (Photo by SSPL / Getty Images)

In the 1960s, Allen pushed Richard out of the firm and stepped back from day-to-day management; except when he feared the new managers were taking the imprint in the wrong direction. When Penguin published a cheeky volume by the French cartoonist Maurice Sinet, Allen broke into his own warehouse at midnight and destroyed the whole stock of the book.

Allen Lane was knighted in 1952, for Penguin's services to literature and literacy, and by the 1960s, Penguin had become a British institution, something like a privately held BBC. The *Guardian*'s literary editor observed, in 1967, that Penguin was "more than a business, arguably the most important publishing house in Britain and certainly a national cultural asset whose value can be calculated (worth how many universities, opera houses, art galleries?)."

The Lane brothers' achievements depended on multiple innovations in the creation and management of intellectual property. The brothers pioneered an approach to licensing that allowed them to use others' copyrighted works. With hardback publishers, Penguin negotiated first right of refusal on the paperback rights for their titles. The low-cost, high-volume business model allowed Penguin to profit nearly as much from single-book authors as from household-name authors like Virginia Woolf, Graham Greene, and Agatha Christie.

Like every successful start-up, the roll-out of Penguin's new business model was well timed. The venture's ingredients came together at precisely the right moment. The reading public was growing and hungry for good books, social norms and class barriers were breaking down, and the Great Depression made printers and retailers ready to support a low-margin product on a very large scale.

The firm has occasionally ventured outside this model. Thirty years after its commencement, the firm launched a hardback imprint, "Allen Lane The Penguin Press." A major departure from the seminal, iconic Penguin paperback, the new imprint enjoyed only mixed success.

No matter. Today, Penguin Books is associated with two things: its paperback books, with their bright bands of color, their cheerful format, and their iconic logo; and for utterly changing the world's reading habits. ◆

Further Reading

Steve Hare (1995) *Penguin Portrait: Allen Lane and the Penguin Editors, 1935–1970*. London: Penguin Books.

Stuart Kells (2015) *Penguin and the Lane Brothers: The Untold Story of a Publishing Revolution*. Melbourne: Black Inc.

Jeremy Lewis (2005) *Penguin Special: Life and Times of Allen Lane*. London: Penguin Books.

Jack E. Morpurgo (1979) *Allen Lane: King Penguin*. London: Hutchinson.

1800   1900   2000

--/-----/-----/-----/-----/-----/--/---/-----/-----/-----/-----/-----/----

24 Ferragamo Wedge

Marianne Dahlén

On the left: A contemporary reinterpretation of the classic Ferragamo "F wedge," Collection FW 2017. (Courtesy of Salvatore Ferragamo S.p.A.)

THROUGHOUT THE 1940s, wedge heel shoes—also known as "wedgies" or "lifties"—dominated feminine shoe fashion, and they have remained popular ever since. They were patented by Salvatore Ferragamo (1898–1960), "the shoemaker of dreams," and the success of the design depended on a lucky combination of form and function. Ferragamo was born in a poor peasant family from a small village outside Naples, but worked in Hollywood and eventually became one of the most influential shoemakers in the 20th century by making extravagant shoes for celebrities. However, the Ferragamo wedge does not owe its genesis to the lavish lifestyles of movie royalty, but to the troubled economic reality of Italy between the wars, and a strategic emphasis on patenting that was ahead of its time.

Salvatore Ferragamo was born in the small southern Italian village of Bonito. He began making shoes at the age of 10 and, at the age of 15, he moved to the United States to join his siblings who ran a shoe-repair shop in Santa Barbara, California. In the period before World War I, Santa

Barbara was one of the main capitals of the American film industry, and young Salvatore began designing shoes for historical films. He was gifted: he knew what shoes would fit the styles of historical film productions, but he made them modern in both fit and material. When the American Film Company moved to Hollywood in 1919, Ferragamo followed suit. Producing shoes that didn't harm the foot of the wearer obsessed him, and he attended anatomy class at the University of Southern California with the purpose of adapting his shoes to the human foot, instead of forcing the foot to adapt to the shoe. As a result, Ferragamo became very popular among film people, making shoes not only for the movies but also for the stars' private use, and many of his famous movie clients became his personal friends.

In 1927 Ferragamo returned to Italy. After some difficult years during the Depression he managed to get his business together again, and by 1938 he had moved his shop to Palazzo Spini Ferroni in Florence—the headquarters of the Ferragamo family business to this day. The wedge heel

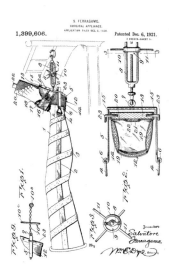

was born out of necessity, brought on by a scarcity of quality materials as a result of Italy's colonial war in Ethiopia and a political environment that demanded Italian self-sufficiency. Under fascist rule in the 1930s, the Italian economy became increasingly nationalized and corporatized. In 1935 the League of Nations imposed sanctions against Italy as a reaction to Mussolini's aggressive war in Ethiopia and, although the sanctions were never fully implemented, they provided Mussolini with an excuse to impose autarkic controls on the Italian economy. Autarky—the political doctrine of limited international trade and domestic self-sufficiency—was significant to Mussolini's corporatist economic politics, and it dictated that Italian producers and consumers should only use or buy Italian products. Laws were introduced that compelled textile and fashion companies to Italianize the major part of the production, and a corporation for fashion was set up in Turin, Ente Moda Italiana, with the assignment of creating a national fashion. Every clothing company was obliged to use only Italian material, and to indicate the Italian origin of the product.

As a consequence of both war and autarky, the materials on which Ferragamo depended were unavailable; but from scarcity emerged a range of new materials and designs, and an extended period of innovation. Ferragamo experimented extensively, using everything that came to mind: paper wrappings from his mother's favorite Sunday chocolates, cellophane, raffia, fishing line, even fish skin.

Although he was surely at the forefront of shoemaking, in both design and comfort, Ferragamo was not alone. A number of contemporary innovative shoemakers—in Italy, France and the United States—created models similar to his. However, Ferragamo stands out for his extraordinary combination of skills: an interest in human anatomy, exceptional artisanal and artistic skills, a restless creativity, incredible entrepreneurial instincts, and an extensive command of the Italian patenting system. The archives of Fondazione Ferragamo contain a shoe-library of more than 20,000 models, and we know that he patented more than 400 inventions and designs. Ferragamo did not see himself as a *stilista*—a fashion designer—but as an "artisan-artist." His first patent, approved in 1921,

Above, left: Ferragamo's 1921 patent for a surgical appliance, US Patent No. 1,399,606.

Above, right: Salvatore Ferragamo at his Via Manelli workshop in Florence. (Alamy)

Above: Handmade lasts for Ferragamo shoes. (Photo: Fedele Toscani / Toscani Archive / Alinari Archives Management, Florence)

was a "surgical appliance," invented to improve his recovery from a complicated leg fracture caused by a car accident. The invention is still in use to this day.

His first footwear patent, issued in 1932, was the steel shank, used to support the arch of the foot; previously the shank was made of leather and did not give the right support to make the shoe comfortable. But the strictures of Mussolini's Italy made this patent useless to Ferragamo. So, he replaced the shank, filling the empty space between the heel and sole with Sardinian cork. Not only did this solve the problem with the shank, but it also gave the arch firm support, was extraordinarily comfortable, and provided ample space for decoration. Notwithstanding these benefits, he suspected this new look would be a hard sell. In order to promote it he asked one of his most prominent clients, a Florentine *contessa*, to let him make a pair for her. At first she refused—she found them too ugly—but he insisted, and after trying them on she was convinced by their superior comfort.

From this rocky start, the wedge heel quickly went global. It soon became popular among the Hollywood film stars and fashionable women all over the Western world. The wedge heel is epitomized in the iconic "Rainbow" sandal tailor-made for Judy Garland in 1938, inspired by the Academy award-winning song "Over the Rainbow" from THE WIZARD OF OZ. The shoe is now part of the collection of the Metropolitan Museum of Art in New York. The Rainbow had a wedge heel and a high platform sole made of cork layers covered with rainbow-colored suede and straps of golden kidskin.

Ferragamo first patented the wedge heel in 1937. On 17 September 1937 he filed an application with the title "*calzature con tallone rialzato senza tacco isolato*" ("shoes with high heel without isolated heel"), and Patent No. 354,889 was granted on 13 December 1937. In the application Ferragamo claimed that the new model offered not only "*novità estetica*" ("aesthetic novelty") but also a perfectly stable foundation supporting the entire foot without

any "auxiliary parts" or reinforcement of the arch. It was, the application read, "absolutely practical" both for sport and for "every use." The patent covered wedge heels of "any suitable filling," not only cork.

In his autobiography, *Shoemaker of Dreams*, Ferragamo writes that he patented the wedge heel in "most of the countries of the world," and that he took action "against the first shoemaker who stole it." That shoemaker was his competitor, Edoardo Frattegiani, a prominent artisan with shops in Florence, Rome, and Venice, who, like Ferragamo, produced handmade shoes of artistic design. Seven months after Ferragamo's patent was approved, Frattegiani filed a patent application for a wedge heel in wood, which was granted in July 1938 as Patent No. 16,133.

The lawsuit Ferragamo refers to began as a criminal case in 1937 and finished as a civil case in 1941. The court records of the civil case—conserved in the Archivio Statale di Firenze—reveal that action was taken *against* Ferragamo by Frattegiani, seeking compensation based on a preliminary ruling of the prosecutor's office. In December 1937 Ferragamo had charged Frattegiani with counterfeiting his design, and had directed the Florence police to confiscate a pair of wedges from Frattegiani's shop window. Ferragamo sought an order that Frattegiani stop making and marketing wedge heels. Ferragamo based his accusations on the grounds that Frattegiani's shoes were identical to Ferragamo's patented model, and that Frattegiani's father had ordered identical cork

Above: Ferragamo's "Rainbow" kidskin sandal with layered cork sole and heel covered in suede. This shoe was designed for Judy Garland, 1938. (The Metropolitan Museum of Art / Art Resource)

Above: A pair of Frattegiani rainbow sandals. This pair hasn't been precisely dated, so it is unclear whether they are from before or after Ferragamo's rainbow sandals. (Galleria degli Uffizi Gabinetto Fotografico)

wedges from Ferragamo's Sardinian cork supplier. Frattegiani claimed that he had produced a pair of wooden-heeled wedges in August 1937, predating Ferragamo's patent. According to Frattegiani, other shoemakers in Florence at the time were already producing similar models. Frattegiani also claimed that, in December 1937, a "*signorina,*" identified as one of Ferragamo's employees, came to his shop to order a pair of wedges. Allegedly she asked for the shoes to be produced with cork, but Frattegiani refused this request. The prosecutor's office dismissed Ferragamo's charges against Frattegiani, stating that the wedge heel had existed since antiquity, initially for sandals and mules, and later on orthopedic shoes. The prosecutor further indicated that Ferragamo's lawsuit was unjust, causing damage to Frattegiani by defamation and a loss of clients—hence, Frattegiani was entitled to damages in an amount to be determined by a civil court.

In the subsequent civil case, Frattegiani sued Ferragamo for compensation. Ferragamo countersued, arguing that Frattegiani's shoes were identical to Ferragamo's patented model. Ferragamo claimed damages, and demanded that a copy of the sentence be published in *La Nazione*. Ferragamo also sought a declaration that he was a leading inventor of women's footwear, that the wedge heel was a novelty, that he was its inventor, and that Frattegiani had copied the design. Frattegiani insisted that he had disclosed his model one month before Ferragamo's patent application, and argued that Ferragamo's accusations were only aimed at eliminating a dangerous competitor.

We don't know how the case was finally decided. The archives show that Frattegiani's claims for compensation were rejected by the court, and that three experts from the Italian shoemaking region of Varese were to be appointed in order to determine Ferragamo's counter-action. But the trail goes cold after this point, and there is nothing in the Archivio Statale showing the disposition of the case. Ferragamo writes in his autobiography that he won the dispute, but says that, by then, the wedge design had already conquered the world and it was useless to fight for his patent.

Ferragamo writes that, by the beginning of the 1940s, wedges dominated the American market and that "86% of the women's shoes sold were wedgies." He comments that if he had received a royalty for only a penny a pair, he would have "become a millionaire many times over," but he never received a cent. However, this never bothered him. The wedge provided him with "immense creative satisfaction," it was received as "utterly different," "completely new," and as "a revolution." Ferragamo's business was bankrupt in the inter-war years, but the wedge heel brought

it back to life, even without the exclusive rights he sought.

The competition between Ferragamo and Frattegiani did not end here. Both shoemakers were celebrated for their creative designs and for their innovative use of materials such as wood, raffia, and cellophane. And they were both aware of the importance of protecting their designs with patents. One of Frattegiani's models is very similar to the Rainbow sandal, except it doesn't feature the wedge heel. It is conserved in the Museo della Moda e del Costume at the Palazzo Pitti in Florence. Although it is given an indicative date of "1935–1940," we don't know if the design came before or after Ferragamo's Rainbow sandal. Was it inspired by the Rainbow, or the other way round? Was it a copy or a totally different model? Either way, it was Ferragamo who was met with international fame, and became the "shoemaker of dreams." Years later, when Italian postwar fashion became a global phenomenon at the famous 1951 Florence runway shows, Ferragamo showcased his patented "Kimo" design. This time, Frattegiani sued Ferragamo for infringement. It seems, however, that he was unsuccessful: Ferragamo still held the patent by the end of the 1980s.

The wedge heel was a brilliant design made by a brilliant shoemaker, or maybe by several brilliant shoemakers. It was not created in a vacuum; it was literally a product of its time. It was a creature of the Italian patenting system, and the intellectual property strategies of artisans like Ferragamo and Frattegiani. It emerged from the intersection of the Italian artisanal tradition, the Hollywood film industry, and the political and economic situation in fascist Italy that created a difficult climate for business and a scarcity of primary materials—the autarkic echoes of which resonate down the ages to the newly nationalist and authoritarian age that we now seem to be living in.

But it wasn't, perhaps, as revolutionary as Ferragamo insisted in his patent filings. In his autobiography, he admits that he later learned that the wedge heel had existed since at least the 14th century. When Boccaccio's villa near Florence was excavated after a bomb attack during World War II, nine pair of wedge heel shoes emerged. Ferragamo writes approvingly of them: he might have designed them himself in a previous life, he says. ◆

Further Reading

Carlo Marco Belfanti and Elisabetta Merlo (2016) "Patenting Fashion: Salvatore Ferragamo Between Craftmanship and Industry," *Investigaciones de Historia Económica*, 12(2), pp. 109–119.

Salvatore Ferragamo (1985 [1957]) *Shoemaker of Dreams: The Autobiography of Salvatore Ferragamo*. Florence: Centro Di.

Sofia Gnoli (2014) *The Origins of Italian Fashion, 1900–45*. London: V&A.

Stefania Ricci (ed.) (2004) *Ideas, Models, Inventions: The Patents and Company Trademarks of Salvatore Ferragamo from 1929 to 1964*. Livorno: Sillabe.

Stefania Ricci and Carlo Sisi (2017). *1927 The Return to Italy: Salvatore Ferragamo and the Twentieth-Century Visual Culture*. Milano: Skira Editore.

Om the left: Series of Salvatore Ferragamo shoe prototypes at Palazzo Spini Feroni, Florence, Italy. (Alamy)

25 Aspirin Pill

Catherine Bond

On 30 August 1915, parliamentarian William Kelly took to the floor of the Australian Federal House of Representatives, troubled by an issue that he felt was plaguing the Australian war effort: enemy-owned trademarks.

Kelly could not believe that his fellow countrymen were so willing to promote the property of the enemy, and was adamant that no product bearing such trademarks should be sold in Australian stores:

The point I want to make is, if during the war we kill a trade mark, we can kill the trade absolutely … If, by using the same trade mark, and by still requiring people to ask for the same things, they [the enemy owner] can keep the trade alive until after the war, they will have achieved their purpose. Take the case of aspirin … the public [has] been educated to ask for aspirin, and the enemy want to make the public ask for it until the war is over.

Kelly's statement highlights the power of registered trademarks in early 20th-century consumer culture, and, more specifically, the power of Australian registered

On the left: Argentinian poster for Bayer aspirin, showing a woman lifting off a mask of a crying face to reveal her smiling face. (Achille Mauzan / Library of Congress Prints and Photographs Division)

trademark 829, for the word ASPIRIN. Australia was not the only country that grappled with a reliance on German products and German-owned intellectual property during World War I. Many countries were caught on the horns of this dilemma, and, more often than not, aspirin was at the center of the struggle—as an object, as a product, as a recipient of multiple forms of intellectual property protection. How this object achieved global dominance, and how it continues to maintain a market presence today, is a story that spans multiple countries and centuries.

Like many legends, aspirin—the object, product, and name—has a mythical, disputed origin story. There is no dispute, however, as to the company it originated from: in 1863 Friedrich Bayer and Johann Friedrich Weskott established Friedrich Bayer & Company, entering the lucrative dye market dominating German industry in the mid-19th century. When Bayer and Weskott died—in 1880 and 1876 respectively—the company was taken over by Bayer's son-in-law, Carl Rumpff. Among a group of new employees appointed under

Rumpff was Friedrich Carl Duisberg, commonly known as "Carl," who was originally involved in dye manufacture but ultimately proposed the company's transition to chemical and medicinal research. On Rumpff's death in 1889, Duisberg assumed control of Bayer and, within ten years, the company would create its most famous product—a medicinal remedy named "aspirin."

Until recently, the much-publicized origin story of aspirin involved a sole player, Felix Hoffman. Hoffman was deeply affected by the struggles of his father, who had rheumatism. Doctors had prescribed the father sodium salicylate, which combatted his rheumatic symptoms but irritated his stomach. It was once thought that the son Hoffman created aspirin by himself, inspired by the wish to help his father, but it has since been established that the drug was more likely developed by a trio at

Bayer, comprising Hoffman *fils*, Heinrich Dreser, and Arthur Eichengrün.

Hoffman was a member of Eichengrün's team, which began researching consumable alternatives to salicylic acid around 1897. For centuries, if not thousands of years, naturally occurring versions of this acid—an effective painkiller—had been derived from plant products like meadowsweet or the bark of the willow tree. Still, there had been little success in any chemical reproduction of this composition, at least in ways that would not also corrode the stomach. Hoffman found a way to combine salicylic acid and acetic anhydride, resulting in a form of acetylsalicylic acid that was purer, more stable, and better than any of the alternatives.

After extensive experimentation and testing, with the product nearly ready to enter the market, one issue remained: what

Above: Meadowsweet (filipendula ulmaria): flowering stem. Color nature print by H. Bradbury. (Wellcome Collection, CC BY)

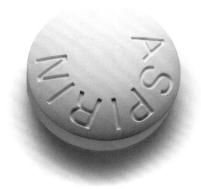

tablets. Product awareness grew as doctors, pharmacists, and, ultimately, consumers began to embrace this remedy that could be used to combat a growing number of medical conditions, including body pain and headaches.

As was the frequent practice of the time, the launch of this product was accompanied by numerous applications for patent registration for the invention itself, and trademark registration for the name. These applications were made in Germany but also in a range of other countries, including Great Britain and the United States. In Britain, patent application 27,088 was lodged on 22 December 1898 and granted to a British resident, Henry Edward Newton. In the United States, Patent No. 644,077—lodged on 1 August 1898 and granted 22 February 1900—was issued to Felix Hoffman. Despite being essentially the same invention, when Bayer initiated infringement action in courts in Britain and the United States, and the defendants countersued for revocation of the patents, those courts reached different opinions on their validity.

In the 1905 English case *Farbenfabriken vormals Friedrich Bayer & Co.* v. *Chemische Fabrik Von Heyden*, Justice Joyce found the plaintiff's patent invalid on account of a lack of novelty, the invention having already been made public in an 1869

Above, left: A nurse dropping an aspirin pill into a glass of water, advertising soluble aspirin. Lithograph by Maurice Cliot, ca. 1910. (Wellcome Collection, CC BY)

Above, right: An aspirin pill. (Getty Images)

should it be called? The chosen name, "aspirin," was a composite: *A* to indicate the acetyl element; *Spiraea*, the Latin name for the genus of plants that included the meadowsweet plant from which naturally occurring salicylic acid was derived; and *In*, a suffix used to help the word roll off the tongue, and one that was widely used to complete medicinal names in the late 19th century. With the name established, the product was launched in July 1899, first in powder form, and then later as

Above: A box of Aspro among falling autumn leaves by Damour, ca. 1930. (Wellcome Collection, CC BY)

article by Kraut and Prinzhorn. In contrast, five years later and across the Atlantic, in *Farbenfabriken of Elberfield Co. v. Kuehmsted*, District Judge Sanborn took note of the British decision but rejected the argument that Kraut's work preempted Hoffman's patent. An appeal to the Seventh Circuit Court of Appeals confirmed the validity of the patent, and a subsequent application to appeal to the US Supreme Court was denied. Thus, at the end of this spate of litigation, Bayer held no patent protection in Britain, but a valuable trademark for the word ASPIRIN; whereas, in the United States it held a valuable trademark for the word, as well as a valid patent.

The ASPIRIN trademark became particularly important when, in 1914, a large majority of countries became involved in the first outbreak of global conflict that would come to be known as World War I. One of the first areas affected by the outbreak of war was international trade, impacting the supply of food, metals, and medicinal products around the world. Allied countries, while resentful of the

success of many German companies like Bayer, were reliant on them for stocks of medicines like aspirin. With no new stock forthcoming, and existing stock selling out, it became apparent to the governments of many Allied countries that the only way to solve the "aspirin crisis" was to give the public an incentive to create new acetylsalicylic products—which is to say, by allowing them to sell such products under the German-owned, ASPIRIN trademark.

This approach manifested itself in two ways. In Britain, the government completely suspended the registered ASPIRIN trademark. Consumers were more familiar with the word "aspirin" than "acetylsalicylic acid," and now any individual or

Above, from left to right: An effervescent tablet. (Getty Images); Roger Moore about to need said effervescent tablet. (Photo by Peter Ruck / BIPs / Getty Images)

business producing this medicine could therefore name the product "aspirin." Unfortunately, few of the locally created aspirin products were as effective as the drug from Bayer.

The other approach to dealing with the ASPIRIN trademark was implemented by the Australian government. When it was announced that the Australian government would suspend enemy-owned intellectual property in favor of local individuals and businesses, many eager parties applied for permission to use the ASPIRIN mark. However, the Australian government established a policy that it would only grant permission to use the trademark where an applicant could prove that he or she had created a product identical to that made by Bayer. The submitted product would be tested by a government chemist to ensure its purity and the consistency of the product, and the applicant would be

able to use the ASPIRIN trademark only after the government official was satisfied.

Enter George Nicholas and Harry Woolf Shmith, two gentlemen who in 1915 successfully produced a local aspirin, identical to its German acetylsalicylic acid counterpart. Nicholas and Shmith were subsequently permitted to use the ASPIRIN trademark. However, production and consumption of the local aspirin waivered as the war progressed, amid concerns that permitting local use of the German-owned trademark was perpetuating goodwill in this enemy brand and associated business. Eventually, the Australian government revoked permission to use the ASPIRIN trademark and the local Australian product was subsequently renamed "Aspro." Ironically, 100 years later, every box of Aspro today features both the "Bayer cross" device trademark and the ASPRO word trademark—the brand having been

E. Ruscha 1971

acquired by Bayer, the company it was intended to usurp.

When the United States joined the war, in April 1917, the Office of Alien Property confiscated all enemy-owned assets, including tangible and intellectual property. A different approach entirely was adopted by the US government in dealing with enemy-owned intellectual property: to ensure a continuing supply of essential enemy-produced products like medicines, it arranged for the sale of a large number of these assets. In late 1918, Sterling Products paid a multimillion-dollar figure to acquire Bayer and its assets, including the ASPIRIN trademark. The 1919 Treaty of Versailles cemented what the United States had done in relation to enemy-owned physical and intellectual property, with little hope for German companies to regain those international assets.

For Sterling Products, aspirin was both a blessing and a curse. The product was in constant demand, but its German origins immediately brought the war to mind. This problem was illustrated when, in 1921, Judge Learned Hand limited the context in which the ASPIRIN trademark could be used. In *Bayer Co., Inc.* v. *United Drug Co.*, Hand found that physicians and pharmacists associated the term "aspirin" with the Bayer product, but consumers of the product considered the term to mean any acetylsalicylic acid product. As a result, where a product was marketed toward consumers, anyone could use the word "aspirin"; a finding which presumably took some of the shine off Sterling's multimillion-dollar acquisition.

In the interwar period, the German pharmaceutical and chemical industry not only recovered, but ultimately regained global dominance. In the mid-1920s Bayer was one of six German companies to merge into a conglomerate known as Interessengemeinschaft Farbenindustrie

Above: Aspirins, 1971, gunpowder and pastel on paper, 29.2 × 73.7 cm, Los Angeles County Museum of Art; gift of the Modern and Contemporary Art Council.
(Photograph © 2002 Museum Associates / LACMA
© Ed Ruscha)

Aktiengesellschaft, more commonly known as "IG Farben." Carl Duisberg, responsible for so much of the success of the aspirin product, helped facilitate the merger and subsequently became an IG Farben board member. While each company continued to make its own products—Bayer continued to produce aspirin—IG Farben achieved both worldwide success and immense fame and privilege within Germany, becoming a contributor to and beneficiary under the Nazi regime.

After World War II, IG Farben—like its country of origin—was investigated, and ultimately divided. In the early 1950s Bayer regrouped and reappeared, and as the century progressed it once again became one of the dominant players in the world pharmaceutical market. While paracetamol and ibuprofen have subsequently come to dominate the consumer painkiller market over the course of the 20th century, studies today are still establishing new and beneficial uses of aspirin, particularly in reducing the occurrence and impact of stroke and heart disease.

A century ago, William Kelly may have had the best intentions in seeking to kill the ASPIRIN trademark. But as an object, aspirin continues to yield benefits for both its owner and the community to this day. ◆

Further Reading

David B. Jack (1997) "One hundred years of Aspirin," *The Lancet*, 350, pp. 437–439.

Diarmuid Jeffreys (2005) *Aspirin: The Remarkable Story of a Wonder Drug*. New York: Bloomsbury.

Kathryn Steen (2014) *The American Synthetic Organic Chemicals Industry: War and Politics, 1910–1930*. Chapel Hill, NC: University of North Carolina Press.

1800　　　　　　　1900　　　　　　2000

--/-----/-----/-----/-----/-----/----/-/-----/-----/-----/-----/-----/----

26 Bell Transistor
Beth Webster

On the left: Replica of the first working transistor invented in 1947 by John Bardeen, William Shockley, and Walter Brattain at Bell Laboratories in the United States. They discovered that by placing two contacts close together on the surface of a crystal of germanium, through which an electric current was flowing, a device that acted as an amplifier was produced. (Photo by SSPL / Getty Images)

The transistor is arguably one of the most profound enabling technologies to be invented in the 20th century. It enhances long-distance telephony and forms the basis of the microchips that enable computers. Without transistors we would not have computers, the internet, cloud computing, artificial intelligence, or the emerging "internet of things." In fact, I would not be writing this entry on my PC.

The story of how the transistor was developed is a classic case of big business technological development: problem-driven research, scientific jealousy, egg-shell egos, government largesse, bonhomie, betrayal, the power of induction over deduction, savvy research management, and the emergence of what we nowadays call "Silicon Valley." The transistor spawned major enterprises for those who had both the early insight to spot its technical potential and the skill to manage people. Our story also fills that sweet juncture of successful curiosity-driven discovery and use-driven research.

Transistors are tiny switches. If triggered by electricity they can do two things: amplify sounds—hence the transistor radio or "tranny" that burst onto the consumer market in the mid-1950s—or store information in binary format. Millions of transistors can record millions of zeros and ones. Combined with the mathematics described by Shannon's Information Theory, these binary numbers can record integers, letters, sentences, and a range of information. If you can miniaturize the size of the transistor, a single chip can contain billions of them and thus store considerable information.

Transistors were invented to solve the telephonic problem of sound amplification. In the 1930s, Mervin Kelly, the research director of the research and development arm of AT&T—the famed Bell Labs—recognized that the telephone market was not going to grow unless there was a better way to amplify sound over long distances. He felt that the answer might lie in a newly discovered class of materials called semiconductors. In 1936, he hired Bill Shockley to pursue this idea.

Although Kelly appointed a whole scientific team to work with Shockley, two

people were pivotal: John Bardeen, a theoretical physicist, and Walter Brattain, an experimental physicist. The whole team was close-knit, but in December 1947 Bardeen and Brattain jointly made the first practical transistor, a device known as a point-contact transistor. Shockley had played a large part in the project but he was furious at their partnership and felt excluded. Shortly afterwards, in an action arguably motivated by spite, he single-handedly made an advance on this early transistor and developed the junction transistor, a much better device than the Bardeen–Brattain transistor.

What had begun as an amicable and productive collaboration descended into bitterness, recriminations, and lawyers. As is common when an idea is built on complementary inputs, all of which are necessary but none of them individually sufficient for a working whole, the allocation of credit became muddled and disputed. Shockley began a major campaign with Bell Labs' lawyers to patent the transistor exclusively under his own name. Shockley believed that Bardeen and Brattain had betrayed him by taking his ideas without credit, and he subsequently kept Bardeen and Brattain as far removed from his own work as possible.

Three patents were filed. The Bardeen and Brattain transistor patent was filed on 17 June 1948 followed shortly by Shockley's patent on 26 June 1948, and a subsequent Shockley patent in September 1948. The assignee in each case was Bell Labs.

Timing is everything. These were not the first patents for transistors, just the most celebrated. Austrian-Hungarian physicist Julius Edgar Lilienfeld filed a patent in Canada in 1925, but his work was ignored by industry. German physicist Oskar Heil patented a transistor in

Above, from left to right: Nobel Prize-winning American physicists John Bardeen, William Shockley, and Walter Brattain. (Photo by Hulton Archive / Getty Images)

Above: Female employees using microscopes to view transistors on the OC81 line at the Southampton factory of Mullard Electronics, 1961. (Photo by Walter Nurnberg / SSPL / Getty Images)

1934 but also appeared to be ignored by industry. Arns has argued these discoveries were overlooked because the timing was wrong. At the time, the vacuum tube provided sufficient sound amplification and the Depression had reduced business appetite for high-risk investment. World War II changed this. Developments in radio, radar, and electronically controlled weapons had shown that electronics could reliably handle both complexity and size within the envelope of lower power requirements.

According to Arns, affidavits from the Bell Labs patent show that Shockley had built operational versions from Lilienfeld's patents but never cited him. Both the Bardeen–Brattain and Shockley patents had examiner-only citations to Lilienfeld's patents, as Bell Labs' patent attorneys had deliberately omitted to cite them.

Although much has been written about the personalities involved in the creation of the transistor, considerable credit should be given to the organization that funded and managed the research. The 20th century was the heyday for grand research in large for-profit R&D labs. In the United States, there were the descendants of the Edison industrial research laboratory—notably General Electric, and the Radio Corporation of America—as well as similar labs that developed in General Motors, IBM, Kodak, and Du Pont. In Europe there was Marconi, ICI, AEG, IG Farben, BASF, and Bayer, among others. These companies challenged the idea that basic research was not profitable for industry and therefore had to be undertaken through an open-science organization, such as a university or nationally-run laboratory. Their success

also runs counter to the economists' theory that monopolies will become lazy and technologically inefficient. The creation and translation of frontier technologies at Bell Labs was truly astounding.

Gertner suggests that much of this success should be attributed to the embedded culture of technological leadership at AT&T and the insight and acumen of the director of research Mervin Kelly. Early in the 20th century, AT&T realized that low costs and superior quality was the only way it could keep competitors at bay, and the only way it could meet these strategic goals was through investment in technology. The company's size—its revenues were, in some cases, greater than those of some nation states—gave it the capacity to not only invest patiently in basic science but also to translate this science into commercial products. Kelly realized as early as the 1930s that amplification technologies were going to limit market demand and new, radical solutions would be needed. He had a hunch that this solution lay with the newly discovered semi-conductor materials and the emerging field of solid-state physics.

Kelly's formula was simple: hire the best people, point them in the right direction,

and leave them alone. Behind the scenes it was not that simple. He was dictatorial about the organizational structure and the layout of the office. In fact, the whole New Jersey campus of Bell Labs was designed to encourage physical connections between groups. He made sure people bumped into each other. The magic of invention could not be concocted in formal, codified terms.

With this said, invention isn't all magic, and is clearly not just a matter of effort. As the earlier transistor patents show, lone inventors with limited access to colleagues who can improve and refine their ideas, and complementary technologies, are less likely to succeed. Successful innovators not only need an appropriate composition of supply-side ingredients, but they also need control over market demand to ensure a reasonable payback. In this respect, AT&T shored up its downstream markets using both the patent system, vertical integration, and its nexus with the government's defense needs.

Funding for the discovery and development of the transistor, as well as other notable Bell inventions—such as the solar cell and the laser—hinged on compliance and collaboration with the US government.

On the left: An assortment of transistors, 1961. (Bettmann / Getty Images)

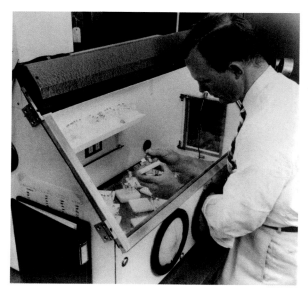

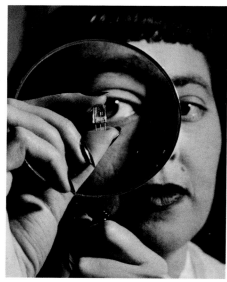

The US government tolerated AT&T's many telephone monopolies in part because its research worked for the public interest. To protect its monopoly profits from anti-trust legislation, the company needed to show it was civic minded. Hence, by a consent decree, it licensed the transistor patents to manufacturing competitors.

Of course, this was not entirely about civic duty. By harnessing the skills of many manufacturers, AT&T reduced the costs of transistors and found new uses and thus more demand for them. According to Watzinger and others, generous licensing deals led to widespread use of the technology, but not to follow-on invention within the telecommunications industry. Follow-on invention was curtailed not by the patent system, but by the vertically integrated monopoly power of AT&T.

The government also assisted AT&T in another profound way. It gave Bell Labs military contracts to create and develop frontier technologies. These contracts, which emphasized quality over cost, underwrote the high-risk, high-cost end of many innovations that later metamorphosed into civilian use.

Our transistor story does not end with Bell Labs. Shockley became increasingly difficult to work with. He left Bell Labs and returned home to Palo Alto to set up his own transistor-making company. Although it was not commercially successful, two of his employees, Robert Noyce and Gordon Moore, went on to found Intel, the world's biggest microchip manufacturer.

Bardeen, Brattain, and Shockley shared the 1956 Nobel Prize in Physics. Nothing was heard of Lilienfeld and Heil again. ◆

Further Reading

Robert G. Arns (1998) "The Other Transistor: Early History of the Metal–Oxide–Semiconductor Field-Effect

Above, left: A "dry box," a dust proof compartment that eliminates possible contamination by dirt, is used by an engineer to assemble new miniature ultra-high frequency transistors at Bell Laboratories. (Bettmann / Getty Images)

Above, right: A lab technician using a magnifying glass to inspect a new transistor the revolutionary electronic amplifier, 1948. (Bettmann / Getty Images)

Above: Transistor radio being used swinging from monkey bars. In the 1950s transistors began to replace thermionic valves in radio receivers, allowing much smaller, more affordable portable radios to be produced. (Photo by A.Y. Owen / The LIFE Images Collection / Getty Images)

Transistor," *Engineering Science and Education Journal*, 7(5), pp. 233–240.

Christopher Freeman (1998) "Technology and Invention," in Richard Bulliet (ed.) *The Columbia History of the 20th Century*. New York: Columbia University Press, pp. 314–344.

Jon Gertner (2013) *The Idea Factory: Bell Labs and the Great Age of American Innovation*. New York: Penguin.

Martin Watzinger, Thomas Fackler, Markus Nagler, and Monika Schnitzer (2017) "How Antitrust Enforcement Can Spur Innovation: Bell Labs and the 1956 Consent Decree," *CEPR Discussion Paper No. 11793*. Available at: https://cepr.org/active/publications/discussion_papers/dp.php?dpno=11793

US Patent No. 1,745,175 (issued Jan. 28, 1930), "Method and apparatus for controlling electric current," describing a device similar to a MESFET.

GB Patent No. 439,457 (first filed in Germany on Mar. 2, 1934), "Improvements in or relating to electrical amplifiers and other control arrangements and devices."

US Patent No. 2,502,488 (issued Apr. 4, 1950), "Semiconductor amplifier."

US Patent No. 2,524,035 (issued Oct. 3, 1950), "Three-electrode circuit element utilizing semiconducting materials."

US Patent No. 2,569,347 (issued Sept. 25, 1951), "Circuit element utilizing semi-conductive material."

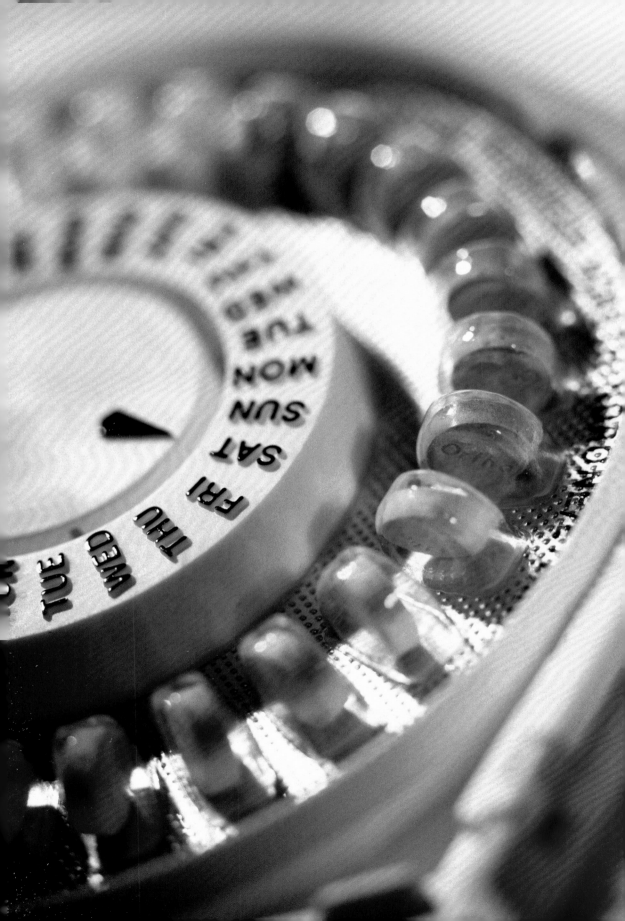

--- *The Consumption Age*

-- *Patent*

- *United States*

1800   *1900*   *2000*

--/-----/-----/-----/-----/-----/-----/-----/-----/-----/-----/-----/----

225

27 Oral Contraceptive Pill

Melanie Brown

IN THE CENTURY since women were finally granted the right to vote, the women's liberation movement has continued to demand equality between the sexes. The recent "Time's Up" and #MeToo campaigns highlight that these issues are still far from resolved, but it was in the 1960s that the single biggest revolution for women occurred. It transformed women's lives across the globe, and was central to the revolutionary gains that women made throughout the 1960s, 1970s, and 1980s. It was, of course, the development of the Pill.

The first version of the Pill, Enovid, was licensed as a contraceptive in the United States in 1960. It contains artificial versions of estrogen and progesterone, hormones that occur naturally in women. It mimics the effects of pregnancy by preventing ovulation, thickening cervical mucus to create a barrier to prevent sperm from reaching the womb, and by thinning the lining of the womb, which lowers the chance of a fertilized egg implanting itself. These combined effects mean that a woman has only a 1 percent chance of becoming pregnant when using the pill as intended. This success rate drops slightly when used imperfectly, but is still more successful than other contraceptives.

The social campaign for contraception arguably started with the social activist Margaret Sanger, who had been campaigning for women's rights to contraception for a long time before the Pill was invented. In 1916, she opened the first birth control clinic in the United States, and for a number of years, she was repeatedly arrested and jailed for maintaining a "public nuisance"; but she reopened the clinic each time she was released.

The political push for better birth control operated in conjunction with medical and pharmaceutical research. Progesterone was identified as the vital hormone for preventing ovulation in the 1930s. Methods for extracting progesterone from yams were developed, but the dosage had to be extremely high to work as a contraceptive. Progestin could be derived from progesterone, and could be given as a contraceptive in much smaller doses. Various individuals sought to invent a contraceptive pill using a synthetic progestin, but it was the Mexican

On the left: Oral contraceptive pills with an indication for the days of the week. (Getty Images)

chemist Luis Miramontes who led the way. Using yams, he generated a semi-synthesis of the hormone progesterone, a progestin called norethindrone. In conjunction with his co-inventors at Laboratorios Syntex SA, Carl Djerassi and George Rosenkranz, he filed a patent application for the invention in Mexico in 1951.

The race to be the first to market the drug was on. Syntex's research had led the way, but the company faced difficulty in finding a manufacturing company in the United States, due to various legal and religious issues. Sanger reappears here, along with Gregory Pincus, an endocrinologist, and John Rock, a gynecologist. Sanger convinced Pincus to develop a contraceptive pill, and Rock worked with him, as he had already been testing chemical contraceptives with his patients. This research was underwritten by Katherine McCormack, a wealthy feminist activist.

The efforts of Sanger, Rock, Pincus, and McCormack led to development of a separate semi-synthetic progestin called northynodrel. This was licensed to GD Searle, which brought the first commercially available Pill to market under the name "Enovid." Searle had beaten Syntex, and went on to reap the financial rewards. The drug was first approved by the US FDA in 1957 for "menstrual disorders," but was finally approved as a contraceptive in 1960 following extensive social campaigning. The path to widespread use was, inevitably, hampered by social conservatism and religious concerns. A 1965 Supreme Court decision granted married couples the right to use the Pill, but this right did not extend to unmarried women. Finally, in 1972, the Supreme Court in *Baird* v. *Eisenstadt* legalized birth control for all women in the United States, regardless of marital status.

The role of intellectual property in the success of the Pill wasn't limited to patents over the drug itself. There were also patents for the Pill's dispensers, which represented the first pharmaceutical compliance packaging in the world. David Wagner patented two Pill dispensers in 1964, one circular and one rectangular. His invention came about as a way of helping his wife remember if she had taken her Pill that day. The

Above, from left to right: Some of the less successful forms of contraception; a stem pessary, a contraceptive sponge, and a cervical cap. (Science Museum, London / Wellcome Collection, CC BY)

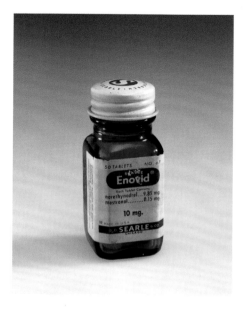

Above, right: Bottle of Enovid tabs 10mg, early 1960s. (Photo by Science Museum / SSPL / Getty Images)

large pharmaceutical companies refused to license his design, instead developing their own, very similar, products. Wagner sued them for infringement, eventually settling out of court.

The formulation of the Pill was still being refined by scientists throughout the 1960s, partly to increase efficiency, but also to lower production costs. Herchel Smith innovated a fully synthetic method for producing progestins, without the need to harvest progesterone from yams. This led to the development in 1968 of Ovral, the first contraceptive made only with synthetic hormones. The connection between intellectual property and the Pill continued: Herchel Smith eventually used the royalties from his patent to endow academic positions in the study of intellectual property at Cambridge and Queen Mary University of London.

The Pill also revolutionized safety standards for pharmaceuticals. The initial testing of northynodrel occurred in Puerto Rico, where there were no laws banning contraceptives. These tests are widely considered now to have been unethical and exploitative, because of the severe side effects of the initial versions of the Pill. These side effects were ignored not only for the women in the study, but also later when drug companies pushed for the Pill to be approved. The side effects were similar to those experienced by women today, such as significant mood swings and nausea, but these were far more severe in the early version of the drug due to the higher dosages. The most severe side effect was an increase in blood clotting, and three women died during the trials. Many more women were injured or killed in the subsequent years of commercial use, and eventually regulators and pharmaceutical companies woke up to the problem. Due to concerns about the serious side effects of the Pill, the dosages of estrogen and progesterone were significantly lowered at the beginning of the 1970s. It was from these challenges from feminists in 1970 that pharmaceutical companies started to include information leaflets discussing possible side effects in all drugs.

If the Pill had a profound effect on intellectual property and pharmaceutical safety, its social impact has been colossal. It enabled a woman to make decisions about her own body and her life choices, something men had been able to do for centuries. A woman could, for the first time, choose whether or not she wished to have children—either delaying pregnancy, or choosing not to have children at all. This signaled a pivotal shift in society in gender roles: a woman was no longer duty-bound to bear as many children as possible as soon as she was married, but could decide to pursue a professional career. She could, of course, choose not to have that career and instead raise a household of children. Or choose when to have that household of children. Either way, she had the ability to *choose*.

This led to a range of options for both women, and for couples. They could choose not to have children for a range of reasons: to avoid passing on mental or physical conditions, because they already had children, because of complications that some women can suffer in pregnancy, for lifestyle choices or for careers, or because they simply didn't want children. For the first time it also allowed women to protect against pregnancy if forced into sex, either during a sexual assault or whilst in an abusive relationship.

In this way the Pill was revolutionary. The ability to choose increased opportunities for women to study for advanced degrees and to begin careers in typically male-dominated fields such as medicine, law, business, and the sciences. A study by economists Goldin and Katz in 2002 showed that as each US state allowed women to access the Pill freely, the percentage of women studying for professional courses raised dramatically, as did their wages. This widening of access to professional study has continued to the present day. In 2009, an article in *The Economist* found that women had earned 60 percent of all undergraduate degrees across the United States and Europe,

On the right, from left to right: The first DialPak manufactured by the Ortho Pharmaceutical Corporation of Raritan, NJ, in 1963 The DialPak, designed by Wagner, contained a monthly regimen of 20 white pills. The DialPak was the first oral contraceptive package to incorporate a "memory aid," which Ortho advertised as "the

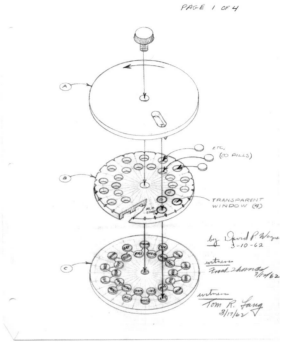

ackage that remembers 'or her." The circular calendar in the center f the DialPak reveals he day of the week nd aligns with a pill n the outer ring. The user turned the dial to 'ispense the next pill, nd the user could eadily see if she had aken her daily pill; Vagner's original rawing of dispenser, 1962. (Division f Medicine and Science, National Museum of American History, Smithsonian nstitution)

especially in the United Kingdom, Denmark, and Germany.

The effect of the Pill on female empowerment via higher education can be seen in the difference between these numbers and the cases of Italy and Japan. In those two countries men still have a 20 percent lead in the workforce participation. Although there are a range of reasons why this might be so, there is a strong correlation between the low employment rate for women in these countries and their historic resistance to the Pill. Italy's strong Catholic beliefs have led to opposition to contraception, with a 2015 UN study finding that only 48.9 percent of women in Italy were using modern contraceptives such as the Pill. This is in contrast to 72.2 percent of women in France and Switzerland.

With a similar gender-inequality rating as Italy, Japan is remarkable in that it only approved the Pill in 1999, decades after the rest of the world. An indication of the gendered nature of pharmaceutical regulation can be seen in the difference in the speed of approval for the Pill and for Viagra in Japan. Women had to wait almost 40 years to access the Pill after its invention. A few months after Viagra was approved in the United States, Japan approved it, too.

The Pill has evidently had a massive impact on women's liberty and economic independence, but it has also impacted on society as a whole. The close ties between the law and the church began to weaken, with changes in legislation in many countries now legalizing contraception and abortion. This divorce from the church and religious doctrine led the way for future

liberalizations of the law, including decriminalizing homosexuality, criminalizing marital rape, and legislation outlawing discrimination in the workplace.

The Pill has proven its usefulness beyond being a contraceptive; its hormone content has been useful for some women to treat severe acne, to regulate and lighten heavy periods that interfere with a woman's daily life, and to ease the symptoms of PCOS and endometriosis. But now, almost 60 years after the Pill was first made available to women, its significance and usage are once again under scrutiny. Due to concerns about the side effects of the Pill (indeed, of any pharmaceuticals) and a rise in the number of women seeking more natural, healthy lifestyles, some women are now choosing not to take the Pill. There are concerns about its extensive possible side effects and links to some cancers.

Whilst some critics might view this as an indicator that it is losing significance for women, this slight decline in usage is rather the Pill's greatest legacy: women can choose what to do with their bodies, and women are able to question the authority of the state, the church, and pharmaceutical companies in deciding what is best for them. The Pill's invention was a major breakthrough in the medical and intellectual property fields, but it is its enduring liberalization for women that has been its most significant success. ◆

Further Reading

Claudia Goldin and Lawrence Katz (2002) "The Power of the Pill: Oral Contraceptives and Women's Career and Marriage Decisions," *Journal of Political Economy*, 110(4), pp. 730–770.

Tim Harford (2017) *Fifty Things that Made the Modern Economy*. London: Little, Brown.

Lara Marks (2010) *Sexual Chemistry: A History of the Contraceptive Pill*. New Haven: Yale University Press.

United Nations, Department of Economic and Social Affairs, Population Division (2015) *Trends in Contraceptive Use Worldwide 2015* (ST/ESA/SER.A/349).

On the left: Belly of a pregnant woman. (Getty Images)

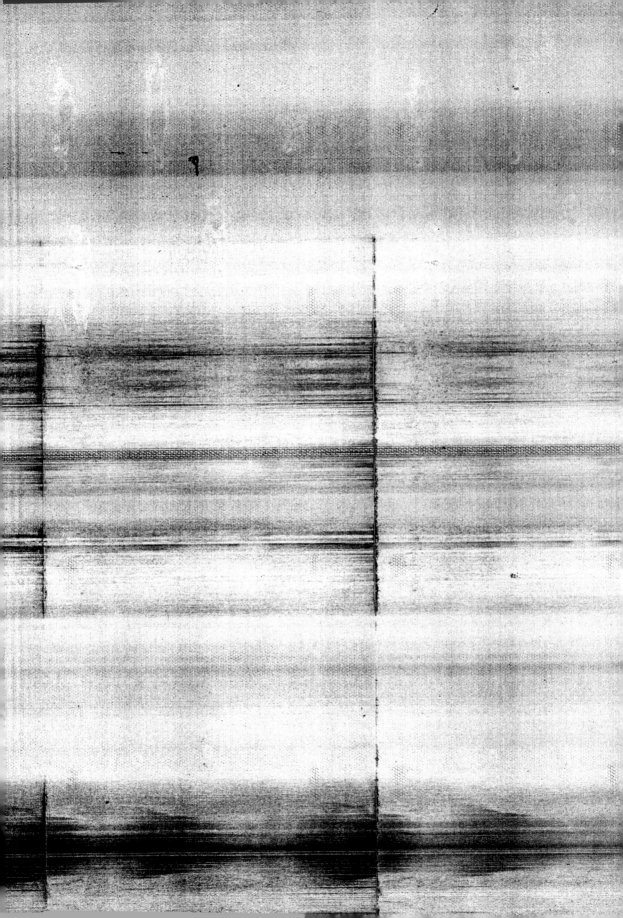

1800   *1900*   *2000*

--/-----/-----/-----/-----/-----/-----/-----/-----/-----/-----/-----/----

28 Photocopier
Jessica Silbey

THE STORY OF the invention of the photocopy machine—or the "Xerox machine" as many call it—dramatizes both cherished and contested features of intellectual property. It dramatizes the myth of the lone inventor, here Chester Carlson, born poor and disadvantaged, who made his fortune from the invention but not before toiling in a patent office and in his own start-up for decades. But the development of the Xerox machine is also the story of collaboration and teamwork, which is essential to most innovation with social impact. The origin of the Xerox machine demonstrates how need, a passion for puzzles, and the creative spirit motivate everyday inventors. And its success in the marketplace implicates the role of business leverage and profit in productive creativity and innovation. The story is about rivals and claims of stealing ideas as well as about inevitable influence and borrowing, both which structure and inform incremental and ground-breaking invention. And if these tensions aren't enough, the intellectual property that protected the Xerox machine forbids copying and yet the Xerox

On the left: A photocopy. (Getty Images)

machine is used to make copies. While the Xerox machine is a tool for making exact copies, it often facilitates transformative creativity from innumerable writers, artists, and musicians. The story of the Xerox machine is a microcosm of debates surrounding the proper purpose and scope of intellectual property and an object lesson in how irreconcilable dualities inform the everyday practice of intellectual property.

Chester ("Chet") Floyd Carlson was born in Seattle, Washington in February 1906 into a family struggling with illness and poverty. Until he left for college, Chet looked after his parents both physically and financially. In high school, he fell in love with science. An early gift of a typewriter from his aunt and, later, the hand-cramping he experienced from verbatim copying of science and law books while taking night classes to advance his career prospects, made him dream of a device that could swiftly produce and copy text. In college, Chet studied physics and chemistry, as well as law, eventually moving to New York to work in the patent department of P.R. Mallory & Co., a manufacturer of electrical components. It was while working by day in that patent department and by night in his home laboratory in Astoria, Queens, when he invented the copying machine. As he describes it: "with the problem so sharply defined, the solution came almost as an intuitive flash."

And yet, the Xerox machine was not invented by one person alone. Although the idea of the copy machine arguably originates with Chet, he did not succeed with his experimentation and prototypes until partnering in 1938 with Otto Kornei, a young German physicist. Together, on 22 October 1938, they made the first xerographic copy on a piece of wax paper, which today is displayed in the Smithsonian Museum of American History. And in 1945, Chet partnered with Battelle Memorial Institute (a private nonprofit research company) to shepherd and develop his invention on which he had already filed several patents. In 1948, the first public demonstration of xerography was given jointly by Battelle, the Optical Society of America and the Haloid Company (a Rochester, New York-based photo-paper company that would later become Xerox). The term "xerography" was coined by a classics professor consulting for Haloid—it derives from the Greek *xero* (dry) and *graph* (write). In 1950, Haloid began selling xerographic equipment and in 1952, Haloid trademarked the term "Xerox" for its line of copying machines. Reducing the invention to practice and bringing it to the public for productive, efficient, and widespread use and sale was a team effort.

Chet retired in Rochester a comfortably wealthy man because of the patent royalties he shared with Battelle and Haloid and the stock he owned in Haloid. The patent that brought him the most money covered an invention in the 914-model machine, released in 1959, the success of which was due largely to its user-friendly design and its low operating costs (it did not require

special paper). Further, Haloid's business model was based on renting the machines, making the machine affordable for most businesses and thus facilitating its wide distribution. The 914 took off and Chet retired shortly thereafter. He described his financial success as satisfying, but not nearly as rewarding as seeing his initial dream of developing a working and usable copy machine to solve everyday problems brought to fruition and the public. From his early days working in an office, to his struggles with hand-cramps as a student, and his later trials with prototypes that failed, the actualization of the affordable desktop copy machine was a dream come true:

The need for a quick, satisfactory copying machine that could be used right in the office seemed apparent [...]—there seemed such a crying need for it—such a desirable thing if it could be obtained. So I set out to think of how one could be made.

Chet was addressing a real need in the world, playing with physical, chemical and manufacturing puzzles and driven by a passion for science and engineering and the desire to design useful products for ordinary tasks. Motivated intrinsically, Chet was also rewarded with substantial financial wealth for his copy-machine inventions because of the collaboration and financial support of Battelle and Haloid, which were essential to bringing the 914 to offices around the world. Although the patent reward and the wealth it may bring inventors is often considered the principal incentive for innovation, Chet's story and the development of the xerography machine as a ground-breaking invention for everyday use tells a more complicated tale about internal drive, personal commitments, and collaborative enterprises. Remember Otto Kornei, who worked with Chet in 1938 in his Astoria "laboratory"

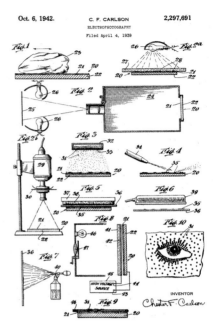

Above, left: Chester Carlson standing next to woman using the dry copying process that he invented. (Getty Images)

Above, right: Carlson's patent for electrophotography, later called xerography, which would eventually revolutionize office copying; US Patent No. 2,297,691.

On the following pages: Everyone's fun at the office—a face on a photocopier. (Alamy)

(a space that was really Chet's mother-in-law's apartment)? Kornei left shortly after helping build the successful prototype to work at IBM. Thirty years later, IBM introduced a competitor xerographic office copier and Haloid (now called Xerox) sued IBM on 21 April 1970 for patent infringement. Xerox eventually won this lawsuit, but it dragged on for years, in part "because the invention of xerography had made it possible for lawyers to turn pretrial discovery into an open-ended orgy of photocopying." One of the other ironies of the lawsuit was that Chet himself borrowed and developed ideas from previous inventors, such as the Hungarian physicist Paul Selenyi, from whose research papers Chet drew substantial information and inspiration, and who himself competes for the title of "father of xerography." Origins

of ideas cannot be traced to a single person or moment, and yet Chet's patents, licensed to Xerox, named him the inventor and not Kornei as a joint-inventor or Selenyi as the grandfather of the original idea. Intellectual property is a grant of title in an invention or creative expression to one person or a group of persons, despite the inevitable reality that all innovation and creativity is iterative and borrows from what came before.

Chet licensed his patents to Battelle and Haloid, which leveraged the time-limited patent exclusivity to prevent competitors (such as IBM) from making close copies of the copy-machine and from diminishing its market dominance. For decades, the patents and Xerox's related market dominance prevented competitors from building machines similar to the Xerox machine, which competition would have reduced the price of the machines and provided consumers with more choices. Not until the patents expired did we see effective competitors. To be sure, Chet, Battelle, and Haloid benefited from the patent protection, but whether the decades

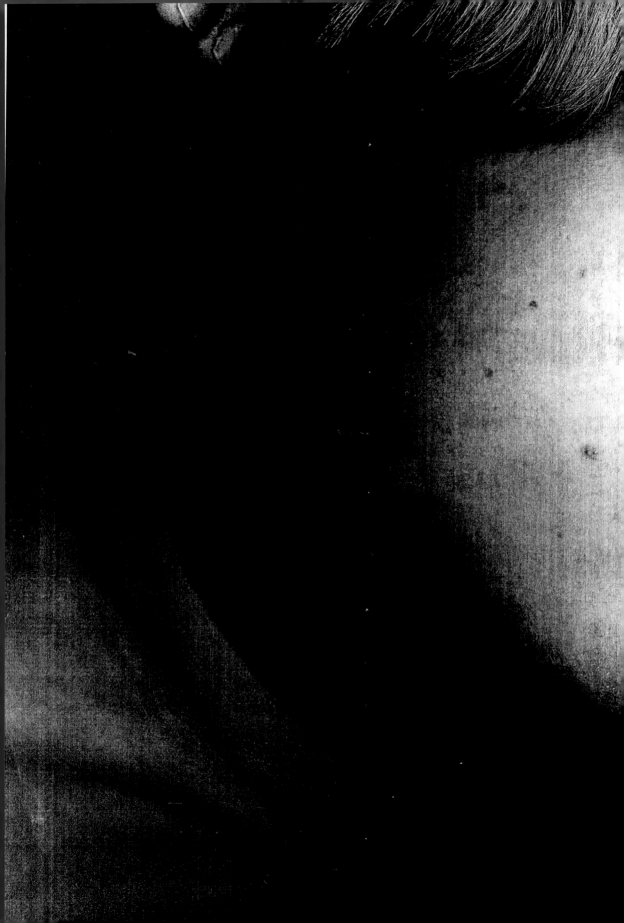

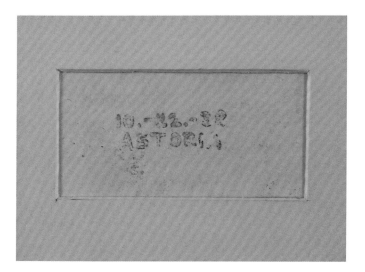

of lost competition was essential to the progress of science and the useful arts as intellectual property is intended remains an important question.

It is ironic that the original copy-machine that could not be copied was built to make copies—copies of texts, photographs, and even instructions for making or using copying machines. And for this reason, although Xerox closely protected its patents from infringement by competitors, the patented technology facilitated infringement of other intellectual property, such as copyrights. It took the 1984 Supreme Court decision *Sony Corporation of America* v. *Universal City Studios* concerning the legality of the video-cassette recording (VCR) machine to clarify that the makers of the copy-machines such as the Xerox, as well as of other "staple articles of commerce" such as cameras, typewriters, and audio recorders, were not liable for their contribution to copyright infringement stemming from the use of the copy-facilitating invention. But today, still, *users* of these machines remain liable for intellectual property infringement depending on the nature of their use of the copies made. In other words, copy-shops and their customers may be copyright infringers, but Chet's copying invention that could not be copied (until the patent expired) remains immune from liability for the copying it facilitates.

The distinction between users and device manufacturers still frame conflicts between stakeholders, such as between the Recording Industry Association of America and music audiences (including downloaders), or the Motion Picture Association of America and movie audiences (including those who share, stream and record video files). All means of recording, storing, and streaming copyrighted work, from MP3 players to peer-to-peer file sharing networks, have roots in copying devices such as the Xerox machine and the conflicts over their design.

Chet's original conception of the copy-machine was to assist with business, education, and research. He imagined verbatim copying for productive uses. Quickly, however, the copy-machine was put to all sorts of uses, many verbatim and productive, some frivolous, and countless transformative and new. In 1967, John Brooks wrote in the *New Yorker* that "one rather odd use of xerography insures that brides get the wedding presents they want" now that stores with bridal registries are equipped with Xerox copiers and lists can be made, remade, and distributed with ease. Photocopying was also a tool for art. Place objects on the plate glass and you don't know what will come out, but surely something provocative and fun. As Pati Hill, an artist who used photocopiers as paint and brush, said: "When I show [the copier] a

Above: First electrostatic Xerox print. (Photographic History Collection, Smithsonian's National Museum of American History)

Above: Pati Hill installing "Common Objects" at Kornblee Gallery, New York, 1975. (Photo: Rollie McKenna; Courtesy Estate of Pati Hill)

hair curler it hands me back a space ship, and when I show it the inside of a straw hat it describes the eerie joys of a descent into a volcano." In addition to quotidian and high art, the photocopier facilitated justice. Famously, Daniel Ellsberg used a copier to reproduce the Pentagon Papers. And grass-roots organizations like ACT-UP gained traction because they could plaster their fliers (made at the day jobs of the organizers) all over the streets of New York City. Where would leafleting and political organizing be today, to say nothing of do-it-yourself publishing and the possibilities of self-expression, without copy-technology? Marshall McLuhan wrote in 1966: "Xerography is bringing a reign of terror into the world of publishing, because it means that every reader can be both author and publisher." And that is a good thing. Patented copy-technology birthed the explosion of copying for everyone. And copying, far from producing copy-cats, transformed the world.

The intellectual property history of xerography demonstrates that copying, which intellectual property rights prevent, is better promoted than prevented. It is a story about how intellectual property's contested boundaries are and should be flexible given the contrasts that animate its realities. And

it is a story about how problems, puzzles, collaborations, and change promote innovation and creativity. ◆

Further Reading

David Owen (2004) *Copies in Seconds: How a Lone Inventor and an Unknown Company Created the Biggest Communication Breakthrough Since Gutenberg. Chester Carlson and the Birth of Xerox.* New York: Simon & Schuster.

Meredith Sellers (2016) "The Personal and Poetic Prints of a Female Pioneer of Copier Art," *www.hyperallergic.com*, 20 April. Available at: https://hyperallergic. com/292378/the-personal-and-poetic-prints-of-a-female-pioneer-of-copier-art/

Jessica Silbey (2015) *The Eureka Myth: Creators, Innovators and Everyday Intellectual Property.* Palo Alto: Stanford University Press.

Clive Thompson (2015) "How The Photocopier Changed the Way We Worked—and Played," *The Smithsonian Magazine*, March.

William Yardley (2014) "Pati Hill: An Author Turned Artist Dies at 93," *New York Times*, 24 September, p. A29.

29 Elstar Apple

Jeroen Scharroo

A T THE FOOT of the Tian Shan mountains in central Asia, wild trees grow. By the end of each summer the trees are full of fruits, in colors that range from yellow to red, and in size from that of a marble to that of a tennis ball. Some are inedibly bitter and sour, but some are sweet and aromatic. Our ancestors' preference for the sweet, large, and attractive specimens of the wild apple—*Malus sieversi*—led to the sorts of modern apples we now know and love. But when people first plucked apples from trees over 10,000 years ago, they surely gave little thought to the debates that would emerge of the intellectual property of apple species, and presumably never considered the way that millennia of breeding would be a vital aspect of food security in the 21st century. Yet, the way that we have domesticated apples and how we have chosen to protect apple varieties is deeply significant to our ability to feed humanity.

It would be difficult to reconstruct the birth of the modern apple, but the processes were likely very similar to the methods applied to other agricultural crops. Gatherers took the tastiest apples to their settlements and shared them with their communities to eat. Careless, they threw away the cores, allowing new trees to grow close to their home, where others could continue to pick them and continue the cycle. Generation after generation, our ancestors nurtured the trees bearing tasty and sweet apples, favoring those whose yields were high, and culling the poor producers. Over time this selection process led to a grouping of early domesticated apples.

From their home in central Asia, apples traveled the Silk Road to the West. Along the way, apple cores and seeds ended up beside the road, and the trees from this migration cross-bred with local, wild apple varieties. These crosses often happened with the European crabapple *Malus sylvestris*, leading eventually to our current species of apple, appropriately named *Malus domestica*. We know that medieval monks in Europe devoted themselves to the cultivation of tasty new apple varieties, and took as parent material the apples that grew in the neighborhood or those that they could readily exchange with other monasteries.

The serendipitous crossbreeding of apples was noticed and so, in time, enthusiasts, farmers, and horticulturists consciously took up the breeding of apples. These breeders all made free use of the work of previous breeders—after all, the seeds from the core of a tasty apple are all one needs to begin growing an apple tree. Breeders could easily cross two promising parents, from which they could select the offspring's best specimens to breed further. In the 19th and 20th centuries, breeders freely used the available varieties as parent material without worrying about their origin or ownership. And thanks to modern legislation, contemporary plant breeders are free to use existing apple species in their breeding programs, with only a few restrictions that we will explore later.

Important in the early development of apple breeding was a knowledge of grafting, described as early as an account by Cato the Elder. A cut branch of a promising tree is grafted onto the established rootstock of another tree, making it possible to grow many genetically identical specimens from just one apple tree. A successful crossing can thus be multiplied into as many apple trees as are needed for an entire orchard. Grafting makes breeding fast and easy, and so, in the 20th century, more than ten thousand apple varieties were bred. Their names are almost as appealing as the apples themselves: Belle de Boskoop, Cornish Gilliflower, Geheimrat Doktor Oldenburg.

One romantic story concerns an apple variety introduced in this century, the Bardsey Island Apple. Bearing a lemon-like aroma, it comes from the windy Bardsey Island in North Wales. It is said that, in 1998, a fowler named Andy Clarke was working with mist nets to catch and ring birds. In his nets he found some fallen apples that seemed absolutely perfect. The ancient tree from which the apples originated was free of diseases, a rarity in North Wales. Clarke's friend and fruit grower Ian Sturrock did not recognize the apples and sent them for identification to the British National Fruit Collection, which determined the apples to be specimens of a unique variety. And so a legend was born—the media spoke of "the rarest tree in the world," and Sturrock now sells grafted clones from the old tree. Accounts of the origin of the apple are mainly speculative: according to one account, the old tree is the last surviving specimen from an orchard of a monastery that stood on the island a 1,000 years ago.

Above: "New Life," a grafted tree. (delihayat / Getty Images)

Apple breeders follow the desires of consumers, and have a list of qualities that the perfect apples must possess: apples must be beautiful, large, sturdy, hardy, balanced in both acid and sugars, and resistant to rot. In addition, breeders select properties that are of interest to growers and traders. It is important that apples are resistant to diseases such as apple scab. Affected trees give lesser yields and their fruits exhibit black or grey-brown spots. They are edible, but few consumers are willing to pay for imperfect apples. There are some breeds of wild apples that do not suffer from scab, such as the Japanese flowering crab apple. Breeders have worked tirelessly to crossbreed a range of varieties, to create new varieties that exhibit the same scab resistance.

Breeding apples is time-consuming: it requires about six years for a seedling to bear fruit, and so it takes this long to assess a new variety for taste, growth, and yield. Not only are apples big business, but they are also important at the national

EEN APPEL AAN EEN BESSE BOOM GEGROEYT
BUYTE ALCMAAR 1759

Above, left: "Spring Farm Work," grafting wood engraving by Winslow Homer. (Corbis via Getty Images)

Above, right: "Een appel aan een besseboom gegroeyt" ("apple growing on a berry bush"), anonymous, 1759. (Rijksmuseum)

On the following pages: Elstar apple trees. (Alamy)

level. The Netherlands has, for instance, maintained a breeding program financed by the government since 1948. Its most important product is a cultivar, crossed in 1955 by Arie Schaap from Elst, that is still popular in the Netherlands. Initially called "Elstarie," it became known in its later renown as "Elstar."

Thousands of apple breeds have been documented, and the explosion of varieties has been made possible by an unusually open approach to the protection of plant breeds. The International Union for the Protection of New Varieties of Plants (UPOV) was founded in 1961, with the mission to maintain the intellectual protection of plant varieties. To enjoy exclusive protection, a plant variety must be new, distinguishable from other varieties, uniform in character, and must retain its characteristics after propagation. For the majority of crops the plant breeder's right applies for 25 years but, due to the long generation period, for apples it's 30 years.

Although UPOV is an advocate for intellectual property over plant varieties, it has generally taken the view that the community of breeders needs access to all forms of breeding material to sustain the greatest progress in plant breeding, and to maximize the use of genetic resources

for the benefit of society. To promote the development of new varieties, an important part of plant breeders' rights is the breeder's exemption. This states that anyone can use a right-protected breed as a starting material for their own breeding program. If a breeder succeeds in cultivating a new, distinctive, uniform, and stable breed from this material, then they may acquire intellectual protection over the variety.

Without the breeder's exemption, there would certainly have been fewer apple varieties. For example, the Elstar is the result of a cross between the Danish apple "Ingrid Marie" and the American "Golden Delicious." When Arie Schaap's employer applied for plant breeder's rights over the Elstar in 1972, it did not have to pay license fees to Denmark or the United States. And neither did the Dutch grower who in 1987 introduced to the market the "Reinders," a smooth version of the Golden Delicious. This grower did not even have to perform crossbreeding: the new apple was discovered in the village of Panningen in 1962 by M.H. Reinders. Its appearance was a spontaneous change—in technical terms, a mutation—in the genetic material of a Golden Delicious tree. In the vast majority of cases, a mutation does not lead to perceptible new features, and even if

it does, the resulting new characteristic is often undesirable. Reinders' discovery was an exception, and his Reinders apple has a skin more attractive to consumers than that of the parent variety. By multiplying the find by grafting, one mutated tree became the basis of a whole new variety. A lucky break, from which, thanks to the breeder's exemption, consumers could benefit directly.

The Golden Delicious itself is also a lucky break, but of a different order. Just like Granny Smith, Red Delicious, and Braeburn, this variety is a random seedling: an unintended cross between two parent trees. The American grower Anderson Mullins discovered the apple that would later be called Golden Delicious at the end of the 19th century. Propagating the tree by grafting, he eventually sold the rights to the variety to Stark Brothers Nurseries for $5,000, which brought it on the market in 1914 as Golden Delicious. Obviously Mullins himself had not paid for the parent material of his breed, an instance of a nonformalized form of breeder's exemption.

Plant breeding was historically a matter of small entrepreneurs and enthusiasts, and small breeders still contribute to the rich diversity of new plant varieties. The breeder's exemption, as it has existed informally for centuries and is now legally established, guarantees their access to basic material, as it prevents a situation where only rich parties can afford new varieties.

This also benefits society at large, as UPOV notes. Thanks to the breeder's exemption, there is now an extensive range of varieties, in which all sorts of beneficial properties are combined in different ways. From these varieties farmers choose those that produce a large, healthy crop on their soil, for which they pay a reasonable price. For the consumer, this means a diverse and affordable range of produce in the supermarket.

In addition, a diversely planted agricultural area reduces the risk of major crop failures. For example, if all farmers planted one variety that was vulnerable to drought, a year with little rain could cause an entire crop to fail. Because different farmers choose different varieties, the risk of crop failure is smaller. Perhaps an apple mis-harvest could be endured, but for other crops the consequences are greater. Only fifteen staple crops, among them wheat, rice, and maize, provide 90 percent of the worldwide plant-based calorie intake. Variation in cultivars for these crops thus contributes to the food security of large parts of the world's population. And so the breeder's right has contributed in no small way to the food security of vast tracts of the world's population.

Of course, large corporations would like to carve out monopolies for their creations, in order to better guarantee returns

Above: "De appelschilster" ("Girl Peeling an Apple"), by Cornelis Bisschop, 1667. (Rijksmuseum)

from their investments in new varieties. In Europe it is not possible to be granted a patent on a plant variety, but the emergence of biotechnology has offered new opportunities. Since 1998, European legislation has made it possible to apply for a patent on genes and new natural breeding techniques, and similar laws exist in many countries. Thus, for example, patents have been granted for a tomato containing less water, for broccoli with extra glucosinolates, and for a red pepper with a resistance to whitefly. And so, competitors were initially not allowed to use these varieties in their breeding programs.

However, this type of legislation continues to be challenged. The owners justify their patents by arguing that they are necessary due to the investment required in costly long-term breeding processes.

Critics have long argued that patents will lead to a decrease in the number of new varieties to come on the market. So, in June 2017, the European Patent Office concluded that the breeder's exemption trumps patent law. This ruling makes existing varieties available as starting material for new varieties. We cannot expect to soon find thousands of apple varieties in the supermarket, but this decision can make an important contribution to the future of diversity within agriculture and to food security for the planet. ◆

Further Reading

Dutch Centre for Genetic Resources Netherlands (CGN) *Apple Collection*. Available at: www.wur.nl/en/Expertise-Services/ Statutory-research-tasks/Centre-for-Genetic-Resources-the-Netherlands-1/ Expertise-areas/Plant-Genetic-Resources/ CGN-crop-collections/Apple.htm

Erika Janik (2011) *Apple. A Global History.* Chicago: University of Chicago Press.

Jay Sanderson (2017) *Plants, People and Practices: The Nature and History of the UPOV Convention.* Cambridge: Cambridge University Press.

--- *The Consumption Age*

-- *Trademark*

- *France*

1800   1900   2000

--/----/----/----/----/----/----/-/----/----/----/----/----/----

249

30 Chanel 2.55

Jeannie Suk Gersen

FREUD SAID THE purse was a symbol of female anatomy, a receptacle for the mysterious and hidden. A woman who went out into society carrying one was clutching her womb, so to speak.

The Chanel 2.55 bag—timeless object of purse-envy—was a kind of rebirth. It was not the first bag created by Coco Chanel. Her first, in 1929, caused scandal. Having become "fed up with holding my purses in my hands and losing them," and inspired by military satchels, she sewed on an extended strap to allow women to carry the bag hands-free and over the shoulder. Making a shoulder bag socially acceptable for ladies offered new freedom of movement and a nod to sexual liberation in Jazz Age Paris.

Chanel was famous for many things, including her romantic liaisons with the likes of Stravinsky and British royalty. Her 2.55 bag, named for its appearance in February 1955, had a secret zippered compartment in its front flap for keeping love letters. The bag's long shoulder straps were made of linked metal chains, and its quilted leather body resembled the

pattern on jockey jackets. Its inner lining was the burgundy color of Chanel's childhood Catholic-school uniforms. Inspired by her girlhood impressions of horses' bridles and harnesses, and of the keychains of the caretakers at her orphanage, the bag expressed both freedom and restraint, mastery and submission. As *Vogue* noted in 2013, "The genius of the Chanel bag can be found in its versatility—it has managed to be the perfect accessory, be its wearer in jeans or black-tie, artfully disheveled or painstakingly put together, for more than half a century, invading not only our wardrobes but our cultural consciousness as well."

The bag was part of Coco Chanel's fraught 1950s comeback, 15 years after she closed her business as World War II began. It proved to be an emblem of Chanel's own ability to rise again, unscathed, after her wartime collaboration with the Nazis. In a social set in which anti-Semitism was pronounced, Chanel had been a secret agent for the Germans and mistress to a German intelligence officer. She had also tried to exploit the Nazi Aryanization of property,

On the left: A Chanel 2.55 bag during Paris fashion week 2016–2017. (Alamy)

by suing her Jewish business partner and backer, Pierre Wertheimer, in an attempt to legally exclude his rights to the Chanel No. 5 perfume empire—unsuccessfully, as he'd already signed over control to a non-Jewish proxy before fleeing France for New York so the company wouldn't be considered Jewish or abandoned.

After the war, Chanel was somehow spared the public shaming, to which many French women who'd slept with the enemy were subjected, with head-shaving and forced march in the streets. After brief investigation by French authorities of her wartime activities, and following a post-war Swiss self-exile, she was back in Paris at the age of 71 reviving the House of Chanel. The ease of Chanel's reintegration into French society has struck many as puzzling, with some crediting the possible intervention of her friend Winston Churchill, her name's close association with French chic, and the desire of postwar France to forget and move on. But it was, most practically, her former partner Wertheimer's decision to financially back her again, despite her wartime conduct, that enabled Chanel's

On the left: Coco Chanel, ca. 1936. (Photo by Lipnitzki / Roger Viollet / Getty Images)

reestablishment. (The Wertheimer family owns the controlling interest in the Chanel company today.)

For all the French forgiveness, it was the Americans who rapturously embraced her return. *Life* magazine declared that "Chanel is bringing in more than style—a revolution," and the *New York Times* remarked that "the look of her return collection was just what American women wanted." Hers was the look of modernity, combining simplicity, ease, line, and movement. If the French found it somewhat familiar by then, the American reception gave Chanel a second life.

The French Syndicate of Haute Couture was the association that controlled who was permitted to use the designation of "Haute Couture," and organized protection of those fashion houses from design piracy. Soon after her comeback, Chanel resigned her membership in the organization because of an intense feud on the issue of design copying. The Syndicate had strict rules to restrict copying. Her fellow couturiers went to great lengths to guard against piracy, even requiring steep

security deposits from potential buyers before allowing them to view collections. But Chanel had perennially thumbed her nose at such anxieties by releasing drawings of her designs to the press, inviting seamstresses to come sketch and take notes, and openly encouraging the copying of her work. "Let them copy. I am on the side of women and seamstresses not the fashion houses," she proclaimed. "What rigidity it shows, what laziness, what unimaginative taste, what lack of faith in creativity, to be frightened of imitations!"

The 2.55 bag's iconic status through the decades is evident in photographs of its various versions on Jackie Kennedy, Elizabeth Taylor, Audrey Hepburn, Brigitte Bardot, Jane Fonda, Mia Farrow, and Princess Diana. Chanel is reported to have said both that "Fashion must come up from the streets," and that "Fashion does not exist unless it goes down into the streets—without imitation there is no success." And down into the streets the bag has gone—as counterfeits on Canal Street. "If people can't afford to buy a real Chanel," she said, "I'd rather they bought a fake Chanel with the idea of Chanel in mind." Her preference was realized with a vengeance.

As the popularity of fake Chanel bags rose in the 1980s, Chanel, Inc. was much less forgiving of copyists than Chanel herself had been. By the mid-1990s, the company was spending millions annually to fight counterfeiting, and has since consistently pursued alleged infringers of Chanel's more than 50 registered trademarks, on handbags and other goods, through litigation, private investigations, and cease-and-desist letters. The company has even successfully sued an Indiana beauty-salon owner named Chanel Jones, to demand that she change the name of her business, Chanel's Salon.

Above: Actress Brigitte Bardot with her 2.55 in London in 1963 during the filming of Une ravissante idiote *(*Agent 38-24-36; F / I 1964, Dir. Édouard Molinaro*). (Photo by Sydney O'Meara / Evening Standard / Getty Images)*

A NOTE OF INFORMATION AND ENTREATY
TO FASHION EDITORS, ADVERTISERS
COPYWRITERS AND OTHER
WELL-INTENTIONED MIS-USERS OF
OUR **CHANEL** NAME.

CHANEL was a designer, an extraordinary woman who made
a timeless contribution to fashion.

CHANEL is a perfume.

CHANEL is modern elegance in couture, ready-to-wear,
accessories, watches and fine jewelry.

CHANEL is our registered trademark for fragrance, cosmetics,
clothing, accessories and other lovely things.

Although our style is justly famous, a jacket is not 'a CHANEL jacket' unless it is
ours, and somebody else's cardigans are not 'CHANEL for now.'

And even if we are flattered by such tributes to our fame as 'Chanel-issime,
Chanel-ed, Chanels and Chanel-ized', PLEASE DON'T. Our lawyers positively
detest them.

We take our trademark seriously.

Merci,

CHANEL, Inc.

Above, left: Chanel's trademark ad, as originally published in "Women's Wear Daily." Fair-use image; Chanel denied permission due to objections to our discussion of Coco Chanel's WWII history.

Above, right: Counterfeit designer handbags on sale in Marbella, Spain. (Alamy)

Ads in *Women's Wear Daily* have warned against using the Chanel name, in terms like "Chanel-ized," "Chanel-ed," or "Chanel-issime," saying "we are flattered by such tributes to our fame," but "our lawyers positively detest them."

The fame of the Chanel bag, though, is largely attributable to the widespread imitation and accessibility encouraged by its creator. A Chanel bag seen on a woman is more likely assumed a fake than a genuine article. At the same time, the resale market for an original 2.55 bag is very robust; its value has risen more than 200-fold in the past 15 years. The bag is both the paradigmatic original and the archetypal copy—an embodiment not only of authentic and rarified luxury, but also of fakeness, repetition, reproduction, and substitution.

Amidst the proliferation of copies, the bag's duality—going high and low, old and young, prim and louche, class and mass—has made it an ever-present, if ambivalent, receptacle for cultural meaning. In 2005, after decades of permutations of the design, the bag was reissued in near-original form for its 50th anniversary under the name, "Reissue 2.55"—as if to commemorate its origin as always already a rebirth. To mark the occasion, in 2008, the House of Chanel, helmed by Karl Lagerfeld, held an exhibition of art inspired by the bag and contained in a mobile structure, designed by architect Zaha Hadid, that traveled to Hong Kong,

Tokyo, New York, London, Moscow, and Paris. The artworks, commissioned from contemporary artists, included a gigantic reproduction of the 2.55 bag, and the soundscape featured Jeanne Moreau talking about the secrets inside a woman's purse. In the blurring of fashion, art, architecture, and advertisement, the commercialization of the 2.55 as aesthetic object was a kind of rejoinder to Chanel's 50-year-old derision of "dressmakers who consider themselves artists."

If the ongoing debate about copying in fashion could have its own trademark, it would likely be the 2.55 bag. Coco Chanel's philosophy favoring copying, expressed in her famous quip that "imitation is the highest form of flattery," has often been invoked to rebuff arguments supporting intellectual property protection for fashion design, currently lacking in the United States. Referring to fashion cycles in which today's objects of desire are doomed to be replaced by tomorrow's, she once said, "The more transient fashion is the more perfect it is." But the Chanel 2.55's power is in its resuscitated longevity, if not immortality—evoking the enduring present of memory, and of forgetting. ◆

Further Reading

Hamish Bowles (2005) "The Chanel Century," *Vogue (US)*, May.

Lisa Chaney (2011) *Coco Chanel: An Intimate Life*. New York: Viking.

C. Scott Hemphill and Jeannie Suk (2009) "The Law, Culture, and Economics of Fashion," *Stanford Law Review*, 61(5), pp. 1147–1199.

C. Scott Hemphill and Jeannie Suk (2014) "The Fashion Originators' Guild of America: Self-help at the edge of IP and antitrust," in Rochelle Dreyfuss and Jane C. Ginsburg (eds.) *Intellectual Property at the Edge: The Contested Contours of IP*. Cambridge: Cambridge University Press, pp. 159–179.

Caroline Palmer (2013) "Visual History: 50 Years of the Chanel Bag on the Street," *Vogue*, 4 December.

Above: Diana, Princess of Wales, greets the crowd on a walking tour of Northwestern University campus in Evanston, Illinois in 1996. (Photo Vincent Laforet / Getty Images

On the right: Street Style Chanel bags. From top to bottom: Berlin, 2017; Paris, 2017; Berlin, 2018. (Photos by Christian Vierig and Edward Berthelot / Getty Images)

1800 *1900* *2000*

--/-----/-----/-----/-----/-----/-----/--/---/-----/-----/-----/-----/---

31 Lego Brick

Dan Hunter and Julian Thomas

On 28 January 1958, a tiny company from a tiny country applied for a patent over a tiny plastic brick. The Lego brick, that tiny block of plastic, has been produced in the tens of billions by the Lego factories since that time. It has been the basis of business school case studies, academic colloquia, and any number of breathless encomia. And it has also been stepped on by countless parents.

The humble brick is, however, much more than just a branded, colored, molded and heat-treated piece of polymer—it is the foundation of a system of control and ownership based on global intellectual property laws. In the early life of the brick, Lego had complete control over its system; but as the patents on the Lego brick began to expire in the mid-1970s, the company had to change its approach. In time it would understand that the thing that mattered was no longer patent but trademark law; and no longer the brick, but the brand.

Beyond this story of corporate evolution, Lego also helps us understand a remarkable legal transformation, that of the global spread of intellectual property laws in the postwar era. The Lego brick has been produced since the mid-1950s, and in its basic form is largely unchanged to this day. In that time, the global intellectual property system has changed from a narrow set of laws that accounted for a tiny percentage of global trade, to one of the foundations of contemporary capitalism. The Lego company and its bricks have been involved in every part of that transformation.

The standard creation story of Lego and the brick begins in 1916 with a master carpenter, Ole Kirk Christiansen, who bought a woodworking shop in rural Billund, Denmark. Over time he came to specialize in wooden toys; and so, in 1934, he named his company "Lego," a contraction of the Danish *leg godt*, or "play well." For more than a decade Lego produced nothing but wooden toys, such as carved wooden cars, trucks, and pull-along ducks.

Lego's first brick-based toy was a knock-off of an earlier system from Kiddicraft, an English toy company created by child psychologist Hilary Page. Lego's 1949 version was made, like Kiddicraft's, from cellulose acetate. It was modified and transformed into the basic unit of the company's "System of Play" in 1955, then redesigned and eventually patented for its stud-and-tube interlocking capabilities in 1958. In its present form, it dates from 1963, when a new polymer called ABS, or acrylonitrile butadiene styrene, replaced the original cellulose material. ABS is wonderfully resilient, bright, and strong. It is now everywhere, but in the postwar period it was new and strange and replete with possibility.

Remarkably, Lego had never created interlocking units with its earlier wooden toys, and the idea of a system was only made possible with the advent of the modern plastics of the postwar period. But once conceived, the idea was impossible to deny. The Lego system promised the interchangeability and reusability of bricks. The more bricks a child acquired, the more valuable their Lego set.

Starting in the late 1950s, Lego sought patents over their basic brick design in numerous countries, including Denmark, the United Kingdom, and the United States. The initial filing was in Denmark on 28 January 1958, but the company was quick to see the significance of international patent protection. Godtfred Kirk Christiansen—the son of Lego's founder—was granted US Patent 3,005,282 on 24 October 1961, for a "Toy Building Brick," relating to "bricks or blocks adapted to be connected together by means of projections

extending from the faces of the elements and arranged so as to engage protruding portions of an adjacent element when two such elements are assembled."

The early stage in Lego's development relied on strong, unitary protection of its intellectual property. The company saw its corporate success defined by establishing formal mechanisms of protection over the brick and other elements, via the patent system. Success for the company came from establishing ever-stronger forms of control, concentrated at a single point at the highest executive levels of the company.

The patent system was uniquely well-developed to deliver this sort of centralized control. And so during the 1960s and 1970s—learning from the success of its first patent over the brick—Lego sought and was granted utility patents over various advances in the Lego system—for rotatable brick elements, or the design of the minifig, amongst many, many other innovations—

Above: A child caught up in his own world playing with Lego bricks on a living room floor. Lego is a contraction of the Danish leg godt, or "play well." (Photo Massimo Calmonte / Getty Images)

*bove: The more
imetic kind of play
ith Lego's sets.
eft: The licensed-in
ntellectual property
f LucasFilm / STAR
VARS. (Photo by
erdaus Shamim /
etty Images).
ight: A set within the
'City" theme. (Photo
y Lya Cattel /
etty Images)

and Lego developed large-scale patent portfolios in countries throughout Europe, North America and Australasia.

But this pattern wasn't to last. In the late 1970s and early 1980s, Lego faced a crisis of control, as its international portfolio of utility patents over the bricks began to expire. A number of competitors sought to take advantage of the installed user base of Lego users, by producing inexpensive brick systems that could interlock with Lego bricks. In the United States, Tyco began marketing its SUPER BLOCK line of bricks to compete with regular Lego and DUPLO bricks. Tyco had copied the basic design of a number of Lego bricks, and began selling its bricks in 1985, noting in its advertising that its product looked and felt just like Lego's, but was cheaper.

Lego sued Tyco under a series of theories, claiming false advertising and unfair competition, based on Tyco's use of Lego marks and designation, as well as

a more interesting claim that Tyco had infringed a common law trademark over Lego's 2 × 4 stud-and-tube configuration. Because of marketing missteps by Tyco, Lego was moderately successful in the false advertising claim; but it failed in its bid to establish a trademark over the brick design. Although the court noted the distinctive nature of the Lego brick, it refused to grant a trademark over it since to give protection to such features would be equivalent to granting a perpetual monopoly over useful features of the product.

Lego also sought to use copyright and designs law to reassert control over the form of the brick, but it was rebuffed at each turn. In the Australian case of *Interlego* v. *Folley*, it unsuccessfully tried to protect the form of its bricks and tiles by claiming copyright in the engineering drawings used to create the dies that stamped out the bricks. While in the Privy Council, in *Interlego* v. *Tyco*, it failed in its bid to use a design registration over the studs-and-tube configuration to stop its competitors from copying.

The conclusion was clear: once its foundational patents had expired, Lego no longer had sole dominion over the form

of the brick. This created the conditions for the company to rethink its approach to intellectual property, and the company began to change its focus. Now it started to think about branding, especially in its sets and themes.

Sets were present at the founding of Lego's brick system, and indeed the product that is credited with creating the idea of the system of play was *Town Plan No. 1*, a cohesive set comprising Lego bricks, figures, cars, trees, and a play mat based around the idea of a town. Over time, sets began to cohere into series, or "themes." Arguably the first theme—these days called *City*—stems from the iconic *Town Plan No. 1* from the 1950s; two other themes, *Castle* and *Space*, emerged in 1978.

These themes emerged more or less organically from the Lego system and they were not planned as an exercise in branding. Within the standard histories of Lego, the emergence of the themes is often explained as a feature of the corporate ethos of creative play, since purchasing a new set that is thematically related to one that a

child already owns gives more opportunities to extend the creations that can be built. But the development of themes led in time to the understanding within the company that it had brands that functioned independently of the individual bricks or system, and that these brands were commercially valuable.

This was an important stage in the evolution of Lego, because it changed the intellectual property focus, from the individual bricks to higher level aspects such as branding. Although the early themes of *Town*, *Space*, and *Castle* operated mostly as a sorting device for the types of bricks inside thematically related sets, later themes began to operate in ways that implemented modern branding practice. Themes generated meaningful consumer associations independent of source identification, and the company started to recognize the potential of these brand lines. The *Town*, *Space*, and *Castle* themes became ever more distinctive throughout the 1980s, with special characters and pieces developed only for sets within those

Above: STAR WARS Princess Leia, Luke Skywalker, and Darth Vader Lego minifigures (CTRPhotos / Levent Konuk / Getty Images.

themes, and new subthemes emerging for each main theme.

Although Lego had internal brands and was aware of their value, it took a long time for it to license-in any outside intellectual property, and it wasn't until 1999 that Lego released anything that featured ideas from another company. The new theme was *Star Wars*, licensed in from LucasFilm and launched to coincide with the release of the first prequel in the STAR WARS canon, EPISODE 1, THE PHANTOM MENACE. It was a huge success, and pointed to a radical change in the company's approach. In 1999 it issued 15 sets of *Star Wars* licensed product; by 2009 it was releasing as many as 24; and in the following years, Lego created huge numbers of sets based on a plethora of outside intellectual property assets, including sets based on RAIDERS OF THE LOST ARK, HARRY POTTER, SPIDERMAN, SPONGEBOB SQUARE-PANTS, and Ferrari cars.

The company's evolution and success tracks the development of the international intellectual property system, from the postwar period to today. It went from an engineering-based toy company that focused on protecting its bricks using patent, designs and copyright law; and ended up a transmedia company, skilled at trademarks and licensing, and dependent on partnerships with a range of intellectual property conglomerates.

Along the way, however, it has been confronted with the difficult truth that it cannot control all uses of its intellectual property. In 1996, Zbigniew Libera approached Lego for a donation of bricks to use for an artwork. The company agreed, but was appalled when their donation resulted in a work called *Konzentrationslager*,

Above: Patent drawings for the Lego minifig, US Patent No. D253,711.

On the right: the Lego minifig patent come to life. (Getty Images)

On the following page: Drawing for Christiansen's patent for a "toy building brick," US Patent No. 3,005,282.

Oct. 24, 1961   G. K. CHRISTIANSEN   3,005,282
                        TOY BUILDING BRICK

Filed July 28, 1958   2 Sheets—Sheet 1

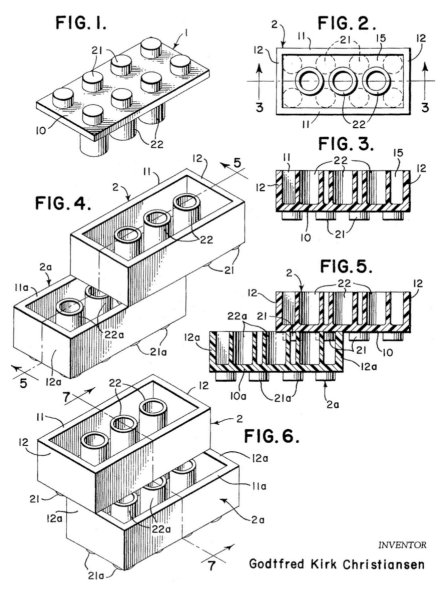

FIG. 1.

FIG. 2.

FIG. 3.

FIG. 4.

FIG. 5.

FIG. 6.

INVENTOR

Godtfred Kirk Christiansen

BY *Stevens, Davis, Miller & Mosher*
ATTORNEYS

Above, left: "LEGO Concentration Camp," by artist Zbigniew Libera. The upper left corner of the box reads "This works of Zbigniew Libera has been sponsored by Lego." This was probably not what Lego had in mind when they provided the artist with bricks. (Photo by Mario Tama / Getty Images)

Above, right: Lego bricks are poured into a car, used as a receptacle for donations of Lego bricks in London, 2015. The collection was organized by Chinese artist and activist Ai Weiwei who, after having his official request for Lego bricks refused, called on the public to donate their bricks as part of his next project. (Photo by Leon Neal / AFP / Getty Images)

comprising a series—a putative "theme" in fact—of fake Lego sets depicting a Nazi concentration camp. The fake sets explored numerous features of a death camp. One box depicted skeletal prisoners behind barbed wire fences—Libera used skeleton minifigs from the *Castle* theme to depict the prisoners—while another showed a minifig being hanged on a gallows. A third set showed skeletons being dragged into a crematorium blockhouse under the watchful eye of a black-clad guard, with the massive crematorium chimneys, too-familiar from Holocaust documentaries, towering above the roofline.

Libera's artistic use of Lego bricks attracted lots of press, was exhibited in the Jewish Museum in New York and was eventually bought by the Museum of Modern Art in Warsaw. Lego initially sought to sue the artist to stop the display of the art—not for the use of the bricks, but rather the appropriation of the Lego trademarks and his claim that Lego had sponsored the work—but eventually backed down once the artist hired a lawyer.

Lego won't make that mistake again—in 2015 it successfully navigated a potential PR-disaster over a fight with the artist Ai Weiwei—and like many successful intellectual property-based companies, it has eventually learned that it will never have total control over its products and ideas. But as it has evolved with the global intellectual property system, it has learnt how to make all the laws snap together, to build a fabulously successful and valuable creation. ◆

Further Reading

John Baichtal and Joe Meno (2011) *The Cult of Lego.* San Francisco: No Starch Press.

Sarah Herman (2012) *A Million Little Bricks: The Unofficial Illustrated History of the Lego Phenomenon.* New York: Skyhorse.

Dan Hunter and Julian Thomas (2016) "Lego and the System of Intellectual Property, 1955–2015," *Intellectual Property Quarterly,* 1, pp. 1–18.

Daniel Lipkowitz (2009) *The LEGO Book.* London: Dorling Kindersley.

Jeremy Phillips (1987) "An Empire Built of Bricks: A Brief Appraisal of 'Lego,'" *European Intellectual Property Review,* 12, pp. 363–366.

David C. Robertson and Bill Breen (2013) *Brick by Brick: How Lego Rewrote the Rules of Innovation and Conquered the Global Toy Industry.* New York: Random House.

1800   *1900*   *2000*

--/-----/-----/-----/-----/-----/-----/--/---/-----/-----/-----/-----/----

32 Barbie Doll

Dan Hunter and Greg Lastowka

THE BARBIE DOLL is a remarkable object—wasp-waisted, flesh-toned, the Venus of Hawthorne, CA, Mattel Inc.'s birthplace. But she is also a lesson in how copyright, trademark, patent can be used by companies to maintain desire. And just as Barbie is the very embodiment of unrequited desire, so too do intellectual property laws constrain consumers in their access to the objects of their lust. Barbie is, then, much more than a doll—she is an object lesson in the connection between lust, laws, money, and flesh-toned plastic.

Born on 9 March 1959, Barbie sprang forth from the imagination of Ruth Handler, one of the founders of the Mattel company and the mother of two children who were, improbably, also named Barbara and Ken. The official Mattel narrative holds that Barbie Millicent Roberts is a wholesome Midwestern gal, a "teenage fashion model" from Willows, Wisconsin. But the creation story of Barbie is more inflected than this, and less wholesome. Barbie was patterned on another doll, "Lilli," which Ruth Handler chanced upon while on a European tour with her family. Spied in a toy store window in Lucerne, Switzerland, the doll-which-would-become-Barbie was anything but a sweet teenage fashionista: she was the embodiment of a lewd cartoon character, created by Reinhard Beuthien for a tabloid German newspaper, *Bild-Zeitung*. The character Lilli was an under-employed secretary who hooked on the side, or at least spent a great deal of time "socializing" with rich sugar daddies to supplement her income—a stereotype distressingly familiar in postwar Europe.

The Lilli dolls, developed by O&M Hausser, were released in 1955 and featured Lilli in various outfits, many of them racy. The dolls weren't intended for children, and were apparently bought by men as gag gifts for bachelor parties, as dashboard adornments, or as suggestive gifts for their girlfriends and mistresses.

On hearing that Lilli was a working girl, some commentators have tut-tutted at the sinful nature of Barbie's birth. But the sin emanated not from the doll, but from her creator. Mattel took the Lilli doll and knocked her off as the Barbie doll, with at best a slight cosmetic alteration: her

On the left: A close-up of a Barbie Doll's face. (Alamy)

hairline was adjusted to have a less pronounced widow's peak, and her eyebrows became less severely arched. Apart from these minor changes, the dolls were identical, even down to the sideways-glancing eyes on both dolls. Years later, Mattel co-founder Elliot Handler—Ruth Handler's husband—was asked whether the Mattel doll was a knockoff of Lilli:

Well, you might call it that, yes. Ruth wanted to adopt the same body as the Lilli doll with some modifications. Changes were made, improvements were made. Ruth wanted her own look [for the doll].

On one level, Mattel's sin is both quotidian and unimportant: many successful products are ripped off from unsuspecting competitors, and this was particularly prevalent in toy and doll manufacture during the middle of the 20th century. Almost inevitably, Mattel's sin was quickly washed clean by later payments to the owners of various Lilli-related intellectual property, a little like medieval parishioners who bought their way out of sin through papal indulgences. The Lilli dolls were quietly forgotten, and a new creation myth of the Barbie doll was officially approved and promulgated.

As soon as this awkward issue was resolved, Mattel began to worship at the altar of intellectual property, seeking to control the concepts of Barbie via patent, trademark, and eventually copyright. Shortly after Barbie's birth, Jack Ryan, the larger-than-life head of Mattel's research and development department, was granted a patent on an invention for doll construction that allowed Barbie to stand upright, and various other patents would be issued

Above: A "modern" Barbie. (Shutterstock)

to him over the years for an articulated waist joint for the doll, for her tinny voice-box, and other innovations. And in time, copyright would be important to protect cartoons, books, comics, and movies that featured the Barbie iconography.

But trademark was always the staple controlling legal technology, and Mattel was thorough in building a huge portfolio of trademarks and was diligent in policing these marks. It has registered marks for all manner of variants of the word "Barbie" for the dolls and for any number of Barbie add-ons—"Barbie Dreamhouse," "Malibu Barbie" (of course), "Barbie Life," "Barbie in Princess Power," and so on. It has registered the distinctive Barbie pink color so that other toy companies can't use it, and has regularly claimed the image and form

of the doll herself as a mark. Barbie's distinctive silhouette with her high forehead and perky ponytail is protected, of course. And as the Web emerged as a commercial force during the 1990s, Mattel quickly secured numerous domain names referencing the word "Barbie": the company maintains its main website for Barbie dolls and related paraphernalia at www.barbie.com, but also holds domain name registrations for barbie.net, barbiedoll.info, barbiedoll.net, and barbieworld.com, amongst others.

Trademarks grant perpetual control over brands, of course, but Mattel came to discover that its control wasn't unassailable. There is a strange fragility at the heart of Barbie, which the company initially failed to recognize. As people came to know of Barbie, they co-opted the doll

and her meaning as their own, in ways which the company struggled to accommodate. It was perhaps not an accident that the timing of Barbie's commercial success intersected with second wave feminism that grew in force from the 1960s, and the blonde-haired doll quickly became a metaphor and symbol for everything that was oppressing women. The arguments are, by now, well known: Barbie is "too tall and too thin … [with] outsize breasts and non-existent hips"; she is a bad role model for girls and she causes eating disorders and body dysmorphic disorders; she discourages girls from taking an interest in math; she teaches girls a certain type of "emphasized femininity" that valorizes niceness and focuses on female

achievement as one that resides only in the aesthetic or sexual realms; her anodyne whiteness and straightness stigmatizes race- and gender-minorities, and forms part of the apparatus of their oppression; and so on.

Barbie wasn't just a lightning rod for criticism, she was also a potent object for artistic reinterpretation in various forms and artists of many types have used Barbie to present all manner of messages. Todd Haynes used Barbie in SUPERSTAR, his portrayal of Karen Carpenter's life, shaving down the limbs and face of the doll to show Carpenter's struggle with, and eventual death from, anorexia. Barbie has been re-imagined in versions of Marcel Duchamp's *Nude Descending a Staircase*, in pastiches of

Above: Barbie as Karen Carpenter in Todd Haynes' 1987 SUPERSTAR. THE KAREN CARPENTER STORY. (Courtesy of Todd Haynes)

Edward Hopper's dystopian cityscapes, as Edouard Manet's *Olympia*, as the *Venus de Milo*, and as Botticelli's *Birth of Venus*.

The uses of the concept of Barbie presented Mattel with a problem of control, the limits of which the company consistently misjudged. Saying nothing about these uses might be seen as a kind of implicit sanction, and so Mattel couldn't ignore every appropriation. But where should it draw the line? The company had to accept that—even outside academic and feminist criticism where it could do little—Barbie's ubiquitous strength and worldwide recognition would mean that she would be re-imagined in all manner of ways. This tension was particularly fraught for the company in dealing with artistic works, and thus began Mattel's 50-year engagement with the policing of Barbie artworks, an engagement that has arced wildly between embrace and reprimand, a dysfunctional relationship that shows varying degrees of tolerance on the part of the company.

The best-known examples of litigation over artistic use of Barbie are familiar. In 1999, the visual artist Tom Forsythe created a series of 78 photos popularly known as "Food Chain Barbie," portraying Barbie dolls in danger of being attacked by various vintage household appliances. Forsythe only managed to sell a small number of the photos as promotional postcards, mostly in his tiny hometown of Kanab, UT, and he grossed the princely sum of $3,659 from the project. (Most of this money apparently came from purchases made by Mattel's lawyers.) Yet Mattel sued Forsythe, for various types of intellectual property evils, seeking millions in damages. The company lost on every count, and was ordered to pay the defendant's court costs and attorney's fees, to the tune of more than $1.8 million.

Then there was the song "Barbie Girl" by Aqua, the Danish pop band of the late 1990s. The band reinterpreted Barbie's image in first person lyrics and a video, in ways that Mattel objected to. Of particular concern were references that Barbie was a "party girl," the suggestion that she wanted Ken to undress her, and a lyric suggesting that she was "a blonde bimbo girl, in a fantasy world / Dress me up, make it tight, I'm your dolly." Mattel sued the band and its recording label, and once again, it suffered a humiliating loss. The strange, but amusing coda to the story is that, Mattel licensed the "Barbie Girl" song for use in an advertising campaign, only a few years after its defeat.

These cases are strange because, seen from the outside one would say that Mattel should have known better. These cases were obvious losers. But Mattel has always

had a blind spot when it comes to Barbie and sex: no matter what the best commercial interests of the company, whenever Barbie is used in a sexualized manner, the company sues or threatens suit. Thus, the company predictably objected when Barbie Benson, a former Miss Nude Canada, created a racy website that included her name. And when Karen Caviale sought to create Barbie Bazaar, a collector's magazine, she had to promise never to show Barbie in a lewd or lascivious manner.

Yet sex suffuses every part of Barbie as cultural object, every part of Barbie as intellectual property. This is obvious in her form and in the nature of the actions that Mattel undertook, as it is in Lilli from whom Barbie was born. But sex is also present in the very intellectual property system itself. Mattel has applied the power of the intellectual property system in very targeted ways. In the hands of Mattel, the intellectual property system has become a technology for the maintenance of desire through control over purity, in this case of Barbie's image.

Mattel's litigation strategy is therefore much more than the simple assertion of control for its own sake. It is directed to two ends: toward commercial control of Barbie and for the control over the sexualized body of her flesh. Mattel came to understand how it could use intellectual property to control access to Barbie and to regulate and maintain consumer desire for both the material object and the concept that Barbie came to represent. The story of Barbie is a particularly vivid example of the deep links between intellectual property laws, desire, sex, and commercial gain.

The intellectual property history of Barbie is thus a story of power and control and money and desire. It is a story of how intellectual property works in reality. And it is the story of a doll from 1959, who is much more than a doll now. ◆

Further Reading

Robin Gerber (2009) *Barbie and Ruth: The Story of the World's Most Famous Doll and the Woman Who Created Her*. New York: Harper.

Orly Lobel (2018) *You Don't Own Me: How Mattel* v. *MGA Entertainment Exposed Barbie's Dark Side*. New York: W.W. Norton.

Yona Zeldis McDonough (ed.) (1999) *The Barbie Chronicles: A Living Doll Turns Forty*. New York: Simon & Schuster.

Jerry Oppenheimer (2009) *Toy Monster: The Big, Bad World of Mattel*. Hoboken: John Wiley and Sons.

On the left: "Malted Barbie" from Tom Forsythe's photography series "Food Chain Barbie." (Courtesy of Tom Forsythe)

It's the real thing. Coke.

1800   1900   2000

--/-----/-----/-----/-----/-----/-----/--/---/-----/-----/-----/-----/----

33 Coca-Cola Bottle

Jacob Gersen and C. Scott Hemphill

JUST OVER A century ago, The Coca-Cola Company faced a major challenge. Copycat colas with similar names and bottle designs—Noka-Cola, Coke-Ola, and the like—openly free-rode on the popularity of the fizzy drink. In 1915 it devised a potent tool to deter knockoffs: the distinctive delivery system that we know today as the Coca-Cola bottle.

A unique bottle, the company hoped, would serve as a versatile and powerful anti-fraud device. If the company's bottlers used only this bottle, and only Coca-Cola was sold in the bottle, consumers could know exactly what they were getting. The company could sue any competitor that dared to use a similar (much less identical) bottle. Better yet, the cost and risk of development might be too great for a knockoff to even attempt.

Today the famous curvy bottle is ubiquitous and synonymous with the product itself. Yet, the whole notion of bottling was actually an afterthought for the company. Early ads showed only fountain Coca-Cola. Company founder Asa Candler thought bottles were low-class

and left the bottling task to others, even going so far as to enter into a perpetual contract for syrup at a set price because he was so dubious of the enterprise. Syrup was sold to bottling franchisees all over the country. Candler miscalculated, as bottle sales soon outpaced fountain sales. Even Americans who would never find themselves seated at the soda fountain could buy a bottle of Coca-Cola for a nickel. While Candler's decision left huge profits on the table, it had the happy side effect of encouraging entrepreneurs to spread the Coca-Cola gospel. Bottling turned out be a force for consumer diversification and mass consumption.

The company needed the bottlers' cooperation and investment to make any switch to a new uniform bottle. Yet bottlers were an unlikely partner in the quest to stamp out free-riders. Early bottles could be any shape or color, required by contract merely to have diamond-shaped paper labels bearing the company's name in capital letters. As agents of the company, some bottlers were faithless in the early days, furtively adulterating the syrup with saccharine.

On the left: Print advertisement, 1975. (Courtesy of The Coca-Cola Company)

(Soda fountains played games too, sometimes quietly swapping a different drink when customers asked for Coca-Cola—thus, Coke's famous advertising campaign to ask for "the real thing.")

A new bottle was urgent, in part, because of infirmities in a second legal tool that the company had used against knockoffs, namely trademark law. The company began filing trademark lawsuits against similar-sounding competitors almost as soon as the first soda fountain glass of Coca-Cola was pulled in 1886. But the company's trademark suits had a weakness. The name Coca-Cola originally referred descriptively to two key ingredients. Coca leaf gave the product its original cocaine kick; the kola nut was known as a source of caffeine. Initially, the company played up the connection with illustrations of coca leaves and kola nuts on bottle labels and advertisements. However, the description was inaccurate. Well before 1915, cocaine had been removed from the "soft" drink, and the kola nut was only used in trace amounts.

The inaccuracy created problems for the company. When it sued a copycat called Koke for using a similar name, it was in turn accused of "unclean hands" for using a misleading mark. The potency of such an accusation, which could prevent enforcement of the trademark, was brought home by a non-IP case. The Food and Drug Administration complained that, because Coca-Cola contained "no coca and little if any cola," it was misbranded, in violation of federal pure food law. The suit, quaintly named *United States* v. *Forty Barrels & Twenty Kegs of Coca-Cola*, ultimately settled. In the meantime, Coca-Cola quietly dropped the coca and kola illustrations. But the case showed the company's vulnerability to a misbranding claim.

The company was in a no-win legal situation. If Coca-Cola had contained cocaine, the company would have been in trouble for the cocaine, which became illegal to distribute without a doctor's prescription in 1914. Absent cocaine and kola, its mark was misleading and arguably its product misbranded. A new bottle thus opened a new, less vulnerable front against knockoffs.

Above: Vintage ads for Coca-Cola. (Left: Photo by API / Gamma-Rapho via Getty Images. Right: Courtesy of Heritage Auctions, HA.com)

Strikingly, Coca-Cola's legal department, rather than marketing, led the charge. At the time, legal was staffed by far fewer than the 100 attorneys that today constitute the internal legal office of Coca-Cola. Harold Hirsch, the company's general counsel, exhorted the bottlers to accept a "bottle that we can adopt and call our own child." In appealing to the bottlers' ambition, he also revealed his own: "We are not building Coca-Cola alone for today. We are building Coca-Cola forever, and it is our hope that Coca-Cola will remain the National drink to the end of time."

The company and bottlers held a design contest with a $500 reward. Eight glass manufacturers accepted the challenge to devise a bottle that could be recognized even in the dark, or in broken pieces on the ground. A team from the Root Glass Company visited the Terre Haute, Indiana, library to find images of coca and kola to somehow incorporate into their design. Bottle designers, it turns out, are

rarely great lawyers. A bottle that conveyed "coca" or "kola" would have invited the same legal headaches the company already faced from its trademark opponents and the federal government. By merciful circumstance, the team found nothing suitable.

Instead, legend has it, they found a picture on a nearby page of the Encyclopedia Britannica—an image of a cocoa pod, from which beans are harvested to make chocolate. Cocoa is a stimulant but otherwise has nothing to do with coca. The distinctive bulge of the cocoa pod was incorporated into the bottle design, yet another instance of (subtle) misdescription of the product. The shape and raised ridges identified the bottle not just by sight, but also by touch.

The Root Glass prototype won the competition and secured a design patent in 1915. The large cocoa bulge of the prototype made the bottle unstable and was slimmed down for production. A slight modification of the production version was

*Above: Andy Warhol's
bottle-inspired art.
(Photo by Ben Rose /
Getty Images)

On the left, and below:
Empty bottles (Alamy);
and the cacao bean that
inspired the bottle's
shape. (SSPL / Getty
Images)*

separately patented in 1923—surprisingly, despite the new patent's resemblance to the prior art. On the eve of the new patent's expiration in 1937, yet a third design, a slight modification of the second, was again separately patented. After three bites at the apple, the design patents finally expired in 1951.

Even without a design patent, the bottle was protected as trade dress. In seeking federal registration for its trade dress, the company cited a study showing that 99 percent of Americans could identify its product by the bottle shape alone, and in 1960, the bottle was accepted for registration. Meanwhile, the company's trademark suits finally escaped the specter of misdescription. The Supreme Court decided that it didn't matter that the Coca-Cola name was once misleading, because consumers understood the name as a signifier of source. Justice Holmes wrote for a unanimous court: "The name now characterizes a beverage to be had at almost any soda fountain. It means a single thing coming from a single source, and well known to the community."

The hourglass-shaped bottle has been fetishized as a design classic. Andy Warhol celebrated the bottle as an American cultural icon, featuring it prominently in his work:

What's great about this country is that America started the tradition where the richest consumers buy essentially the same things as the poorest. You can be watching TV and see Coca-Cola, and you know that the President drinks Coke, Liz Taylor drinks Coke, and just think, you can drink Coke, too. A Coke is a Coke and no amount of money can get you a better Coke than the one the bum on the corner is drinking. All the Cokes are the same and all the Cokes are good. Liz Taylor knows it, the President knows it, the bum knows it, and you know it.

Today, the company embraces Warhol's homage. At the time, however, it was far more suspicious. The company appears to have tolerated the paintings and silkscreens that Warhol produced, but immediately sent a cease-and-desist letter when Warhol took bottles, spray painted them silver,

filled them with perfume, and made them available for sale. Images of the bottle were fine, but any actual use of the bottle had to be fought.

Over the years, the company worked with a range of artists to fashion the Coca-Cola image. Norman Rockwell's well-known "Out Fishin" (1935) portrayed a young boy fishing from his stoop on a tree stump, with his pole, his dog, and a bottle of Coca-Cola. Haddon Sundblum forever stamped his (and Coke's) mark on American cultural consciousness with his soon-to-be iconic Coca-Cola Santa— plump, jolly, and dressed in Coca-Cola red and white.

Although early advertising did emphasize the importance of the bottle for ensuring a cold and refreshing beverage, no one at the time could have imagined just how much the taste of a Coke and its packaging would ultimately merge. When Coca-Cola phased out glass packaging in favor of aluminum cans, customers complained that the product didn't taste the same, even though the formula had not changed. A 2004 study in the journal *Neuron* emphasized the importance of the contour bottle when it concluded that brand loyalty may override factors such as taste. More to the point, participants experienced the taste differently depending on the bottle used to deliver the soda.

Though an unqualified success as a branding device, the bottle has seen mixed results as a tool of legal enforcement. The 1915 design patent blocked some knockoffs and surely discouraged others. But in 1927, the company tested its patent against the makers of "Whistle," another soft drink sold in a slender hourglass bottle. The court considering the case rejected the company's broad claim to bottles with an hourglass shape, pointing to older designs

On the left: Vintage advertisement. (Photo by API / Gamma-Rapho via Getty Images)

with the same general shape. Otherwise, the slender Whistle bottle was deemed quite unlike the "relatively short and stocky" bottle—"giv[ing] to the observer the impression of rotundity"—depicted in the 1915 patent. Much later, the company failed, in litigation in Australia and New Zealand, to prevent Pepsi from using an hourglass bottle.

Actual use of the bottle has waxed and waned. Shortly after registration of the bottle trademark, the company shifted from glass packaging to aluminum cans and plastic bottles. The bottle still appeared in advertisements, and a faint visual echo appeared in the curvy "dynamic ribbon device" printed on bottles and cans. In the 1990s, the shape made a big return, both in glass and, more importantly, in plastic bottles that adopted a version of the hourglass shape. The company attributed a large part of its sales growth during this period to the return of the famous contour bottle. In the 2000s, the company introduced a new aluminum version of the bottle. As the company noted in advertisements touting the bottle's return, sounding an almost apologetic note: "Certain things belong in certain packages. Anything else just doesn't seem right." ◆

Further Reading

Mark Prendergast (2013) *For God, Country, and Coca-Cola: The Definitive History of the Great American Soft Drink and the Company That Makes It* (3rd rev. edn). New York: Basic Books.

Coca-Cola Company v. *Whistle Company of America*, 20 F.2d 955, D. Del. 1927.

US Design Patent No. 48,160 (issued Nov. 16, 1915), "Design for a Bottle or Similar Article."

1800   1900   2000

--/-----/-----/-----/-----/-----/-----/---/--/-----/-----/-----/-----/----

34 Zapruder Film

Brian L. Frye

THE ZAPRUDER FILM is not only the most important home movie ever made, but also the most thoroughly analyzed 26 seconds of film in existence. Shortly after noon on Friday, 22 November 1963, President John F. Kennedy was assassinated in Dallas, Texas. At least 32 people filmed or photographed some aspect of the event, but Abraham Zapruder captured the assassination itself more clearly and completely than anyone else. His film was a key item of evidence in the government's investigation of the assassination, and the subject of lasting controversy, at least in part because copyright made it largely unavailable to the public until 1998.

Abraham Zapruder was a 51-year-old Russian-Jewish immigrant and the co-owner of Jennifer Juniors, Inc., a women's clothing company headquartered in the Dal-Tex Building on Dealey Plaza in downtown Dallas. He was also a Kennedy fan and an avid amateur filmmaker. The morning of 22 November was dark and rainy, so Zapruder left his movie camera at home, but when the rain stopped and the clouds broke, he went home to get it.

Zapruder's camera was a Bell & Howell Zoomatic Model 414PD, loaded with Kodachrome II daylight 8mm roll film. Typically, 8mm film is sold as 25 foot rolls of 16mm film perforated for 8mm. A filmmaker first exposes one half of the width of the film, then reloads and exposes the other half. After processing the film, the lab splits it down the middle, creating two strips of 8mm film, which the lab splices together, creating a 50 foot reel of film. A roll of 8mm film is usually exposed to light when it is loaded and unloaded, so a reel of processed 8mm film typically has light flares at its beginning, middle, and end.

The Zapruder film consists of 486 frames (about 6 feet) of 8mm film exposed over the course of 26.6 seconds at 18.3 frames per second. Actually, it was part of a longer film. Zapruder used the first half of a roll of film at home and at the office. He then reloaded the camera, intending to use the second half of the roll to film the presidential motorcade.

Initially, Zapruder intended to film the presidential motorcade from his office window, but his view was obscured, so he went

On the left: President and Mrs. Kennedy arrive at Love Field, Dallas, Texas on 22 November 1963. (Alamy)

down to Dealey Plaza to look for a better location. While waiting for the motorcade to arrive, he filmed his secretary Margaret Sitzman walking up the grassy knoll and his payroll clerk Beatrice Hester sitting on a bench with her husband Charles, in order to ensure that none of the motorcade was obscured by a light flare. At Sitzman's suggestion, Zapruder then stood on a small concrete pillar on the north side of the plaza, while she stood behind him and held his coat to steady him.

When the presidential motorcade entered Dealey Plaza at 12:30 p.m., Zapruder started filming the advance motorcycle police. He briefly stopped, then resumed filming when the presidential limousine came into view, focusing on Kennedy. A large street sign briefly blocked Zapruder's view of Kennedy. As Kennedy emerged from behind the sign, he raised his hands, and then a spray of blood and gore erupted from his forehead. Zapruder continued filming as the motorcade sped away, taking the mortally wounded Kennedy to Parklane Hospital.

According to the official account of the assassination, as the presidential limousine approached Zapruder, Lee Harvey Oswald fired three shots from a sixth floor window of the Texas School Book Depository. His first shot missed. His second shot hit Kennedy in the neck and Governor Connally in the torso. And his third shot hit President Kennedy in the head.

A few minutes later, Zapruder was walking back to his office when Harry McCormick of the *Dallas Morning News* tried to interview him. Zapruder just said, "I got it all on film." Two Dallas police officers went to Zapruder's office and asked for the film, but he refused to give it to them. Darwin Payne of the *Dallas Times Herald* also went to Zapruder's office and tried to buy the film, but he refused to give it to anyone other than the Secret Service or FBI. McCormick eventually found Secret Service Agent Forrest Sorrels and took him to Zapruder's office. Sorrels asked for copies of the film and Zapruder agreed, with certain conditions: "Mr. Zapruder agreed to furnish me with a copy of this film with the understanding that it was strictly for official use of the Secret Service and that it would not be shown or given to any newspapers or magazines as he expected to sell the film for as high a price as he could get for it."

Later that day, the Eastman Kodak Processing Laboratory processed Zapruder's film, and the Jamieson Film Company made three copies at three different exposures: underexposed, correctly exposed, and overexposed. Zapruder gave the underexposed and overexposed copies to the Secret Service, which shared them with the FBI and CIA.

Notably, the copies did not reproduce the entire image recorded on the original. Zapruder's camera, like many 8mm cameras, recorded unprojectable images between the perforations, but Jamieson could only copy the projectable part of the film. In addition, the image quality of all three copies was lower than the original. A copy of a film is always lower quality than the original, and 8mm color reversal copies are considerably lower quality, blurrier and less detailed. At some point, frames 207 to 212 of the original film were destroyed

Above: The camera used by Abraham Zapruder to film the assination of JFK. (Getty Images)

and restored from the copies. Accordingly, those frames do not reproduce the entire original image and are lower quality than the rest of the film.

Immediately after the assassination, LIFE editor Richard B. Stolley flew to Dallas, hoping to license stills from the Zapruder film for publication. Early the next morning, he went to Zapruder's office and watched the film with two Secret Service agents. Stolley immediately offered Zapruder $15,000, and quickly increased his offer to $50,000, the most he could promise without authorization. Zapruder agreed, and Stolley drafted a three-sentence contract giving LIFE "exclusive world wide print media rights" in the film, but reserving motion picture rights and ownership of the original film to Zapruder. Stolley sent the original film to LIFE's press in Chicago, and took the correctly exposed copy to LIFE's headquarters in New York.

By several accounts, Zapruder agreed to license his film to LIFE because he trusted LIFE not to "exploit" it. On 25 November, he sold his copyright in the film to Time, Inc., the owner of LIFE, for $150,000, payable in six annual installments of $25,000, and 50 percent of all revenue derived from the film in excess of $150,000. The contract also provided that Time would defend the copyright at its own expense. Zapruder asked Time not to disclose the terms of the agreement, and gave the first $25,000 installment to the widow of J.D. Tippit, the Dallas police officer killed by Lee Harvey Oswald.

The cover story of the 29 November, 1963 issue of LIFE was the Kennedy assassination,

illustrated by 30 frames from the Zapruder film, printed in black and white. And on 7 December, 1963, LIFE published a "John F. Kennedy Memorial Edition," illustrated by nine frames from the Zapruder film, printed in color. At Zapruder's request, LIFE did not publish frame 313, which shows the shot to Kennedy's head.

At the time, federal copyright law only protected works published with a copyright notice and unpublished works registered with the Copyright Office. Zapruder never published or registered his film, but Time registered every issue of LIFE, and registered the Zapruder film itself as an unpublished motion picture. However, Time refused to license the Zapruder film, so it was generally unavailable to the public.

On 29 November 1963, President Johnson created the President's Commission on the Assassination of President Kennedy, and appointed Chief Justice Earl Warren chairman. The Warren Commission presented its final report to President Johnson on 24 September 1964, concluding that Lee Harvey Oswald assassinated President Kennedy, acting entirely alone. The Warren Report relied heavily on the Zapruder film, as well as other home movies and photographs of the assassination. Time authorized the Warren Commission to publish stills from the Zapruder film in the Warren Report, but the report did not include a copyright notice.

The Warren Commission was intended to provide the definitive account of the Kennedy assassination. But many people questioned the accuracy of its findings, especially its conclusion that Oswald acted alone. These skeptics became "assassination

Above: Frames of the Zapruder Film. On the left, frame 313, and on the right, frame 371. (The Sixth Floor Museum)

researchers," who studied any information even tangentially related to the assassination, hoping to disprove the Warren Report and expose what "really" happened. The Zapruder film was their holy grail, and many believed it would also be their Rosetta Stone.

In 1967, Bernard Geis published assassination researcher Josiah Thompson's book, *Six Seconds in Dallas: A Micro-Study of the Kennedy Assassination*. Thompson argued that Oswald did not act alone, based primarily on his analysis of the Zapruder film. Geis tried to license frames from the Zapruder film to illustrate the book, but Time refused. So Geis hired an artist to make charcoal drawings of the relevant parts of the frames, and used those instead.

Time sued for copyright infringement. The court found that Time owned a valid copyright in the Zapruder film, and that Thompson had copied frames from the film without permission. But it also found that Thompson's use of the frames was a noninfringing fair use, because it made his argument easier to understand and did not hurt Time.

While Time tried to restrict access to the Zapruder film, illicit copies were available from many different sources. When Time purchased the film, several editors made personal copies. The Secret Service, FBI, and CIA also made additional copies. The Warren Commission deposited a copy in the National Archives. And in 1967, New Orleans District Attorney Jim Garrison subpoenaed a copy from Time, which he improperly allowed assassination researchers to copy and distribute. But the relative scarcity of the Zapruder film still fascinated assassination researchers, and made copies of the film precious relics of the Kennedy martyrology.

Unfortunately, the copies were terrible. Many generations removed from the original, and often poorly made, they provided only an obscured and distorted version of the Zapruder film. But assassination researchers still studied those copies with obsessive zeal, hoping to glean clues about the original. Effectively, they adopted a philological method of studying the Zapruder film, treating each copy as a recension, preparing critical editions, and reading backward to reconstruct the original.

Journalists gradually began to defy Time's refusal to license the Zapruder film. In 1970, Chuck Collins showed a copy on local Chicago TV, and in 1975, Geraldo Rivera showed a copy on his ABC talk show, *Good Night America*. But Time just ignored them.

Abraham Zapruder died on 30 August 1970. He never made another film. In 1975, the Zapruder family sued Time for failing to enforce the copyright in the film, and Time settled the lawsuit by selling the film and the copyright back to the family for $1. In 1978, the Zapruder family gave the original film to the National Archives and Records Administration ("NARA") for preservation, but retained ownership of the film and the copyright, charging Oliver Stone about $85,000 to use it in his film JFK (1992).

The President John F. Kennedy Assassination Records Collection Act of 1992 ("JFK Act") nationalized all records of the Kennedy assassination, including the Zapruder film. When the Zapruder family asked NARA to return the original film, it refused. In 1997, the Assassination Records Review Board determined that the Zapruder film was nationalized by the JFK Act, but the copyright was

Above: An Oak Cliff, Dallas, business closed after the shooting. (The Sixth Floor Museum)

not, and ordered compensation to the Zapruder family. Later that year, the Zapruder family licensed the film for use in the documentary IMAGE OF AN ASSASSINATION: A NEW LOOK AT THE ZAPRUDER FILM (1998), which included several different versions of the film.

The government and the family disagreed about the value of the film, but in 1999, an arbitration panel ordered $16 million compensation. After receiving compensation, the family donated the copyright in the film to the Sixth Floor Museum, which licenses it at reasonable rates. The copyright in the Zapruder film will expire on 1 January 2040.

The story of the Zapruder film raises difficult questions about how copyright should apply to important historical documents, if at all. In theory, copyright is indifferent to social meaning. Either a work is protected or it isn't, and copyright owners have the final say on whether and how people use their works, especially unpublished ones. While fair use can mitigate the problem,

copyright effectively precluded public access to the Zapruder film for 35 years.

Ironically, the philological method adopted by assassination researchers survived the release of the original film to the public. Initially, they used copies of the film to imagine the missing original. Today, they use the original film to imagine the actual event. The Kennedy mystery lives on, secreted in the interstices of the frames of the Zapruder film. ◆

Further Reading

Brian L. Frye (2016) "Reflections on Motion Picture Evidence," *World Picture Journal*, 12: Orthodox.

Josiah Thompson (1967) *Six Seconds in Dallas: A Micro-Study of the Kennedy Assassination.* New York: Random House.

Alexandra Zapruder (2016) *Twenty-Six Seconds: A Personal History of the Zapruder Film.* New York: Twelve.

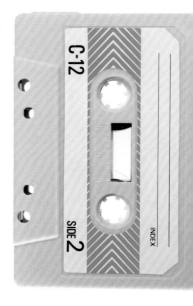

1800   1900   2000

--/-----/-----/-----/-----/-----/-----/---/--/-----/-----/-----/-----/----

35 Audiotape Cassette
Robin Wright

THE AUDIOTAPE CASSETTE arrived on the scene in the same year the Beatles released their first album.

Before this, between the 1930s and the 1960s, amateur use of audio recording technologies had developed slowly, via wire or reel-to-reel tape technologies or with various attempts at cartridge systems like the 8-track. It wasn't until Philips unveiled their prototype audiotape cassette at the 1963 Berlin Radio Show that home recording really took off. Suddenly, for the beat generation, sound reproduction technology was available to everyone. The audiotape cassette was easy to use, and widely available to everyday consumers. Initial problems with sound quality were resolved during the 1970s, and the audiotape cassette soon replaced the 8-track tape cartridge as the media format of choice for Baby Boomers. Between the jukebox of the 1950s and the Spotify playlists of the 21st century, these simple, plastic media objects were the low-tech forerunners of our modern digital media platforms. And they created the framework for music on what we now know as user-generated content sites, social media, and internet streaming.

The development of the audiotape cassette gave music consumers a new, very personal way to interact with recorded music. Along with affordable playback equipment—including battery-operated portable player/recorders, the in-car deck, the Sony Walkman, and the boom box aka ghetto blaster—the cassette tape revolutionized music for the masses. Users could cheaply and easily design and program their own interaction with recorded music, and create an object that reflected their own personal media identity. With an audiotape cassette, fans could change the order of play, add sounds and effects, draw or write on the label, and take and play the tape anywhere. Most importantly, they could create an individual expression of their own musical experience that could be shared with others. The homemade mix tape became a standard trope of musical communication, connecting with friends and family at home, in the car, at a party, or on the beach. The choice of what would go onto a tape was a matter of serious

On the left: Collection of audio cassettes from the 1980s. (Getty Images)

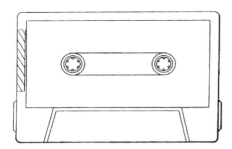

import for romantics across the globe. As they recognized that every mix tape is a love letter.

But this newfound freedom to interact with recorded music had profound implications for the commercial music recording industry. The cassette tape technology produced a huge rise in private home taping of music off the radio, LP records, live performances, and even from other audiotape cassettes. For commercial music producers and copyright owners, the audiotape cassette was the latest battle in the music wars, and its introduction was the opening salvo in a new war against the manufacturers of consumer electronics which allowed the easy, unauthorized copying of copyright works.

In 1988 the British Phonographic Industry—a UK copyright collecting society representing the owners of copyright in commercial sound recordings—took legal action against Amstrad Consumer Electronics and a group of electronics retailers. Amstrad was manufacturing, and the retailers were marketing, a double cassette deck that allowed recording from one tape deck to another at twice the normal playback

speed. BPI wanted to stop Amstrad and the retailers from being able to advertise and sell these tape decks. Advertising for the decks suggested that consumers could use the equipment to copy their favorite sound recordings onto blank audiotape cassettes. At the time UK copyright law didn't permit home copying of sound recordings, and so BPI asked the court for an injunction to halt all advertising and sale of the machines. Amstrad's lawyers countered that the copyright in a musical work or sound recording did not include the exclusive right to manufacture or promote the sale of tape recorders: their argument was that any copyright infringement by a purchaser of the device could only be due to an act by the user, and was not attributable to the manufacturers or retailers of the equipment used to play or record the

Above, left: Drawing of an audiotape cassette in US Patent 5,706,145 (1984).

Above, right: A mixed tape / love letter. (Getty Images)

Above, from left to right: A walkman enjoyed solo, or, shared. (Getty Images)

unlawful purposes. Despite characterizing Amstrad's advertising of the devices as cynical, the court held that selling the equipment did not actually authorize the breach of copyright by a purchaser. A purchaser of the equipment would not believe that the equipment manufacturer had the authority to grant them permission to copy sound recordings. So, the court concluded, it was the operator of the recorder alone who decided "whether he shall copy and what he shall copy."

The case exposed a range of issues that feature large in the music wars to this day. For example, the judgment noted that an injunction against Amstrad selling the device might only reduce the level of home copying, not end it. To completely eliminate home copying would require restrictions on all manufacturers of compact recording equipment. The ubiquitous availability and use of the audiotape cassette had shifted popular custom around the use of recorded music too fast and too far for copyright law to be used to change consumer habits. The same dynamic had played out in the fights over player piano rolls of the late 19th century, and it would be echoed in concerns in later years about CDs, DVDs, VCRs, the internet, and streaming services.

audiotape cassette. The electronics companies claimed that they did not control how a consumer used the equipment, and so they did not have a duty to prevent or deter purchasers from using the device to infringe copyright. Amstrad and the retailers were merely selling the device, they said, and they were not responsible for any copyright infringement that might happen to occur through its use.

In the UK House of Lords, Lord Templeman described the case as a climax of the conflict between two interdependent industries, the makers of sound recordings and the makers of recording equipment. He noted that, at the time, audiotape cassettes and compact recording equipment had been available for at least a decade, and that they could be used for both lawful and

Lord Templeman also observed the difficulty of seeking to enforce a law that was clearly more honored in the breach than the observance. It seemed, he said, that "the beat of Sergeant Pepper and the soaring sounds of the Miserere from unlawful copies are more powerful than law-abiding instincts or twinges of conscience." Rather than the court providing an injunction in an attempt to stop the practice of home copying, it concluded that it would be more appropriate that a law that is treated with such contempt be amended or repealed. The court drew attention to one potential solution to the dilemma that had been adopted in Germany: charging a levy on the sale of blank audiotape cassettes, which could then be used to compensate copyright owners for any loss from the widespread practice of home copying.

A private copying scheme including a levy to compensate copyright owners was introduced in Germany in the 1960s. Similar schemes continue to operate in many European jurisdictions and also in limited forms in Canada and the United States. Most levy schemes involve a copyright exception in the local legislation that permits private copying, operating alongside collection of a levy on blank media or recording equipment. Amounts collected are distributed to copyright owners as a reimbursement for losses from the private use of their work.

The introduction of the German scheme followed a 1955 court case between yet another music collecting society, GEMA—Gesellschaft für musikalische Aufführungs-und mechanische Vervielfältigungsrechte—representing composers, lyricists and music publishers, and the audio equipment

Above: A group of young men carries a portable stereo through Central Park in Manhattan. (Photo by Karl Weatherly / CORBIS / Corbis via Getty Images)

manufacturer Grundig. Just as BPI argued in the UK case, GEMA claimed that by advertising and selling their recording equipment to consumers who might use it to copy musical works onto blank audiotape cassettes, Grundig was jeopardizing the rights of its copyright-owning members. GEMA, like BPI, sought an injunction on the sale of the devices. The court found that home taping was not permitted under the existing private copying exception in German law, and also that authors were entitled to receive just remuneration for any enjoyment of their work, even if the use was private and non-commercial. As a result, in 1965 an amendment was introduced into German copyright law creating the world's first statutory license and levy scheme to compensate copyright owners for the revenue lost as a result of private copying. Oddly enough, however, the scheme wasn't extended to blank audio media, like audiotape cassettes, until 1985.

Private copying levy schemes now operate in 31 countries around the world. There are different opinions about whether they are an effective way to address the issue of revenue lost from private copying of copyright works. But in the digital age, levies on various forms of media storage devices are still delivering returns to copyright owners, particularly in Europe, and there are few calls for their removal. The amounts received as a percentage of overall music revenue are small, and increasingly unpredictable, as blank media items disappear from the market and some levy systems extend to digital devices. Discussion has now turned to the challenges faced by levy systems in an environment where private copies are increasingly stored in the cloud rather than on physical media.

In the early 21st century, the audiotape cassette—just like the vinyl record—is showing a resurgence of popularity. There is a certain nostalgic romance to the idea of recordings held on these inexpensive, lo-fi, analog artifacts. Unsigned bands can release small runs in the cassette tape format to sell or swap, giving an underground, indie buzz, and the feeling of being part of a subculture. And despite commercial sound recording formats moving on, first to

CDs, then remote servers, and now into the cloud, enthusiasts for the homespun, DIY features of the simple audiotape cassette are still out there, keeping the faith.

In 2014, the film GUARDIANS OF THE GALAXY prominently featured a gift mix tape as a plot point, and the soundtrack was released on audiotape cassette. This nostalgic return to the tangible reality of a physical, modifiable, media object suggests an ongoing affection for the symbolic and social importance of a technology that is now more than 50 years old. Despite its ephemeral nature and often-poor quality, the audiotape cassette created an enduring culture that continues to play an emotional role in the production, distribution, and consumption of recorded sound into this century. Some believe that the cassette tape has a unique, "warm" sound, and that its transient nature is part of its charm. But it is the broader historical contribution of this small, portable, immediately identifiable object to our personal interaction with re-corded music that has cemented its place in the history of both intellectual property law and popular culture. The cassette tape was a key part of the media revolution that has brought us into the modern world of digital copying, sharing and an ever-closer con-nection of consumers with the production and distribution of recorded music. It has played a crucial role in our engagement with sound recording, and the evolution of both the international music industry and copyright law in the late 20th and early 21st centuries. An impressive role for such a small, humble, plastic object. ◆

Further Reading

Thurston Moore (2004) *Mix Tape: The Art of Cassette Culture*. Milford: Universe Publishing.

David Morton (1999) *Off the Record: The Technology and Culture of Sound Recording in America*. New Brunswick: Rutgers University Press.

Jude Rogers (2013) "Total Rewind: 10 Key Moments in the Life of the Cassette," *Guardian*, 30 August. Available at: www.theguardian.com/music/2013/aug/30/cassette-store-day-music-tapes

Hester Wijminga, Wouter Klomp, Marije van der Jagt, and Joost Poort (2016) *International Survey on Private Copying. Law and Practice 2016*. Geneva: WIPO. Available at: www.wipo.int/publications/en/details.jsp?id=4183

C.B.S. Songs Limited & Others v. *Amstrad Consumer Electronics Plc* [1988] UKHL 15

GEMA v. *Grundig* 1 ZR 8/54, 17 BGHZ 266, 1955 GRUR 492

On the left: In terms of love declarations, John Cusack set the bar high as Lloyd Dobler in SAY ANYTHING (US 1989, Dir. Cameron Crowe) standing outside his object of affection's window playing Peter Gabriel's "In Your Eyes" on a boombox. (Alamy)

1800   *1900*   *2000*

--/----/----/----/----/----/----/---/--/----/----/----/----/----

36 Action Figure

Jason Bainbridge

Tʜᴇ Aᴄᴛɪᴏɴ Fɪɢᴜʀᴇ is very much the son of Barbie.

He offers the same liminal pleasures of plaything and companion. He allows children to roleplay-as-an-adult, thanks to a scalable world of vehicles and accessories that are capable of replicating most careers and transforming any space into a war-zone, an urban center or an alien world. And, similar to his mother, he is also an important site for articulating copyright and trademark, defining categories that would otherwise appear as liminal as the pleasures he offers. As such, the Action Figure embodies the limits of what his consumers can engage in, policing the boundaries between their imaginations and the IP rights of his creators. But whereas Barbie remains a largely passive receptacle of her consumers' fantasies—and Ken little more than another accessory for her—the Action Figure announces his point of difference in his name: *action*. Sure, he may have the same adult *figure* of a male doll like Ken, but that figure is matched (and his masculinity rigorously underscored) by being articulated and therefore *capable of action*,

On the left: G.I. Joe action figure by toy company Hasbro, US armed forces, 1964. (Alamy)

of performing as an adult rather than just looking like one.

The first action figure, *G.I. Joe*, was originally conceived as a licensed toy. In March 1962 Stan Weston came to toymakers the Hassenfeld Brothers' (later Hasbro) Creative Director of Product Development, Don Levine, with the idea of a "movable soldier" based on the up-coming television program *The Lieutenant* starring Gary Lockwood. Weston's idea was very much informed by Hasbro's rival, Mattel, and their most popular toy, Barbie. Like Barbie, Weston envisioned his moveable soldier as being similarly accessory-based. Observing boys secretly playing with Ken dolls had convinced him that there was a market for boys' "dolls."

Levine, a veteran of the Korean War, liked the idea but worried about linking it to a television program aimed at adults and vulnerable to cancelation. It wouldn't be until February 1963 that he was finally convinced via a chance encounter with a sculptor's wooden mannequin in the display window of Arthur Brown's art supply store. This gave Levine the basic design template for a ball-jointed soldier doll with moveable parts. The connection to *The Lieutenant* was dropped in favor of a movable military figure founded on the classic "razor/razor-blade" model advanced by Mattel's co-founder Elliot Handler: "You buy the razor (the doll), then you've got to buy a lot of blades (the uniforms, the equipment, the vehicles)." Merrill Hassenfeld loved the concept and offered Stan Weston a choice of either a lump sum of $75,000 up front or a 1 percent royalty on the toy line. While Weston negotiated the figure up to $100,000 he missed out on millions in royalties—but he was still to make another important contribution to the history of the Action Figure and the Figure's relationship with IP.

Hassenfeld quickly recognized the problems implicit in marketing the line as "a doll for boys" so he quickly set out to demarcate the *action* element. Each toy was referred to as a "movable fighting man" and through his 21 moveable parts, the figure brought "action" to children's toys in a way that had never been seen before. Boys might have been hesitant to play with a doll, even a male doll, but this toy's capacity for action (to look like he was running, shooting, fighting, basically everything that an adult soldier could actually do) made him socially acceptable. The line was also given a single name for trademark purposes, *G.I. Joe*, inspired in part by the 1945 Robert Mitchum film THE STORY OF G.I. JOE (1945) referring to "Government Issue Joe," the generic term for the common everyman soldier. The name had previously been licensed for comics and candy bars but not toys.

So it was that *G.I. Joe* debuted in 1964 as four action figures, each representing a branch of the US armed forces—Army, Navy, Marines, and Air Force. The 11½-inch (29cm, 1/6 scale) Caucasian figure came in a variety of hair and eye colors and sported a realistic male physique. According to the patent Joe was a "toy figure or doll having movable joints that closely simulate the movable portions of the human anatomy."

The patent was the only time Hasbro referred their new product as a doll and it also threw up a new challenge for Levine. If *G.I. Joe* was to be as successful as he hoped, how could he protect against infringement? How could you trademark the human body? The answer came in two physical imperfections that would subsequently be borne by every *G.I. Joe*—a very manly right cheek scar and, more bizarrely, an early production error—printing the right thumbnail on the underside of the thumb. Both of these became

Above: Gary Lockwood in The Lieutenant, 1963–1964. (Alamy)

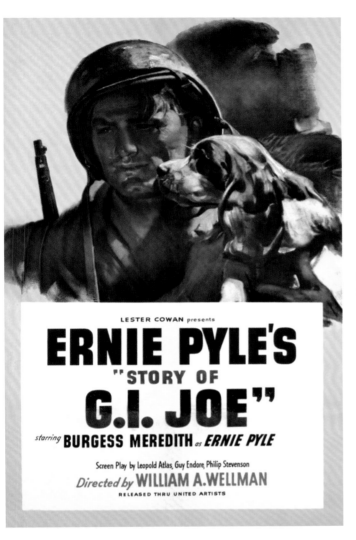

Above: THE STORY OF
G.I. JOE *poster, a 1945
American war film
directed by William
Wellman, starring
Burgess Meredith
and Robert Mitchum.
(Alamy)

protective measures against infringement and were diligently policed by Hasbro; for example, Mego's later *Fighting Yank* was taken off the market after Hasbro successfully sued when the *Yank* was discovered to have the reverse thumbnail as part of his design. Later *G.I. Joe* additions like the Kung-Fu grip (flexible curved fingers), eagle eyes (moving eyes) and "real" hair were as much additional protective measures for trademark purposes as they were points of difference in a rapidly crowded marketplace. *G.I. Joe* proudly carried his trademark on his right buttock. The Action Figure proudly demonstrated that amongst its repertoire of actions was a capacity for legal action, too.

G.I. Joe became an instant sell-out in toy stores, buoyed by television advertising that identified Joe as both "TV's new hero" and more importantly a "male action figure," extensive in-store displays and, by December 1964, a fan club of over 150,000. His subsequent development across the decades is a mirror of the times, a plastic map of the cultural zeitgeist. In 1965 the first African-American Joe appeared and—in addition to the uniform and equipment sets—the first in-scale vehicle, a Jeep. The *G.I. Joe* trademark was licensed across a range of merchandise with the first international license going to English firm Palitoy who would release *G.I. Joe* under the name *Action Man* in the United Kingdom and Australia.

Keeping pace with the times, 1966's Special Forces Fighter Green Beret *G.I. Joe* was modeled after the American soldiers in the Vietnam War. While Levine had feared tying his military toy to a canceled television series, he hadn't foreseen the damage that growing dissatisfaction with American involvement in the Vietnam war would have. By the end of 1966 over 184,000 US troops were in Asia and the war was being lost in the lounge rooms of America. Parents Groups picketed the Toy Fair of 1966 with banners reading "Toy Fair or War Fare?". Hasbro's television advertising was questioned by the Federal Commission. The Action Figure had suddenly become linked to the wrong type of action.

Oct. 11, 1966   S. F. SPEERS ETAL   3,277,602

TOY FIGURE HAVING MOVABLE JOINTS

Filed June 15, 1964   2 Sheets—Sheet 1

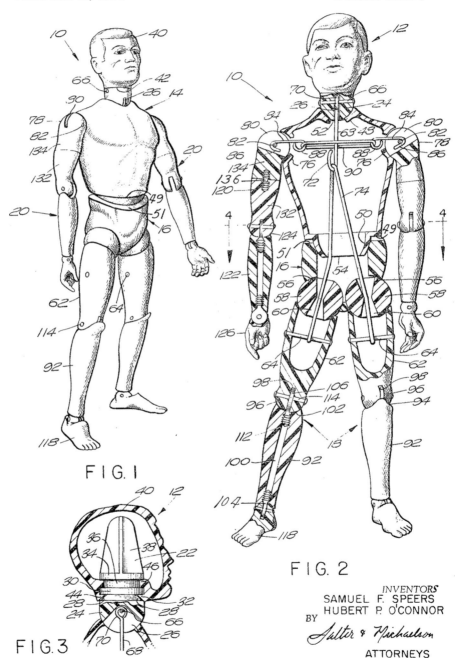

FIG. 1

FIG. 2

FIG. 3

INVENTORS
SAMUEL F. SPEERS
HUBERT P. O'CONNOR
BY
Salter & Michaelson
ATTORNEYS

Hasbro's rivals were also challenging *G.I. Joe*'s sales, including Marx's 1965 *Best of the West* line (western action figures), Mattel's 1967 space-based *Matt Mason* (astronaut action figures) and Joe's own creator Stan Weston, who had used his $100,000 from the sale of the *G.I. Joe* concept to Hasbro to establish his own licensing company, representing DC Comics (then National Periodical Publications), Marvel Comics and Kings Features. This gave him a stable of superheroes from Superman to Spiderman to Flash Gordon. Rather than creating action figures for each of them, Weston presented Ideal Toys with a competitor to Joe; *Captain Action* (originally Captain Magic) a 12-inch action figure that could assume the identity of a variety of superheroes through the standard razor/razor blade model—one *Captain Action* doll and multiple superhero costumes. Not so coincidentally all of those superhero licenses were represented by Weston's own Leisure Concepts company. The superhero Action Figure was born and *Captain Action* went on the market in 1966 as Joe became embroiled in controversy.

Fortunately *G.I. Joe* had been created for a fight. He responded by leaving the military and rebranding himself as an Adventurer in 1970, leading an "Adventure Team" that spent its time capturing pygmy gorillas and searching for white tigers (according to the back of their packaging). But having lost his uniqueness as a military man throughout the 1970s, *G.I. Joe*'s greatest action now became his *re*action to

whatever was the latest trend. At the height of the Kung-Fu craze in 1974 he acquired a Kung-Fu grip. In response to the success of both *The Six-Million-Dollar-Man*'s television series and toy line (developed by rival Kenner) he briefly welcomed Major Mike Powers, the Atomic Man, onto the team. By 1976, when old rival Mego was dominating the toy industry with their *World's Greatest Super Heroes* line, *G.I. Joe* had become a fully fledged super hero himself, fighting alien Neanderthals. Joe was a very long way from the military. But it would actually be his rivals in the *World's Greatest Super Heroes* toy line that would prove just how well the Action Figure could articulate IP laws.

Ideal's *Captain Action* had not enjoyed a long shelf life in toy stores, so Joe's creator Stan Weston had redeployed his stable of super heroes with considerably more success at Mego. Here, a cross-section of DC and Marvel comic heroes and villains, along with *Conan the Barbarian* and *Tarzan*, formed their *World's Greatest Super Heroes* line. While Joe had demonstrated that a human body could be trademarked, these figures would demonstrate that an entire category of people could be copyrighted: Super Heroes.

Despite being most associated with comic books, the first successful attempt to register "Super Hero" was not made by either DC or Marvel Comics but by Halloween costume and rubber toy manufacturer Ben Cooper in April 1966. So when Mego sought to trademark *World's*

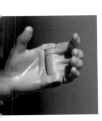

Above: GI Joe's inverted thumb. (www. instructables.com)

On the left: GI Joe deep freeze action figure, Hasbro 1967. (Courtesy of Heritage Auctions, HA.com)

Below: GI Joe action figures at the Hasbro International G.I. Joe Collectors' Convention in California. Hundreds of G.I. Joe fans from around the country attend the convention to buy, sell, and trade G.I. Joe and military action figures. (Photo by Justin Sullivan / Getty Images)

Greatest Super Heroes for their Action Figures they encountered opposition from Cooper. Unwilling to proceed with protracted legal proceedings Mego assigned its interest to rivals DC and Marvel, jointly. By the 1970s, both comic companies had come to realize the value of trademarking the category name "Super Heroes" to develop merchandising revenue. Indeed, they were generating more value from licensing than from comic book sales. With Mego's interest in the WGSH mark jointly assigned to them, DC and Marvel united to challenge Cooper. Cooper withdrew its opposition to the WGSH mark and subsequently assigned its interest in "Super Heroes" to DC and Marvel too. Over the next ten years DC and Marvel would co-operate to enact a joint strategy whereby they gained control of "Super Hero" (and all of its variations) through trademark registration. Thanks to Weston and Mego's Action Figures revealing the value of Ben Cooper's original trademark application, DC and Marvel effectively created a superhero duopoly, enforced through the threat of litigation and without ever being questioned about genericism or their co-registration of the mark.

Ultimately the Arabian oil crisis and the OPEC oil embargo of 1973 made the cost of petroleum prohibitive, forcing the price of raw plastic ever higher. The entire *G.I. Joe* line briefly shrank to 8½ inches to become the science-fiction oriented *Super Joe / Super Adventure Team*. But Joe's embrace of science fiction had come too late and by 1978 both Joe and Mego's *World's Greatest Super Heroes* had entered the one war they couldn't win—STAR WARS. Kenner's 3¾-inch action figures could be used with in-scale playsets and vehicles and,

because of their cheaper price point, made it possible for children to collect the entire range. Perhaps more importantly it also confirmed the value of licensing and the Action Figure as part of a multimedia approach to merchandising. Reportedly 300 million STAR WARS units were sold between 1980 and 1983. While never reaching those sales again, Action Figures remained at the forefront of the multibillion dollar deals Disney did to acquire the Marvel and Lucasfilm licenses throughout the 2000s, while continuing to contribute to the massive merchandising revenue streams that are often more valuable than the film and comic properties themselves.

The intellectual property history of Action Figures is therefore a history of control, from trademarking the representation of the human body to copyrighting an entire category of some of the most recognizable fictional characters in the world. It highlights the importance of licensing, the value of alternative revenue streams for corporate gain and the plastic figures who embody them. ◆

Further Reading

Jason Bainbridge (2017) "Beyond the Law: What Is So 'Super' about Superheroes and Supervillains?," *International Journal for the Semiotics of Law*, 30(3), pp. 367–388.

Mark Gallagher (2006) *Action Figures: Men, Action Films, and Contemporary Adventure Narratives*. New York: Palgrave Macmillan.

Vincent Santelmo (2001) *The Complete Encyclopedia to G.I. Joe* (3rd ed). New York: Krause.

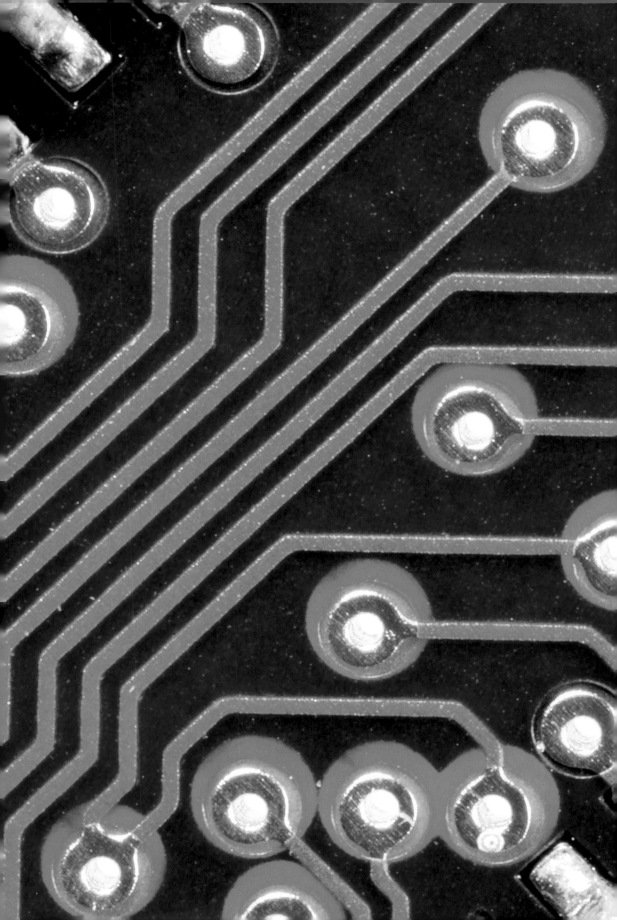

1800   *1900*   *2000*

--/-----/-----/-----/-----/-----/-----/----/-/-----/-----/-----/-----/----

37 RAM-Chip

Jake Goldenfein

DYNAMIC RANDOM ACCESS Memory, or DRAM, was patented by IBM employee Robert Dennard in June 1968, under the title "Field-Effect Transistor Memory." Although invented by an IBM employee, it was first successfully commercialized by Intel in 1970 in their 1103 DRAM-chip—the first RAM technology to bring dynamic electrical memory into the mainstream. It was a remarkable breakthrough in memory technology, but it was also fundamental in reshaping intellectual property law and the way that we regulate the entire technical ecosystem of the digital, hyper-connected, cloud-enabled world we live in today.

Developments in RAM, along with improvements in communication technologies more broadly, have meant that copyright materials are constantly being copied into RAM for the sake of ease of access and use. This single fact became the anchor point for almost every aspect of our digital lives: it was central to the emergence of digital copyright during the 1980s, arguments over reverse engineering, mod-chips, and software piracy in the 1990s, internet browsing, cable television time-shifting, and internet intermediary liability in the 2000s, and live streaming, cloud computing, and the innumerable ways we consume media in current times.

The invention of the Intel 1103 chip was the start of all this. It represented a binary digit—also known as a bit—as a high or low charge on a capacitor paired with a single transistor. In comparison, static RAM systems of the day required up to six transistors per bit. The advantage of the DRAM approach was clearly described in the patent documentation: since only two components are required, the area needed for each bit is extremely small. Thus, very large memory systems could be built on a single chip.

Memory is needed in all digital systems and, prior to the RAM-chip, magnetic core arrays were the preferred means of creating memory systems. These arrays involved grouped donuts of ferrite material suspended on wires, such that they could be magnetized in one of two directions using pulsed electrical charges—the magnetic dipoles of north and south represented

On the left: A close-up of RAM-chip connections. (Alamy)

Above: A magnetic-core memory, the predominant form of random-access computer memory between ca. 1955 and 1975. (Photo by Jud McCranie, CC BY-SA 4.0)

the digital 1s and 0s. DRAM changed the medium of memory from ferromagnetic to electrical, increasing memory density sufficiently to make silicon chips a viable choice. The trade-off for this dramatically smaller medium was the need constantly to refresh the capacitor with electricity to prevent the charge from "leaking," thereby destroying the data.

Prior to the 1103, Intel had already produced several static RAM-chips—notably the 3103 and the 1101—but the 1103 was the first commercially successful DRAM-chip, and the first type of memory chip to challenge magnetic cores. Intel marketed the 1103 with the claim, "The End. Cores lose price war to new chip." The marketing copy was prescient: nine years after the introduction of the 1103, core memory had all but disappeared. And while the low cost of the DRAM-chips was significant for commercial adoption, their truly revolutionary impact is better attributed to their size, which meant they could be joined with central processing units to create integrated computing machines. For instance, the 1103 was combined with

early microprocessors, like the Intel 4004 (released in 1971) and the Intel 8088 (1979), which led first to the development of the minicomputer, and then to the personal computer. While the 1103 used in those early personal computers may have been primitive, the chip was the progenitor of a family of DRAM-chips whose continually decreasing cost and continually increasing memory density drastically changed information and communication technology.

RAM initially became the subject of copyright jurisprudence because of the way that digital processing systems temporarily reproduce data in RAM for subsequent processing by a CPU. In other words, the "copy" ultimately accessed by a computer user is always an ephemeral RAM reproduction. A series of copyright cases in a range of jurisdictions quickly sprouted from this fact, pitting copyright owners against chip manufacturers and others. Those disputes required judges to address vexing questions about what amounted to a "reproduction," especially one that wasn't visible to the naked eye and was merely a set of temporary, evanescent electrical

The following text appears within the advertisement image:

THE END

CORES LOSE PRICE WAR TO NEW CHIP
ASK INTEL FOR PROOF

Intel introduces Type 1103, a history-making 1024-bit RAM made by our silicon-gate MOS process at such high yields that the cost dips below cores.

Just tell us what core memories cost you, and we'll tell you how to build operational Type 1103 memories for less cost in any size from 50,000 bits to 10,000,000 bits.

The Intel 1103 makes a fully assembled memory system that has a maximum access of 300 nanoseconds and a total cycle time of 600 nanoseconds. The chip is fully decoded and dissipates only 100 microwatts per bit, permitting dense packing in compact configurations.

For all of the cost advantage, phone your Intel representative or call us collect at (415) 961-8080. For immediate delivery phone your local Intel distributor, Cramer Electronics or Hamilton Electro Sales. If your distributor isn't stocked, call Intel collect for immediate same-day shipment.

Intel Corporation is in high-volume production at 365 Middlefield Road, Mountain View, California 94040.

intel delivers.

charges. Each case had to contend with some version of the "RAM reproduction" doctrine, a concept notoriously expressed in the 1993 US decision of *MAI Systems Corp* v. *Peak Computer* which held that any reproduction in RAM—a necessity for accessing and processing digital data, irrespective of how transient or ephemeral—would generally constitute an infringing copy.

The necessary implication of this doctrine is constant, massive infringement of copyright by any functioning electronic device. Academic responses to the doctrine were animated, typically railing against the risks of rigid doctrinal approaches and "prehistoric understandings" of copyright. Notwithstanding these concerns, a close reading of the RAM decisions from the late 1980s through to the current day suggests that the courts took a pragmatic approach. In the United States at least, much of the rigidity of the doctrine was ameliorated by case-by-case analyses of the facts, often finding against the copyright holders on the basis of the grant of an implied license or by finding fair use under §107 of the Copyright Act. In Europe, while the 2001 EU Copyright Directive gave owners exclusive right to temporary reproductions, it also exempted transient or incidental reproductions that are an integral and essential part of a technological process.

Although the RAM reproduction doctrine emerged during the era of the personal computer, it has also been central to the control of content in the internet era. The idea that ephemeral copies might still be infringing was fundamental in reconfiguring copyright into a content "access" regime. This first became visible with the development of the internet, but has become crucial to the content and service delivery structures afforded by cloud servers and subscription models. It turns out that RAM's most significant impact on intellectual property then, has been the evolution of copyright doctrine that allows tight control over networked content distribution.

In a digital media environment where information can be stored anywhere and retrieved anytime, this is a profound thing. As early as 1997, Trotter Hardy observed that, in applying the RAM reproduction

Above: Intel successfully targeted its first commercial MOS DRAM at users of older magnetic core memories. (© Intel Corporation / Courtesy of Intel Museum)

doctrine to the networked world, courts were enabling content owners to build business models that gave them control over digital media. That insight presaged a huge shift, away from users getting a material copy of a work, to merely getting access to that work for a limited time—a move that transformed "copy-right" to "access-right." Jeremy Rifkin noted that this new "Age of Access" meant that the market had given way to networks, where there were no buyers or sellers, merely access providers and their users. This has had a substantial impact on the way consumers relate to copyright content and media, as subscription and experience became more important than license and possession. Without the RAM reproduction doctrine there is no Spotify, no Netflix.

Subscription-based media environments rely on a drastically different communications infrastructure from the ones developed in the early days of the RAM-chip. Whereas the 1103 was part of the integration of electronics for personal computing, the role of RAM in the age of access is best understood as part of the dis-integration of components in the "device paradigm." Because data stored in RAM is ephemeral, that data needs a source of storage memory. Personal computing involved multiple integrated components—CPU, RAM and storage—requiring little engineering input from the user. The device paradigm, on the other hand, grants the user control over their personal device, but externalizes storage memory to remote data centers. This exporting of storage has successfully made users' devices "thinner," but also highly dependent on a complex communications network for access to content.

RAM is therefore best understood as a single node within a complex of communications technologies. In terms of content distribution, the most significant of these are the remote data centers—that is, cloud storage systems—and the internet protocols that facilitate high speed, high bandwidth provision of content. This technical constellation enables a permission system that looks more like a metered utility service than a market for intellectual goods. As copies are only ephemeral, copyright focuses less on control over the bits that constitute the content, and more on the temporary display or performance that those bits enable. "Publication" and "performance" become indistinguishable, the material copy fades in relevance, digital content loses its hybrid tangible and intangible character, and the basic unit of consumable media changes.

Whereas the RAM copy constitutes the location of user-experienced data, it is now the remote data center that increasingly organizes how intellectual commodities circulate. Although mainframes and virtualization—the technology that enabled

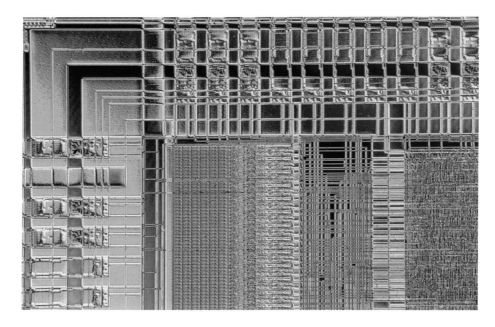

computers to run several applications simultaneously—were commercially available in the early 1970s, the technology was sidelined during the personal computing era, only to reappear in the 1990s when computer networking enabled a client-server model. Uptake of that approach expanded with the proliferation of internet providers and remote server hosting through the 1990s. From the early 2000s, cloud servers and virtual technologies made possible the pooling of storage, network and processing resources to facilitate on-demand allocation of services. The concept of "infrastructure-as-a-service" was updated when increases in server capacity and bandwidth enabled data centers to provide "software-as-a-service" products using subscription models.

The clearest example is Amazon Web Services and the distribution environment associated with, for example, the Amazon Kindle e-reader: these combined systems offer a clear example of the property rights architectures that developed around these networked computing infrastructures.

Sean Dockray describes how the e-reader is not a repository of content, but rather an object that establishes trusted access with electronic books stored in the cloud, and ensures that each and every person purchases their own rights to read each book. Although the user has more and more RAM, the content that they have—or rather the content that they can control—is distinctly less.

As a business, content streaming also took advantage of access to remotely stored data. And even piracy occurs increasingly through streaming rather than downloads. The first live audio stream of a baseball game was of a matchup between the Seattle Mariners and the New York Yankees in 1995. At that stage 56K modem lines were a tangible obstacle to content transmission. And while YouTube began in 2005, streaming really exploded after the development of HTTP adaptive streaming in 2007, through which player applications could monitor download speeds and request media parcels to be delivered in varying sizes in response to

Above: Light micrograph of a detail of a RAM computer memory chip. RAM is a type of computer memory that can be accessed randomly; that is, any byte of memory can be accessed without touching the preceding bytes. This is the most common type of memory found in personal computers and different other electronic devices like cellular phones, USB sticks and printers. Actual size is approximately 1.2 mm across. (Science Photo Library / Alamy)

*Above: The Intel®
1103 DRAM Memory
Die, 1972. The first
DRAM would enable
the explosive growth of
PC's. The production
costs of the 1103 were
much lower than the
costs of a core memory.
It quickly became the
world's best-selling
memory chip, and
was responsible for the
obsolescence of magnetic
core memory. (© Intel
Corporation / Courtesy
of Intel Museum)*

network conditions. The same year, the first Apple iPhone was released, putting a universal media player literally in people's hand. Netflix launched streaming video in 2008, and Blockbuster video symbolically went bankrupt in 2010. The era of the local content repository was over.

In many ways, the combination of data center, distribution network, streaming protocol, and dynamic RAM strain every traditional copyright category. As a concept in copyright doctrine, RAM reproduction became the anchor on which contemporary distribution models depend. And while the RAM reproduction cases were part of copyright's coming into the computer age—something undeniably significant at the dawn of the personal computer in the mid-1970s—it was RAM's tacit reconfiguration of copyright to afford control over access that reflect its true contributions to the history of intellectual property. All those phenomena find their origins in the Intel 1103, the single transistor bit, and the miniaturization of volatile electrical memory. ◆

Further Reading

Albert Borgmann (1984) *Technology and the Character of Contemporary Life: A Philosophical Inquiry*. Chicago: University of Chicago Press.

Sean Dockray (2013) "Interface, Access, Loss," in Laurel Ptak and Marysia Lewandowska (eds.) *Undoing Property?* Berlin: Sternberg Press.

Jane C. Ginsburg (2003) "From Having Copies to Experiencing Works: The Development of an Access Right in U.S. Copyright Law," *Journal of the Copyright Society of the U.S.A*, 50, pp. 113–132.

Jeremy Rifkin (2000) *The Age of Access: The New Culture of Hypercapitalism*. New York: Putnam.

US Patent No. 3,387,286 (issued June 4, 1968), "Field-effect transistor memory."

38 Football

Michael J. Madison

THE FOOTBALL SERVES as emblem, symbol, subject, and object of the ancient, medieval, and modern forms of the game of football (or soccer). It is the one constant in the game's story of change.

The football may be the most widely recognized cultural object in the world. Its status depends partly on its origins as a shared thing and partly on the distinctiveness and exclusivity of its modern attributes. It supplies a focal object through which great themes in intellectual property have shaped the game: its origins, innovation, and standardization, and relationships among law and rules on the one hand, and the organization of society, culture, and the economy on the other.

Games involving a ball and the feet are among the world's oldest. Pre-Common Era antecedents of football have been documented in ancient China (*cuju*), ancient Greece (*episkyros*), and ancient Rome (*harpastum*), among other places. Mob football, sometimes called "Shrovetide" football or "festival" football, was played in England, Scotland, Ireland, Wales and parts of Normandy and Brittany from the 12th century onward.

In medieval times, more formal versions of the game were contested by smaller groups, often organized as clubs attached to taverns. Football was not class-based nor gender-specific, and aristocrats and laborers participated, women and men. "Footeballe" was promoted during the 16th century in England by Richard Mulcaster, headmaster of the Merchant Taylors' School in London, where the play involved kicking, throwing, and possessing a ball. History is vague as to the existence and content of rules at this time, as football was quintessentially local and locally variable.

During the mid-1800s, related developments shaped mob football and its domesticated versions into the game's recognizable modern form. Efforts to systematize the game gradually distinguished between elements of modern rugby and modern football, depending on whether the ball could be possessed and advanced with the use of the hands. Developing and defining the football was central to those efforts, but sharing innovations mattered more than

On the left: Dutch forward Johan Cruyff controls the ball under pressure from a West German player during the World Cup final between West Germany and the Netherlands in Munich, 1974. (Getty Images)

controlling them via intellectual property. The Football Association (FA) was formed in London in 1863, and published a set of rules that year for the so-called "Association game." (The word "Association," in shortened form, generated the label "soccer.") For the first time, the 1863 FA rules formally prohibited handling the ball by carrying or throwing it. Full abolition of the use of the hands followed successive amendments to FA rules and to competing sets of rules of the era, notably the Sheffield Rules.

The first competition rule specifying a type of football was used in 1866, for a match under FA rules between Sheffield Football Club and FA members in London. The teams agreed that the ball should be "Lillywhite's No. 5." That designated a leading English sporting goods retailer and a size, No. 5, that the store used to distinguish among footballs on its shelves. The "No. 5 ball" remains the colloquial label for a match football for adult play.

Early efforts to standardize the football aligned with parallel technological innovations, the most critical of which was the invention of vulcanized rubber by Charles Goodyear. Goodyear secured a US patent on "Improvement in India-Rubber Fabric" in 1844 and put his innovation to use, among other ways, by making inflatable rubber bladders for footballs.

England and Scotland offered the larger entrepreneurial opportunity, both because of growing interest in football and because Goodyear's invention was not patented there. The development and production of India rubber bladders for footballs was pursued during the 1860s by Richard Lindon, a producer of footballs that used inflated pig's bladders. Lindon named his football the "Punt-about Buttonball." He never patented it, but he adapted it into ovoid forms for use in rugby and spherical forms for use in the Association game.

The combination of the rubber bladder and a spherical leather covering gave footballs a standard size and shape. That consistency supported the decision of the FA in 1872 to require that balls used in its new FA Cup competition be spherical, with a circumference of 27 to 28 inches. In 1883, the FA extended that requirement

Above, left: Brazilian football star Pele plays goalkeeper during a practice game in the 1966 World Cup, UK. (Photo by Art Rickerby / The LIFE Picture Collection / Getty Images)

Above, right: A group of West Ham supporters cheering as they leave Waterloo Station for a match at Boscombe, 1929. (Getty Images)

to all matches played under FA rules. In 1889, the FA adopted a standard weight of 12 to 15 ounces.

The size and shape of the football have remained unchanged since 1872. International aspects of football propelled further standardization of the rules and of the football. The International Football Association Board (IFAB) was formed in 1886 by the associations of England, Scotland, Wales, and Ireland, while the International Federation of Association Football (FIFA) was founded in 1904. The laws of each administering body have been added to and modified through to the present day. Law 2 states specifications for the size, shape, pressurization, and weight of the football. The weight was changed in 1937, to 14 to 16 ounces, and the law now makes allowance for the use of materials other than leather for the cover.

Openness and innovation underpinned the growth of football in its early phases, but exclusivity and market capitalism were equally important to the game that we know as football today. The invention of the spherical ball based on the rubber bladder meant that leather panels for the outer covering could be manufactured according to a standard template. Footballs cost less to produce. Manufacturing scale was possible. From the earliest days of the Association game, manufacturers competed to produce the roundest and most durable footballs. Football manufacturing began with English and Scottish producers, including William Shillcock, maker of the McGregor football in Birmingham; Mitre, in Huddersfield; and the Greenbank Leather Works, owned by the Thomlinson family, in Glasgow. Intellectual property appeared and advanced the art of football ball design and production. Producers around the world innovated by varying the number and shape of the football's leather panels. Thomlinson secured patents on his football designs during the late 1800s and later marketed the leather quality of his better footballs as "Tugite," to distinguish them from his "T-model."

In 1962, Eigil Nielsen, a former Danish player and founder of the Danish equipment producer Select Sport, developed the 32-panel icosahedron-based football, featuring a cover of hexagon- and pentagon-shaped panels. (In the 1950s, Nielsen developed a method of eliminating the external lacing that used to close the football's leather cover.) The German firm adidas modified that ball design by coupling black pentagon-shaped panels with white hexagon-shaped panels. Adidas introduced that black-and-white model, which it christened "Telstar"—evoking the Telstar satellites of the early 1960s—as the official ball of the 1970 World Cup finals in Mexico. This tournament was the first World Cup finals to

be broadcast worldwide, and the black-and-white ball became an icon of football in part because it offered better visibility to football fans following matches on television.

Adidas has held the exclusive contractual right to supply official footballs to World Cup competitions ever since. Its current contract with FIFA, the organizer of the World Cup, runs through the 2030 tournament. FIFA and adidas have modified this relationship from time to time based on intellectual property considerations that implicate the expanding influence of market capitalism on football generally. In 1970, FIFA prohibited adidas from including any brand markings on game balls. For the 1974 World Cup finals FIFA removed that restriction. New versions of the Telstar ball were used; the adidas name and logo and the Telstar name appeared on each ball. For the 1974 tournament, FIFA began referring to the competition as the "FIFA World Cup."

For every World Cup finals since 1974, adidas has designed and marketed a new official World Cup football. Football manufacturers now regularly compete with each other to supply the "official" football of clubs and competitions around the world. Adidas and other equipment manufacturers pay significant sums to earn marketing exclusivity and design and brand their footballs to distinguish them on and off the pitch. Experts estimate that adidas' contract with FIFA costs the company US$100 million for each of the World Cup finals, a figure that adidas recovers several times over via the sale of replica footballs. During 2014, when the World Cup finals were played in Brazil, adidas sold more than 12 million footballs, in various sizes. FIFA now adds its own exclusivity by offering certification of match footballs under several marks, including the "International Matchball Standard (IMS)" mark, as part of the FIFA "Quality Program."

In some respects, these systems of exclusivity generate corresponding social benefits in the ways that intellectual property law predicts. Newer balls are innovative. Equipment manufacturers have invested significantly in improvements to virtually all aspects of the football. Leather covers and bladders have been replaced by more durable and more spherical synthetic substitutes. Stitching of the panels has been succeeded by heating and

Above: Italian goalkeeper Lorenzo Buffon makes a save during training at Highbury for a match against England the next day; London, 1959. (Getty Images)

Above: Goalkeeper Briana Scurry of the US women's soccer team drops to her knees and celebrates after the United States defeated China in a penalty kick shoot-out to win the 1999 Women's World Cup final at the Rose Bowl in Pasadena. (Photo by Mike Fiala / AFP / Getty Images)

WILLS'S CIGARETTES

WILLS'S CIGARETTES

WILLS'S CIGARETTES

G. ALSOP (WALSALL)

R. PRYDE (BLACKBURN ROVERS)

A. McSPADYEN (PARTICK THISTLE)

On the left: Collectable Cigarette Cards. George Arents Collection, The New York Public Library. "G. Alsop, Walsall," "Robert Pryde, Blackburn Rovers," "Alec McSpadyen, Partick Thistle." (The New York Public Library Digital Collections)

molding, reducing the football's susceptibility to water retention. Ball surfaces have been engineered to produce truer flight and greater control for the player. The newest, most innovative balls may be fitted with "smart" technology that transmits information about ball performance wirelessly to match officials, coaches, and manufacturers. Footballs bounce better, fly with more accuracy, retain their shape and size, and repel water better than ever. The players' ability to control the football means that the modern game is faster and more fluid. Through various forms of legal exclusivity—partly based on intellectual property laws—the game of football has reached stratospheric levels of popularity and wealth. A steady if slow stream of relevant utility patents, design patents, and trademark registrations have been issued, particularly to the leading equipment producers, adidas and Nike.

Innovation supported by exclusivity and intellectual property comes at a cost. On the pitch, the lure of financial returns from innovation and brand differentiation has confronted claims that play of the game has been compromised. The 2010 World Cup finals, held in South Africa, were marred by players' complaints that the official match ball—the "Jabulani" supplied by adidas—flew unpredictably. Goalkeepers claimed that they could not predict where shots on goal would go; players could

not control the ball as they wished. The 2014 official World Cup match ball, the "Brazuca," was not the subject of similar objections.

Off the pitch, at the top of the economic hierarchy, huge amounts of money and influence now flow to FIFA, the national federations, and the large football equipment manufacturers, via their exclusive involvement in professional football and football equipment. There is little transparency or accountability, and numerous issues concerning corrupt behavior have been raised, directed particularly to FIFA.

At the bottom of the hierarchy, those who produce footballs have enjoyed little of the wealth associated with the new designs. Football manufacturing has shifted over the last several decades from local factories to global supply chains, which are predictably driven by economics and cost structures. The substitution of synthetic materials for leather beginning in the 1980s improved football quality and reduced production costs, facilitating production in developing countries. By the mid-1990s, a substantial percentage of all footballs produced worldwide—some estimates run as high as 70 percent—came from factories located in a single city in Pakistan: Sialkot. Hand-stitching was still the norm. Exploitation of low-wage stitchers, including children, was exposed.

Below: Vintage football and the "Brazuca." (Getty Images)

Above: Young Brazilian man playing barefoot on a dirt court in a favela in Rio de Janeiro. (Getty Images)

Private collaborations to end child labor and increase wages in football production have been undertaken since then, including the Atlanta Agreement negotiated in 1997 among the International Labor Organization, UNICEF, and the Sialkot Chamber of Commerce. FIFA's launch in 2007 of a match ball certification program included manufacturer compliance with a code of conduct for labor standards. Nonetheless, concerns about abusive labor practices and low wages continue to be voiced, even as 21st-century football production depends less than it once did on hand-stitching.

The intellectual property history of the football follows a pattern seen in other objects. Initially, we see tremendous innovation, coupled with technological and cultural openness. This leads to standardization, which evolves over time into innovative improvements and differentiation. Ending, almost inevitably, in wealth production based on intellectual property laws and the exclusivity these bring.

The story of the football, then, both resembles and conflicts in part with the story of the game of football. Both on and off the field of play, for more than a century, football has been linked closely to collective identity and opportunity of many sorts. Not for nothing has it been called "the People's Game." The game of football and the object that is the football may be pursued by almost anyone, at modest cost, in almost any setting. These social and cultural implications have been essential to football's global cultural hegemony. Yet football's global success created the conditions for inflecting the football with the ideologies and practices of intellectual property and market capitalism, both good and bad. The ethos of the marketplace, in turn, arguably has been essential to continuing to link all who play and watch football in an integrated global narrative.

The world, like the football, is round. ◆

Further Reading

Alicia DeSantis, Mika Gröndahl, Josh Keller, Graham Roberts, and Bedel Saget (2014) "The World's Ball," *New York Times*, 12 June. Available at: www.nytimes.com/interactive/2014/06/13/sports/worldcup/world-cup-balls.html

David Goldblatt (2006) *The Ball is Round: A Global History of Football*. London: Penguin Books.

David Goldblatt and Johnny Acton (2009) *The Football Book: The Leagues, The Teams, The Tactics, The Laws*. London: Dorling Kindersley.

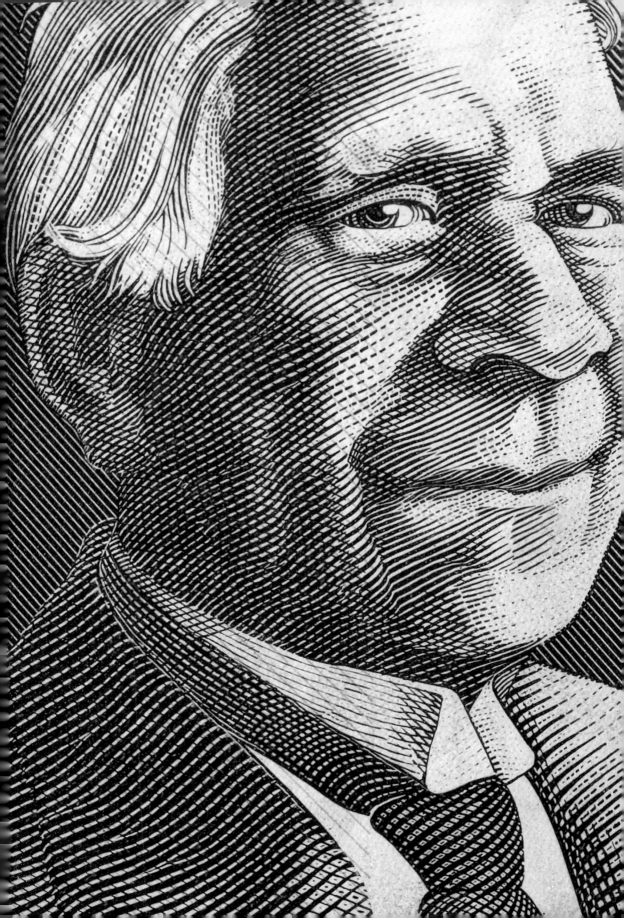

39 Polymer Banknote

Tom Spurling

On the left: Intaglio printing of David Unaipon on the front of Australia's $50 note. Intaglio—one of ten primary security devices in current polymer banknotes—is the family of printing and printmaking techniques in which the image is incized into a surface and the incized line or sunken area holds the ink, the direct opposite of a relief print. (Alamy)

IN APRIL 1963 the Australian government announced that the country would change from currency based on pounds, shillings, and pence to decimal currency, and set 14 February 1966 as the date for the introduction of the new currency. The Reserve Bank of Australia—the country's central bank, responsible for all banknote printing—had imported from Europe the latest in banknote technology and printing equipment, and was astonished to discover on Christmas Eve 1966 that its new state-of-the-art banknotes were forged. The police quickly identified the forgers and the ringleader was jailed for ten years. But the worry remained.

The Governor of the Bank, Herbert Cole "Nugget" Coombs, decided that, since the usual overseas sources of technological innovation had failed to produce a secure banknote, he would enlist the help of eminent Australian scientists in the quest for new technologies. Aside from the recent evidence of Australian forgers' sophistication, Herbert Coombs was acutely conscious of the threat of color photocopiers that had recently come on the market.

So in 1969, the Bank commenced a joint project with the Commonwealth Scientific and Industrial Research Organisation (CSIRO) to develop a more secure banknote. David Solomon, a polymer scientist, and Sefton Hamann, a physical chemist, took up the challenge.

The team worked on two different, but complementary, ideas. The first was the notion of an "optically variable device." Such devices contain images that change color or form according to the viewing angle, and which forgers cannot duplicate by simple scanning techniques. The second idea was to replace the paper substrate with one made from a polymer. A polymer substrate would not only facilitate the inclusion of the optically variable devices and other security features, but also increase durability.

By 1972 CSIRO, with the help of some employees of the Bank, had developed, a proof-of-concept banknote, and it wanted to proceed quickly to turn it into a commercial product. The Bank, on the other hand, was aware both of the risk involved in introducing new banknote technology,

and of the great technical expertise residing in its international banking colleagues and their technology partners. They were skeptical that a group of Australian scientists working in somewhat run-down facilities in Melbourne could, in a few months, come up with an invention that was superior to anything that better-funded and more-experienced international teams could offer.

To convince the Bank that it had invented a unique and useful product, CSIRO decided to patent the invention. The Australian Provisional Specification 73, 762/74 was filed on 26 September 1973. The inventors were Hamann, Solomon, and Brown, the Bank's printing expert. The process of drafting the patent—with its extensive demands on assessing international publications and prior art in the field—eventually convinced the Bank that the project had international significance, and it agreed to go ahead to develop the concept. The patent was accepted on 18 November 1977.

The Reserve Bank did not possess the technical capability to develop the new technology and kept CSIRO involved for the next decade or so. Robert Allen "Bob"

Johnston became the Governor of the Bank in August 1982. He had been present at the 1968 meetings and so was familiar with the project. Upon taking up the role as head of the Bank, his view was that it had spent a lot of money and had been "fiddling around for years." He decided that it was time either for it to adopt the technology, or to stop the project. He therefore built up the capability of the Bank to take over the project from CSIRO, with the aim of releasing the world's first official banknote made from a transparent polymer film on 26 January 1988, the bi-centenary of the landing of the First Fleet on Botany Bay. The decision to issue the first polymer banknote as a commemorative note was both wise, and brave. It was an extremely large-scale field test, in circumstances where the consequences of failure would have been very public and very serious. Fortunately, the technology worked.

Although they look simple, banknotes are sophisticated products. Until 1988, Australia was completely dependent on imported banknote technology and the Note Printing Branch of the Reserve Bank of Australia had no links with the academic or research community. The outcome of

Above: A $10 bicentennial note. The security features of the new banknotes included: a quality paper substrate made from cotton and linen fibres; a 25mm square watermark; a metallize plastic thread that ran through the banknote, and high-quality intaglio printing. (Courtesy of Heritage Auctions, HA.com)

Above: Banjo Patterson, famous Australian bush poet and author, as featured on the Australian $10 banknote. (Photo by Richard McDowell / Alamy)

the polymer banknote project completely reversed that situation. Many countries in the world now use Australian technology for their banknotes, and Note Printing Australia has built up strong links with the research community.

Banknotes have three levels of security devices. Primary security devices are those recognized by members of the public. These include intaglio printing, metal strips, and the clear area in a polymer banknote. Secondary security devices are those that require a machine to detect them. The most common of these is ink that is only visible under ultraviolet light. And then there are tertiary security devices. Only the issuing authority can detect tertiary security devices, and these technologies are closely guarded secrets. They are used to detect undiscovered forgeries when the banknote is returned to the central bank.

The number of primary security devices has increased over the years to cope with the widespread availability of color photocopiers and scanners. The paper note issued by the Reserve Bank of Australia in 1966 had four primary security devices. In contrast, the latest Australian $5 banknote has ten: the polymer substrate, the top-to-bottom window, a three-dimensional image, two optically varying bird images, a reversing number, an image in a small window, intaglio print, very detailed background print, and micro-printing. A portfolio of seven Australian patent families protect these primary security devices.

Retailers also need to recognize and understand secondary security devices. The $5 banknote issued by the Reserve Bank of Australia in September 2016 has a bird, the serial number, and the year of print that fluoresce under UV light. For the latter security feature, Note Printing Australia purchases fluorescing ink from a supplier, and anyone who wants to detect it has to have access to a UV black light

with a wavelength that is centered around 365nm. The fluorescing ink and the detecting device may or may not be patented by their suppliers, and from the forger's point of view the presence of a secondary security device is not a huge technical problem, but it does slow them down. Although many forgers can get access to fluorescing ink, its presence adds one more step in the forger's production line.

The public is not aware of the presence or absence of tertiary security devices. Central banks do not disclose the presence of such a device, and their websites and material explaining security devices and counterfeit detection never mention them. The intellectual property associated with tertiary security devices is highly confidential. If you come across a patent claiming to cover such a device, you should doubt its value: secrecy, not patents, is how these ideas are protected.

Banknote issuing authorities are necessarily very conservative. A secure, reliable currency is essential to the functioning of a modern state. It was Johnston's view that the CSIRO scientists grossly underestimated the "enormity of getting it wrong," when they were proposing the technology for the polymer banknotes. The significance of banknote security to the sovereignty of the state can easily be seen by the typical punishment for forgers during the medieval period: they were simply executed.

While counterfeiting the national currency is no longer a capital offence in most countries except China and Vietnam, it is still a serious criminal offence. Issuing authorities have powerful remedies against forgers, primarily criminal charges followed by long jail terms. Aside from these criminal protections, modern banknote manufacturers also rely on conventional intellectual property protection such as patents, trade secrets and trademarks.

Of course, counterfeiters do not care whether the banknotes they are simulating are protected by patents or not. They simply want to produce them as quickly as possible, release them, and collect as much real money as they can without being detected. Therefore, police forces, not intellectual property laws, are the main protectors of currency. In Australia, this forms part of the duties of the Australian Federal Police, along the various State police forces. Similar arrangements are in place in most countries. The United States is unusual in that it has a special law enforcement agency, the Secret Service, to investigate financial crimes; and its remit covers the prevention and investigation of counterfeit US currency, investigations into scams related to US treasury securities, and the investigation of major fraud. This is in addition to its better-known area of responsibility, to ensure the safety of current and former leaders and their families.

The question remains then: why do the issuing authorities and banknote manufacturers take out patents if they have the police to protect their product? They do so because the production of banknotes is a very lucrative international business, and one subject to lots of competition. Note Printing Australia—a wholly owned subsidiary of the Reserve Bank of Australia—prints banknotes for Australia, as well as for several other countries including Singapore and Papua New Guinea. Canada produces notes for New Zealand. And so on.

There are three main activities associated with the production of banknotes—

On the left: Australian 5, 10, 20, 50, and 100 dollar notes. (Phillip Minnis / Alamy)

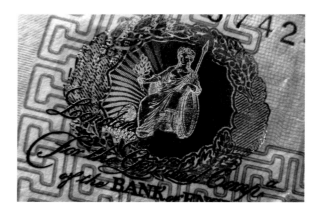

On the left: Details of the new British polymer banknotes. A detail of the holographic foiling on a £5 banknote featuring a brightly colored picture of Britannia, 2016. (Photo by Jim Dyson / Getty Images)

On the right: Australian dollar banknotes from 1966, 1988, and 2016, with increasing security devices, such as the top-to-bottom window. (Getty Images / Alamy / Heritage Auctions, HA.com)

the manufacture of the substrate, the manufacture of the security devices, and the printing of the banknote. Each of these activities is part of a highly complex and competitive international business system. If issuing authorities conducted all three activities exclusively, there would be little need for intellectual property, as national criminal law systems would provide adequate protection. But once the private sector is involved in any of these production processes, inter-firm competition creates the need for intellectual property protection. De La Rue plc, a major producer of banknotes and other secure documents, has more than 1,000 patents covering anti-counterfeiting measures. CCL Secure, a North American multinational, now owns the intellectual property rights associated with the CSIRO-RBA developed polymer substrate. Crane & Co., the company that has produced the paper substrate for US currency for more than 200 years, has an extensive patent portfolio and has used the intellectual property system virtually since its founding. An early patent was US Patent No. 353,666, dated 7 December 1886, for an improved watermarked paper invented by Zenas Crane, Jr.

Compared to paper notes, polymer notes are at least ten times more secure, 75 percent cleaner, and up to five times more durable—despite being only twice as expensive to produce. In 2004, Canadian paper notes had 470 forgeries per million notes in circulation. In 2016, with the introduction of polymer notes, Canada had a forgery rate of ten per million. Yet, despite their superior properties polymer banknotes account for only 3 percent of the world's production of banknotes. Invented in Australia nearly 50 years ago, used around the world in a range of countries, and demonstrably better in every way than its paper-based rival, polymer banknotes still struggle to break the stranglehold of centuries of tradition in the use of paper-based banknotes. ◆

Further Reading

David Solomon and Tom Spurling (2014) *The Plastic Banknote: From Concept to Reality.* Melbourne: CSIRO.

Tom Spurling and David Solomon (2017) "Banknote Security: Keeping our Currency Current," *Chemistry in Australia*, June, pp. 16–19.

US Patent No. 353,666 (issued Dec. 7, 1886), "Watermarked Paper."

US Patent No. 4,536,016 (issued Aug. 20, 1985), "Banknotes and the like."

40 Post-it Note

Stavroula Karapapa

THE POST-IT® NOTE is an excellent example of radical innovation that has achieved a nearly mythic stature in our consumer culture. Invented and manufactured by Minnesota Mining & Manufacturing Company, better known as 3M, the "Post-it" is a piece of stationery consisting of a small piece of paper with a re-adherable strip of adhesive on the back. It is designed for temporarily attaching notes to documents, computer displays, and so forth, and removing them without leaving marks or residue. The iconic Post-it note is a canary yellow three-inch square pad, even though it also comes in various other sizes, colors, and styles. Emerging as a convenient medium for informal note taking, the Post-it sticky notes have revolutionized the practice. Their appeal is tremendous both in the office and in the home, as they are reliable and easy to use.

It is not surprising that the product and its success has found expression in popular culture, such as the 1997 film ROMY AND MICHELE'S HIGH SCHOOL REUNION. Trying to reinvent themselves as successful businesswomen to impress their classmates, the title characters, played by Lisa Kudrow and Mira Sorvino, claim credit for the "Post-it," "a product that everybody has heard about but nobody really knows who invented it." In their imagination, the invention of the Post-it notes was a very simple process: they ran out of paper clips and stuck glue on the back of the paper.

In reality, however, the sticky notes did not always appear destined to set the office supply world alight. Unlike the common assumption linked to inventorship that there is a technical problem that needs solving, the discovery of the glue that is used in the Post-it notes was—according to its inventor—"a solution waiting for a problem to solve."

The making of the repositionable note took around ten years from the discovery of the adhesive to its application. In the mid 1960s, 3M was carrying a four-year program on "Polymers for Adhesives" and one of their chemists, Spencer Silver, started performing experiments on a new family of polymers. Contrary to established scientific principles, which required mixing precise

On the left: A yellow adhesive note. (Getty Images)

ratios of the various elements, Silver mixed an unusually large quantity of the element with the reaction mixture. Through this process he discovered a new polymer that was only partly sticky. Although fascinated by his discovery, Silver could not find a useful application for it.

It was years later, in 1974, that another 3M scientist, Arthur Fry, came up with an application for this unusual glue. This was yet another incidental discovery: Fry was a choir member and one Sunday at church his bookmarks kept slipping out of the hymnbook. That is when he started to wonder if he could create a bookmark that would stick to the page but could be removed without damaging it. He had heard about Silver's adhesive in a seminar at 3M and started creating some prototype products. Later, Fry reportedly observed: "I thought, what we have here isn't just a bookmark. It's a whole new way to communicate." And that was indeed the case.

It took, however, several years before the Post-it note, originally called "Press'n'Peel," went to market. There were further technical issues that needed to be solved, including the fact that the glue would come off unevenly when the two objects joined by the adhesive were separated. In order to solve this problem, 3M scientists had to create a method of priming the substrate on the back of the paper.

The Post-it note also posed a conceptual challenge: people could not see any practical benefit before they used it. Fortunately, Fry's boss, Geoff Nicholson, believed in the success of the product and encouraged him to continue working on it. He also started handing out samples to various 3M departments. Soon his secretary was swamped by requests for more. This was sufficient evidence for the marketing team to decide to put the product on the market. In the product's trial in 1977, consumers

initially were skeptical about its utility. It was trialled in four cities and failed in all of them. It seemed as if people needed to sample the product before starting to buy it. In 1978, a 3M team descended on Boise in Idaho, handing out countless samples and giving demonstrations on how to use the product. The result of the so-called "Boise Blitz" was that 90 percent of those who tried the product said they would be willing to buy it. The following year, 3M changed the name from "Press'n'Peel" to "Post-it" notes, and by 1980 the Post-it note had entered the national market in the United States. Just four years later it became 3M's most successful product, coming in a range of colors, sizes, and styles. The Post-it note created a need in the market that did not previously exist.

The success of the Post-it note did not remain unchallenged. As its popularity grew, competitors started to introduce their own versions of the sticky notes. The same year that ROMY AND MICHELE'S HIGH SCHOOL REUNION was put into circulation, Alan Amron—the distributor of the first battery-operated water gun, the toy that would in time be called the "Super Soaker" and be the subject of its own very famous intellectual property dispute—filed an action against 3M in Federal Court in the Eastern District of New York. He claimed that he had invented the sticky note in 1973, one full year before the 3M scientists developed the product that became the Post-it. Amron said that he had been looking for a way to stick a note on his fridge for his wife and used a chewed piece of gum, gaining the inspiration to create the adhesive that would be used on his product, which he called the "Press-on Memo." According to his claim, he took the sticky notes to a New York trade show in 1973, where he briefly met with two 3M executives; but nothing came of the meeting. Although Amron settled the lawsuit against 3M under

On the left: Poster for ROMY AND MICHELE'S HIGH SCHOOL REUNION *(US 1997, Dir. David Mirkin). (Touchstone Pictures / Alamy)*

On the following pages: An epic mic drop across the windows of multiple stories brought the Post-it war between Havas Worldwide and Harrison & Star on Canal Street in Lower Manhattan to an end in 2016. (Photo by Nicholas Hunt / Getty Images)

terms that remain confidential, he brought a new suit in 2016, seeking $400 million in damages, and claiming that the company breached its previous agreement not to take credit for the sticky-backed paper products. His understanding of the 1997 settlement agreement was that 3M had considered that neither he nor 3M was the inventor of the sticky note, whereas 3M later made statements that its scientists had invented the Post-it note. These statements, Amron alleged, defamed him and harmed his ability to attract funding for developing other inventions. District Court judge James Cohn in the Southern District of Florida dismissed Amron's complaint on the basis that the previous settlement "unambiguously cover[ed]" Amron's claims. Not only that, but Amron never patented his invention; 3M held the patent over the adhesive that made the sticky note commercially viable.

The patent on the adhesive is not the only intellectual property right on the sticky note: 3M holds a number of trademarks both on the word "POST-IT" and for the distinctive canary yellow color (US TM Reg. No. 2,390,667; EU TM Reg. Nos. 655,019 and 2,550,457). Interestingly, the story goes that even the iconic color of the Post-it note was chosen by happenstance and was not part of an elaborate consumer research strategy. During the making of the sticky note, a lab next door only had scrap yellow paper on hand, which came to be the iconic color of the Post-it note. Although successful color trademark applications are relatively rare, the 3M registration demonstrates the potential value of a color mark and the possibility for single

colors to function as marks for widely used products. The company has successfully blocked the importation into and sale in the United States of certain canary yellow self-stick, repositionable note products on the basis of the protection provided by its color mark registration.

The trademarked name of the product has also become the definitive term for the sticky notes, increasing its exclusionary power against potential competitors. The Trademark Trial and Appeal Board (TTAB) of the US Patent and Trademark Office refused to register the term "Flag-it!" on 17 July 2014 for a line of similar re-adhesive labels. In rejecting the application of Professional Gallery Inc., the Board relied on the fame of 3M's sticky notes.

Besides the pioneering nature of the sticky notes and 3M's investment in advertising, the Post-it note has also made unsolicited appearances in numerous films, TV shows, and print publications. As the TTAB stressed, "the references in the television programs and the movie ROMY AND MICHELE'S HIGH SCHOOL REUNION reflect the writers' and producers' views that the 'Post-it' mark is so well-known that viewers will immediately understand the reference." Another example is in *Sex and the City*, when Carrie Bradshaw, infuriated, announces to her friends Charlotte, Miranda, and Samantha, that Berger broke up with her "on a Post-it."

The enduring strength of the POST-IT mark, alongside its original canary yellow color, is a paradigmatic example of how a

Above: In the sixth season of Sex and the City, Berger famously breaks up with Carrie "on a Post-it," which has been a popular culture reference ever since.
Fair-use image; in response to our licensing request, HBO communicated that it "does not license its images to be used in published or digital books be it for personal, educational, or for profit-generating uses." (Frame-grab from DVD, S6E7, "The Post-It Always Sticks Twice.")

product can build sufficient goodwill and rely on trademark protection to successfully remain in the market, long after the initial patent expired (which, in this case, was over 20 years ago).

The Post-it repositionable notes have also inspired artistic interpretation, with the sticky notes becoming a medium of creative expression. In celebration of the Post-it note in 2000, various artists were invited to make artworks on the notes; R.B. Kitaj created perhaps the most expensive sticky note in the history of the product, selling it for £640 in an auction. Other artists have used Post-it notes as platforms for creative expression. Rosa Maria Arenas drew one Post-it note a day every day for over a decade during temporary jobs as part of one-minute meditations. Her "Yellow Stickee Diary of a Mad Secretary" consists of more than 2,000 drawings on Post-it notes, some of which were exhibited at the Michigan Institute of Contemporary Art Gallery in the summer of 2013. And in 2001, California artist Rebecca Murtaugh covered her whole bedroom with $1,000 worth of notes, whereby ordinary canary-yellow notes would depict objects of less value and neon-colored notes more important objects in the room.

The Post-it note has also migrated into the digital world. As part of its Windows product, Microsoft developed a feature that would enable users to create digital equivalents of the sticky note. This led to a temporary conflict between 3M and Microsoft over the creation of digital versions of the Post-it note—but in 2004, the companies announced a collaboration that established the Post-it brand more firmly in the Windows world, and 3M has recently launched a free mobile application that allows users to capture, organize, and share their notes

from their iPhone or iPad. The app uses a revolutionary technology designed to support digital representation of sticky notes, for which 3M has been granted a patent (US Patent No. 8,891,862). The patent develops a method of extracting content from notes by use of a computer system that receives image data of a scene with a plurality of notes and generates multiple indications corresponding to various color classes. This method aspires to bridge the gap between the use of the physical Post-it notes and how they are organized with electronic tools.

The story of the Post-it note is one of a powerful idea brought to fruition by accident. Unlike what is commonly thought of the inception of innovative products, the Post-it note did not start from the identification of a need or a well-thought out strategy—it was in fact a compilation of ideas and hard work that followed an initial experiment that failed. It challenges common assumptions about the creation and management of intellectual property objects and shows that persistence can be as rewarding as the eureka moment itself. ◆

Further Reading

Royston M. Roberts (1989) *Serendipity: Accidental Discoveries in Science.* New York: John Wiley and Sons.

James Ward (2014) *Adventures in Stationery: A Journey Through Your Pencil Case.* London: Profile Books.

Neil Wilkof (2010) "The Wonderful IP Story of the 'Post-it' Note," *IPKat blog,* 10 October. Available at: http://ipkitten.blogspot. co.uk/2010/10/wonderful-ip-story-of-post-it-note.html

The Post-it brand remains a registered trademark and, unlike the escalator, has not become generic. Those working in the IP industry are often familiar with the officially 3M-approved language (adhered to in this chapter). References to the Post-it note in popular culture, however, tend to pluralize or fail to add a proper generic descriptor to the Post-it brand: in ROMY AND MICHELE'S HIGH SCHOOL REUNION, *Michele claims to have "invented Post-its"; in the Romy and Michele musical, there's a song called "I Invented Post-Its," and Carrie Bradshaw proclaims in the episode of Sex and the City mentioned above that "There is a good way to break up with someone, and it doesn't … involve … a Post-it!"*

WATCH WHATEVER WHENEVER

With Sony's Betamax SL-8600 vi[c]
recorder, you can see any TV show y[ou]
want to see anytime you want to se[e].

Because Betamax, which plugs i[nto]
any TV set and is easy to operate, [can]
videotape a show up to three-ho[ur]
long (with the L-750 videocassette) wh[ile]
you're doing something else—ev[en]
while you're out of the house, by setti[ng]
the electronic timer.

It can also videotape something [on]
one channel while you're watchi[ng]
another channel.

And remember, Sony has more [ex]
perience in videorecorders than anyo[ne]
(over 20 years!). In fact, we've sold m[ore]
videorecorders to broadcasters and [in]
dustry than any other consumer ma[nu]
facturer. We even make our own tap[es].

For years you've watched [TV]
shows at the times you've h[ad]
to. Now you can wat[ch]
them at the times y[ou]
want to.

SONY BETAMAX
THE LEADER IN VIDEO RECORDING
© 1978 Sony Corp. of America. SONY and Betamax are registered trademarks of Sony Co[rp.]

--- *The Digital Now*

-- *Copyright*

- *United States*

1800   1900   2000

--/-----/-----/-----/-----/-----/-----/-----/-----/-----/-----/-----/-----/----

337

41 Betamax

Julian Thomas

On the left: The Sony Betamax was marketed as a machine for timeshifting, as exemplified by this prominent print advertising campaign from the late 1970s, using the slogan "Watch Whatever Whenever." (Rubenstein Library Rare Book and Manuscript Library, Duke University)

THE SCENE IS middle-class suburbia, in the late 1970s. We are in a comfortable family living room, anywhere in North America, Europe, or Australia. The signs of postwar affluence: earthy colors, plush sofas, carpet, an elegant wooden Scandinavian coffee table, a stereo system complete with turntable and a collection of records. A television, of course, perhaps a 19-inch Sony Trinitron (then still under patent), with its distinctive cylindrical screen. The TV is not new, but next to it sits a striking indication that this domestic order is about to change: a Betamax videotape cassette recorder, a bulky electronic box, also produced by the Japanese company Sony. It is the first of its kind to find its way into middle-class households in large numbers.

A sense of promise and possibility resonates in this machine's low hum. It has a wood-grain finish, a blinking digital clock, a hatch on top for loading tapes, and a group of large control keys. A cable attaches the Betamax to the TV. A few paperback-sized plastic videotape cassettes sit beside it. On the sleek coffee table we find a remote control and a TV schedule.

A thin wire connects the remote to the recorder. We can see at once that this new thing is part of an array of objects: the tapes, the remote, the device itself, and the connected television set are all elements in a video ecology. We're not sure at this stage what this array of things can or might do. Will we all now become video producers? Video librarians and curators? All sorts of imaginary video futures are attached to this object. We know now that some possibilities were realized, some not. But the video recorder changed entertainment for good. It had ramifications around the world for the screen industries, visual culture, for technology and intellectual property. Its effects remain with us today.

What did the Betamax mean for the owners and consumers of video content? And how did it become the center of a huge battle between its Japanese manufacturer and the Hollywood studios? In the famous 1984 case of *Sony Corp of America* v. *Universal Studios, Inc.*, the US Supreme Court found that the home recording of television programs was not unlawful. It was a form of fair use, and as a result the technology

Above: Children watching TV in the 1970s. (Alamy)

companies that supplied the recording equipment were not responsible for any infringement. The Court took a broad and enabling view of the Betamax and its many uses. It placed users in the position of control. The decision has been a focus for analysis ever since—it is seen as both revisionist and generative, opening a path into the new century's polarized debates over the control of digital property and how we manage all kinds of multipurpose consumer technologies, whether these are electronic objects or, increasingly, software.

In order to understand what was extraordinary about the arrival and impact of the Betamax, we need to remain for a moment in that lost postwar world of broadcast television. The TV set then was a dedicated, single-purpose device, a specialized video display with a built-in tuner and controls designed solely to allow viewers to select a broadcast program on a single channel. The set allowed a sole input, intended for a radio-frequency signal from an antenna or a cable system. It was part of a whole TV system, an end-to-end broadcasting model that had been adapted without significant change from the pre-war era of radio. In that system, streams of licensed programs were transmitted in real-time to millions of television sets in people's homes.

The legal, regulatory, and business structures of broadcasting created a multisided economy of scarcity, aggregating vast audiences for a small number of commercial or public service channels. In the commercial model, advertisers paid the broadcasters to air their commercials, broadcasters made or licensed the programs, and viewers paid for the (often expensive)

Above: The Magnavox Odyssey, the very first video game console. Released in 1972, the Odyssey was a device that generated shapes on the television that could be controlled and interacted with. It only produced black and white graphics and had no sound. (Photo by Evan Amos)

On the right: A BBC teletext page. (Alamy)

hardware necessary to enjoy the content. Governments regulated the number of channels and their content, and paid for public service broadcasting. Apart from the occasional cultural critic, neoliberal economist, or frustrated media entrepreneur, everyone loved TV. Viewers, advertisers, broadcasters, film studios, governments, television manufacturers, and rights holders were all united in their delight in the model. Trouble was just around the corner, in the shape of that box.

That expensive TV set was a dumb receiver, but there was no reason why it couldn't be used for things other than just watching live TV, and the 1970s was a time when there were many ideas about how that could happen. The decade produced not only Betamax and the competing VHS format, but a raft of ingenious new television-based technologies: teletext systems, the first games consoles, the first home computers, the first comparatively inexpensive video cameras. All of these were designed to use the consumer's sunk cost of the television set as a general-purpose video display that went

far beyond the limits of broadcast TV. The technologies needed to give TV new tricks were maturing fast. Solid-state electronics meant miniaturization, and helical scanning made videotape cassette recording practical. Sony failed in its first attempt at a home video recorder in the 1960s; by the mid-1970s the idea of a compact combination of a tape recorder, tuner and timer priced for consumers was a reality. And it could be manufactured in the millions by Japan's booming consumer electronics industries.

Betamax and the devices around it transformed television in several remarkable ways, and at the same time raised many

questions about intellectual property. First, the recording capability gave the television set a memory. The reception of the TV signal and the viewing of the TV content were separated in time. What was broadcast could now be preserved, segmented, and detached from the sequential flow of the broadcast. In the form of the collectible plastic cassettes, Betamax also offered a reasonably durable storage system for recorded content, something that might become a video library rather like a domestic collection of books or records. This had never been possible before.

Second, with the machine's clock, timer, and electronic controls, the TV became a programmable device. Broadcast content was governed (then and now) by its transmission and reception in real time and by its fixed program schedule; but now a viewer could control and program the actions of the receiver in advance. This profoundly changed the

viewer's relationship with the content that they were watching—they were suddenly granted a degree of autonomy over how and when and where they could consume the content. And, of course, they could share their tapes with others within their friend and family groups, presaging the rise, many years later, of the sharing economy and internet social media.

Third, the recorder's tuner took control of that function from the TV. The Betamax pretended to be a broadcaster, plugging into the TV's RF input and appropriating an unused channel. The viewer could change channels and the video source through a remote control connected to the recorder. Remotes were not new to video recorders (and not all early models included them), but they were popularized by them. Combined with the video recorder, remotes gave viewers a new level of ready control over recorded content, fast forwarding, pausing, and rewinding. They enabled easy

Above: Akio Morita, co-founder and President of Sony handling the recording device, 1979. (Photo by Financial Times / ullstein bild via Getty Images)

recording, and easy channel changing: another revolution in media autonomy for most viewers.

How then can we sum up the significance of the VCR's capacities? These devices redistributed power in the TV system. They shifted agency from the center of the broadcasting network to its edges, from the TV broadcasters to the viewers and consumers who bought TVs and made places for them in their homes. Some of the new power also now lay with new commercial actors, and this shift involved a contentious globalization of the entertainment industry, and a redrawing of the industry boundaries around entertainment and technology. Once it was the case that the only players who mattered were Hollywood-based film and television studios and the New York-based broadcast networks. But the Japanese

company Sony designed the new recording system. If the Betamax made it easy to fast forward through ads, it was because Sony had made it so; if recording a program was a prominent capability, that was also Sony's choice, not that of the US studios or networks.

Sony's power also derived from something less tangible than the device itself: it controlled the Beta format, which defined the physical and technical dimensions of the recording system, a format that could be licensed to other manufacturers. This determined, for example, the length of the tape, and ultimately the quality of the recorded content; and since Sony controlled the hardware and the key formats, the question arose as to who had control over the content itself. The new video ecology brought with it a host of new video industries, all built around the production, distribution, and circulation of video, in pre-recorded, bootleg, or amateur forms, from mainstream movies and television to video art, educational and technical content, underground and bootleg productions, pornography and politics. The

contemporary video culture of the internet traces its origins to that protean world of analog video; all made possible by the Betamax and the videotape cassette recorder formats that followed.

If everyone loved TV, would they also love Betamax? It seems that Sony actually thought so, because it was convinced that Betamax would increase TV watching. Sony ads highlighted the convenience of timeshifting, and of accumulating a personal library of favorite programs. The machines—in common with the VHS format competitors produced by Sony's Japanese rivals—were enormously popular with consumers. By the early 1980s, in the United States alone, over three million had been sold.

But everyone did not love Betamax. For broadcasters, Betamax appeared to be designed to help viewers skip ads, and kill their business model. For rightsholders, the box enabled unlicensed recording, and encouraged the appearance of a new, subterranean economy of informal video sharing, copying, renting, and distributing. For economic nationalists, the VCR

represented a foreign threat to America's trade. All these bubbling fears and resentments were condensed in movie industry lobbyist Jack Valenti's remarkable testimony before a 1982 congressional committee on home taping. In the middle of the protracted litigation against Sony, Valenti set out the existential threat posed to America's dominant entertainment industry by "a thing called the video cassette recorder and its necessary companion called the blank tape." According to Valenti, the movie industry was a defenseless woman alone at home at night, and the VCR was the Boston strangler. But if the living room was a crime scene, where would that leave those millions of Americans who were already wielding their remote controls, busily taping their way to happiness?

Intellectual property, technology, and popular culture all took a different direction in 1984, the year of the *Sony* v. *Universal* case. Valenti was right about the significance of the Betamax, but wrong about the nature and consequences of the transformation. Advocates for the movie and broadcasting industries focused on

Above: Jack Valenti at home in Washington. As Lucas Hilderbrand notes in his excellent book "Inherent Vice," when Time reported the Supreme Court's decision on Sony v. Universal, the magazine showed a bit of sass by illustrating the article with a picture of MPAA president and piracy paranoiac Jack Valenti smiling in front of his own VCR. Not only is the machine a VHS; the tape in his hand is also a pre-recorded film classic, and not a home recording from television. (Time, 30 January 1984, p. 67.)

Above: A young girl stretches out to pick out a film at the video rental store. (Alamy)

Betamax as a dangerous device. They saw a reflection of their own economic impulses and fears. The Supreme Court was ultimately interested in something else, in the diverse practices of home copying, in how this device was embedded in domestic life. That approach showed a new way of thinking about the emerging world of electronic consumer technologies and property.

The Betamax never achieved its potential. Sony exercised too much control over the format, and fell behind its many competitors. We now live with many other dangerous devices, including the descendants of the VCR: streaming services, personal media recorders and players that are also phones, a huge proliferation of global

online video services. Some of these tools are now entirely software, but many still involve some kind of physical object, an electronic appendage connected to the TV just as the Betamax once was. Behind these devices are vast global businesses. The history of the Betamax suggests that, in intellectual property as elsewhere, it's not the objects that matter, but what we do with them. ◆

Further Reading

Lucas Hilderbrand (2009) *Inherent Vice. Bootleg Histories of Videotape and Copyright.* Durham: Duke University Press.

James Lardner (1987) *Fast Forward: Hollywood, the Japanese, and the VCR Wars.* New York: W.W. Norton.

James Lardner (1987) "Annals of Law. The Betamax Case I/II," *New Yorker*, 6/13 April.

Richard Stengel (1984) "Decision: Tape It to the Max," *Time Magazine*, 30 January.

1800   *1900*   *2000*

--/----/----/----/----/----/----/----/----/----/----/----/----

42 Escalator

Megan M. Carpenter

GREAT TECHNOLOGICAL DEVELOPMENTS create a universe. The invention of the escalator was, literally, groundbreaking. It expanded our concept of space and time— and, accordingly, redefined the possibilities for commerce.

For those within the intellectual property system, the escalator is famous for its association with the phenomenon of "trademark genericide." Trademark genericide occurs when trademarks become so famous that they cease to identify the source of goods or services in the minds of consumers and instead become names for the goods themselves. "Escalator" is right up there with "aspirin," "cellophane," and "kitty litter" as an example of a brand that morphed into its product. And it's true that the intellectual property story of the escalator is, in part, how Charles Seeberger's brand of moving staircases grew to symbolize the thing itself. But the larger story is about the cultural phenomenon, an invention that transformed the way we interact with the world. How people move. How sales are made. How the built world is constructed.

Before the escalator was invented, commerce and transportation were largely one-dimensional. Stairs and elevators were for the committed and purposeful, their limitations constraining vertical expansion, above and below ground. Stairs require patience and effort. Elevators have a unique, precise, and tightly constrained mission. The invention of the escalator changed everything: suddenly, a constant flow of people could ascend into the air, or descend to the depths. The escalator modified architecture itself, creating fluid transitions into spaces above and below. Now, in commerce and transportation, neither the sky nor the ground would be the limit.

The first conceptual articulation of an escalator was "An Improvement in Stairs," described in an 1859 US patent issued to Nathan Ames. Ames was an inventor with several patents, including a railroad switch, a printing press, and a combination knife, fork, and spoon. Ames' patent made claim over an endless belt of steps revolving around three mechanical wheels that could be powered by hand, weights, or steam.

On the left: Spiral escalators in a shopping mall in Shanghai, China. (Getty Images)

This version of the moving stairway didn't gain much momentum, however, and was never built.

As the 20th century drew near, urbanization transformed society, and the development of the escalator was inextricably connected with the new way that people were living and working. Architecture responded to increasing populations in cities through the development of skyscrapers, department stores, and urban planning. Mass transit facilitated movement via electric streetcars, elevated trains, and the promise of subway systems. Revolutions in printing and photography heralded an explosion of advertising and new ways to sell goods.

These cultural and economic developments coincided with the most important technological improvement in the moving staircase: the use of a linear belt, invented by Jesse Reno. Reno was an engineer, working at the time on a plan for a subway system in New York City, involving slanted conveyors to move passengers underground. After the city declined to adopt his plan, he focused instead on the

technology. Granted a patent in 1892 over an "Inclined Elevator," he demonstrated the design at Coney Island in 1896: riding his invention, passengers leaned forward and stood on a conveyor belt of parallel cast-iron strips, powered by a concealed electric motor. During two weeks at Coney Island, 75,000 people were elevated seven feet. It was a sensation. Building on this success, a Reno Inclined Elevator was installed at the Brooklyn Bridge the following year.

As so often happens when cultural movements and technological innovation intersect, another inventor contemporaneously created a different version of the moving staircase. George Wheeler's "Elevator" was similar to what we know as the modern escalator, and it was the one that took hold in the market. It comprised steps that emerged from the floor and flattened at the end. Wheeler's patents were purchased by Charles Seeberger in 1899, who quickly struck a deal with elevator manufacturer Otis to produce moving staircases. Seeberger also coined the term "escalator"—from the French "l'esca-

Above: "Luna Park," Coney Island, by Eugene Wemlinger, 1909. The mechanical escalator to the top of the Helter Skelter, where an attendant handed out a small mat that would facilitate the downward slide. (Brooklyn Museum)

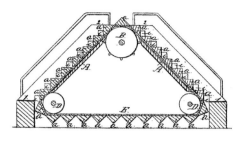

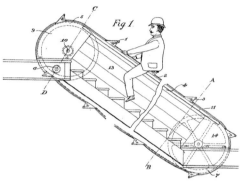

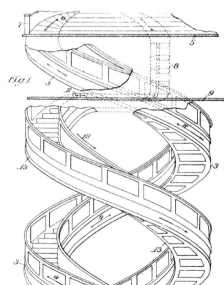

On the right, top: The Nathan Ames patent, US Patent No. 25,076-0, an "improvement in stairs."

On the right, middle: Jesse Reno's patent for an "inclined elevator," which he demonstrated in Coney Island. US Patent No. 708,663-0.

On the right, bottom: Otis' patent for a duplex spiral escalator (Engineer: Charles Seeberger). US Patent No. 999,885-0.

lade," to signify climbing—and registered the trademark ESCALATOR (US Reg. No. 34,724).

The Harvard Design School Guide to Shopping notes that the escalator is among the most important innovations in retail marketing, remarking that no invention has had more impact on shopping. It's not hard to see why. The elevator can transport a small number of people between floors. The stairway is constrained by the effort and commitment it requires from consumers to move between floors. But the moving staircase democratizes all levels; upper floors become indistinguishable from lower. Retail traffic flows seamlessly between levels, so that the consumers can access higher floors with little more effort than entering on the first floor. The Siegel Cooper Department Store in New York was the first to recognize its revolutionary potential, installing four of Reno's inclined elevators in 1896.

A universe of possibility opened when moving staircases were introduced to the world at the Paris Universal Exposition of 1900. The World's Fair long served as the place where innovators demonstrated breakthrough technologies on the world stage—the show introduced the world to the Colt revolver (London, 1851), the calculator (London, 1862), the gas-powered automobile (Paris, 1889), the Ferris Wheel (Chicago 1893), the ice cream cone (St. Louis, 1904), and both atomic energy and television (San Francisco, 1939).

The Paris Exposition of 1900, in particular, has been called one of the most important of them all. At the time, though,

organizers and government officials were concerned how this Exposition would make its mark—after the introduction of the Eiffel Tower at the fair in 1889, how could the one 11 years later compete? Officials entertained many bizarre proposals, many of which involved alterations of the Eiffel Tower itself including the potential additions of clocks, sphinxes, terrestrial globes, and a 450-foot statue of a woman with eyes made from powerful searchlights to scan the 562-acre fairgrounds. Instead, rather than beams-of-light from a giantess, what shone brightest at the 1900 Paris Exposition was the moving staircase. It won Grand Prize and a Gold Medal for its unique and functional design.

After the Exposition the invention spread internationally. Bloomingdale's in New York removed its staircase and installed an inclined elevator in 1900. Macy's followed suit in 1902. The Bon Marché in Paris installed the European "Fahrtreppe" in 1906. Escalators made department stores commercially viable entities in ways that stairs and the elevator simply could not. Vertical expansion of the stores into upper levels was now as

viable as horizontal expansion, but at a fraction of the cost.

The escalator did not simply revolutionize the shopping experience through vertical movement; it also created a new universe of human activity. Escalators transformed public transportation when they were installed in underground railway stations in New York and London in the early 1900s. In 1910, the *Boston Sunday Globe* included a series of illustrated comics providing a caricature of human behavior on the escalator, including "The Timid Lady Who Keeps the Crowd Waiting," and "They [Who] Are Unable to Pass the Stout Party." The newspaper noted that the "sport of escalating" is "a simple thing when you know how" but could fool "many an agile man."

Within the workplace, the changes were equally revolutionary: throughout the first half of the 20th century, escalators quickly became a tool of workplace efficiency. They enabled rapid transition between shifts, and were installed by owners to maximize efficiency for workers on a two- to three-shift system. Yet the benefit to the workers was real, and, from mills in

Above: The escalator going down into the Dupont Circle Metro station in Washington, DC on a sunny day. (Karen Bleier / AFP / Getty Images)

Massachusetts to the factories of the Soviet Union, escalators were often adopted as a potent symbol of the proletariat.

With post-World War II prosperity and a renewed hunger for shopping in the United States, the escalator found an expanded market. An Otis advertisement at the time captured the spirit of the moment, when "the Escalator polished up its manners, put on a new dress of gleaming metal in the latest streamline fashion, and went out in quest of new jobs." Otis marketed directly to consumers, and its advertising was widely recognized and very successful: an "Advertising Times" columnist of the day wrote of the triumph of the Otis marketing strategy, and the wisdom that the company had shown recognizing the power of "straight out-and-out advertising."

Ironically, Otis' marketing success in making its escalator a household name cost the company one of its most important assets. In 1950 its competitor, the Haughton Elevator Company, petitioned the US Patent and Trademark Office to cancel the ESCALATOR trademark, on the basis that the term had become generic to engineers, architects, and the general public. In court, Otis' ads were used against the company—one ad described "The Meaning of the Otis Trademark" in the following terms:

To the millions of daily passengers on the Otis elevators and escalators, the Otis trademark or name plate means safe, convenient, energy-saving transportation ... To thousands of building owners and managers, the Otis trademark means the utmost in safe, efficient economical elevator and escalator operation.

The USPTO found that the advertisements showed that Otis treated the term "escalator" in the same generic and descriptive way as the term "elevator." The mark no

On the right: Metro riders descend the escalator at the Dupont Circle Metro stop as the snow streams from the sky. (Sarah L. Voisin / The Washington Post / Getty Images)

longer represented the source of the product; it represented the product itself. Consequently, the mark was canceled—and to this day when you think of the word "escalator" you are unlikely to call to mind the Otis company.

The modern market for escalators has increased dramatically. As cities around the world increase in density, they often rely on the escalator as a key architectural element, both above and below ground. In Hong Kong the Central Mid-Levels Escalators span an entire hillside—a 2,625-foot set of moving sidewalks lined by open-air markets, stores, and apartment towers. The number of escalators in the world doubles every ten years: Otis continues to be a major player, although by 1993 its nemesis, the Haughton Elevator Company (now owned by Schindler) claimed to have

the largest market share of escalators. Yet, amazingly, the basic form of these new escalators has barely changed from the design sketched out in the early Wheeler patents.

The revolutionary has become ordinary, and escalators are now simply part of the background cultural radiation of modern life. Movies are replete with escalator scenes, from AN AMERICAN WERE-WOLF IN LONDON, to RAIN MAN, to THE HANGOVER's parody of the RAIN MAN escalator scene. Perhaps the movie ELF best encapsulates our relationship with the escalator. In that movie, Will Farrell plays a human raised by elves, who visits New York City to find his biological father. Alien to modern technology, he does not know how to step on an escalator at a department store and, after several aborted

Above: Mid-level escalator system over a busy street in the Central District, Hong Kong. (Getty Images)

Above: Cyclists on the escalator into the Maastunnel in Rotterdam, NL, in 1959, which at the time was only one of two bike connections between the city's north and south bank. (Photo: Aart Klein / Nederlands Fotomuseum)

attempts that interrupt the flow of traffic and irritate those around him, he steps on with one foot, holding onto the rails with his arms. His front foot escalates while the rest of him drags behind. The scene is a reminder of the strange wonder that is the escalator; one we now take for granted. It could be a scene by Buster Keaton, or drawn from the 1910 *Boston Sunday Globe* comic: "Man Who Forgets to Step with Both Feet." The scene is funny precisely because it calls up both the marvel and banality of the moving staircase.

We take the escalator for granted, in part, because it is that possibility realized; we all now inhabit the world of the escalator, with no longer a sense of its radical nature. The escalator may be the most important invention in shopping, but its impact reaches well beyond commerce. It has conquered space itself. ◆

Further Reading

Chuihua Judy Chung, Jeffrey Inaba, Rem Koolhaas, and Sze Tsung Leong (eds.) (2001) *Harvard Design School Guide to Shopping.* New York: Taschen.

"The Sport of Escalating," *Boston Sunday Globe*, 25 December 1910.

Haughton Elevator Co. v. *Seeberger* (Otis Elevator Co. substituted), 85 U.S.P.Q. 80, 1950.

43 3D Printer

Dinusha Mendis

THE 3D PRINTER is not new: the technology dates back to the 1970s. Initially controlled by a thicket of patents, it only became commercially significant when the main patents expired and a range of homebrew developers saw the benefit in the widespread adoption of a range of 3D printing technologies.

The first patent for the technology was granted on 9 August 1977 to Wyn Kelly Swainson, an American. Although it did not lead to a commercially available 3D printer at the time, it paved the way for the manufacturing of 3D parts. Shortly thereafter, Hideo Kodama of Nagoya Municipal Industrial Research Institute published his work in producing a functional rapid-prototyping system using photopolymers, a photosensitive resin that could be polymerized by a UV light. In a process that is now familiar to most, a solid, printed model was built up in layers, each of which corresponded to a cross-sectional slice in the model. Kodama never patented this invention, and the first commercial 3D printer was launched in 1988 by Charles Hull—

On the left: The author scanned and 3D printed in Palo Alto, California in 2015. (Courtesy of Dinusha Mendis)

another American—following a patent for "Stereolithography" granted to him in March 1986. In 1988, at the University of Texas, Carl Deckard brought a patent for a different type of 3D printing technology, in which powder grains are fused together by a laser. From these three different approaches, and the patents that protected them, 3D printing born.

The 3D printer, and the process of 3D printing, has caused a great deal of hype in recent times for a range of reasons. The technology became widely accessible because of a move away from commercial and industrial printers to low-cost desktop printers, a movement caused by the expiration of the foundational patents. This gave rise to the "Maker Movement"—similar to the homebrew computer clubs that formed around personal computing in the 1980s— that made 3D printing more accessible and appealing, and which captured the imagination of the consumer. In 2005, Neil Gershenfeld predicted that "personal fabrication will bring the programming of the digital worlds we've invented to the physical world we inhabit." Barely more

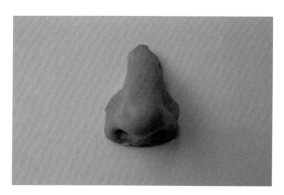

than a decade later, Gershenfeld's prediction has become a reality.

Although the 3D printing movement as we know it was created by patents (and their expiration), the present and the future of 3D printing is intrinsically linked with intellectual property. This is true although the current laws were not designed with 3D printers in mind; however, the rise of desktop 3D printers and the emergence of the do-it-yourself Maker Movement changed the 3D printing landscape. Equipped with tools of design and production, consumers were empowered to become "prosumers"—both producers and consumers at the same time—with the ability to 3D print toys, jewelry, food, make-up, phone cases, and spare parts, all within the comfort of their home. The 3D printer caused a disruption to manufacturing and business, and the presence of low-cost consumer 3D printers in supermarkets, schools, and community centers in countries like the United Kingdom demonstrates that the trend is very much on the rise.

What does this explosion of interest mean for intellectual property laws, for rightsholders, and for users? The functioning of a 3D printer is heavily reliant on a design file, which describes what the printer should print; and so the future potential of 3D printing rests on the creation and dissemination of design files. Computers will play a critical role in the 3D modelling, designing, and printing process. For a 3D printer to have any value, it will require instructions from a computer coupled with a printable design file, just as we use a 2D printer for printing a Word, Powerpoint, or Keynote document. In other words, the functioning of a 3D printer depends on it being fed a well-designed electronic design file, typically a Computer Aided Design (CAD) file, which tells it where to place the raw material. The importance of the CAD file is summed up by Hod Lipson and Melba Kurman in their book *Fabricated*, noting that "a 3D printer without an attached computer and a good design file is as useless as an iPod without music." Protecting the software and design file is, therefore, just as important as the hardware. However, whilst many academics, practitioners, and policy makers have

Above, right: A prosthetic arm made with biodegradable plastic corn starch by volunteers of the nonprofit project "Do it yourself" of Foundation of Materialization 3D, in Bogota, Colombia, 2017. A group of volunteers provide hands and arms to those born with missing limbs or who lost them in war, disease, or natural disaster, at the Build It Workspace studio, which teaches people how to use high-tech printers creating their own superhero arms for children. (Photo by Juancho Torres / Anadolu Agency / Getty Images)

Above: Cleopatra, a leopard tortoise, whose shell is deformed because of malnutrition, wears a prototype 3D printed prosthetic shell in Golden, Colorado, 2015. (Photo by R.J. Sangosti / The Denver Post via Getty Images)

On the left: Prosthetic nose on display at the 3D printing show, held at Metropolitan Pavilion in New York, 2014. The medical applications for 3D printing is increasing, especially in the area of reconstructive surgery. (Photo by Timothy Fadek / Corbis via Getty Images)

commented on this point, the legal status of a CAD file continues to be uncertain.

At the same time, the increase in the number of online platforms dedicated to sharing design files has significant intellectual property implications. CAD files can be disseminated effortlessly using online platforms, causing consequences for all types of rightsholders. A 2016 report for the European Commission pointed out that the two main areas for enforcement against unauthorized 3D printing are with the intermediaries involved in facilitating the download of potentially infringing files, and in their eventual reproduction by the end-user. It can be challenging and costly to enforce rights against end-users, due to the decentralized nature of the activity, and so the report suggests that pursuing intermediaries, particularly online hosting sites, is probably a more streamlined and effective choice for rightsholders. This issue is compounded by the emergence of 3D scanners, and the proliferation of accessible scanning capabilities leading to real-time photogrammetric and cloud-based data processing, which has begun to eclipse the more traditional laser-scanning solutions. We can expect the number of design files to increase dramatically over time.

The 3D printing process—from the design file to the 3D printer—allows physical goods to be customized. The widespread use of web-based software tools has therefore meant that users have the opportunity to customize products, and the intellectual property concerns of this behavior are particularly noticeable in the customization of jewelry, accessories, headwear, and shoes. Whilst the concept of mass customization appears attractive—who could be against providing freedom of design to consumers?—it nonetheless raises questions of authorship and ownership, issues at the core of many intellectual property laws.

The story of the 3D printer is much like the stories of ages past: intellectual property laws attempting to keep pace with new technologies, with law-makers seeking to strike a fair balance between protecting the effort of the creator and providing opportunities for the user. As the market for 3D printed objects continues to expand and the technology continues to develop, existing intellectual property laws will need to be reviewed for their adequacy in balancing the interests of creators and users. New licensing schemes in this sphere should be embraced and welcomed, as these new technologies create the opportunity for a new and innovative regulatory structure for intellectual property in the years to come.

But apart from intellectual property laws, 3D printers give rise to other concerns and prospects. For example, what does 3D printing mean for the future of the environment

Above, right: The world's first 3D printed bus stop in Shanghai, China, 2018. The 3D printed bus stop with a unique closed-loop design looks like a rectangular frame. (Photo by VCG via Getty Images)

On the left: An Apis Cor 3D Printer prints a house on the grounds of the Stupino Aerated Concrete Plant, Russia, 2016. (Photo by Maxim Grigoryev / TASS via Getty Images)

and sustainability? Widespread acceptance and implementation of 3D printing would reduce the costs of the transportation of goods, as manufacturing shifts away from centralized factories to regional 3D printing facilities, or even consumers' own homes. It might also eliminate a large amount of the waste that exists within current manufacturing processes and supply chains.

There is also a range of ethical and legal issues, where regulators may have to get involved. Jasper Tran provides a hypothetical example to highlight this point by asking what would regulators do, should 3D printing technologies be used to "cloneprint" mammals, especially extinct animals? Whether one is "animal-friendly" or "environment-friendly," for the sake of human health and safety, the welfare of animals, and the integrity of the environment, countries will look to regulators to set appropriate standards in relation to research and development, and the application, of new technologies such as 3D printing. Similar issues will arise from the bio-printing and potential trafficking of human organs. In the United States,

also health and safety concerns arising from 3D printing have been brought to the forefront; for example, with an attempt by a libertarian 3D printing advocate who sought to post his design online for a 3D printed gun. These are challenging matters that need addressing as the technology continues to develop.

Finally, there is the issue of product liability. Up until now, it has not been possible for the average consumer to manufacture products requiring machinery, due to the cost involved. Product liability laws are premised on the basis that the party best able to shoulder the burden of liability is to be held liable, and this is typically the well-heeled manufacturer. However, as consumers become prosumers, this assumption no longer necessarily holds true. For example, if person A downloads a CAD design file for a toy car, which has been uploaded by person B on to an online sharing platform and modified by persons C, D, E, and F, and then has it 3D printed at the local supermarket, who would be liable when A's child is injured by the toy car when playing with it? As 3D printers continue to

develop and become more technologically advanced, regulatory issues and product liability laws will need to be reviewed and reformed to tackle such concerns.

Although 3D printing will give rise to challenges, it also has the potential to pave the way for exciting new opportunities. The ability to customize products to an individual's need is one of the many benefits which 3D printing affords. Mass customization has the potential to become a norm amongst consumers and, as the technology develops, the cost of mass customization will decrease. There is also the promise of 3D printers being more environmentally friendly.

On the other hand, 3D printers will throw up challenges for intellectual property laws, product liability, and ethics. Lipson and Kurman liken 3D printers to the magic wand of childhood fairy tales, as it offers the promise of control over the physical world. It will be some time before this becomes a complete reality. However, in a 3D printed world, people will have the opportunity to make what they need, when and where they need it. Therefore, legislators, regulators and policy makers must be ready for that to happen.

Undoubtedly, reform will be required to deal with these issues. However, an impulsive or a reactive call for legislative and judicial action in the realm of 3D printing could stifle the public interest in fostering creativity and innovation, and threaten the right of manufacturers and content creators to protect their livelihoods.

The history of 3D printing was born from intellectual property laws. It's clear that its future is equally bound up with them. ◆

Further Reading

Jos Dumortier *et al.* (2016) *Legal Review on Industrial Design Protection in Europe.* Brussels: European Commission.

Dinusha Mendis, Mark Lemley, and Matthew Rimmer (eds.) (2019) *3D Printing and Beyond: Intellectual Property and Regulation.* Cheltenham: Edward Elgar.

Dinusha Mendis, Davide Secchi, and Phil Reeves (2015) *A Legal and Empirical Study into the Intellectual Property Implications of 3D Printing.* Newport: UK Intellectual Property Office.

OECD (2017) *The Next Production Revolution: Implications for Governments and Businesses.* Paris: OECD.

Above: Airbus unveiled THOR (short for "Test of High-tech Objectives in Reality," rather than a reference to the Norse god of thunder), a 13-foot plane made entirely out of 3D printed parts. The small plane, which is shaped like a miniaturized version of a commercial airliner, weighs about 50 pounds, and took four weeks to print and build. (Photo by Tobias Schwarz / AFP / Getty Images)

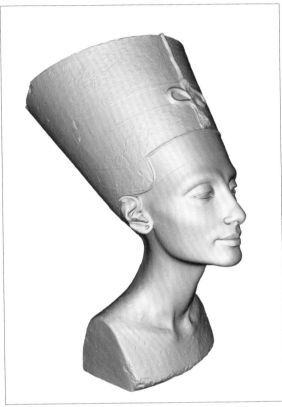

Above: " *You wouldn't steal an ancient Egyptian relic." Artists Jan Nikolai Nelles and*
Nora Al-Badri have added to an ongoing conversation about "plundered" art objects.
Whether this story concerns a surreptitiously taken scan or a stolen digital file, by
providing a free download of the 3D scan of the Nefertiti bust held by the Neues Museum
in Berlin, the artists question the belonging and possessing of objects of other cultures, the
museum as a repository of secret knowledge, and the meaning of the public domain.
Left: Nefertiti's bust in the Neues Museum, Berlin. (Getty Images);
Right: 3D scan of the bust. ("The Other Nefertiti." Available at: http://nefertitihack.
alloversky.com, Public Domain Mark 1.0)

44 CD

Matthew David

THE COMPACT DISC is, literally and figuratively, a mirror reflecting the power of intellectual property in late 20th-century society, and a prism refracting it into the early 21st century. Physically more robust than vinyl and—at least at its inception—less prone to copyright infringement than the audiocassette, the introduction of the CD created an unprecedented flood of profits for the recorded music industry. This unanticipated windfall financed intense vertical and horizontal integration within the sector, and gave rise to the expectation that the good times would last forever.

However, the CD is just the physical medium for the delivery of unencrypted digital content, and its development supercharged the revolution that would become central to the digital media age we live in today. The ability to detach the tangible expression—that is, the content—from the tangible object—the shiny Mylar disk—meant that the CD eventually took away all of the benefits that it initially conferred on the music industry. In providing the unencrypted digital content that came to populate peer-to-peer systems, torrents, and streaming services, the CD's mirror-like image masked the danger that lay a few microns under its surface.

Intellectual property protection has been central to the music industry for centuries. Copyright on sheet music in England goes back over 200 years. But the nature of the protection and the methods of infringement of the early days of music protection were utterly different from those that the CD created. The act of copying-out sheet music by hand was time consuming, whilst access to printing presses required commercial investment. Just as was later the case with early sound recording cylinders and records, making copies of sheet music required industrial machinery. The initial focuses of musical copyright and its enforcement were aimed at regulating commercial rivalry, and piracy was defined in terms of infringement for commercial gain.

The 1930s saw the development of audiotape, but this technology was not generally available to consumers; it was only in the 1960s that eight-track tapes

On the left: The CD reflecting and refracting the power of IP. (Alamy)

and later still the compact audiocassette became widely available to the ordinary user. By the 1970s, the proliferation of home taping was a central concern to the music industry, and so the development of the digital compact disc—created independently initially by Philips and Sony, but then commercialized as a collaboration between the two companies—was seen as a godsend by the industry. It offered a new format that promised to return control to the music labels and other copyright holders, at the same time as offering something of the flexibility and portability of the compact cassette.

The CD was launched with great fanfare as an alternative to vinyl and audiocassettes in 1982, and the period from its introduction until the advent of Napster in 1999 saw unprecedented profitability in the recorded music industry. The cost of production of CDs was initially higher than for that of vinyl, but this rapidly fell; and the losses due to breakages fell away quickly too—though "deductions" for breakages at vinyl rates continued to be taken from artists' royalties. Digital content could be more easily distributed, and encoding the content onto the discs could be done anywhere in the world, and in any quantity. Music fans had to restock their record collections in the new format, and this increased the value of back-catalogues. Sales rocketed. All this, and then there was the fact that CDs were considerably more expensive for customers to buy. In the space of little over a decade, Sony went from being a manufacturer of playing devices, to being the largest manufacturer of the discs being played; it ended up, in time, becoming the largest producer of recorded content in the world.

Selling CDs came to dominate the musical economy. Awash with cash, the major record labels set about using their new-found wealth buying up all the major music publishing companies. As a result, artists' publishing rights are now almost always owned by their record companies. This has led to "360 Degree" contracts, where failure of royalties (themselves being only five, ten, or at best 15 percent of net sales) to recoup the total cost of production, marketing, and management allows

Above: Sheet music and records required manufacture. As Marion Holland plays the piano, Money the cat joins in the singing. (Bettmann / Getty Images)

Above, left: The path not taken; a Digital Audio Tape (DAT). (Getty Images)

Above, right: The CD's unencrypted encoding of digital content enabled a new digital mode of distribution to replace it. (Photo by Bruno Vincent / Getty Images)

record companies to take artists' additional revenues, such as those from publishing and performance. In addition, the profits afforded by the CD saw major labels buying out independent labels if the indies found or fostered new talent. Rich labels simply bought out their nascent competitors, and incorporated these buyout costs into the advances that artists then had to recoup from their still-diminutive royalties' rates. This ended the concertina-like fluctuation of the death of established labels and the rise of new ones, a pattern that had characterized earlier eras of creative destruction in the business. As a result of the CD boom years, the industry became extremely concentrated on a small number of major labels.

That digital content was so easy to work with, circulate, produce, master, and embed was its great advantage—as long as it was contained in the containers sold by record companies. But, as one record company executive ruefully observed after the fact, people in the industry were too busy counting the money to worry about the fact that they were, in effect, giving away their master copies with every sale. Where the compact audiocassette had led to a panic over home-taping in the 1970s, cassettes were never seen to be the

equivalent in quality to vinyl recordings. By 1987, when Sony sought to release its Digital Audio Tape system, the industry had started to wake up to the problem it had created for itself: the DAT-format was not adopted by any major record label, for fear that its high recording quality, combined with the consumer's ability to make their own copies, would lead to even more problems than they were beginning to face with CDs.

Digital copies of digital content offered far higher fidelity than analog formats; even if early forms of compression limited the quality of reproduction. The digital shift created by CDs quickly changed the way the industry saw copyright infringement. At first its concern was the same as that which animated the sheet music industry 200 years before. The 1994 Trade Related Aspects of Intellectual Property Agreement (TRIPS) coda to the multinational trade agreement still framed copyright infringement in music primarily in terms of commercial "piracy." Two years later, the 1996 WIPO Copyright Treaty, was alive to the threat from cheap home CD-burners. The subsequent mass copying of content from CDs onto the internet saw the record industry's years of feast turn into famine.

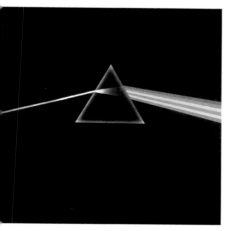

Above: The profit storm. Reformatting from vinyl to CD made record companies rich—and made back catalogues (and copyright on old works) more valuable than a label's current artists. Left: Cover artwork for Pink Floyd's "The Dark Side of the Moon," 1973. (Photo by Michael Ochs Archives / Getty Images); Right: Beatles albums on sale at Tower Records in New York City, 2001. (Photo by Mario Tama / Getty Images)

On the left: A broken, or rather, microwaved, CD. (Photo by Dan Brandenburg / Getty Images)

The problem, many said, was encryption. Content wasn't encrypted on the CD, in order to provide a common set of standards by which all record companies and manufacturers of players could operate. (The film and TV industries learned from this mistake, and so the subsequent standard for DVDs mandated encryption—although it never worked very well.) The absence of encryption on CDs facilitated the diffusion of the format; but this initial benefit became an Achilles heel once compression formats and increased broadband speeds enabled internet users to copy content from CDs and share it online. This came to a head in 1999 with the development of Napster, a service that the industry fought bitterly and was eventually able to shut down, due to its centralized control. Subsequent infringement mechanisms—such as torrent-based systems and remote streaming from foreign jurisdictions—have posed more intractable difficulties for the music business.

Faced with the rise of infringing sharing services, record companies were eventually willing in 2004 to make a deal with Apple to license their content for iTunes, but only on the proviso that the MP4 files were themselves encrypted. However, research by Apple revealed that 85 percent of content on iPods was lifted from freely shared online content that was originally copied from unencrypted CDs. This led Steve Jobs to announce in 2007 that iTunes would cease to encrypt its files, as, he said, record companies' own unencrypted CDs were creating unfair competition for the iTunes service. Record labels protested at the time, but no major record label withdrew its content when Apple removed its "Fairplay" encryption software in 2008. Today's legal streaming services likewise seek to tame free-sharing by emulating what they cannot prevent. The CD let the sharing genie out of the bottle.

At its inception, the CD reflected the interests of the dominant record labels like a mirror, and it came to concentrate that power like a magnifying glass. Ironically, with the detachment of tangible expression from physical container, the CD ended up

Above, right: iTunes
music gift cards
of different values
displayed for sale.
(Photo by Roberto
Machado Noa /
LightRocket via Getty
Images)

On the left: A
pedestrian passes a wall
covered with Apple iPod
advertisements in San
Francisco, California,
2005. (Photo by
Justin Sullivan / Getty
Images)

acting like a prism, fracturing the power it had initially reflected and which it had helped to concentrate. The paradox of digitization, initiated by the CD, lies in the increased detachability of tangible expressions from the physical objects used to contain them; but which no longer constrains them.

Since the end of the Cold War intellectual property—and in particular copyright—has seen a large expansion in the control given to copyright holders: extensions in duration, increased geographical reach, global harmonization toward stronger protection, and greater depth of coverage. Whilst these expansions have sought to extend protection over musical content, it was the CD which planted the seeds of revolution for the music industry, and which undermined the very profit flood it had created.

As the sales of CDs have declined, and free online sharing of music has exploded, artists can deliver their music to a much larger audience, anywhere in the world. As a result, the number of live concert tickets sold has increased, as has the price charged for live shows. International tours are no longer only the province of the world's most-popular

artists, and nowadays indie bands and musicians have fans—and play to packed houses in clubs and venues—thousands of miles from their home. This new, democratic musical scene has benefitted artists and performers greatly; but it has helped the labels less. Thanks to the introduction of the CD, these once-mighty record labels have struggled. They have found it difficult to capture the value of live performances, even as so many of their recordings are now distributed for next-to-nothing.

Or for free. ◆

Further Reading

Marie Connolly and Alan B. Krueger (2006) "Rockonomics: The Economics of Popular Music," in Victor A. Ginsburgh and David Throsby (eds.) *Handbook of the Economics of Art and Culture*. Amsterdam: Elsevier, pp. 667–720.

Matthew David (2010) *Peer to Peer and the Music Industry: The Criminalization of Sharing.* London: Sage.

Matthew David (2017) *Sharing: Crime Against Capitalism*. Cambridge: Polity.

1800   *1900*   *2000*

--/-----/-----/-----/-----/-----/-----/-----/--/---/-----/-----/-----/----

45 Internet
Jonathan Zittrain

IN A BOOK chartered to demonstrate intellectual property in objects, what concrete thing can represent the internet, a phenomenon that exists only as a well-elaborated idea? Perhaps the best physical representation of the genius of the Internet—and in particular, "Internet Protocol"—is found in an hourglass.

Internet Protocol is the essence of today's global worldwide network, and it's a very different kind of "IP" than the one this book is about. The Internet Protocol suite is a freely available set of standards for how digital devices and the software running upon them might talk to one another, and the internet exists because the makers of those devices and software, and the networks to which they're connected, have decided to implement those standards. The internet is a collective hallucination that functions because millions of people and companies believe in it.

The hourglass on the left is from late 18th-century Italy, a time before the waisted glass shape could be blown as a single piece of glass. Instead, two glass ampules were joined by wax, covered with cloth, and

On the left: A late 18th-century Italian hourglass. (Harvard University Collection of Historical Scientific Instruments)

secured by threads. That junction, which Jon Evans calls a "bubble-gum-and-baling-wire" construction, is where Internet Protocol can be found.

The metaphor of hourglass architecture is fundamental to understanding how the internet works, though its origins are a bit obscure. The US National Research Council's magisterial *Realizing the Information Future: The Internet and Beyond* from 1994 is one of the earlier conceptions, and it introduces the idea of a network built in layers. The number and nature of the layers has evolved over time, but its essence is three, mapping to the top, middle, and bottom of an hourglass. The bottom represents the range of physical media, wired and wireless, through which communications can take place. It's broad because it's meant to encompass any form of physical conveyance of data.

The top represents applications—what we might do when we can exchange data with one another, whether email, web browsing, or videoconferencing. It grows every time someone comes up with a new use for the internet.

And the middle is the "bearer service," the translator that links the top to the bottom without either having to know anything about the other. Companies can build networks without needing to know specifically how they'll be used; developers can write software without having to know anything about how the network that the software depends on is supposed to work. So long as each side knows a small amount about Internet Protocol, they're good to interoperate.

This technical design reflected not only the desire to occasion a network that would be ecumenical about the pipes it could run upon, and the applications that could in turn run upon it, but it also embedded the values of the cooperative and academic environment from which Internet Protocol sprang. As the 1994 NRC report put it:

This separation of the basic bearer service from the higher-level conventions is one of the tools that ensures an open network; it precludes, for example, a network provider from insisting that only a controlled set of higher-level standards be used on the network, a requirement that would inhibit the development and use of new services and might be used as a tool to limit competition.

So the hourglass represents layers designed to operate independently from one another—while still interconnecting thanks to the middle. And that middle is meant to be narrow. Steve Deering unpacked that narrowness in a 2001 presentation to the Internet Engineering Task Force, or IETF, which is the open, non-membership organization that develops and stewards internet protocols. According to Deering, the middle layer is narrow because it "assumes [the] least common network functionality to maximize [the] number of usable networks." By keeping the protocols simple and straightforward, and evolving very slowly, many unrelated parties who build networks and software can easily adapt to use Internet Protocol. As Bob Braden put it in 2001: "The lesson of the Internet is that efficiency is not the primary consideration. Ability to grow and adapt to changing

Above, left: The top and the bottom of the hourglass. (Harvard University Collection of Historical Scientific Instruments)

Above, right: The "bearer service" of the hourglass. (Harvard University Collection of Historical Scientific Instruments)

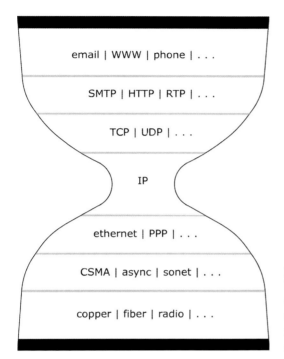

email | WWW | phone | . . .

SMTP | HTTP | RTP | . . .

TCP | UDP | . . .

IP

ethernet | PPP | . . .

CSMA | async | sonet | . . .

copper | fiber | radio | . . .

Above: Hourglass architecture of the internet. This version of the hourglass is derived from "The Internet's Coming of Age" by the Computer Science and Telecommunications Board of the National Academies of Sciences, Engineering, and Medicine, The National Academies Press (2001).

requirements is the primary consideration. This makes simplicity and uniformity very precious indeed."

This principle of simplicity goes hand in hand with the principle that new features for users are typically best implemented not as additions to Internet Protocol, which would expand the waist of the hourglass, but rather through a given piece of software built on top of it, running at two or more communicating endpoints.

Unlike the textbook story of IP-driven innovation, where creativity is inspired by the prospect of the creator monopolizing its fruits for a while, today's global network only exists thanks to its far-flung inventors disclaiming any property interest in its success.

Internet protocols have been devised by an open, unincorporated group—the IETF—which has sought to make those protocols as freely usable by the world as possible. That's a near-inversion from

previous network architectures, which were built by a single company or consortium and then protected as much as possible to allow for exclusive rights in selling deployments of those networks. By contrast, in copyright terms, participants in the IETF grant an irrevocable and perpetual nonexclusive license to an IETF Trust which, in turn, grants that license to everyone else in the world. Patent rights are a bit more complicated; here the IETF seeks maximal disclosure of rights implicated by a technology proposed for inclusion in an internet standard, with an opportunity for IETF participants to weigh whether the burdens of such rights are worth it. But according to the IETF's Best Current Practice Memo, the overall thrust remains that "IETF working groups prefer technologies with no known IPR claims or, for technologies with claims against them, an offer of royalty-free licensing."

As a competitor to proprietary network models and services, the internet not only offered a particular technology that the market might determine to be superior, but at least as important, a technology that could be adopted by anyone without concern for demands for licensing from its progenitors. (The risk of patent

claims by third parties remains for any technology.) Internet Protocol was designed to be ubiquitous and invisible, an all-important transparent glue piecing together disparate networks, devices, and applications. And that vision has not only been realized, but replicated among some of the still-most-common applications and services running at the "top" of the hourglass: the servers and clients following the protocols of Tim Berners-Lee's World Wide Web—described by James Gleick as the "patent that never was"; the mediawiki software and Wikipedia, a global encyclopedia in multiple languages to which anyone can contribute, and for which all contributions are licensed freely; and bitcoin, a cryptocurrency whose underlying blockchain protocols can be themselves found in a wiki, based on a paper written by a pseudonymous author who licensed them freely.

The signal disruption to the status quo as the internet became mainstream was its impact upon copyright enforcement. The move from analog to digital meant that the physical vessels of books, CDs, and DVDs that lent themselves to the scarcity on which IP is premised became unnecessary to convey their contents. A different network architecture—one designed and managed by a single company, for example—could have facilitated the design of digital bottles meant to decant their contents at least as discriminatingly as their analog forbears. The NRC's pro-competitive idea behind the layers of the internet hourglass translated to a reality that anyone could write an application to convey data, and network providers would serve no gatekeeping role.

Thus in 1999 an 18-year-old college student could devise "Napster," a song-sharing program, and freely share the program itself over the internet. The program

Above: The middle part of an hourglass consisting of one piece of glass. (Harvard University Collection of Historical Scientific Instruments)

was not one friendly to limiting access to music only to those who paid for it, and those who ran it soon found themselves able to trade music back and forth. When Napster was shut down, that broad and open top of the hourglass meant that any number of successors could take its place, many using fully peer-to-peer technologies such that once a copy of the software was obtained from any source, users could communicate directly with one another to swap files, making enforcement of any successful infringement claim difficult because there was no one central point of intervention to halt the activity. This resulted in some enforcement actions by the music and movie industries against individual users rather than intermediary software writers or service providers. Over time, it appears that the carrot of simple (and significantly cheaper) legal licensing schemes, such as those occasioned through the Spotify music subscription service, have had more of an impact on users' behavior than the stick of direct threat of lawsuit for using peer-to-peer services to trade copyrighted material.

For material born digital and intended to be shared by its makers, the free software movement pioneered licenses that would permit the sharing of software and the making of derivatives—so long as those derivatives, if shared, would be similarly free. Creative Commons came about in 2001 to facilitate the sharing and remixing of text, photos, and other nonsoftware creative works. In 2016 Creative Commons reported 1.2 billion licenses in use. In the meantime, legally blessed repositories that could index and aggregate old books in new ways—as compared to music and movies—have been difficult to achieve.

Internet Protocol has proven extraordinarily resilient as it has gone from experimental to universal, and even as its openness to innovation elicited seismic counter-reactions from incumbents whose interests or rights have been threatened, with copyright as a bellwether. By keeping its narrow waist, neither trying to optimize for particular applications, nor adding features to address concerns by rightsholders, Internet Protocol and the values of openness behind it have reigned.

These values are now tested as some applications at the top of the hourglass have become so popular as to constitute

constructive networks unto themselves. In 2017 Facebook crested two billion active users, including some who think it to *be* the internet, according to surveys conducted by *Quartz*. For better or worse, the internet's structure is akin to a monolith rather than an hourglass: innovation is channeled as business relationships by Facebook rather than anything goes, and bad behavior can be defined by the company and monitored and acted against in a way not possible on the internet at large. Bad behavior itself constitutes another test for the open internet; if the open tools to preclude it are outstripped by the tools to facilitate it and the energy to conduct it, users themselves may be driven away. There have been open implementations of social networks to compete with those like Facebook, and none have succeeded.

Finally, the Internet of Things confronts us with design choices originally made for the transport of "mere" bits. It's one thing for my 1998 PC to crash because of too much generativity in its amenability to running malware; it's entirely another for my car to crash for the same reason. The eccentric openness of groups like the IETF will be hard to apply in the world of traditional devices and vendors. The things joining the internet might yet be linked to their vendors by Internet Protocol, but not to one another in the free-for-all of the 1990s and early 2000s. ◆

Further Reading

Scott Bradner (2003) "A Short History of the Internet" (presentation, NANOG, February 9), http://www.sobco.com/presentations/n30.history.pdf. Archived at https://perma.cc/U36F-66JB.

Steve Deering (2001) "Watching the Waist of the Protocol Hourglass" (presentation, IETF 51 London, August), https://www.ietf.org/proceedings/51/slides/plenary-1/sld003.htm. Archived at https://perma.cc/2XLV-J66M.

The US National Research Council (1994) *Realizing the Information Future: The Internet and Beyond*. Washington: National Academies Press. www.nap.edu/read/4755/chapter/4. Archived at https://perma.cc/G56F-BFV8.

Jonathan Zittrain (2008) *The Future of the Internet and How to Stop It*. London: Penguin. http://yupnet.org/zittrain/2008/03/05/chapter-2-battle-of-the-networks/#15. Archived at https://perma.cc/7XZX-29WW.

On the left: An early 19th-century French hourglass (1800–1850) without a bearer service. (Harvard University Collection of Historical Scientific Instruments)

1800   1900   2000

--/-----/-----/-----/-----/-----/-----/----/--/---/-----/-----/-----/----

46 Wi-Fi Router
Terry Healy

EVEN THE CHEAPEST laptop no longer needs a cable to access the internet; you just walk into a place and, somehow, magically, the device you are carrying connects automatically with a Wi-Fi hot spot. This happens in cafes, at home, on a train, on a plane. Wi-Fi routers are everywhere, to the point where it feels odd when you find a spot where you actually *can't* find a Wi-Fi hot spot to watch movies, stream music, search the internet, or do emails.

The name "Wi-Fi" is the trademark popularized by the Wi-Fi Alliance to describe radio systems used to access the internet, with billions of devices now connected and growing. Wi-Fi uses a set of industry standards adopted by the Institute of Electrical and Electronics Engineers or "IEEE," a body that not only promulgates standards, but also records patents relevant to Wi-Fi. By now Wi-Fi-related patent families number a few hundred; but one stands out.

This is the story of the core patent, the one that showed how to make fast and efficient Wi-Fi. The patent journey took 25 years, and it took many twists and turns. In the end, it is a tale about how much hard work is involved in taking a great idea to market, how long it takes, and how, often, obtaining a patent may be merely the first salvo in a long war of attrition.

The story began with a small group of scientists in Australia, working in the esoteric field of radio astronomy. They were searching for gravitational waves associated with exploding black holes. That research lead to the filing in August 1987 of a patent application for "A Transform Processing Circuit," for a semiconductor chip that could perform two types of signal processing on data streams: Fast Fourier Transforms (FFT) and Inverse Fast Fourier Transforms (IFFT). The inventors were employees of CSIRO, Australia's primary scientific research body.

It's not clear whether the researchers who were named on the patent ever thought that the invention would be significant in communications, but a few years later one of those researchers, John O'Sullivan, was involved in a commercialization project at CSIRO. Along with a group of other researchers, O'Sullivan was tasked with the creation of a new, very fast wireless

On the left: "No Wi-Fi" sign in shop window (Stockimo / Alamy)

network technology. The CSIRO team set itself an ambitious target: to create a system with speeds matching those of the best wired networks of the time, about 100Mb/s. To carry this much data they had to use very high frequency radio waves—1GHz or more—but at these frequencies the waves tend to bounce around indoor environments, causing echoes, which prevent clear transmission. To overcome this, the team focused on a radical solution, using FFT and IFFT to solve this "multipath" problem.

The use of FFT and IFFT in communications was not unheard of at the time, but it tended to be limited to desktop computers and other fixed-location products, since the limited battery technology of the time meant that most solutions were impractical for portable devices. However, based on the earlier patent and subsequent research, the CSIRO team knew that they could make an FFT/IFFT system work on a semiconductor chip, a solution that was inherently energy efficient and radically better than competing alternatives.

By 1992 the CSIRO team had invented a radio transceiver system implementable on a chip, capable of transmitting and receiving data over multiple subchannels simultaneously. The scientists wrote up their work, filed patent applications, and embarked on the process of finding commercial partners to take the system to market.

CSIRO talked with a range of industry leaders, but other than IBM, was met with deep skepticism. Despite clear evidence, many simply did not seem to believe that the system could work as promised. CSIRO started work with a small start-up company called Radiata, and by 2000 was commercially demonstrating the world's first functional microcircuit embodying the invention.

By that time, the IEEE had promulgated two new standards, one of which was built around the concepts of the CSIRO invention. CSIRO had not objected to this

Above: Several children using their smartphones. (Getty Images)

Above: A woman doing paperwork with laptop in coffee shop. (Gang Zhou / Getty Images)

On the following pages: Young girl with headphones at cafeteria studying on laptop. (martin-dm / Getty Images)

and in fact had agreed with the IEEE that it would grant licenses under its patents to firms practicing the standard.

Firms needed to make written requests and CSIRO would then license them on "reasonable and non-discriminatory" terms, a common form of patent licensing intended to allow widespread adoption.

Initially, the most successful wireless local area network standard was not the CSIRO-based one. It was the "b" standard (IEEE 802.11b). The "b" standard inherently had comparatively slow data transfer rates but it was allowed to operate at 2.4GHz, which gave it an early commercial advantage. The CSIRO-based standard (802.11a) operated only at 5GHz, which was more difficult to implement. However, by 2005, regulatory authorities permitted Fourier-transform technologies to operate at 2.4GHz, opening the way to yet another standard, 802.11g, which

included the CSIRO invention. The "g" standard took off and quickly made the "b" standard commercially redundant. We now have the "n" standard—802.11n—among others; but all use the technology covered by the CSIRO patents.

Perhaps naively, CSIRO expected firms to take licenses under its patents and pay modest royalties. But, oddly, no one signed a license; even though many were using the technology.

Mystified by the stonewalling, CSIRO decided to initiate a test case against Buffalo Technologies, a mid-sized infringer based in Japan. The first proceedings were filed in February 2005, in the Eastern District of Texas, a common location for US-based patent infringement proceedings.

A few months later, a pair of defensive lawsuits was filed against CSIRO, seeking declarations that its US Wi-Fi patent was invalid and/or that the plaintiffs did not infringe. The plaintiffs were Apple, Microsoft, Hewlett-Packard, Intel, Dell, and Netgear. If CSIRO ever needed confirmation that its Wi-Fi patents were indeed very valuable, then it clearly had it.

The litigation lasted for 12 years, with endless parties, suits, and countersuits—including several excursions to the appeals courts in the United States, and actions in Japan and Germany. Several

attempts to invalidate the patents before national patent offices failed, with the patents remaining in force in 32 countries until their expiration in 2013. All cases ultimately settled, mostly on the steps of the trial court, with royalty payments to CSIRO totaling more than AUD$500 million.

In addition to the satisfaction of knowing that billions of products worldwide now use its Wi-Fi technology, CSIRO was left with cash as the primary recompense for its world-changing invention. One notable mechanism for reinvestment of the cash was the rejuvenation of an endowment fund that had been created by the Australian government in 1926. The Science and Industry Endowment Fund

("SIEF") had initially been well funded but nearly a century of inflation had reduced the value of its capital to almost nothing. The proceeds from CSIRO's Wi-Fi litigation changed that. In 2009, CSIRO presented AUD$150 million to SIEF to support a range of challenging scientific research projects that are now being carried out by Australian universities, CSIRO, and others.

Governments agree that innovation is the key to the future, particularly for advanced economies. Perhaps the most important policy instrument for encouraging innovation is the patent system, and it remains under siege. In the United States, major firms in the so-called technology industries have lobbied vociferously to

Above: Harry Bliss, The New Yorker Collection. (The Cartoon Bank, originally published in The New Yorker, 3 September 2018)

Above: Free Wi-Fi and Beer sign outside a cafe, Hyderabad. (Alamy)

weaken the patent system, particularly for organizations like CSIRO, which never intend to make products from their patents, but rather to license them. Over the 12 years of CSIRO's litigation, the context for patent assertion in the United States changed radically. Some of the changes came through the America Invents Act of 2013, but most came from the courts.

The movement to reduce the strength of the patent system has been remarkably successful over the past decade or so. It remains to be seen whether or not the pendulum will swing back any time soon. In the meantime, the success of CSIRO's Wi-Fi litigation demonstrates that it is still possible for research to win. But it is not a game for the fainthearted.

Wi-Fi exists today due to brilliant, basic research into astrophysics, a strong patent system, and the tenacity of the CSIRO in prosecuting the patent. Had it not been for these things, we would all be poorer off; and no-one would ever have heard the query of houseguests and office visitors the world over:

"What's your Wi-Fi password?" ◆

Further Reading

Brad Collis (2002) *Fields of Discovery: Australia's CSIRO.* Clayton: CSIRO Publishing.

Jon Gertner (2013) *The Idea Factory: Bell Labs and the Great Age of American Innovation.* New York: Penguin.

Wolter Lemstra, Vic Hayes, and John Groenewegen (2010) *The Innovation Journey of Wi-Fi: The Road to Global Success.* New York: Cambridge University Press.

Marc Watt (2014) *What to Do When the Wi-Fi is Down: Ideas to Pass the Time When You Can't Access the Internet.* Amazon Media EU Sarl.

www.wi-fi.org/

1800   *1900*   *2000*

--/-----/-----/-----/-----/-----/-----/-----/-----/-----/-----/-----/----

47 Viagra Pill

Graham Dutfield

VIAGRA IS A remarkable pharmaceutical object, and an even more remarkable social phenomenon. Its 1998 release was accompanied by media attention on a scale barely precedented for any medicine, let alone one that doesn't actually save lives. It swiftly became a global social phenomenon, turning an embarrassing and sometimes distressing personal condition into a recognized medical problem, susceptible to a pharmaceutical solution. "Erectile dysfunction" went from being a condition that people rarely talked about, to one that they couldn't stop talking about. In doing so, Viagra helped extend the boundaries of medicalization, accelerating the trend to label any deviation from supposedly normal human well being as a condition for which medical treatment, in some form or another, should be available.

What then *is* Viagra? It cannot be *wholly* defined by what it is made of, what it is for, by what it looks like, or by what it does when the human body absorbs it—essential features though these might be. But these aside, Viagra's identity, status, and value are determined by the regulatory regimes

that control its use, and the intellectual property rights used to protect it. Although we can describe Viagra as a "sildenafil-containing erectile dysfunction treatment in the form of a blue diamond-shaped tablet," the drug is a kind-of legal construct created by intellectual property law, whose boundaries are defined by the scope of these rights, the freedoms of others, and the edges of the public domain.

Viagra is a highly specific product in pill form containing a single active ingredient and other substances called "excipients," which protect the active ingredient on its journey through the body, control its rate of absorption, and enhance palatability. Scientifically, the active ingredient can be identified as 1-[[3-(6,7-dihydro-1-methyl7-oxo-3-propyl-1H-pyrazolo[4,3-d]pyrimidin-5-yl)4-ethoxyphenyl]sulphonyl]-4-methylpiperazine or $C_{22}H_{30}N_6O_4S$; and it has the generic pharmaceutical name of "sildenafil citrate."

To say that Viagra is sildenafil citrate is a simple statement of fact, but it obscures the range of ways in which Pfizer has used the intellectual property system to shape

On the left: A despairing statue in the Tuileries gardens of Paris. (Brendan Hunter / Getty Images)

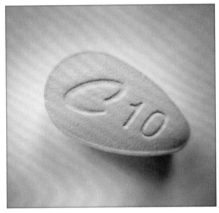

On the left: A Viagra pill, distributed by the pharmaceutical company Pfizer. (Getty Images);
A Cialis pill, a sildenafil containing anti-impotence tablet. (Getty Images)

our understanding of Viagra. Sildenafil purposely disrupts a naturally occurring enzyme called phosphodiesterase type 5 (PDE5), and the drug was developed initially to deal with disorders like hypertension and angina. It was intended as a better version of a failed, and now largely forgotten, drug candidate called zaprinast. Sildenafil's initial results from tests on patients started in 1991, and they were disappointing, in part due to the chemical's short half-life in the body which made its effects too temporary. However, a group of people given the substance—in some tellings of the story, a group of Welsh miners—described increased incidences of erections. It turned out that PDE5 inhibition enables the flow of blood into the penis by relaxing certain muscles in the erectile tissue.

Medicines must be *for* something; but what then was Viagra for? Aphrodisiacs are not medicines. Consequently, the medical condition of erectile dysfunction (ED) had to be invented in order for sildenafil to become the prescription medicine "Viagra," instead of a recreational drug like ecstasy. Of course, the name "erectile dysfunction" is both mechanical and reductionist, although it does get to the point: it's the penis, after all, that needs fixing. Pfizer did not invent ED, but it invested huge sums in promoting the medicalization of the condition, one previously thought either to be too trivial or too inherently psychological to deserve its own drug. This of course suited many men who could point to their "condition" as a medical problem, one for which they should not be blamed.

Central to any marketing strategy in the pharmaceutical industry is to have a good name for the product, one that directs people purchasing drugs to that product, and not to any alternative. Without question, Viagra® as a product name and trademark has been hugely successful, generating vast sums of money for Pfizer. Registration of the word mark is the first step in protecting the name of your drug, but being ready to guard the mark—through enforcement actions and oppositions to the registration of similar marks—is also essential. Pfizer's strong policing of the mark has ensured

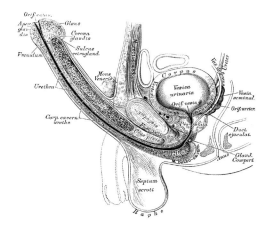

Above: Scientific illustration of the male pelvis section. (ilbusca / Getty Images)

that there is no legal recognition, for example, of "Natural Viagra"—notwithstanding the constant efforts of internet sellers of herbal remedies of varying levels of dubiousness to tempt the unwary. Keeping control over use of the term "Viagra" in the market place helped prevent it becoming a genericised synonym of "aphrodisiac," something that was assisted by Pfizer's educational program to enhance public awareness of ED as a condition. Here trademark and patent strategy supported each other, as they often do in the pharmaceutical business.

Until Pfizer informs us otherwise, Viagra's defining characteristic is that it *must* consist of sildenafil citrate, a substance patented in the early 1990s. On the other hand, when sildenafil citrate is prescribed for pulmonary arterial hypertension (PAH), it is not Viagra® but Revatio®. All Viagra is sildenafil citrate, but not all sildenafil citrate is Viagra. In this sense one can say that Pfizer is narrowing the boundaries

of its monopoly to accommodate another one, so that it is Viagra *only* when indicated for erectile dysfunction. But in a sense it is even more specific than this. Pfizer has numerous trademarks relating to Viagra, including ones covering the blue-colored and diamond-shaped appearance of the tablet. It even has a European design right. Thus in the minds of the consumer and the general public Viagra is that "little blue pill." And so Viagra's appearance will prevent generic firms from making their sildenafil pills look like Pfizer's original product.

Pfizer, as one would expect, did its utmost to expand the scope of its monopoly on the product as much, and for as long, as possible. The challenge facing the company was that, after its initial discovery as a novel substance with a plausible medicinal use, it turned out to be much more effective for something else—in this case, for its main reported side effect. Thankfully for the industry it is possible to file patent applications for new medical indications of substances that themselves lack novelty, having been discovered earlier. Pfizer availed itself of this possibility in those areas of the world where such patenting is allowed.

As the first inhibitor of PDE5—or as it's sometimes styled, PDEV—and the first

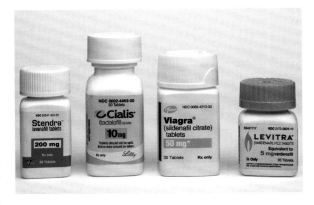

Above: Erectile dysfunction drugs Strenda (avanafil), Cialis (tadalafil), Viagra (sildenafil citrate) and Levitra (vardenafil HCI). (H.S. Photos / Alamy)

for treating erectile dysfunction, Pfizer was understandably keen to associate its invention with PDE5 inhibition as a unique feature. Otherwise it would have been impossible for Pfizer to block the market entry by competitors of follow-on PDE5 inhibitors. It sought to do this by claiming in its new use patents a class of compounds of which sildenafil citrate was one member sharing the ability to inhibit the action of PDE5. However, doing so helped to render these patents vulnerable to attack. Consequently, Pfizer was unable to prevent the market entry of me-too rivals Cialis® and Levitra®.

Although successful to a limited extent, Pfizer was unable to use the patent system to carve out a complete monopoly for this new use. The United Kingdom and European patents were revoked or successfully opposed, primarily on grounds of obviousness. The Chinese State Intellectual Property Organization revoked the counterpart Chinese patent in 2004 on similar grounds. In 2012, the Canadian Supreme Court revoked the patent there for insufficient disclosure.

The fate of the US patent on the use of Viagra for ED—which remains in force until 2019, albeit with reduced scope—is particularly fascinating. In February 2010, the Board of Patent Appeals and Interferences of the US Patent and Trademark Office decided on an appeal by Pfizer relating to the following rejected patent claim:

A method of treating erectile dysfunction in a male human, comprising orally administering to a male human in need of such treatment an effective amount of a selective cGMP PDEV inhibitor, or a pharmaceutically acceptable salt thereof, of [*sic*, or] a pharmaceutical composition containing either entity.

Four of the references used by the examiner to reject the claim on the basis of "anticipation"—that is, the information was known prior to the invention, meaning that the invention was not novel and therefore not patentable—disclosed use of Yin Yang Huo or "horny goat weed," in traditional medicine. For the Board, the key point at issue was whether or not these

references "describe oral administration of the selective PDEV inhibitor *icariin* in an amount effective to treat ED."

In his rejection of the claim, the examiner had relied on expert testimony showing that Ying Yang Huo contains *icariin*, and that this substance is effective as a cGMP PDEV inhibitor. The question arose of whether or not the Yin Yang Huo oral preparations, as used in traditional Chinese medicine as an aphrodisiac, that were described in the publications effectively delivered *icariin* to the patients and therefore anticipated the claim. Of the four relevant publications one of them did not mention *icariin*; evidently the preparation was not well known to this author by its chemical composition. In arguing its case, Pfizer observed that this article, "disclosed treatment comprises a mixture of Yin Yang Huo and Tu Si Zi, as well as yellow rice wine, genital massage, rest, bathing in a

herbal mixture, and abstinence from intercourse and, therefore, does not establish that the treatment effect was due to Yin Yang Huo alone." Accordingly, Pfizer's lawyers claimed, this was not enabling of the invention, and consequently not relevant in anticipating the patent. The Board rejected this view, concluding that the disclosure just had to enable the oral delivery of enough of the enzyme inhibitory substance to treat erectile dysfunction, which it did. Therefore, each of the four publications held by the examiner to anticipate the claim was accepted also by the Board.

Even without a perfect patent foundation, Viagra is still potent. The market—and marketing—power generated by the drug's intellectual property rights allows a large measure of control over how the product is represented to the public as a medical entity. However, what patents

and trademarks could never do is enable Pfizer to control all of the narratives, stories, meanings, and representations about Viagra. Consumers, social commentators, and comedians have all had much to say about Viagra and erectile dysfunction. Viagra is the subject of endless chatter, discussion, articles, and gossip. Jokes about it abound.

That is a measure of its success. Viagra, whatever it is and whatever it is for, has joined aspirin, Valium, Prozac, and, of course, the Pill as a cultural icon, one that has been extraordinarily profitable for Pfizer. Viagra may well be the first billion-dollar-a-year drug whose sales were as much attributable to direct-to-consumer publicity and attendant media hype, as they were to a creative mix of patents and trademark protection. And it is probably the only such drug for an incidental side-effect of its original use. ◆

Further Reading

Hossein Ghofrani, Ian Osterloh, and Friedrich Grimminger (2006) "Sildenafil: From Angina to Erectile Dysfunction to Pulmonary Hypertension and Beyond," *Nature Reviews Drug Discovery*, 5, pp. 689–702.

Meika Loe (2004) *The Rise of Viagra: How the Little Blue Pill Changed Sex in America.* New York: New York University Press.

Annie Potts and Leonore Tiefer (eds.) (2006) "Special Issue on Viagra Culture," *Sexualities*, 9(3), pp. 267–272.

1800　　　　　*1900*　　　　*2000*

--/-----/-----/-----/-----/-----/-----/-----/-----/-----/-----/-----/----

48 Qantas Skybed
Mitchell Adams

A LOT OF thought goes into what we sit on. From the design of the office chair to the cafe bench, kitchen stool, or couch where we watch television. For consumers, even more thought goes into what we sit on when we fly. Either domestic or international, we all have our preferences. Starting with which airline, then the location within the aeroplane—either up front or behind the wing. Finally, our preference for aisle or window, but never choosing a middle seat. Choice matters and can influence passengers to pay more than an economy fare. Design also plays a part and can affect a consumer's experience when flying. Good design can also play a role in linking innovation and the commercial success of products and services. Airplane seating is no exception.

Less thought goes into understanding the importance of design. Qantas Airlines Australia, however, recognized the importance of design and equally its protection and with the inception of the Skybed, it changed the perception of international business-class travel and what it means to fly. Design played a key role and created a

consumer experience that was more functionally efficient and more aesthetically pleasing. The Qantas Skybed is an illustrative example of the unseen connections between industry, designer, consumer experience and design law.

In 2001, Qantas approached Marc Newson, a designer famous for his Lockheed Lounge and Embryo chair, to create a new business-class seat. The seat would need to recline and produce a flat bed. Qantas knew what drove customers to choose business class: comfort, privacy, and flexibility. The Newson seat would achieve all this, but also create a new sense of space for passengers either while working, relaxing, sleeping, or being entertained. Newson designed a retro-futuristic business-class seat with a sculpted carbon fibre back shell. Although not the first flatbed business-class seat—British Airways introduced the first in 1999—the Skybed was the longest at two meters fully reclined. The innovative design went on to win the Good Design Award from the Chicago Athenaeum Museum in 2003 and, a year later, an Australian Design Award. Following the successful

launch and acclaim of the Skybed, Qantas asked Marc Newson back to redesign the entire cabin interior of Qantas' new A380 fleet. To Qantas, the Skybed was the crown jewel of a $385 million modernization process. For Newson, this was an opportunity to design a mini-world. Nothing was spared and included all aspects of the interior, including hundreds of accessories. During the redesign, Newson took on the economy-class seat, recreating it to echo the Skybed. Again, Newson found new ways to play with space: a reduction in bulk in the seat provided extra foot room and the capacity for a larger screen. Six years after the initial success of the Skybed design, the Qantas A380 Economy seat went on to win the 2009 Australian International Design Award.

Design not only provides for product and service differentiation, but it determines a user's experience with the product or service. The Skybed encompassed aesthetics,

ergonomics, and comfort. By integrating design, Qantas signaled a superior value, offering over and above its competitors. For Qantas, the Skybed design provided an opportunity to attract the attention of consumers and presented an image of quality, which reinforced the reputation of the company.

The Skybed and the A380 cabin was not the first time Qantas had integrated design to create a new airline experience. By the early 1970s passengers were sick of flying and reminiscent of the experience a decade earlier. Time spent at airport terminals became longer, the lines for check-in grew, space reduced, and noise increased. The introduction of the Boeing 747 "Jumbo Jet" exacerbated this. The Jumbo's promise of increased cabin space allowed the airlines to accept more passengers; but shortly after its introduction, a recession, coupled with increased fuel prices, meant that airlines with large Jumbo Jet

Above, left: The Lockheed Lounge. (Photo: Karin Catt; Courtesy of Marc Newson Ltd.)

Above, right: The Embryo Chair. (Photo: Fabrice Gousset; Courtesy of Marc Newson Ltd.)

fleets had too many seats and too few passengers. For Qantas, price-cutting was out of the question. They needed new customers and were desperate to hold on to the loyal ones.

Retaining the full fare business passengers was Qantas' priority. A handful of airlines began offering more for these passengers. Pan Am established the "Clipper Class" in 1978: full fare business customers were allowed to access the First Class lounge. Air France followed, offering free champagne, cognac, and French cheeses on-board. British Airways introduced "Club Class," with a new cabin between economy and first, offering new English-inspired cuisines. Each of these innovations catered to their business passengers and provided additional amenities above what was available to economy passengers. Even so, these offerings were not akin to the business-class experiences we know today.

Qantas challenged the status quo and announced in 1979 a new way to fly between Australia and the United States—a new service called "Business Class." A new, exclusive cabin was designed. It had bigger seats and more legroom. Passengers were never far from the aisle, with seats arranged in pairs. Qantas Business Class passengers enjoyed a special menu, a bar, in-flight entertainment, separate check-in with shorter queues, and priority baggage collection. All these amenities were available for merely 15 percent above the economy fare. Qantas gave birth to the first business-class service, and at the centre of this was the world's first business-class seating, designed with its travelers specifically in mind.

The consumer-centric design of this first Business Class offering presages the achievement of the Newson design seen three decades later. Comfort and flexibility in the use of space were paramount. Qantas incorporated seating with a retractable leg rest that stowed beneath the seat; previously, foot and leg rests were a problem for aeroplanes with space and safety limitations. Clever use of integrated design solved the problem.

What then of the protections of these innovative designs? Design law was a much-misunderstood area of intellectual

property for many years. The protection of design involves the registration of the overall appearance of a product. The overall appearance may include the shape, configuration, pattern, and ornamentation which, when applied to a product, give it a unique visual appearance. Qantas was an early leader in the use of designs law to marshal and control its investment in design. In September 1979, the airline filed three design applications for business-class seating: first in Australia, for the design of "an aircraft-seating unit" and thereafter with filings in 1980 in the United Kingdom and the United States.

Although not the only airline to register their designs, Qantas placed their flag in the ground with the first business-class seat. Subsequent patterns in design applications and registrations show just how important design is to global competition. In particular, trends relating to the international protection of aircraft seat design reveal how the Qantas Skybed design innovation caused reverberations in the industry and led to an increased interest in design. For the Skybed, Qantas made application to protect the design in Australia on 24 September 2002—the "seating module" AU 200,202,967—an application which was subsequently registered in June 2004. True to its purpose as an international business class seat, Qantas quickly sought protection for the design with registrations in the United States (D493,294) and in Europe (000,013,727).

After the registration of the Skybed design in 2004, interest intensified in the protection of designs for aircraft seating. Previously, worldwide applications for aircraft seating was relatively steady from 1977 to 1995, with only 43 filed applications. A minimal increase was seen between 1996 to 1999 with both British Airways and Qantas filing applications. However, after Qantas' Skybed application, filing activity rose markedly, with an average of 40 design applications filed each year between 2006 and 2016. These applications make up 80 percent of the total applications submitted. The interest in design protection was driven, not by Qantas or British Airways, but by Airbus, Etihad, Japan Airlines, Virgin, and Air

Above, left: The "orginal" Skybed. (Courtesy of Marc Newson Ltd.)

Above, right: Accessories for the Qantas A380. (Photo: Fabrice Gousset; Courtesy of Marc Newson Ltd.)

New Zealand. The Skybed caused renewed interest and competition in design
among the airlines. Interestingly, Qantas
never filed for any design-related protection
after this point.

What then was Qantas seeking to protect with the Skybed design application,
and why was there a marked drop-off by
this company in its design applications
after the Skybed filing? Some argue the
importance of design protection is limited,
and suggest that the registered designs system is the poor cousin of the patent system.
In an age of patent dominance, the tendency is to identify innovations as discrete
units of invention that can be protected by
the patent system. Design is, however, easy
to describe but difficult to define. Consider
the case of a company manufacturing a
kitchen chair. If it uses the same materials, the same construction methods and
the same manufacturing technology to
make a new kitchen chair, as it does with
its other chairs (and its competitors), what
sets its product apart? Design is the unique
outward appearance that differentiates the
product from its competitor's products.
Design here is an intangible factor that
adds value and contributes to the overall
success of a company. The registration of
a design can capture this critical dimension to a product, its higher-than-average
market value.

Others have insisted on increased
protection; principally where intellectual
property laws do not easily protect the
design in objects such as furniture and
fashion. Design as intellectual property is of
a hybrid nature, having much in common
with the other major intellectual property

paradigms but struggles to occupy any
of them. At its essence, design registration only protects the original ornamental features of an object. However, it has
been argued that this is the most direct
way companies can communicate brand
and personality with customers. The rise
of modern design practices has therefore
led to strategic behaviors from businesses
around the use of intellectual property
protection.

In registering the design of the Skybed,
it seems that Qantas was seeking to secure
an aura of authenticity in the business-class
seat. The collaboration with Marc Newson
and the design application assured Qantas'
investment in integrating design within the
company and ensured it was first to market
with their innovative design. Consequently,
the market followed. Qantas initiated a culture of design innovation linked to design
protection, which saw its apotheosis in the
Skybed but goes back even further to the
introduction of Business Class. Theirs is a
culture where design links innovation and
commercial success. ◆

Further Reading

Dan Hunter and Suzannah Wood (2016)
"The Laws of Design in the Age of
Mechanical Reproduction," *Adelaide Law
Review*, 37(2), pp. 403–429.

Malcolm Knox (2005) *I Still Call Australia
Home: The Qantas Story 1920–2005*. Sydney:
Focus.

Conway Lloyd Morgan (2003) *Marc Newson*.
London: Thames & Hudson.

1800   *1900*   *2000*

--/-----/-----/-----/-----/-----/-----/-----/-----/-/----/-----/-----/----

49 Mike Tyson Tattoo

Marie Hadley

MIKE TYSON'S FACIAL tattoo has been described as one of the most distinctive tattoos in North America. It has attracted controversy as an example of the cultural appropriation of *ta moko*, the sacred culturally embedded tattooing practice of the Maori people of Aotearoa/New Zealand. It has also attracted much media attention for its place at the heart of *Whitmill* v. *Warner Bros.*, a rare litigated instance of a tattooist enforcing their copyright in a tattoo design. More than this, though, Tyson's tattoo is an excellent example of the tensions that emerge over the protection of traditional knowledge, and the difficulty of claiming one truth in an intellectual property world that was born in the Western philosophical tradition, and is only now beginning to come to terms with its colonial heritage.

Mike Tyson's "warrior" tattoo was inked by Las Vegas tattooist S. Victor Whitmill in 2003. From the time of Tyson's first public appearance with the tattoo, Maori activists and scholars were critical of it as a cultural appropriation of *ta moko*. Tyson's tattoo is monochrome, curvilinear, features two spiral shapes, and was placed around his left eye. Whitmill has described the "flow" of Maori art as a design influence, and he created it after showing Tyson pictures of Maori *moko*. In Maori culture, facial *moko* is a privilege reserved for respected cultural insiders, and it represents and embodies the wearer's sacred genealogy and social status. Appropriating an individual's *moko* is profoundly offensive and akin to identity theft.

But the controversy from the original tattoo wasn't the last of it. In THE HANGOVER PART II an exact copy of Tyson's tattoo was featured on the face of actor Ed Helms as part of a humorous plot device. Whitmill was outraged, and claimed copyright over his tattoo. In 2011 he sued Warner, arguing that they had violated his exclusive right to authorize derivative works. Whitmill's decision to sue stirred lingering resentments in Aotearoa/New Zealand around the tattoo's cultural content: in response to the litigation, Maori politician Tau Henare tweeted that it was a "a bit rich" that Tyson's tattooist was claiming someone had stolen the design, given

402

that he had copied it from Maori without permission. Maori arts scholar Ngahuia Te Awekotuku's criticism of Whitmill's assertion of copyright ownership was widely reported:

It is astounding that a Pakeha tattooist who inscribes an African American's flesh with what he considers to be a Maori design has the gall to claim ... that design as his intellectual property.

The tattooist has never consulted with Maori, has never had experience of Maori and originally and obviously stole the design he put on Tyson. The tattooist has an incredible arrogance to assume that he has the intellectual right to claim the design form of an indigenous culture that is not his.

Given the Western intellectual property system's miserable colonial record, it should come as no surprise that the claim of cultural appropriation was irrelevant to the trajectory of the *Whitmill* proceedings. Whitmill asserted that he was the author and owner of the copyright in an original artistic work, comprising the tattoo on

Tyson's face. Warner did not dispute that Whitmill created the tattoo or question its provenance, but argued that copyright does not subsist in tattoos. At the preliminary hearing, Judge Perry refused to grant Whitmill's request for a preliminary injunction to prevent the release of the film; but she did accept the basis of Whitmill's claim, stating that "of course tattoos can be copyrighted." As a result she ruled that Whitmill had a strong likelihood of prevailing at trial.

The only time that a connection with *moko* was mentioned was after the preliminary hearing when Warner released a media statement that it would be pursuing pre-trial discovery to determine whether Tyson's tattoo was derivative of preexisting Maori designs. This investigation never eventuated however, as the case settled soon after. In any case, there is no evidence to suggest that Whitmill copied an existing *moko*.

The invisibility of the claim of Maori cultural appropriation and the primacy of Whitmill's rights suggest that copyright law is not interested in the aesthetics of

Above, left: Actor Ed Helms at the Los Angeles premiere of THE HANGOVER PART II at Grauman's Chinese Theatre in Hollywood, California, 2011. (Photo by Jon Kopaloff / FilmMagic)

Above, right: Dick Cherry photographed with THE HANGOVER PART II poster. Cherry, while working for Tinsley makeup and prosthetics studio, was responsible for the Mike Tyson tattoo recreation of Whitmill's design on the actor's face. (Photo by Don Kelsen / Los Angeles Times via Getty Images)

imagery, the source of artistic inspiration, or the possibility of competing cultural rights to indigenous design forms. In legal scholarship, this bias in copyright's functioning is typically attributed to the inherent philosophical conflicts between Western intellectual property systems that are focused on private economic rights and financial gain, and indigenous approaches to intellectual rights and heritage that tend to be centered on collective interests, reciprocal obligations, and respect for natural resources. These divergent underpinnings mean that, in this case, while individual *mokos* are protected by copyright the same as any other tattoo art, copyright's cornerstone principles of limited duration, idea/expression dichotomy, material form, and preference for individual ownership will not protect indigenous cultural imagery and art styles from appropriation by Westerners. Whitmill was legally permitted to adopt the visual markers of *moko* by using curvilinear lines that flow with the contours of the body, a monochrome color scheme, and by placing *koru* motifs in the negative space—so long as he did not directly copy a substantial part of an existing, copyright *moko*.

At first glance, then, Tyson's tattoo is just another version of the familiar story of Western appropriation of indigenous culture: a taking without remuneration, or even recognition. This age-old story of colonial plunder seems worse when one considers the fact that ownership of traditional knowledge was never mentioned during the *Whitmill* legal proceedings. *Ta moko*, it seems, had been cast into the public domain, a domain where everything is free for Westerners to take without payment.

But a closer look at the controversy that surrounds the tattoo's cultural content revealed that the foundations of the cultural appropriation allegations were contested from within. Some Maori *ta moko* practitioners considered Tyson's tattoo to be an inoffensive tribal design, and the *ta moko* industry was, and is, reasonably open to outsider engagement. Taking and re-using *moko*-inspired tattoo imagery is not necessarily problematic, and the depth of cultural contestation that surrounded Tyson's tattoo illustrates a dynamic discussion that occurs within cultural appropriation claims.

Within Aotearoa/New Zealand there was a strong counterclaim from *ta moko* practitioners that Whitmill created merely a "tribal" tattoo for Mike Tyson, and did not misappropriate *ta moko*. "Tribal" is a Western tattoo genre that offers a contemporary interpretation of traditional Pacific, Asian, and African tattoo imagery. Henriata Nicholas, a female *ta moko* artist and *uhi* practitioner, suggested that Whitmill's design was likely inspired by traditional Maori art, but stated that she

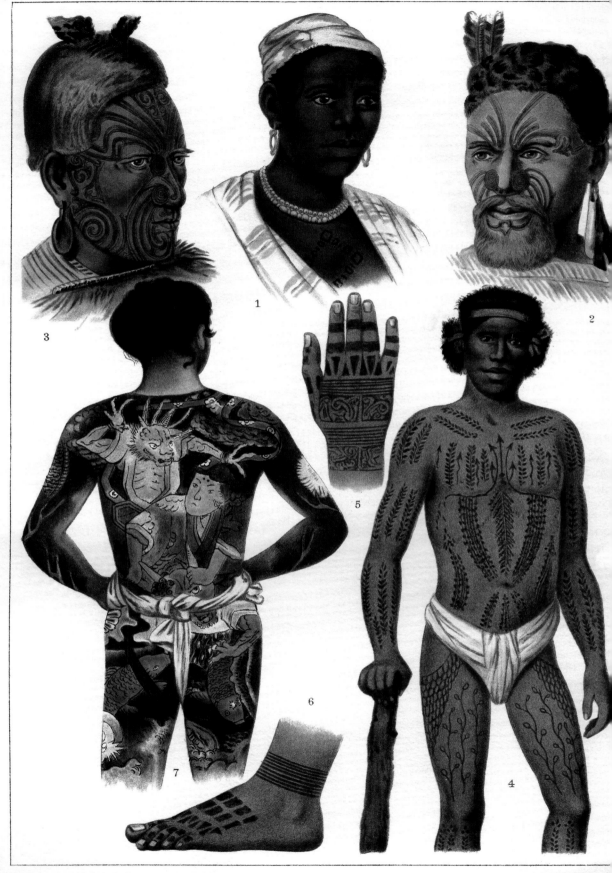

1. NEGRESS. 2. NEW ZEALAND CHIEFTAIN. 3. NEW ZEALAND KING. 4. CAROLINE ISLANDER. 5, 6, HAND AND FOOT OF DAYAK OF BORNEO. 7. JAPANESE.

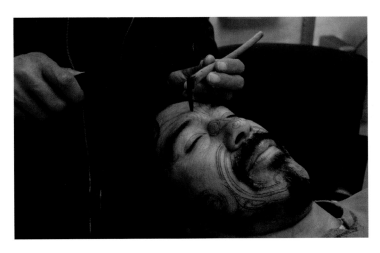

Above: Shane Jones receives a moko—a Maori traditional skin carving. (Photo: Aroon Thaewchatturat / Alamy)

On the left: "Tattooing 1800–1900." Engraving to illustrate different tattooing styles from around the World. Original print by the Bibliographisches Institut, Leipzig. (Photo by The Print Collector / Print Collector / Getty Images)

couldn't connect it solidly back to her own imagery. Award-winning *ta moko* practitioner Richie Francis considered the design a tribal hybrid: an "intelligent" mix of the Maori *koru* and the solid black of Hawaiian and Tahitian motifs. For Francis, the media reporting of the tattoo as cultural appropriation was, in fact, an indictment of how poorly the media were educated about *ta moko*.

Rangi Kipa, a renowned artist, sculptor and *ta moko* practitioner, did not recognize any Maori elements in the tattoo. He regarded it as heavily influenced by traditional Papua New Guinean tattoos, and said that it had very little to do with *moko*, despite its placement on the face, a placement that implies a Maori connection. It seems then that Tyson's tattoo was not necessarily perceived to be appropriative of Maori culture, even if it was inspired by *moko*, is monochrome, and contains *koru* motifs.

There is also a cultural contest around whether intercultural engagement with *moko* is permitted. *Moko's* circulation as fashion has been criticized by some Maori as inconsistent with *moko's* sacred function and cultural importance. It is suggested that it is inappropriate for cultural outsiders like Tyson to wear *moko*-inspired designs because they have no connection to Maori culture. Yet *ta moko* practitioners themselves

appear open to this type of intercultural engagement. They regularly apply *moko* to cultural outsiders. *Ta moko* practitioners might vary in how they conceptualize this work—for example, some use the word *kirituhi* to describe *moko* for outsiders that is devoid of spiritual power—however, it remains the right of the *ta moko* practitioners to conduct their business how they please, including whom they decide to tattoo. This suggests that *moko* is not as closed to outsiders as the Maori cultural appropriation allegations against Whitmill might imply.

It is also unclear whether non-Maori using *moko* as design inspiration is culturally problematic. Reproducing existing *mokos* and ancestral imagery is taboo for Maori and non-Maori alike, but taking cultural imagery is not necessarily troubling to Maori. While some tribes have "signatures," and use or combine patterns in a certain way, *moko* is not a heraldic device. In Aotearoa/New Zealand, *pakeha* tattooists regularly create *moko*-inspired work and it does not appear that *ta moko* practitioners regard them as direct competitors. Tattoos that are merely moko-inspired are perceived to be visually recognizable from the work of insiders, and are generally seen as poor quality. For example, *ta moko* artist Jack Williams likens outsider tattoo work to "a page of spelling mistakes." He believes

that if a customer values authenticity and wants the real deal, they will seek out an experienced Maori practitioner. Similarly, Rangi Kipa, who describes imitative work as third-rate, does not worry about competition from non-Maori tattooists. He suggests the answer is in *ta moko* artists continuing to innovate and develop their narratives and meanings as they progress. These perspectives suggest that as long as *ta moko* artists are the source of quality *moko*, commissioning outsiders like Whitmill to create imitative work is unlikely to cause financial harm or be misrecognized as authentic, and so cannot threaten Maori cultural integrity.

The cultural appropriation controversy that surrounds Mike Tyson's *moko*-inspired "warrior" tattoo is a fascinating microcosm of the concerns around traditional knowledge, and the inability of the Western-created intellectual property systems to account for all the nuances of other cultures. It is an indication of the gap in intellectual property systems to account for anything other than that which fits into a western ideological framework. Tyson's tattoo, and the furor that surged around it, is as neat a depiction as one could imagine of the problems that occur from the erasure of indigenous cultural imagery and art styles from protection. But it is also a picture of the internal tensions within indigenous

On the left: Maori Chief Tamati Waka Nene by Gottfried Lindauer 1890, oil on canvas, Auckland Art Gallery, New Zealand. (Photo by VCG Wilson / Corbis via Getty Images)

cultures, and a consideration of it facilitates a secondary, more complex reading of this cultural terrain as marked by multiple, conflicting cultural perspectives and interests. Cultural appropriation allegations, as well as critiques of law's Western bias, can mask the dynamism of culture.

The simple design in ink means so much more than its face value. ◆

Further Reading

APN Holdings NZ Limited (2003) "Concern Over Ignorant Use of Maori Moko," *New Zealand Herald*, 27 February. Available at: www.nzherald.co.nz/nz/news/article.cfm?c_id=1&objectid=3198136

Leon Tan (2013) "Intellectual Property Law and the Globalization of Indigenous Cultural Expressions: Maori Tattoo and the Whitmill versus Warner Bros Case," *Theory, Culture and Society*, 30(3), pp. 61–81.

Whitmill v. *Warner Bros*, ED D Mo, 4:11-cv-752, 2011.

The quotes from ta moko practitioners used in this chapter are drawn from fieldwork that was conducted in the North Island of Aotearoa/New Zealand in 2012, as part of the author's PhD project (forthcoming, University of New South Wales, Australia).

1800   *1900*   *2000*

--/-----/-----/-----/-----/-----/-----/-----/-----/--/---/-----/-----/----

50 Bitcoin
Primavera De Filippi

On 12 January 2009 a pseudonymous entity signed a transaction that instructed a distributed network to transfer a small amount of digital currency to Hal Finney, one of the key figures of the cypherpunk movement. After a few minutes, the transaction was recorded on a distributed public ledger, permanently updating the balance of both parties. This transaction—the first Bitcoin transaction—marked the beginning of a new era of decentralized payment systems, ushering in a variety of financial services that do not depend on any centralized clearinghouse or other financial middleman.

Bitcoin is regarded by many as a powerful technological innovation that could disrupt many sectors, in the realm of finance and beyond. But the underlying technology on which the network operates, the Bitcoin *blockchain* can do much more than that. Just as the internet did in the early-1990s, blockchain technology carries with it a whole new range of promises concerning how decentralization can support and promote individual freedoms and autonomy. Blockchain proponents believe

that Bitcoin and other cryptocurrency platforms will revolutionize mechanisms of value exchange in the same way that the internet transformed information sharing, by providing a platform for people to exchange digital resources, in a secure and decentralized manner without the need to rely on any intermediary or trusted authority. But this revolutionary potential also carries with it serious implications for censorship, intellectual property, and the regulated flow of information.

A blockchain is a decentralized database of transactions maintained by a distributed network of computers, which all contribute to the verification and the validation of transactions. Once accepted, these transactions are recorded inside a "block" of transactions, which incorporates a reference to previous blocks. This creates a long chain of blocks—a "blockchain"—that stores the history of all transactions in a chronological order. Every block contains information about a particular set of transactions, a reference to the preceding block in the blockchain, and the answer to a complex mathematical puzzle that is

On the left: Several bitcoins on a table. (Photo by Minchen Liang / EyeEm / Getty Images)

used to validate the data associated with that block. A copy of the blockchain is stored on every computer in the network, making it virtually impossible for anyone unilaterally to modify the data stored on this decentralized database: if anyone tries to modify any transaction the fraud will be immediately detected by all other network participants. The initial implementation of the idea of a blockchain is found in the first Bitcoin whitepaper. Released on 31 October 2008, it was attributed to "Satoshi Nakamoto," a pseudonymous entity who has managed to keep his or her (or their) identity secret, despite numerous attempts by the media to unmask them.

While no one owns the Bitcoin network, many people own Bitcoins, the virtual currency that enables this network to operate in an open and distributed manner. But what does it mean to "own" a Bitcoin? With cash, things are relatively simple: if you have a $10 bill in your wallet, you probably own it, since ownership of physical objects is closely related to, and often synonymous with, possession. Ownership of digital things is much more complicated, however, not because possession is difficult to assess but because in the digital world possession doesn't really line up neatly with ownership. I might possess a copy of an MP3 sound recording, but I may not have purchased it—and even if I have it's not clear that I own it. (Because what, exactly, does it mean to "own" digital content? While the intellectual property regime has to some extent resolved the question of ownership for information goods, no such regime exists for dealing with the ownership of digital content—which I may only have a right to for a short period.)

Intellectual property is a legal layer of artificial scarcity imposed over specific types of information, in order to facilitate the trading of those information goods.

Above, left: A clerk at Lloyd's of London, manually updating his centralized ledger. (Getty Images)

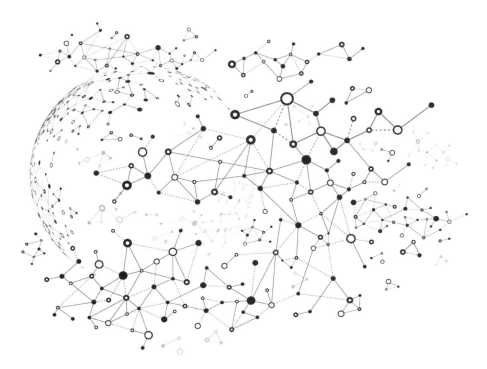

Above: An illustration of a distributed global network. (Ani_Ka / Getty Images)

Its goal was to re-align the properties of information—a non-rival good—with the properties of the medium into which it had been embodied—typically, a physical, and therefore rival good. This model broke down with the advent of the internet and digital technologies. Digital resources are, like all information, inherently non-rival: they can be held and consumed by multiple people at the same time, without this affecting the opportunities for others to enjoy the same resource. The non-rivalry of the digital world is one of the wonders of the information age, and is fundamental to our ability to use the internet to share knowledge with one another.

Solving the digital scarcity problem is at the core of Bitcoin. Although a Bitcoin is nothing more than a series of bits stored on a decentralized public ledger that is associated with someone's Bitcoin account, because of the design of the underlying blockchain network no one has the ability to reproduce or multiply their Bitcoin in the same way as they could reproduce a digital file. With the blockchain, therefore, we gained the ability to create digital resources

that are inherently scarce, such that they cannot be digitally copied or reproduced. Before Nakamoto's Bitcoin protocol, it was only possible to *reproduce* digital assets, since transferring a digital file over the internet still allowed the original owner to keep a copy of the file. With Bitcoin, it is now possible to *transfer* digital assets, without copying them.

The development of Bitcoin has thus marked the beginning of a new era, an era of digital scarcity where digital bits can be transferred over the internet, without losing their scarcity, and without recourse to the artificial scarcity of intellectual property laws. The first great advance ushered in by Bitcoin is, therefore, that it enables us to apply the notion of property to digital assets, for the first time.

This revolution has led to the emergence of many new cryptocurrencies—such as Ether, XRP, Litecoin, and Bitcoin itself—which have been the subject of enormous media and public interest. But the significance of the blockchain is not limited to digital currency: less than ten years after the first Bitcoin transaction, the

blockchain protocol has inspired a large variety of new applications, many of which extend well beyond the realm of finance. From decentralized registries, recordation systems, marketplaces, and peer-to-peer value exchanges, the blockchain protocol is being used as the underlying transaction layer for the trading of numerous digital assets in a secure and decentralized manner.

The range of opportunities is seemingly endless, and the blockchain protocol is particularly valuable in the management of property, especially intellectual property and digital property. In the context of copyright, for instance, a blockchain can be used to manage the rights in artistic works that are recorded in a digital format. It was until now essentially impossible to create limited editions of a digital work, since anyone in possession of one of these editions could simply make multiple identical copies. But by recording the unique identifier of each legitimate copy of a work

on the Bitcoin blockchain, any given copy can become forever associated with a Bitcoin transaction—even if it is only worth a few cents—so that the ownership details of that copy are forever recorded. Of course, people still retain the ability to reproduce the digital work and distribute it as they wish, but only the recipients of the relevant Bitcoin transactions will be able to prove that they are the legitimate owners of that authorized copy of the work.

The technology underpinning Bitcoin can also be applied to revolutionize trademark law: rather than rely on brands and marks to distinguish the source of goods, companies can rely on the blockchain in order to prove the authenticity of their products, by associating them with a particular Bitcoin transaction. For instance, Armani or Louis Vuitton could transfer a small fraction of Bitcoins along with the purchase of any of their designer clothes, which would serve as a seal of authenticity

Above: Mining rigs of a super computer are pictured inside the bitcoin factory "Genesis Farming" near Reykjavik, 2018. At the heart of Iceland's lava fields stands one of the world's largest bitcoin factories at a secret location rich in renewable energy, which runs the computers creating the virtual currency. (Photo by Halldor Kolbeins / AFP / Getty Images)

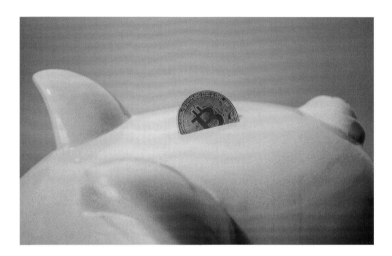

Above: Cryptocurrency and saving. Piggy bank with golden bitcoin coin virtual money. (Nejau Photo / Getty Images)

to prove that these products are, indeed, authentic. When selling these products on the secondary market, the original purchaser would also need to transfer these Bitcoins to the new buyer; who would then be able to prove and verify that the product is not a counterfeit. Initiatives of this kind already exist to prevent the counterfeiting of luxury goods, in markets such as diamonds, for instance. Today, a diamond's authenticity is guaranteed by paper certificates, which can easily be forged. The company Everledger is using the Bitcoin blockchain to register diamonds, thereby increasing the transparency and traceability of diamond supply chains, giving people the possibility to trace the movements of these diamonds as they pass from hand to hand.

This usage of the Bitcoin blockchain offers new opportunities to artists, eager to distribute their digital works over the internet while preserving the scarcity and authenticity of these works. Using the blockchain, digital objects can be imbued with a greater degree of rivalry and may be traded or exchanged in ways that are roughly equivalent to tangible property. Secondary markets are likely to emerge, where copyright owners can transfer title to digital resources—e-books, digital movies, music files, and so on—which will potentially lower the price of these resources and increase their public availability. The Bitcoin blockchain is, therefore, much more than a decentralized payment system: it is a decentralized ledger that makes it possible for anyone to exchange scarce digital resources in a secure and decentralized manner, without the need to rely on any trusted authority or centralized middleman.

At first glance, Bitcoin might therefore appear as a powerful tool for the enforcement of copyright in the digital world. Yet Bitcoin's relationship with intellectual property laws is ultimately a double-edged sword. The same properties that make Bitcoin so valuable for exchanging value in a secure and decentralized manner also make it a powerful tool to disseminate information in a way that cannot be retroactively deleted or modified. By recording data on the Bitcoin blockchain, a user can

be sure that, as long as the blockchain exists, these data will remain permanently and persistently available to anyone who holds a valid copy of the blockchain. Any attempt by a third party to censor the information will be doomed to failure, since the network will simply ignore the request. The underlying protocol of the Bitcoin network makes it extremely difficult for censorship to occur in the first place, since it requires a coordinated action of more than 51 percent of the computational power of the network to alter the blockchain retroactively.

Because of the disintermediated nature of a blockchain, law enforcement authorities do not have the ability to restrict the flow of online communications using traditional means. In the context of most centralized online platforms, enforcement authorities can exert pressure on service providers or intermediary operators, who are generally responsible for taking down any illicit content from their platforms. In a decentralized network like Bitcoin, the lack of a central authority in charge of managing the network makes it virtually impossible for any single party to control the information that can be posted onto the network, or subsequently to censor or block that information. Whether it is copyright-infringing material, cyber-bullying, or hate speech, all information recorded on the Bitcoin blockchain will forever exist, outside the reach of the long arm of the law.

It is this dichotomy, between blockchain technology as a *regulatory technology* and its potential use as an *unregulatable technology*, that makes the blockchain so interesting—and so worrying—from a legal perspective. The distinctive features of a

On the left: Bitcoin Mining. Miniature people digging on valuable coin. (coffeekai / Getty Images)

blockchain—its transparency, its resiliency, and its incorruptibility—can be regarded simultaneously as a gift and a potential curse to intellectual property. The Bitcoin blockchain may strengthen the ability for rightsholders to enforce their intellectual property interests; but it may also lead to the demise of the current copyright regime, as well as many other laws aimed at restricting the flow of information. ◆

Further Reading

Primavera De Filippi and Aaron Wright (2018). *Blockchain & The Law: The Rule of Code*. Cambridge, MA: Harvard University Press.

Primavera De Filippi and Samer Hassan (2016) "Blockchain Technology as a Regulatory Technology: From Code is Law to Law is Code," *First Monday*, 21(12). Available at: http://firstmonday.org/ojs/index.php/fm/article/view/7113/5657

Jessica Litman (2001) *Digital Copyright*. Amherst: Prometheus Books.

Satoshi Nakamoto (2008) *Bitcoin: A Peer-to-Peer Electronic Cash System*. Available at: https://bitcoin.org/bitcoin.pdf

Don Tapscott and Alex Tapscott (2016) *Blockchain Revolution: How the Technology Behind Bitcoin is Changing Money, Business, and the World*. New York: Portfolio Penguin.

Hal R. Varian (1999) *Markets for Information Goods*. Tokyo: Institute for Monetary and Economic Studies, Bank of Japan.

About the Contributors

HEE-KYOUNG SPIRITAS CHO

Spiritas Cho is Professor at Hongik University College of Law in Korea, where she teaches intellectual property law, competition law, and arts and law, and where she helped to establish a Masters of IP program in the graduate school. Spiritas obtained a degree in international relations from Cambridge University, and she is admitted as an attorney in Australia, England, and New York. Before joining academia, she worked as an IP litigator in private practice and as a government affairs specialist.

STEFANIA FUSCO

Stefania Fusco is a Senior Lecturer at the University of Notre Dame Law School, where she teaches International Intellectual Property and Corporate Finance. She earned a J.S.D. from Stanford Law School, where she was a Kaufmann Fellow and a Transatlantic Technology Law Forum Fellow. Her research interests include the impact of patent protection on financial innovation, the activity of Non-Practicing Entities (NPEs) in the United States and Europe, and the historical origin of the patent system.

ANDREA WALLACE

Andrea Wallace is a Lecturer in Law at the University of Exeter. She earned her PhD in Cultural Heritage Law at CREATe / The University of Glasgow in partnership with the National Library of Scotland, focusing on the intersections of copyright, cultural institutions, and the public domain. She holds an LL.M from Radboud University, NL, a J.D. from DePaul University College of Law in Chicago, and a B.F.A. from the School of the Art Institute of Chicago. She is also a registered attorney with the Illinois Bar.

JANE GINSBURG

Jane C. Ginsburg is the Morton L. Janklow Professor of Literary and Artistic Property Law at Columbia Law School, and faculty director of its Kernochan Center for Law, Media and the Arts. She teaches legal methods, copyright law, international copyright law, and trademarks law, and is the author or co-author of casebooks in all four subjects, as well as of many articles and book chapters on domestic and international copyright and trademark law. In 2011, she was elected to the British Academy.

MICHAEL PUNT

Michael Punt is Professor of Art and Technology at the University of Plymouth, where he is the founding convenor of the Transtechnology Research group. He is an international co-editor for *Leonardo*, Editor-in-Chief of *Leonardo Reviews*, and founder of *Leonardo Quarterly Reviews*, an experimental publishing platform published through MIT Press and UT Dallas. He is the author of *Early Cinema and the Technological Imaginary* (2000, Postdigital Press) and co-editor of *Screen Consciousness: Cinema, Mind and World* (2006, Rodopi).

AMANDA SCARDAMAGLIA

Amanda Scardamaglia is Associate Professor and Department Chair at Swinburne University Law School. Her area of research is intellectual property law with a special focus on empirical and historical studies in trademark law, branding, advertising and the consumer. She is the author of *Colonial Australian Trade Mark Law: Narratives in Lawmaking, People Power and Place* (2015, Australian Scholarly Publishing). Her second book, *Charles Troedel: From Stone to Print* will appear with Melbourne Books in 2019.

ADAM MOSSOFF

Adam Mossoff is Professor of Law at Antonin Scalia Law School at George Mason University, where he teaches a wide range of subjects in property and intellectal property law. He is a founder of the Center for the Protection of Intellectual Property (CPIP). He has published extensively on the theory and history of intellectual property with his scholarship focusing on patents as private property rights and on private-ordering institutions for commercializing innovation.

LIONEL BENTLY

Lionel Bently is the Herchel Smith Professor of Intellectual Property Law, Director of the Centre for Intellectual Property and Information Law, and Professorial Fellow of Emmanuel College at the University of Cambridge. He has been the Yong Shook Lin Visiting Professor of Intellectual Property law at the National University of Singapore and the BNL Professor of European Law at Columbia University. He is the one of the authors of *Intellectual Property* (5th edn, 2018, Oxford University Press).

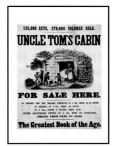

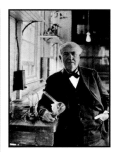

PETER JASZI

Peter Jaszi is Professor Emeritus at American University Law School. He was a founder of the school's Glushko-Samuelson Intellectual Property Law Clinic and its Program on Intellectual Property and Information Justice. Since 2005, he has been working with Patricia Aufderheide to help creative communities develop fair use guidance documents that reflect their problems and practices. A new edition of their book, *Reclaiming Copyright*, was published in 2018 by the University of Chicago Press.

KARA W. SWANSON

Kara W. Swanson is Professor of Law at Northeastern University School of Law. Her main research interests are intellectual property law, gender and sexuality, the history of science, medicine, and technology and legal history. She is the author of *Banking on the Body: The Market in Blood, Milk and Sperm in Modern America* (2014, Harvard University Press). Her current book project investigates the centrality of inventive ability to American nationhood and citizenship.

CHRISTOPHER BEAUCHAMP

Christopher Beauchamp is Professor of Law at Brooklyn Law School. He teaches and publishes in the areas of intellectual property and legal history. His first book, *Invented by Law: Alexander Graham Bell and the Patent That Changed America*, was published by Harvard University Press in 2014. He is also working on a book about the history of patent law and litigation in the US, entitled *Technology's Trials*. His recent scholarship has been published in the *Stanford Technology Law Review* and the *Yale Law Journal*.

STEF VAN GOMPEL

Stef van Gompel is senior researcher and lecturer in intellectual property law at the Institute for Information Law at the University of Amsterdam, where he also received his doctorate. His dissertation, titled *Formalities in Copyright Law: An Analysis of their History, Rationales and Possible Future*, was published by Kluwer Law International in 2011. He is specialized in national and international copyright law, and is national editor for the Netherlands of the *Primary Sources on Copyright (1450-1900)* project.

MEGAN RICHARDSON

Megan Richardson is Professor of Law at the University of Melbourne. Her research and publication interests include intellectual property, privacy and personality rights, law reform and legal theory. She is currently Co-Director of the Melbourne Law School's Centre for Media and Communications Law (CMCL) and the Intellectual Property Research Institute of Australia (IPRIA). She is the author of *The Right to Privacy: Origins and Influence of a Nineteenth-Century Idea* (2017, Cambridge University Press).

JESSICA LAKE

Jessica Lake is a Lecturer in Law at Swinburne University, and researches at the intersection of law, technology and gender. She is the author of *The Face that Launched a Thousand Lawsuits* (2016, Yale University Press), demonstrating that women forged a "right to privacy" in the United States in the 19th and 20th centuries by bringing cases protesting the unauthorized use and abuse of images of their faces and bodies. In 2016–2017, she was the Karl Loewenstein Fellow in Political Science and Jurisprudence at Amherst College.

RONAN DEAZLEY

Ronan Deazley is Professor of Copyright at Queen's University Belfast. He is the author of *Rethinking Copyright: History, Theory, Language* (2006, Edward Elgar), and co-editor of *Privilege and Property: Essays on the History of Copyright* (2010, Open Book Publishers). He is the principal contributor to the *Copyright User Portal* (copyrightuser.org) and *Copyright Cortex* (copyrightcortex.org), independent online resources that make UK copyright law more accessible to creators, media professionals, and the general public.

CLAUDY OP DEN KAMP

Claudy Op den Kamp is Senior Lecturer in Film and faculty member at the Centre for Intellectual Property Policy & Management (CIPPM) at Bournemouth University, and Adjunct Research Fellow at Swinburne Law School. Her research interests include the role of copyright in film restoration and access to archival collections. She is the author of *The Greatest Films Never Seen. The Film Archive and the Copyright Smokescreen* (2018, Amsterdam University Press). She is co-editor of this book.

MAURIZIO BORGHI

Maurizio Borghi is Professor of Law at Bournemouth University, where he is also Director of the Centre for Intellectual Property Policy & Management (CIPPM). He formerly taught at Brunel University and Bocconi University. His research interests cover theoretical and empirical studies on copyright, data protection, and the role of law in the information society. He is co-author of *Copyright and Mass Digitization* (with Stavroula Karapapa), which was published with Oxford University Press in 2013.

DEV S. GANGJEE

Dev Gangjee is an Associate Professor in Law and Director of the Oxford IP Research Centre at the University of Oxford. Dev's research focuses on intellectual property, with a special emphasis on branding and trademarks, geographical indications and copyright law. His research interests include the history and political economy of IP, collective and open innovation, and the significance of registration for intangibles. He is one of the authors of *Intellectual Property* (5th edn, 2018, Oxford University Press).

PETER DECHERNEY

Peter Decherney is Professor of Cinema & Media Studies and English at the University of Pennsylvania. He holds a secondary appointment at the Annenberg School for Communication and an affiliation with the Center for Technology, Innovation, and Competition at Penn Law School. He is the author or editor of multiple books, including *Hollywood's Copyright Wars: From Edison to the Internet* (2013, Columbia University Press) and *Hollywood: A Very Short Introduction* (2016, Oxford University Press).

STINA TEILMANN-LOCK

Stina Teilmann-Lock is Associate Professor in the Department of Management, Politics and Philosophy at Copenhagen Business School. She was formerly a patent manager, a Carlsberg Research Fellow at the Danish Design School, and a Postdoctoral Fellow at the Centre for Information and Innovation Law at the University of Copenhagen. She has published widely on copyright, art, and design. Her book, *The Object of Copyright: A Conceptual History of Originals and Copies in Literature, Art and Design*, was published by Routledge in 2015.

BRAD SHERMAN

Brad Sherman is Professor of Law at The University of Queensland. His previous academic positions include posts at the London School of Economics, and the University of Cambridge. His research expertise encompasses many aspects of intellectual property law, with a particular emphasis on its historical, doctrinal and conceptual development. In 2015, he was awarded an Australian Research Council Laureate Fellowship. He is a co-author of *Intellectual Property* (5th edn, 2018, Oxford University Press).

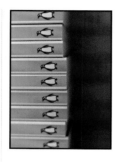

STUART KELLS

Stuart Kells is Adjunct Professor at LaTrobe Business School in Melbourne. He has a PhD in Law from Monash University as well as degrees in Commerce from the University of Melbourne. He authored multiple books, including *Shakespeare's Library: Unlocking the Greatest Mystery in Literature* (2018, Text Publishing Company), *The Library: A Catalogue of Wonders* (2017, The Text Publishing Company), and *Penguin and the Lane Brothers: The Untold Story of a Publishing Revolution* (2015, Black Inc.).

MARIANNE DAHLÉN

Marianne Dahlén is Associate Professor in Law at Uppsala University, where she teaches comparative legal history and conducts research within two strands: the history of international child labor law, and intellectual property law and fashion in comparative and historical perspective. Her current project focuses on trademark legislation in a globalized world at the turn of the previous century. Her most recent work has been published in *Business History*, and the *Queen Mary Journal of Intellectual Property*.

CATHERINE BOND

Catherine Bond is a Senior Lecturer in the Faculty of Law, UNSW Sydney, where she teaches intellectual property courses. Her research focuses primarily on historical intellectual property issues, and specifically on the relationship between intellectual property and war. Her first book, *Anzac: The Landing, The Legend, The Law*, which explores the 100-year history of the regulation of the word "Anzac" in Australia and internationally, was published by Australian Scholarly Publishing in 2016.

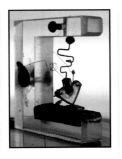

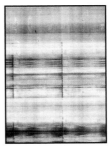

BETH WEBSTER

Beth Webster is Director of the Centre for Transformative Innovation at Swinburne University, where she is also Pro Vice-Chancellor for Research Impact and Policy. Her expertise centers on the economics of the way knowledge is created and diffused through the economy. Her work has been published in multiple journals, including *The RAND Journal of Economics, The Review of Economics and Statistics, Oxford Economic Papers, The Journal of Law & Economics,* and the *Journal of International Economics and Research Policy.*

MELANIE BROWN

Melanie Brown is a PhD researcher at Bournemouth University, where her research involves a consideration of copyright law and the film industry within the European Digital Single Market. She graduated from Aberystwyth University with a degree in Criminal Law, and obtained a Master's degree in Human Rights Law from Sunderland University, during which she explored compulsory licensing of essential pharmaceuticals in public health emergencies. She previously worked as a corporate paralegal.

JESSICA SILBEY

Jessica Silbey is Professor of Law at Northeastern University School of Law, where she is also co-director of the Center for Law, Innovation and Creativity (CLIC). Her research and teaching focus on law's entanglement with other disciplines such as the humanities and social sciences. She is a 2018 Guggenheim Fellow; the author of *The Eureka Myth: Creators, Innovators and Everyday Intellectual Property* (2015, Stanford University Press); and co-editor of *Law and Justice on the Small Screen* (with Peter Robson, 2012, Bloomsbury).

JEROEN SCHARROO

Jeroen Scharroo works in the communication and marketing department of the Faculty of Science at Leiden University as its Editor-in-Chief. Previously he was editor at *Bionieuws,* a biweekly Dutch newspaper for biologists, as well as campaign leader at Greenpeace in Amsterdam. He has also been a freelance journalist. He was educated in Plant Breeding and Crop Protection at Wageningen University, and holds a Master's degree in Journalism from the University of Amsterdam.

JEANNIE SUK GERSEN

Jeannie Suk Gersen is the John H. Watson, Jr. Professor of Law at Harvard Law School, where she teaches constitutional law, criminal adjudication, family law, and the law of fashion and the performing arts. She is the author of *A Light Inside: An Odyssey of Art, Life and Law* (2013, Bookhouse Publishers), *At Home in the Law: How the Domestic Violence Revolution is Transforming Privacy* (2011, Yale University Press), and *Postcolonial Paradoxes in French Caribbean Writing* (2001, Oxford University Press). She is a Contributing Writer for NewYorker.com.

DAN HUNTER

Dan Hunter is the founding dean of Swinburne University Law School, and has previously held positions at QUT Law School, New York Law School, the University of Melbourne Law School, the Wharton School at the University of Pennsylvania, and Cambridge University. He is author of *The Oxford Introductions to U.S. Law: Intellectual Property* (2012, Oxford University Press) and co-author of *For The Win: How Game Thinking Can Revolutionize Your Business* (2012, Wharton Digital Press). He is co-editor of this book.

GREG LASTOWKA

Greg Lastowka was a Professor of Law at Rutgers Law School. His scholarship helped to define the field of cyberlaw: his book *Virtual Justice: The New Laws of Online Worlds* (2010, Yale University Press) is regarded as a landmark treatise on the complex intersection of law and virtual worlds. The book identified and addressed compelling and new legal questions about such issues as owning virtual assets and preventing virtual crimes. He was originally going to be an editor of this book, but passed away in April 2015.

JACOB GERSEN

Jacob Gersen is Sidley Austin Professor of Law at Harvard Law School, Affiliate Professor in the Department of Government, and Director of the Food Law Lab, which supports academic research on the legal treatment of food in society. He is co-author of *Food Law: Cases and Materials* (2018, Wolters Kluwer), co-editor of *Food Law & Policy*, and his current teaching and research focuses on food law, remedies, regulation, and international arbitration. His work has also appeared in the *New York Times*, *Wall Street Journal*, *Time*, and *Forbes*.

C. SCOTT HEMPHILL

Scott Hemphill is Professor of Law at NYU School of Law, where he teaches and writes about antitrust, intellectual property, and regulation of industry. His scholarship has been cited by the US Supreme Court and California Supreme Court, among others, and formed the basis for congressional testimony on matters of regulatory policy. His writing has appeared in law reviews, peer-reviewed journals, and the popular press, including the *Yale Law Journal*, *Science*, and the *Wall Street Journal*.

BRIAN L. FRYE

Brian L. Frye is the Spears-Gilbert Associate Professor of Law at the University of Kentucky College of Law, where he teaches classes in professional responsibility, intellectual property, copyright, as well as a seminar on law and popular culture. He is also a filmmaker. He produced the documentary OUR NIXON (2013), which was broadcast by CNN and opened theatrically nationwide. His critical writing on film and art has appeared in *October*, *The New Republic*, *Film Comment*, *Cineaste*, *Senses of Cinema*, and *Incite!*

ROBIN WRIGHT

Robin Wright is the Manager, Licensing, Acquisitions and Copyright at Swinburne University of Technology. She holds an LL.B (Hons) from La Trobe University. Her research interests include the intersection of copyright and digital technologies in the education and cultural sectors. She has published on copyright and cultural institutions, digital television, and open access. She was project leader on the Open Education Licensing project supporting the use of open educational resources at Australian universities.

JASON BAINBRIDGE

Jason Bainbridge is Professor of Media and Communication and Head of the School of Creative Industries at the University of South Australia. He holds a PhD in Media Studies and a Bachelor of Laws. His research and publication interests include popular representations and understandings of law; superheroes, justice and comic book culture; and the study of merchandising and material culture in relation to media convergence, particularly the function of toys and play in mainstreaming fan culture.

JAKE GOLDENFEIN

Jake Goldenfein is a Lecturer in Law at Swinburne University, and a Postdoctoral Research Fellow at the Digital Life Initiative at Cornell Tech, Cornell University. He received his PhD from the University of Melbourne, in which he investigated the histories of state surveillance technologies and the legal regimes governing them. His current research addresses the nature and role of law in computation society and cyber-physical systems.

MICHAEL MADISON

Mike Madison is Professor of Law, and Faculty Director of the Innovation Practice Institute, at the University of Pittsburgh, where he teaches and researches intellectual property law and policy and institutional governance of knowledge and innovation. He is co-author of *The Law of Intellectual Property* (5th edn, 2017, Wolters Kluwer), co-editor of *Governing Medical Knowledge Commons* (2017, Cambridge University Press), and *Governing Knowledge Commons* (2014, Oxford University Press).

TOM SPURLING

Tom Spurling is Professor of Innovation Studies at Swinburne University. He is a scientist with experience in managing the process of translating research into commercial products. His current research interests include the use of social network analysis in understanding how best to commercialize public sector research, and the use of case studies to tell the story of Australian innovation. He is a co-author of *The Plastic Banknote: From Concept to Reality* (with David Solomon, 2014, CSIRO).

STAVROULA KARAPAPA

Stavroula Karapapa is Professor of Intellectual Property and Information Law at the University of Reading, where she also serves as the Executive Director of the Centre for Commercial Law and Financial Regulation (CCLFR). Her research interests include copyright doctrine and policy; digitization, big data and the internet; European Union trademark law; and law and the arts. She is the author of *Private Copying* (2012, Routledge), and co-author of *Copyright and Mass Digitization* (2013, Oxford University Press).

JULIAN THOMAS

Julian Thomas is Professor of Media and Communications at RMIT University. He works on the history and regulation of communications and information technologies, with a longstanding interest in media piracy, grey and black markets. These are explored further in *The Informal Media Economy* (2015, Polity; co-authored with Ramon Lobato). He recently led the *Australian Digital Inclusion Index* team (2016–2018), and is the author of *Internet on the Outstation* (2016, Institute of Network Cultures).

MEGAN CARPENTER

Megan Carpenter is Dean of the University of New Hampshire School of Law. Her research interests include intellectual property, with a particular focus on entrepreneurship, branding, and the arts. Prior to joining UNH Law, she was founder and co-director of the Center for Law and Intellectual Property at Texas A&M University School of Law, where she also served as Professor of Law. She is the author of *Entrepreneurship and Innovation in Evolving Economies: The Role of the Law* (2012, Edward Elgar).

DINUSHA MENDIS

Dinusha Mendis is Professor of Intellectual Property and Innovation Law at Bournemouth University, where she is also Co-Director of the Centre for Intellectual Property Policy & Management (CIPPM). She is co-editor of *3D Printing and Beyond: Intellectual Property and Regulation* (2019, Edward Elgar), has conducted research on 3D printing and IP Law for the UK IPO, and is currently leading a project on the IP implications of the development of industrial 3D printing for the European Commission.

MATTHEW DAVID

Matthew David is Associate Professor of Sociology at Durham University. He has undertaken research and has published in the areas of new social movements, online data-services in higher education, online training in rural areas, and forms of free online music sharing. He is author of *Sharing: Crime Against Capitalism* (2017, Polity), co-author of *Owning the World of Ideas* (2015, SAGE), and author of *Peer to Peer and the Music Industry. The Criminalization of Sharing* (2010, SAGE).

JONATHAN ZITTRAIN

Jonathan Zittrain is the George Bemis Professor of International Law at Harvard Law School and the Harvard Kennedy School of Government, Professor of Computer Science at the Harvard School of Engineering and Applied Sciences, Director of the Harvard Law School Library, and Faculty Director of the Berkman Klein Center for Internet & Society. He is a co-author of *Access Contested* (2011, MIT Press) and author of *The Future of the Internet—And How to Stop It* (2008, Yale University Press).

TERRY HEALY

Terry Healy is Adjunct Professor on the CSIRO History Project in the Centre for Transformative Innovation at Swinburne University. CSIRO is a vital part of Australia's National Innovation System and the research on the History Project concentrates on the evolution of CSIRO since World War II, and the main factors that have driven changes in the organization. The project is assisting CSIRO to document its rich and important history, including contributions by key CSIRO personnel.

GRAHAM DUTFIELD

Graham Dutfield is Professor of International Governance at the University of Leeds School of Law. His areas of expertise include intellectual property, human rights, sustainable development, health, agriculture, genetics, and biotechnology. He is co-editor of *Knowledge Management and Intellectual Property Concepts, Actors and Practices from the Past to the Present* (2013, Edward Elgar), and *Intellectual Property and Human Development: Current Trends and Future Scenarios* (2012, Cambridge University Press).

MITCHELL ADAMS

Mitchell Adams is a Research Associate at Swinburne Law School, and the Research Centre Manager of the Centre for Transformative Innovation at Swinburne University. He is a registered Trademarks Attorney and Australian Solicitor, and has previously worked at CSIRO in the Intellectual Property and Commercialization group. As a Research Associate he is involved in conducting empirical research into the various Australian intellectual property registration systems, examining the registered trademark and designs systems.

MARIE HADLEY

Marie Hadley is a PhD researcher in the Faculty of Law, UNSW Sydney, where she researches cultural appropriation claims, and the protection of indigenous visual imagery by copyright law. Previously, she has worked as a research assistant on intellectual property law projects at UNSW law. Marie currently works as a research assistant at the Centre for Crime Policy & Research, Flinders University, and teaches law at Macquarie University, where she has previously worked as a research assistant at the Centre for Research on Social Inclusion.

PRIMAVERA DE FILIPPI

Primavera De Filippi is a permanent researcher at the National Center of Scientific Research (CNRS) in Paris, a faculty associate at the Berkman-Klein Center for Internet & Society at Harvard University, and a Visiting Fellow at the Robert Schuman Centre for Advanced Studies at the European University Institute. Her research interests include legal challenges raised by decentralized technologies. She is co-author of *Blockchain and the Law* (with Aaron Wright, 2018, Harvard University Press).